W9-BNB-575

Pottery & Porcelain Marks

GORDON LANG

American Consultant:
Ellen Paul Denker

MILLER'S

**Miller's Pocket Fact File:
Pottery and Porcelain Marks**

Gordon Lang

First published in Great Britain in 1995
by Miller's, a division of Mitchell Beazley,
both imprints of
Octopus Publishing Group Ltd.
2–4 Heron Quays
Docklands
London E14 4JP

Executive Editor Alison Starling
Executive Art Editor Vivienne Brar
Editor Katie Piper
Art Editor Geoff Fennell
Illustrator Amanda Patton
Indexer Richard Bird
Production Heather O'Connell
American Consultant Ellen Paul Denker

Marks of British pottery and porcelain
manufacturers are reproduced from
*Encyclopaedia of British Pottery and
Porcelain Marks* by Geoffrey A. Godden
(Barrie & Jenkins, 1991), by permission
of the author and his publishers.

Set in Granjon and Helvetica Neue
Produced by Toppan Printing Co., (HK) Ltd.
Printed and bound in China

Contents

Graphic marks 18

Staffordshire-type marks 268

Name & initial marks 284

Chinese marks 330

Additional information 338

How to use this book

This book is divided into a number of sections. Within each section, each entry includes the dates when the factory or potter was in production, the types of wares produced, and details of different marks used. Where the same maker is featured more than once, cross-references indicate where the main entry can be found. The sections are as follows:

Graphic marks

This section illustrates different types of marks which can stand alone as a guide to a piece's origin. These are based on written letters or words, and on symbols or devices.

Single letters lists marks featuring one letter or multiples of the same letter in alphabetical order.

Initials lists marks featuring initials only in alphabetical order.

Monograms lists monogram marks used by makers alphabetically, according to the most dominant letter in the design. If the monogram on your piece does not appear to have one dominant letter, it is advisable to check this section under each letter visible within the monogram.

Written name & signature marks lists alphabetically, marks that are, or appear to have been, handwritten, according to the surname of the individual potter or the title of the firm. Where the firm or potter's name in unclear, the entry has been placed under the first letter that appears.

Letters & devices lists marks comprising devices or symbols, that appear with the initial or initials of a factory or potter. The initials appear in alphabetical order. The devices appear in the order detailed on the contents page.

Devices lists marks comprising devices or symbols that appear either on their own, or with the name of a factory or potter. The devices appear in the order detailed on the contents page. To aid identification, devices that have a similar form or style appear together so that subtle differences can be detected.

Staffordshire-type marks include the Royal Arms, the Garter mark, and the Staffordshire knot mark. While these types of marks usually appear on British pottery and porcelain, they were also used by manufacturers in the USA and in Europe. For each type, there is an alphabetical list of the factory name or initials that appear with the device. Many factories used these marks; those featured here used them as one of their principal marks.

Entries in Graphic marks appear as follows:

Charles Waine (& Co.), Longton, Staffordshire, UK
Formerly Waine & Bates, this company produced porcelain 1891-1920. This printed mark appeared c.1913-20.

The name of the firm or producer is given first; additions or changes to the style of the manufacturer appear in brackets. The location of the manufacturer appears next, including the county, state or region, followed by the country of origin.

Name & initial marks

The marks of many factories are characterized by distinguishing name or initial marks. These may appear on their own or in combination with graphic marks. These may be stencilled, incised, impressed, painted or transfer-printed. Several manufacturers detailed in this section used a large number of marks, many of which were characterized by the same name or initials. The name and initial marks in this section appear alphabetically, according to the form in which the name appears in the mark; variations of the names used by the same potter or factory may appear in brackets, or on a new line.

Entries in Name & initial marks appear as follows:

A. CADMUS/CONGRESS POTTERY/SOUTH AMBOY N.J.

> **Abraham Cadmus/Congress Pottery**, South Amboy, New Jersey, USA
> Cadmus's pottery (active 1849-54) made Rockingham and yellow ware in table and kitchen forms and is especially known for his pitchers, one of which has a fire brigade marching around the sides. The mark was impressed.

The first line contains the written details of the mark, followed by the name and location of the firm or maker.

Chinese marks

The Chinese Ming dynasty (1368-1643) represents the first systematic marking of ceramics. This section illustrates the marks used during the reigns of the emperors of the Ming and Qing (1644-1916) dynasties, together with information on the types and styles of wares produced during each period, and details of any other marks that may appear on Chinese ceramics.

Additional information

This section includes the following:

Fakes & copies details of fakes and copies of ceramics from China, Italy, France, Germany, Holland, Britain and the USA.

Maps showing the main pottery and porcelain-producing centres in China, Italy, France, Northern Europe, Britain and the USA.

Appendices containing information on British Patent Office Registration Marks, and details of the year marks and cyphers used by Derby, Minton, Sèvres, Wedgwood and Worcester. A list of important painters', gilders', sculptors' and potters' monograms and symbols found on pieces made at Sèvres, is also included.

Glossary a detailed list of terms used in ceramics.

Further reading a list of more specialist texts which supplement the information found in this book.

Index a useful point of access for the identification of marks. If the name of the maker appears on the piece, the index will contain page references for each time that manufacturer is mentioned in the book.

Introduction

The production of ceramics is one of the world's oldest crafts, together with the making of flint tools, basketry and textile weaving. Archaeological evidence of these skills provides us with the basis of our social history. It is the durability of ceramics that set them apart, however, and they play a vital role in helping us to understand the origin of, and the history on which our cultures rely.

Decoration found on pottery and porcelain can tell us a great deal about earlier times, and the prevailing beliefs and fashions that ruled them. For instance, very many pieces of Italian *istoriato* maiolica (tin-glazed earthenware decorated with narrative subjects), show scenes from the history of Greece and Rome or from mythology. There are very few examples of early 16thC maiolica painted with biblical or religious subjects, suggesting that the influence of the Church was relatively weak at this time, and that the Classical world was an area of great interest. In the 17thC, the vast output of blue and white, rather than polychrome, tin-glazed earthenware in Delft, Holland, is visible proof of the extensive trading links with the Far East, and especially the porcelain of China. In the following century, the delicate porcelain tea and coffee services made at Meissen and Sèvres, tell us of sophisticated people with time to dawdle and converse over a cup of a fashionable drink. In the 19thC, the Industrial Revolution is evident not only in the mechanized methods of production, but also in the decorative motifs that were used on many pieces, such as railways, ships and bridges. Therefore, the collecting and studying of ceramics gives us at least a glimpse of life at other times and places.

Unless one concentrates on early pottery such as Greek or Roman or pre-Tang Chinese ware when pieces were rarely marked in any way, marks are very important in helping to establish the date and place of manufacture. The word "helping" is a deliberate choice: unfortunately marks are not sacrosanct, and one soon learns for example that the crescent mark based on the arms of the city of Worcester, and used on pieces by the porcelain factory located in the city, was also used by the factories at Bow and Lowestoft, and there are many similar examples. Anyone venturing into the study of Chinese ceramics will soon find that very few reign marks are contemporary with the date of manufacture. Thus, one should not get too excited upon the discovery of the reign mark of the emperor Chenghua (1465-87): as the porcelains of this period were among the finest ever made, the mark was frequently added by later potters to humbler porcelains. The fact that later potters in China practised this type of "forgery" almost as a matter of course, is widely understood today, and most people seeking advice on pieces with important reign marks, do so with a healthy amount of scepticism.

During his or her professional life, a dealer or specialist will acquire a knowledge of those marks which are most commonly faked, as well as some of the more obscure forgeries. Within a relatively short period of time, most people can learn important examples of the former: Emile Samson's 19thC copies of Worcester, Meissen or Chelsea; Paris hard-paste fakes of early Sèvres soft-paste; and the Dresden pastiches of early Meissen. Almost all of these are inscribed, often with marks deliberately designed to resemble the original. However, the material and the quality of the painted decoration should not fool anyone with even a little experience. For example, while Samson copies of Worcester feature the Worcester crecent, or square. flag-shaped seal mark, the greyish, glittery, hard-paste porcelain of the Samson version is quite unlike the irregular, speckled surface, and softer appearance of the Worcester original. Likewise, a Samson copy of a Meissen figure will have a very smooth, slightly brushed, pure white surface, which contrasts with the grey-white, flecked, textured Meissen body. Note too, that what looks like the crossed swords of Meissen, may simply be the crossed batons of Samson. A random dip into the pages of this book will soon bring the reader to an awareness of the difficulties presented by some types of marks. The understandable, but dubious practise adopted by some of the smaller pottery or porcelain manufacturers, of imitating the marks of a successful contemporary factory, such as the crossed swords of Meissen, or the crescent of Worcester, does present difficulties. Therefore it is essential to study the different pastes and colours of each factory in order to be more certain of making a correct attribution.

In order to gain a fuller understanding of ceramics, it is absolutely necessary to develop a method for examining items. As well as looking at the mark, a piece should be studied from the base upwards, taking the following into consideration: the type of material used, the colour of the material, the appearance of the glaze, the tone of the white glaze, how the piece has been made, the colours used in the decoration. These factors will reinforce an attribution made on the basis of a particular mark. Remember also, that there may be variations in colour or glaze on pieces made in the same region, or even at the same kilns, due to such factors as the temperature of the part of the kiln at which a particular piece was fired.

With experience the collector will begin to understand the complexities, and begin to make sense of ceramics. Using a book such as this one, together with a close examination of all the elements of a piece, should make this area of collecting a fascinating and rewarding one.

The Scope of the Book

There are a good number of books covering marks on ceramics: some of them appear in the suggestions for further reading at the end of this book. While many are excellent in their way, covering British, European, American and oriental pottery and porcelain, few of them cover the number of areas included here, and certainly not in such a portable form. This book contains more information than any other book of comparable size on the subject, and will be a handy companion when looking around antique shops, auction rooms, and even car-boot sales.

The range of material covered in this book includes factory marks, and other marks commonly used by individual potters or manufacturers which may help to identify the origin of a particular piece. Also included are date marks, such as Chinese reign marks (see pp.330-37), details of the design registration marks used on British ceramics (see p.360), and a number of examples of dated inscriptions which may be typical of a group or period. Specialist year marks (numbers, letters or cyphers) used by certain major manufacturers are also included (see pp.361-62, pp.373-74).

The marking of pottery and porcelain is an erratic and often inexact science. The marks included in this book have been arranged in the most logical order possible, but this has not always proved to be the most straightforward exercise. When looking up a particular mark in this book, it is always worth a closer look at the mark on the piece to see whether the main factory name is present, however small, as the index will then refer you to all the different entries for that particular manufacturer. If the factory name does not appear on the mark, but it does feature a symbol or a device (such as a crown, anchor, crescent, triangle, or bird), the mark may be included within the two sections on devices. Where the device appears with the initials of the maker, you should refer to "Letters & devices"; where no initials are present then go to "Devices". Sometimes, where a manufacturer uses a large number of different devices, or no device at all, the name or initials used by the firm may be located in "Name & initial marks".

Marks that have been omitted include those which may hinder or confuse the collector, such as the majority of individual workman's or decorator's marks, which may appear as monograms on pieces by particular factories. (Important marks that appear on wares decorated at Sèvres, France, have been included however, and appear on pp.363-72.)

With few exceptions the marks illustrated are representative of a factory, pottery or an individual. With early, handwritten marks there is inevitably some variation on each piece, and it is not unusual to see abbreviations or omissions of secondary names on some pieces. For example, Francesco Xanto Avelli da Rovigo, a leading painter of *istoriato* designs on Italian maiolica in the second quarter of the 16thC, sometimes signed his name in full, but is also known to have shortened it to "Fran: Xanto.A.Roui", "Fra: Xanto. A", "F. X. A. R." or one of several other combinations. Where variations exist, we have tried to include as many as possible.

Chinese reign marks from the Ming and Qing dynasties have been included in this book. It is worth noting that these have been copied extensively both by later Chinese potters, and by manufacturers in Japan. Factory marks were not used on early Japanese pottery and porcelain. Those that do appear are numerous and confusing: as well as marks copied from Chinese ceramics, a large number of artist's signatures and other marks were used, often a seal, or written characters. The fine Japanese porcelains of the 18thC (Kutani, Kakiemon, Nabeshima and Hirado), rarely feature marks.

Marks on other south-east Asian (such as Korean, Cambodian and Thai) and Islamic pottery and porcelain are not included in this book. Factory marks are virtually unknown in these areas, although individual inscriptions are quite often found on examples of Islamic pottery.

The proliferation of factories in the 19th and 20thC renders it impossible to include them all, as many of these concerns were either short-lived or relatively unimportant. Furthermore, well-established manufacturers often made regular changes to their trademarks, and to include all the variations of the marks of factories with a high output would occupy more space than is available here.

Pattern numbers began to appear at the end of the 18thC and can be extremely useful when making attributions: the larger factories often used distinctive forms, such as Ridgways in Staffordshire, and Coalport in Shropshire, who have both used fractional numbers. In the second quarter of the 19thC pattern names began to appear on mass-produced transfer-printed wares, and these can help to identify pieces in the absence of the main factory mark. There are, however, so many of them that it is beyond the scope of this book to include them all, and it may be necessary to consult specialist texts for a more comprehensive list.

The intention of this book is to give a concise history of the main pottery and porcelain factories in Europe and the USA, together with a general overview of the most important factory, name and trademarks used, and their different variations. Cross-references indicate where the main entry for a particular maker can be found, and the index lists all the entries for that factory that appear in the book.

Pottery & Porcelain Marks: A Brief History

Marks on ceramics fall into several categories which may determine one or more of the following: where a piece was made; who made it (the potter, decorator, factory or factory owner); when it was made; and for whom it was made.

Types of pottery & porcelain marks

Incised (or scratched): where a mark is cut into the body of an unfired piece with a sharp tool, leaving a thin line. Until the late 18thC, most marks were executed by hand.

Carved: where a mark is cut into soft clay leaving conspicuous trenches with sloping sides.

Impressed: where marks are inscribed by pressing a mould, stamp or stencil, made from metal or wood, into the surface of unfired clay.

Painted: where marks are painted onto the surface of pottery or porcelain. This may be under the glaze or over the glaze. Most painted (and printed) marks appear in cobalt-blue, the oxide most tolerant of high kiln temperatures. The other most common colours mare manganese-brown or iron-red.

Printed: where marks are created by covering a copper engraving with coloured pigment, transferring the image to thin paper, and from there onto the ceramic surface, either Before or after glazing.

China

It is not until the Chinese Ming dynasty (1368-1643) that we see the first systematic marking of ceramics. Reign marks were chosen after a new emperor ascended the throne and date from the beginning of the first new year after his accession. This system remained in use for 500 years. Early marks are either incised into the clay or painted in slip or pigment. By the Song dynasty (960-1278) some pieces are stamped or impressed. In the early 18thC form seal marks were introduced which were used concurrently with conventional script.

Europe & the USA

Pottery The earliest devices and marks are found on Italian maiolica. Marks appear on the grandest pieces of their type. In northern Europe, the earliest marks are found in the mid-16thC: the date 1559 is the earliest encountered in German ceramics. In the 17thC, the potters of Delft in Holland were more consistent in inscribing factory or proprietor's initial marks on their products. The first marks used on Delftware appear around the middle of the 17thC. In the British Isles the 16th and 17thC delftware potteries never marked their wares, and it was not until the late 18thC that Josiah Wedgwood introduced proper factory marks. The practise was subsequently adopted by most ceramics manufacturers in Europe and the USA.

Porcelain The first porcelain factories began to mark their wares fairly quickly. These marks could be based on the area, the patron or the proprietor of the factory. For example, Meissen used the famous crossed swords, derived from the arms of Saxony. These hand-painted symbols or initials are typical of almost all European porcelain factories until the early 19thC, when printed or impressed marks became standard. A few factories such as Derby, Spode and Meissen continued to use handwritten method.

Patent Office Registration Marks By the mid-19thC, plagiarism forced British ceramic manufacturers to adopt a registration system to protect their designs and forms. The registration of a design safeguarded its copyright for a period of three (or after 1883 five) years, after which it was no longer protected unless the patent was renewed. (For further details, see p.360 in Additional information.)

Dating pottery & porcelain marks
There are a number of general rules for dating ceramic marks (this list primarily concerns marks used by British manufacturers). These include the following:
* Printed marks that include the Royal Arms date from the 19th or 20thC.
* Printed marks that incorporate the name of the pattern of a particular piece were made after 1810.
* Any English mark that includes "Ltd." after the firm's title or initials must have a date later than 1855.
* The words "Trade Mark" indicates a date subsequent to the Act of 1862.
* The inclusion of the word "Royal" in a firm's title or tradename suggests a date in the second half of the 19th or 20thC.
* In 1891 the United States introduced the McKinley Tariff Acts, whereby any exported pottery or porcelain should be marked with the country of origin. Later, probably to avoid confusion, the words "Made in" were also added.
* The inclusion of the words "Bone China", "English Bone China" and other similar styles indicates a 20thC date.

Pottery & porcelain forms The following four pages feature illustrations of characteristic forms found in both porcelain (pp.14-15) and pottery (pp.16-17). These can help a collector to identify the country of origin and the date of production of a particular piece.

Baluster vase
China, early 17thC

"Yen Yen" vase
China, 1662-1722

Hexagonal vase
China, 1662-1722

Bottle vase,
China, 1662-1722

Bottle in transitional style
China, mid-17thC

"Gu"-Shaped Beaker Vase
China, late 17thC

Rouleau vase
China, c.1700

Moon flask
China, 18thC

Bottle vase
China, 18thC

"Kendi"
China, 18thC

Baluster Vase
China, mid-18thC

"Hu"-shaped Vase
China, mid-18thC

Meissen
Germany, c.1725-30

Meissen
Germany, c.1730-35

Meissen
Germany, c.1730-40

Kloster-Veilsdorf
Germany, c.1770

Kloster-Veilsdorf
Germany, c.1770

Vienna
Austria, c.1740-50

Vincennes
France, c.1755

Sèvres
France, c.1756-58

Chelsea
Britain, c.1744-49

Worcester
Britain, c.1770

Worcester
Britain, c.1772

Coalport
Britain, c.1830-40

Helmet-shaped ewer
Rouen
France, 18thC

Two-handled jar
Florence
Italy, 15thC

Covered Jug
Orisini-Colonna,
Italy, 16thC

Two-handled vase
Italy, 16thC

Wet drug-jar
Castel-Durante
Italy, 16thC

Pharmacy bottle
Italy, 16thC

Pilgrim vase
Urbino
Italy, 16thC

Oviform jar
Venice
Italy, 16thC

Oviform albarello
Palermo
Sicily, 17thC

Campana-shaped vase
Italy, 18thC

Pharmacy jar
Italy, 17thC

Tankard
Germany, 17thC

Apostelhumpen
Germany, 17thC

Stoneware jug
Germany, late 16thC

Bartmannkrug
Germany, 16thC

Stoneware jug
Germany, 16thC

Jug
Germany, 17thC

Schnelle
Germany, 16thC

Enghalskrug
Germany, 18thC

Tureen
Strasburg, 18thC

Jug
Delft, Holland, 18thC

Vase
Delft, Holland, 18thC

Posset pot
Britain, early 18thC

Agateware vase
Britain, late 18thC

Graphic marks

The marks shown here have an illustrated form, which can stand alone as a guide to a piece's origin. First are those that are (or appear to have been) written, incised or painted by hand (Single letters, Initials, Monograms, Written name & signature marks). Second are those that feature devices or symbols, with initials (Letters & devices), or on their own or with the name of the factory or potter (Devices). The third category are Staffordshire-type marks (the Royal Arms, Garter marks, and Staffordshire knot marks).

Ansbach, Bavaria, Germany
Hard-paste porcelain was produced 1758-1860;
the factory was transferred to Bruckberg (Bavaria)
in 1762. Best pieces made c.1767-85. This mark is
late and appears in blue. This mark may also
appear with a shield or an eagle.

Rue Thiroux, Paris, France
Hard-paste porcelain manufactured by Leboeuf
c.1775-19thC, initially under the protection of
Queen Marie Antoinette (1755-93). The mark
registered in 1776 was the letter "A" stencilled in
red. "A" with a crown in underglaze blue is also
used.

Bow China Works, Stratford, London, UK
Porcelain was made from c.1747-76. Forms of
functional wares are imitative of Chinese, Japanese and Meissen pieces, rococo-style decoration,
figures copied from Meissen. Before 1760 the
palette was delicate and original: opaque light
blue, emerald-green, and crimson-purple; a soft
shade of yellow was added later. The quality of
the painting decreased towards the end of the
period. This mark appeared on figures and late
pieces in underglaze blue.

Alcora, Valencia, Spain
This factory made faience c.1727-85, and later
hard-paste porcelain and cream-coloured wares.
The factory mark of a letter "A" was used only
from 1784 when rival establishments were set up
in the area. The mark above is incised; the mark
below appears in gold.

Alderney Pottery, Alderney, Channel Islands, UK
Studio-type pottery by Peter G. Arnold was first
made at Leatherhead in Surrey 1958-62, and the
Alderney Pottery, Alderney, Channel Islands from
1962. Painted mark used from 1958.

Avoncroft Pottery, Hampton Lovett, Nr. Droitwich,
Hereford and Worcester, UK
Established by Geoffrey Whiting, studio-type
earthenwares were made from 1952. This
impressed seal mark appears within a circular
outline.

"Amphora" Porzellanfabrik, Turn, Bohemia,
Czech Republic
General pottery was made by Riessner & Kessel
from 1894. This is one of many marks used.

St Agnes Pottery, Cornwall, UK
Earthenwares were made at the St. Agnes Pottery by A. and N. Homer 1953-57. This seal mark was used by A. Homer.

François-Antoine Anstett, Baden-Baden, Germany
A factory producing faience and porcelain was founded here in 1770 by Zacharias Pfalzer, but this undertaking was abandoned in 1778. In 1793 a new factory was established by Lorenz Müller, who made English-style earthenware. In 1795 he was succeeded by François-Antoine Anstett who became sole proprietor in 1800. His glazed earthenware featured this mark.

Jacques Vermonet, Boissette, Seine-et-Marne, France
Faience was made in Boisette from 1732. Hard-paste porcelain was produced in the abandoned faience factory by Jacques Vermonet and son 1778-c.1792. This mark on porcelain appears in underglaze blue.

Jacques Féburier and Jean Bossu, Lille, France
Faience was made here from 1696-1802, in a factory founded by Jacques Féburier (d.1729) and Jean Bossu, a painter. This mark was used.

Boscean Pottery, St Just-in-Penwith, Cornwall, UK
Studio-type stonewares made by Scott Marshall and Richard Jenkins (both formerly worked at the Leach Pottery) from 1962. Impressed seal mark.

Antoine Bonnefoy, Marseilles, Bouches-du-Rhône, France
Antoine Bonnefoy (d.1793) ran one of a number of faience factories in Marseilles in the late 17th, and first half of the 18thC. Bonnefoy's factory operated between 1762 and c.1827. Bonnefoy's son Augustin took over after his death. Porcelain was made after 1803.

Johann Valentin Bontemps, Nuremberg, Bavaria, Germany
Faience was made in Nuremberg 1712-c.1840. This is believed to be the mark of faience painter Johann Valentin Bontemps (1698-1775), whose work is recorded at Nuremberg in 1729, and who also worked at Ansbach and Bayreuth.

Bow China Works, Stratford, London, UK
See p.21. This mark is a rough, incised workman's mark, c.1750-60.

B

Worcester Porcelains, Hereford and Worcester, UK
This the main factory at Worcester produced porcelains from c.1751. The history of the factory is classified by periods, the first or "Dr. Wall" period c.1751-83 is named after one of the founders, Dr. John Wall who worked closely with the first manager William Davis. The second or "Flight" period, 1783-92 is named after Thomas Flight, the firm's London agent who bought the factory for his sons. The third period, "Barr and Flight & Barr" (c.1792-1807) occurs after the Flight brothers went into partnership with Martin Barr, and with the admission of more members of the Barr family, the fourth and fifth periods were named "Barr, Flight & Barr" (c.1807-13), and "Flight, Barr & Barr" (c.1813-40). c.1852-62 is the Kerr and Binns period. The company was known as the Worcester Royal Porcelain Company Ltd. (Royal Worcester) from 1862. Output includes table wares and decorative wares; figures were rare before the late 19thC. This incised "B" mark, found on tea wares, was used c.1792-1807.

·B
ℬ

Belvedere factory, Warsaw, Poland
Faience made from 1774 at the Belvedere factory. Chinese, and Japanese Imari-style items, imitating German pieces, especially Meissen, were made.

·B·

Basing Farm Pottery, Ashington, West Sussex, UK
Studio-type pottery by John N.S. Green from 1962. This is an impressed pottery seal mark.

β

Booths (Limited), Tunstall, Staffordshire, UK
Earthenwares were made at the Church Bank Pottery in Tunstall from 1891-1948. The company incorporated the Swan and Soho Potteries from c.1912. This painted or printed mark appeared on reproductions of antique Worcester porcelains made from opaque earthenware.

Ƀ

Cafaggiolo, Nr. Florence, Italy
Maiolica made from late 15th-mid-18thC. The palette includes a dark red, a strong dark blue, orange- and lemon-yellows, and a strong, transparent green. This mark appears on a piece dated 1506, painted with gothic foliage.

C

Moscow, Russia
Porcelain factory run by Safronoff from c.1820. The Cyrillic "C" (for "S") of this mark is sometimes mistaken for the "G" of Gardner (see p.27).

Capel Ceramics, London, UK

Established by Anthony and Elizabeth Lane in 1962, this workshop produces Studio-type pottery, jewellery, dishes, etc. They used this impressed seal or painted initial mark.

Caughley Porcelain Works, Nr. Brosely, Shropshire., UK

Good porcelain made in the Worcester style c.1775-99. In 1799 the works were taken over by the Coalport factory. These printed and painted "C" marks were used 1775-95, and are sometimes mistaken for the Worcester crescent mark (see p.230).

Münden, Hanover, Germany

A faience factory was established here c.1737 by Carl Friedrich von Hanstein, which remained in operation until 1854. This mark based on the arms of von Hanstein was used 1737-93. May appear in conjunction with a painters' mark.

Höchst, Nr. Mainz, Germany

The Höchst factory was established when Adam Friedrich von Löwenfinck, with the financial backing of two Frankfurt merchants, Johann Christoph Göltz and Johann Felician Clarus, obtained permission from Elector Emmerrich Joseph von Breidenbach to begin production. Löwenfinck was a porcelain painter, who had previously worked in Meissen, Bayreuth, Ansbach and Fulda. Löwenfinck left in 1749 after Göltz had become sole proprietor. After Göltz's death the factory was taken over by the elector until the stock was sold in 1796. Plates, dishes, jugs, tureens, vases and figures were made in faience and porcelain. The distinctive wheel mark was used with painters' marks. The letter "C" with the Höchst wheel (see also p.225), is the mark of painter Lothar Charlot, c.1748. This mark appears in crimson.

Flörsheim, Nr. Frankfurt-am-Main, Germany

A faience factory was founded here in 1765 by Georg Ludwig Müller, and was sold in 1763 to the Carthusian Monks of Mainz, who leased the premises until they were sold in 1797. The factory still exists today. Made functional wares in blue or high-fired colours. Cream-coloured earthenware was made in the later period. The mark seen here, is a painters' mark found on faience made at Flörsheim.

Derby Porcelain Works, Derbyshire, UK
The original factory at Derby was founded c.1750 by William Duesbury, and closed in 1848. A new company was formed in 1878, and is still in existence. Periods of production are broken down into the Duesbury period (1750-c.1820), the Bloor period (c.1820-48). The Crown Derby Porcelain Co. was formed in 1878, and the prefix "Royal" was added after 1890. Although most pieces made c.1750-80 were unmarked, this incised mark was used.

D

Hamburg, Germany
One of the earliest German faience factories existed here for around 50 years from c.1625. Much of the output consisted of large jugs and dishes, painted in blue with yellow, and more rarely green and brownish-red. Painters' marks, such as this one from c.1625-30, are found.

D+·

Barthélémy Dorez, Lille, France
This mark is found on faience and soft-paste porcelain made at the factory run by Barthélémy Dorez, between 1711 and c.1820.

D

Damm, Nr. Aschaffenburg, Germany
White and cream-coloured earthenware was made in a factory founded by Anna Maria Müller and continued by her son, from 1827. It is chiefly known for its reproductions of Höchst figures (see p.24) that featured the Höchst wheel together with the letter "D".

E

Hubert Letellier, Rouen, Seine-Inférieure, France
Mark used by potter Hubert Letellier from 1781. After 1805 he made cream-coloured earthenware and other imitations of English wares.

E E

Ginori Factory, Doccia, Nr. Florence, Italy
The potteries at Doccia were founded in 1735 by the Marquis Carlo Ginori. The factory has remained in the hands of the Ginori family. All types of pottery and porcelain were made in the 19thC. These incised marks appear on porcelain from c.1810.

Fürstenberg, Brunswick, Germany
A porcelain factory was founded here in 1747 by Duke Carl I of Brunswick; its principal period was between 1770 and 1814, but it is still in operation today. The mark above is an example of an early mark, and appears in blue. The mark below

was used by the factory in the late 18th and early 19thC, and appears in blue.

Kastrup Factory, Copenhagen, Denmark
The Kastrup factory, situated on the island of Amager to the east of Copenhagen was started by the Danish Court Architect Jacob Fortling. The factory produced faience, initially under the guidance of J. A. Hannong of Strasbourg. The mark of a letter "F" in manganese was used by Fortling, and subsequently by his widow after his death in 1761.

Cornelius Funcke, Berlin, Germany
The factory of Dutchman Cornelius Funcke (d.1733), was founded in Berlin in 1699. He made faience wares in a distinctive style, especially vases with scrolls or baroque panels on coloured grounds. Otherwise decoration is similar to Delft wares in the Chinese style. The factory closed c.1760. This mark was one of those used.

Joseph Fauchier, Marseilles, Bouches-du-Rhône, France
Joseph Fauchier I established a factory in Marseilles in 1711 making faience painted in blue in similar style to Rouen wares. After his death in 1751, his son Joseph Fauchier II took over the factory.

Doccia, Nr. Florence, Italy
See p.25. These incised marks are found on fine-paste porcelain, 1792-1815.

Count Ferniani, Faenza, Emilia, Italy
The factory of Count Ferniani and his descendants, 1693-1900, made maiolica decorated with Chinese and French-style designs. This mark was used in the 18thC.

Joseph Fouque, Moustiers, Basse-Alpes, France
Joseph Fouque (1714-1800) founded a factory in partnership with Jean François Pelloquin (1715-75). Fouque also acquired the Clérissy factory in 1783, and the operation continued until 1852. This mark is attributed to the factory.

Giuseppe and Andrea Fontebasso, Treviso, Venezia, Italy
From the late 17th to the early 18thC soft-paste porcelain was made at Treviso by brothers Giuseppe and Andrea Fontebasso, who later went

on to produce cream-coloured earthenware.
This mark has been found with the date 1779.

Flaminio Fontana, Urbino, Italy
Maiolica was made in Urbino c.1520-18thC. The
area is know for its narrative *istoriato* wares,
which are characterized by a rich amber yellow.
This mark is attributed to painter Flaminio
Fontana, dated 1583.

Fancies Fayre Pottery, Staffordshire, UK
This Staffordshire pottery made earthenwares,
figures and "fancies" at Hanley (c.1946-51), and
Shelton (from c.1951). This impressed or printed
mark was used from 1950.

Berlin, Prussia, Germany
In 1761 the porcelain factory in Berlin begun by
Wilhelm Wegely in 1752 with the backing of
Frederick the Great (1712-86), was taken over by
financier Johann Ernst Gotzkowsky. In 1763 he
sold the undertaking to the King, together with a
large stock of unglazed wares. It is therefore not
certain that all the marked pieces (figures and
table wares) with the Gotzkowsky mark seen
here, were painted in this period. The factory has
remained state property to the present day.

Moscow, Russia
The main porcelain factory in Moscow was
established c.1765 by an Englishman, Francis
Gardner. High-quality porcelain was made, and
figures modelled in a characteristic, vigorous style.
The factory remained in the Gardner family until
1891. This mark was used, together with the
Cyrillic letter "G" in the Russian alphabet.

Gera , Thuringia, Germany
A porcelain factory was founded in Gera in 1779
by Johann Gottlob Ehwaldt and Johann Gottlob
Gottbrecht, but was taken over by the Greiner
family. Thuringian porcelain is generally greyish
in tone, and most was intended for the mass
market. Hard-paste porcelain table wares and
figures were made. This mark appears.

Countess Anna Barbara von Gaschin, Glienitz, Silesia, Germany
Faience production began in 1753 in a factory
owned by Countess Anna Barbara von Gaschin.
This mark was used 1767-c.1780. A double- "G"
was also used representing "Gaschin-Glienitz".

Gotha, Thuringia, Germany
Hard-paste porcelain was first produced here in
1757 in a factory owned by Wilhelm von Rotberg,
and run by a succession of proprietors. From
c.1805 the "G" mark appears in blue or enamel
colour.

Tavernes, Nr. Moustiers, Var, France
A faience factory existed here between 1760 and
1780. This mark was used.

Gera, Thuringia, Germany
A great deal of faience, and later porcelain, was
made in towns in Thuringia. Faience is characte-
rized by strong, high-temperature colours;
cylindrical tankards are the most common form.
Faience was made here c.1752-80, by Matthias
Eichelroth, and subsequently by Johann Gottlieb
Gottbrecht. This mark was used.

Louis H. H. Glover, Barnsley, South Yorkshire, UK
Studio-type pottery made from 1930. This
impressed or painted initial mark from 1946.

Doccia, Nr. Florence, Italy
See p.25. This mark was used on general pottery
made at the Ginori factory 1874-88.

Three G's Pottery, Worthing, West Sussex, UK
First established c.1953 in Rowlands Castle,
Hampshire, this pottery, run by Mrs. Lloyd, made
earthenwares. This incised mark was used.

Holitsch, Hungary
A faience factory was established here in 1743 by
Francis of Lorraine, the consort of the Empress
Maria Theresa (1717-80). Wares were made in the
style of French faience. Pieces were marked with
an "H" or a double- "H". White and cream-
coloured earthenware was made after 1786

Pierre Heugue, Rouen, Seine-Inférieure, France
Pierre Heugue and his family of potters based in
Rouen, 1698-19thC used this mark.

Pierre Antoine Hannong, Faubourg Saint-Denis,
Paris, France
A porcelain factory was founded here in 1771 by
Pierre-Antoine Hannong who registered this
letter mark, as well as a capital letter "H". He left
in 1776 and the factory, owned by the Marquis
d'Usson, operated under a number of directors.

Benedict Hasslacher, Alt-Rohlau, Bohemia, Czech Republic
From 1813, this factory made cream-coloured earthenware and hard-paste porcelain. Proprietor from 1813-23 was Benedict Hasslacher, whose mark appears here.

St Petersburg, Russia
After her accession in 1762, Empress Catherine II (1729-96) revivified the porcelain factory that was originally established in St Petersburg by her predecessor, Empress Elizabeth (1709-62) in 1744. The Imperial factory then began to flourish. This mark was used by Nicholas II 1894-1917.

Harborne Pottery, Birmingham, West Midlands, UK
Established by E. M. and B. Bloomer in 1956 to produce pottery and tiles. This impressed seal mark was used from 1956.

Thelma P. Hanan, London, UK
This potter worked in London in 1947, and then moved to the Island Pottery, Portsmouth, in 1951. This incised or painted mark was used from c.1947-53.

Henry F. Hammond, Farnham, Surrey, UK
Produced Studio pottery and stonewares at the Oast Pottery and the Farnham School of Art. This incised or impressed mark was used from 1934.

Höchst, Nr. Mainz, Germany
See p.24. This "H" denotes Georg Frederick Hess, "arcanist" and painter at the Höchst factory, 1746-50 (or his son Ignatz, c.1750).

Kelsterbach, Hesse Darmstadt, Germany
A faience factory was founded in Königstädten, near Kelsterbach, in 1758 by Wilhelm Cron and Johann Christian Frede. Frede went into partnership with Caspar Mainz in 1759 when Cron withdrew, and the factory moved in 1760 to Kelsterbach. Thereafter the factory changed hands a number of times. All kinds of faience and porcelain were made. This mark was used on early faience, denoting "Kelsterbach" or "Königstädten".

Klosterle, Bohemia, Czech Republic
In 1794 a porcelain factory was founded here on the orders of Count F. J. Thun, the forestry superintendent. From 1797-1803 the factory was

leased to Christian Nonne. Pieces were made with good quality decoration. This mark was used 1794-1803. Production continues today.

Edwin M. Knowles China Company, East Liverpool, Ohio, USA

This pottery produced high quality table and toilet wares in semi-porcelain and ironstone with good printed or decal decorations. The first pottery plant was in Chester, West Virginia. Offices remained in East Liverpool until 1931. Knowles was the son of Isaac M. Knowles of Knowles, Taylor & Knowles. This mark should not be mistaken for one used by Knowles, Taylor & Knowles.

Langenthal, Switzerland

Porcelain was made at Langenthal from 1906; this "L" mark appears on hand-decorated wares.

Langewiesen, Thuringia, Germany

Hard-paste porcelain was made here in the 19thC. This mark appears.

M. Landais, Tours, Indre-et-Loire, France

Faience was made at Tours from c.1750, and later porcelain and earthenware. This mark was used by M. Landais who made copies of Palissy and "Henri II" wares in the 19thC.

Jean-Joseph Lassia, Rue de Reuilly, Paris, France

Hard-paste porcelain was made at this factory at the end of the 18thC, c.1774-1787, by Jean-Joseph Lassia who registered the "L" mark in 1774. This mark appeared in gold or colour.

Andreas Dolder, Bero-Munster, Switzerland

Andreas Dolder ran a faience factory here 1769-80, which was subsequently moved to Lucerne. The factory produced faience decorated in the Strasbourg style. This mark denotes Münster.

Magdeburg, Hanover, Germany

A faience factory was founded in Magdeburg by Philipp Guichard in 1754. Early wares were made from faience, and included characteristic open basketwork (also made at Munden); later wares were made from glazed earthenware in the English style. These marks were used on faience 1754-86. The letter "M" also appears on cream-coloured earthenware 1786-1839.

M

Patrick McCloskey, Hove, East Sussex, UK
Studio-type pottery, slip-decorated wares and
figures were made from 1948 with this impressed
seal-type mark.

William S. Murray, London, UK
Made Studio Pottery in London and at various
addresses in England; lived in Southern Rhodesia
from 1940. This impressed seal mark was used
1919-40 in England.

Theophilus Brouwer, Middle Lane Pottery, Long
Island, New York, USA
Brouwer (active 1894-1932) made earthenware art
vases with a variety of lustre and metallic effects
first in East Hampton and later in Westhampton.
His pottery making was steadier during the
earliest years, but as time went on he developed
additional interests, particularly as concerned cast
concrete. The mark mimics the jawbone of a
whale that made the gate to his studio in
Westhampton.

N.

Niderviller, Lorraine, France
The original faience factory in Niderviller that
was founded in 1735, was bought by Baron Jean-
Louis de Beyerlé in 1742. Porcelain and faience
were produced, but by c.1765 production almost
exclusively comprised porcelain. The factory was
bought in 1770 by Adam Philibert, Comte de
Custine. François-Antoine Anstett, a former pupil
of Paul Hannong managed the factory 1754-79.
Later it was directed by Claude François Lanfrey
1802-27. Faience wares were strongly influenced
by Strasburg, but the palette was softer. Tureens
and figures were made in both faience and
porcelain. Porcelain was not produced after 1827.
This "N" mark which appears in black has been
used on pieces from the start of production. The
town name also appears impressed in full, and as
an abbreviation "Nider" in black.

P

Bonnin and Morris, Philadelphia, Pennsylvania, USA
Although the making of porcelain had been
attempted previously several times, this pottery
is the first for which any ware survives. Gousse
Bonnin and George Morris hired potters from
the English Bow factory to make porcelain in
Philadelphia, 1769-72. Although the ware was
a reasonably good copy of the English original, the
cost for making it in America was prohibitive and
the venture failed within few years of opening.

Sargadelos, Spain
White and cream-coloured earthenware was
made in Sargadelos between 1804 and 1875. This
"P" mark was used 1835-42.

Prague, Czech Republic
A factory producing English-style lead-glazed
earthenware was set up in 1795. This mark was
used 1795-1810.

Count Leopold von Proskau, Silesia, Germany
A faience factory was founded in Proskau in 1763
by Count Leopold von Proskau who was killed in
a duel in 1769. The factory was taken over in 1770
by Johann Carl von Dietrichstein, following a
short period of closure, who owned the premises
until 1783 when they were sold to Frederick the
Great of Prussia. The factory was managed and
then leased by Johann Gottlieb Leopold 1783-93.
In 1788 the factory began producing earthenware,
and the manufacture of faience was discontinued
after 1793. The factory continued until c.1850.
The mark above was used 1763-69; the mark
below was used during the Leopold period
1783-93.

Deruta, Umbria, Italy
Maiolica was produced at potteries in Deruta
from c.1490. This mark has been found on pieces
from a group of wares known as the "petal-back"
class: plates and dishes with a distinctive type of
floral pattern on the reverse. Other initials also
appear in this style.

Cafaggiolo, Nr. Florence, Italy
See p.23. This mark found on a plate depicting a
procession that includes the Medici Pope Leo X,
made c.1513.

Tuscany, Italy
Maiolica was made in Tuscany from the 15thC
onwards, especially around Florence and
Siena. The double-"P" mark (above) was found
on an armorial vase with Spanish-style flower
decoration. The single "P" mark (below) has
been found on pieces that feature characteristic
"Hispano-Moresque" and "Gothic" foliage.

Palgrave Pottery, Broome, Suffolk, UK
Run by Mr and Mrs J. Colliers, this pottery made
Studio-type wares from 1953. This "P. P." initial
mark was used from 1953.

Miragaya, Nr. Oporto, Portugal

A faience factory existed here in the late 18thC. This mark has been found.

Robert's Factory, Marseilles, Bouches-du-Rhône, France

Joseph-Gaspard Robert founded a faience factory in Marseilles c.1750. He produced hard-paste porcelain from 1773. The factory operated until at least 1793. Many variations of this factory mark were used on both faience and porcelain.

De Roos, Delft, Holland

This factory (The Rose) operated from 1662-1755 under various proprietors. The mark above was principally used in the early 18thC on Chinese-style blue and white wares. The mark below was also used in the 18thC.

Pierre-Joseph Prudhomme, Aire, Pas-de-Calais, France

Faience was made in Aire from c.1730-90, in a factory founded by Pierre-Joseph Prudhomme. This mark was used by Prudhomme c.1730-55. After 1755 the factory was taken over by his son-in-law François Dumetz, who continued the concern until c.1790.

Roseville Pottery Company, Roseville and Zanesville, Ohio, USA

During its earliest years the company produced utilitarian stoneware at two potteries in Roseville and within a few years painted ware in Zanesville. In 1900, their famous "Rozane" glazed ware was begun in Zanesville, and by 1910 all pottery production was moved to that city. The firm was active 1892-1954. A variety of glaze effects was made under the Rozane name. In 1918, the trademark "Roseville U.S.A." was adopted and the moulded floral wares, such as Pine Cone, Wisteria, Dahlrose, etc., were added. F. H. Rhead produced an elaborate art line called Della Robbia during the early 1900s.

Roeginga Pottery, Rainham, Kent, UK

This pottery operated 1938-39 producing earthen-wares. It was reopened in 1948 by Alfred Wilson Ltd. This incised mark was used 1938-39.

Bow China Works, Stratford, London, UK

See p.21. This is a rough, incised workman's mark, c.1750-60.

Nuremberg, Bavaria, Germany
Evidence suggests that maiolica was made in
Nuremberg during the 16thC, by Augustin
Hirschvogel. Records show that in 1531 he
worked in partnership with Hans Nickel and
Oswald Reinhard (who had worked in Venice).
This mark attributed to Reinhard was found on a
dish painted with Samson and Delilah, with the
date 1526.

Sargadelos, Spain
See p.32. This mark is found on white and cream-
coloured earthenware 1804-29.

Sipiagin, Moscow, Russia
Vsevolojsky and Polivanoff operated a porcelain
factory in Moscow from 1813-55. This is the mark
of Sipiagin, proprietor from 1820.

Georg Matthäus Schmidt, Erfurt, Thuringia,
Germany
Faience was made in Erfurt c.1717-92. Privileges
were granted, notably to J. D. Fleischhauer in
1717, which were then taken over by Laurentius
Silberschlag in 1718. Silberschlag's factory was
bought in the same year by Johann Paul Stieglitz
(also a pewter manufacturer) who obtained
another privilege in 1734. Stieglitz's son and
grandson continued the factory until it closed
in 1792. Tankards, dishes, jugs, and more
rarely, figures, all painted in the characteristic
Thuringian palette, were made. Painters' marks
appear, such as this one by Georg Matthäus
Schmidt.

Souroux, Rue de la Roquette, Paris, France
Production of hard-paste porcelain took place
here, made by Souroux who registered this mark
in 1773.

Sinceny, Aisne, France
A faience factory was established in Sinceny in
1733 by J. B. de Fayard, and was managed by
Denis-Pierre Pellevé of Rouen. Fine quality
faience, including *grand-feu* Chinoiserie was
produced which is very similar to wares from
Rouen. The factory operated until 1864. This
mark was used in the first period, 1733-75.

Cafaggiolo, Nr. Florence, Italy
See p.23. This mark appears c.1480, on a jug in the
Ashmolean Museum, Oxford, painted with the

arms of Alessandro dei Alessandri, on a ground which imitates Hispano-Moresque ware.

Schlaggenwald, Bohemia, Czech Republic
A porcelain factory existed here from c.1793-1866. This marks was used in the early 19thC.

Caughley Porcelain Works, Nr. Brosely, Shropshire, UK
See p.24. Blue painted or printed "S" marks, often appearing with a small cross or circle, are found on underglaze blue decorated wares, c.1775-95.

Guiseppe Sinibaldi and Lodovico Santini, Trieste, Italy
From 1783-early 19thC creamware was made in Trieste by Guiseppe Sinibaldi and Lodovico Santini, who used this double- "S" mark.

Stockhardt & Schmidt-Eckert, Kronach, Bavaria, Germany
This mark was used on hard-paste porcelain made by Stockhardt & Schmidt-Eckert from 1897.

Tettau, Franconia, Germany
A porcelain factory was founded here in 1794 by Georg Christian Friedmann Greiner from Kloster Veilsdorf. Early utility wares were then joined by coffee, tea, chocolate and table services, many with floral decoration. From 1915 the factory was known as Porzellan-fabrik Tettau AG. This 19thC mark and other variations appear in blue.

Johann Samuel Friedrich Tännich, Mosbach, Baden, Germany
The faience and creamware manufactory at Mosbach was established in 1770 by Pierre Berthevin under the protection of the Elector Palatine Carl Theodor. Between 1774 and 1781 the factory was run by Johann Samuel Friedrich Tännich, and he was succeeded by Johann Georg Friedrich List who formed a company to take over the factory. From 1787-1836 the proprietors were Roemer and Co., thereafter it was owned by Heinrich Stadler. The early, mainly tableware or other domestic ware was based loosely on the Strasburg style with scattered flowers or landscape vignettes in a polychrome palette. Towards the end of the 18thC the factory switched to the production of cream-coloured earthenware which continued until the closure of the factory in 1836. This "T" mark stands for Tännich.

Vianna do Castello, Portugal
This "V" mark appears in blue on faience that was produced here from 1774.

Nathaniel Friedrich Hewelcke, Venice, Italy
From 1758-63 hard-paste porcelain in the style of Meissen was produced by Dresden dealers Nathaniel Friedrich Hewelcke and his wife Maria Dorothea. The privilege was granted on condition that they mark their pieces with the letter "V". This mark was either incised or painted red.

Nicholas Vergette, London, UK
Working at the Camberwell School of Art and other posts 1946-58, Vergette used this incised mark.

Varages, Vars, France
Faience was made here in the 18thC in the Moustiers and Marseilles style. This mark was used.

Villegoureix, Noël & Co., Limoges, Haute-Vienne, France
Founded in 1922, this firm became Villegoureix & Cie (1924-26), and S. A. Porcelaine Villegoureix (1928-29).

Pierre Verneuilh, Bordeaux, Gironde, France
Porcelain was made in Bordeaux from 1781, when a manufactory was established by Pierre Verneuilh and his nephew Jean, until 1787 when it was taken over by Michel Vanier in partnership with Allaud of Limoges. This continued until 1790, and made porcelain similar to wares from Paris. This double- "V" mark was used.

Wiersbie, Silesia, Germany
A small faience factory existed in the neighbour-hood of Glienitz with a painter Fialla 1775-83, making pieces similar to those from Proskau. This mark was used.

Würzburg, Lower Franconia, Germany
A porcelain factory was established c.1775 by Johann Caspar Geyer, and seems to have lasted until 1780. This mark appears in black.

Johann Jacob Wunderlich, Erfurt, Thuringia, Germany
This mark was used by Wunderlich (d.1751), a painter at Erfurt from 1730.

W

Anne Wedd, Brixton, London, UK
Studio-type pottery made from 1955. This
impressed seal-type mark was used from 1961.

W
W

Worcester Porcelains, Hereford and Worcester, UK
See p.23. The painted mark above is rare, and was
used c.1870-85. Several variations of the "W"
mark below appear c.1755-70, painted or printed
in underglaze blue.

Y

Michael Leach, Yelland Manor Pottery, Devon, UK
Trained by his father Bernard Leach, Michael
Leach made Studio-type pottery from 1956. This
impressed seal mark was used.

Y

William Absolon, Great Yarmouth, Norfolk, UK
Absolon worked at The Ovens and 25 Market
Row in Yarmouth 1784-1815, decorating earthenwares and glass. He used this painted Yarmouth
mark.

Z
3

Zürich, Switzerland
A porcelain and faience factory established near
Zürich at Schoren by a company in 1763. After
1790 faience and lead-glazed earthenware were
the principal output. Both faience and porcelain
were made in the 18thC marked with a "Z" with
or without dots, as seen here.

Z

Zerbst, Anhalt, Germany
A faience factory here was one of those founded
by Johann Caspar Ripp of Hanau. A factory
operated under various owners until 1861. This
factory mark was used.

Z

Leipzig, Saxony, Germany
A hard-paste porcelain decorator, Oscar Zenari
worked out of Leipzig from 1901 and used this
mark.

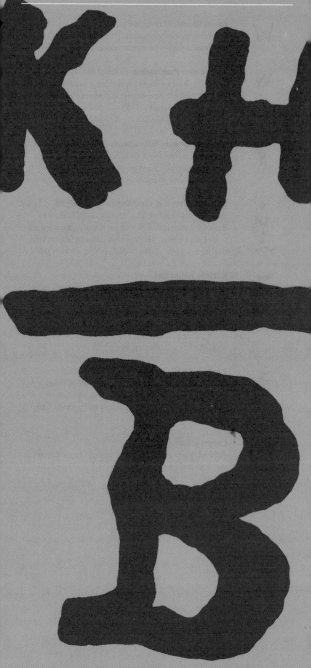

Adam Clemens Wanderer, Bayreuth, Germany
One member of a family of potters who painted
brown and yellow wares at Bayreuth in the 18thC.
These are typically decorated with fired-on gold
and silver, with high quality painting. Motifs
include scrollwork and monograms.

Bow China Works, Stratford, London, UK
See p.21. This is a rough, incised workman's mark
c.1750-60.

Johann Georg Christoph Popp, Ansbach,
Bavaria, Germany
Johann Georg Christoph Popp (b.1696, d.1791)
became the proprietor of the faience factory at
Ansbach (established 1708-10) in 1769. He had
been a painter at the factory since 1715, and was
manager from 1737-69 (with Köhnlein 1737-47).
In 1770, his son Johann Gottfried Popp became his
partner. The factory remained in the hands of the
Popp family until 1807. This mark, which denotes
"Ansbach-Popp", was used after 1769.

Aprey, Haute-Marne, France
See p.68. The initials "A. P." were not always
used. This mark and the monogram are common
on modern copies.

Arras, Pas-de-Calais, France
A soft-paste porcelain factory was founded here in
1770 by Joseph-François Boussemaert of Lille (see
p.70). The factory was taken over in 1771 by four
female faience dealers called Delemer. The factory
closed in 1790. Only tablewares were made, and
are painted in blue or crimson monochrome with
flowers, coats of arms, and festoons. The mark
appears in crimson or purple.

Annette Fuchs, London, UK
Studio-type pottery was produced from 1961 with
this painted initial mark.

Albrecht von Erberfeld, Aumund, Hanover, Germany
A faience factory existed here for a short time
from 1751-61. The third owner was Albrecht von
Erberfeld (from 1757), whose mark appears here.
Output included rococo tureens and cylindrical
tankards, painted in blue or *grand-feu* colours.

Alan Wallwork, London, UK
Based at the Alan Gallery, Wallwork's workshop
produced Studio-type pottery and architectural

ceramics from 1959. This incised initial mark appeared on his individual pieces. The letter "W" was also used, and appears as an incised, impressed or painted mark.

B.
C

Duke Karl of Brunswick, Brunswick, Germany
See p.83. In 1756 the Brunswick faience factory was purchased by Duke Karl who retained it until 1773. This second ducal "B" mark was used at this time and later as one of the conditions of the privilege granted to Johann Benjamin Heinrich Rabe (who ran the factory from 1773) in 1781.

B & C

Bougon and Chalon, Chantilly, Oise, France
M. Pigorry founded a factory in 1803, and produced utility ware and tea services. From c.1818, Jacques Louis Chalot and Pierre-Louis-Toussaint continued the concern; their pieces feature this mark.

B.F.S.

Adolf Fränkel and Johann Veit Schreck,
Bayreuth, Bavaria, Germany
The factory at Bayreuth produced some of the most important German faience during the early 18thC. It was established with the help of potter Johann Kaspar Ripp (who also worked at Hanau, Ansbach and Nuremberg) and possibly a merchant called Johann Georg Knöller in c.1713. Kaspar Ernst Hild was named as manager in 1723. In 1724 the concern was taken over by the Margrave of Brandenburg-Kulmbach, who appointed Johann Nicolaus Grüner as manager. The Margrave died in 1726, and two years later Knöller once again took over the factory, and it became a profitable concern, supplying a large amount of high quality brown-glazed ware to the Court. Knöller died in 1744, and between 1745 and 1747 the factory was run by Adolf Fränkel (d.1747) and Johann Veit Schreck, who used this mark.

B&G

Bing & Grøndhal, Copenhagen, Denmark
Founded in 1853, this factory produced artistic and domestic porcelain and earthenwares. A successful factory, this business still exists today. This mark appears.

-B-X-

Adolf Fränkel and Johann Veit Schreck,
Bayreuth, Bavaria, Germany
See above. This mark is one of those used during the Knöller period, 1728-44. The initials "B. K." often appear in conjunction with painter's marks.

Bernberg, Thuringia, Germany
A faience factory existed c.1725-75, with the patronage of Prince Victor Friedrich of Anhalt-Bernberg. There is no written record of the factory, but a set of Chinese-Delft style vases have been found with this mark.

Bernard Leach, St Ives, Cornwall, UK
Active 1921-79, Bernard Leach was one of the most famous English Studio-potters. He also trained a large number of potters at his studio in St. Ives. He made pieces with a strong Oriental feel, with simple painted, *sgraffiato* or trailed decoration. These personal marks were used by Leach 1921-79.

Bernard Moore, Stoke, Staffordshire, UK
Formerly Moore Bros. (c.1872-1905), a company that made decorative porcelains at Longton, the firm was continued by Bernard Moore, c.1905-15, who produced fine glaze effects on porcelain and earthenwares. This painted initial mark was used in several forms 1905-15.

Baldassare Manara, Faenza, Emilia, Italy
A member of a well-known family of Faentine potters, Baldassare Manara decorated a number of pieces of maiolica dated between 1530 and 1536. His initals appear on some of the pieces.

De vergulde Blompot, Delft, Holland
Founded in 1654 by J. G. van der Houve, *De vergulde Blompot* (The Golden Flowerpot) operated until c.1778. Successive owners included van der Houve's widow, Jacob Pijnacker (see p.91), and M. van den Bogaert. This factory mark is one of several used.

Johann Georg Pfeiffer, Bayreuth, Bavaria, Germany
See p.40. In 1747, the faience factory in Bayreuth was taken over by Johann Georg Pfeiffer, who worked in conjunction with Adolf Fränkel's widow until 1760 ("Pfeiffer & Fränkel" period, see mark below), and on his own 1760-67 (see mark above). During the "Pfeiffer" period the factory was very prosperous, and after his death in 1767 Pfeiffer's widow and children remained as owners until 1783, when the financially-troubled business was taken over by State officials. In 1788 C. A. Wetzel bought the concern, and produced cream-coloured earthenware, as well as faience, until 1806.

B & R

Johann Heinrich Reichard and Johann Erich Behling, Brunswick, Germany
See p.83. From 1749-56, the proprietors of the factory at Brunswick were Johann Heinrich Reichard and Johann Erich Behling, and the mark used was "B & R" or "R & B".

B.S.

Bartholomäus Seuter, Augsburg, Swabia, Germany
Independent faience and porcelain painting was one of many crafts practiced by Bartholomäus Seuter (1678-1754). His work is found on faience jugs and tankards, and features flowers and figures arranged in panels or cartouches, executed on manganese purple or brown and yellow. Other characteristic colours include crimson, egg-yolk yellow and blue. His later work on porcelain includes figure subjects in black, red and especially gilding.

BX

Bayeux, Calvados, Normandy, France
First established at Valognes in 1793 by Le Tellier de la Bertinière, this hard-paste porcelain factory was transferred to Bayeux in 1810 by Joachim Langlois, and continued by his family after his death in 1830. Owned by François Gosse from 1849, the factory was then taken over by Jules Morlent in 1878, who, together with his descendants, continued until 1951. This mark denoting the Morlent period appears, sometimes within a circle.

C.A.

Eckernförde, Schleswig, Germany
Founded first at Criseby in 1759 by Johann Nicolaus Otte and his brother Friedrich Wilhem, a faience factory operated at Eckernförde from 1765-85. This mark has been atributed to the early period 1759-64.

CA

Arzberg, Bavaria, Germany
A hard-paste porcelain factory was founded at Arzberg by Carl Auvera from 1884. Pipe bowls were made with this mark.

C.A.P. Co.

Cincinnati Art Pottery, Cincinnati, Ohio, USA
A variety of art wares was produced at this pottery (active 1879-1891) on various earthenware bodies, including "Hungarian Faience" with an elaborate overall polychrome pattern or "Kezonta", the Indian name for turtle, that was an ivory-colored faience with hand-painted polychrome flowers or gilt scrolls. Some of their ware was furnished in the white to decorators.

C ∙ B

Coburg, Thuringia, Germany
A small faience factory was established here in
1738 by Johann Georg Dümmler of Bayreuth
under privilege from the Duke of Saxa-Coburg-
Gotha, who took over the factory himself in 1760.
The concern contiued until 1786. This mark
appears on general Thuringian-style faience, and
has been ascribed to Coburg.

C B

Clive Brooker, Stanmore and Enfield, London, UK
From 1956, Clive Brooker has produced Studio-
type pottery that features an incised or impressed
signature mark (1956-60), or this impressed seal
mark (from 1960).

C:BM

Cornelius Boumeester, Rotterdam, Holland
Tiles and faience were made at Rotterdam in
the 17th and 18thC. Faience manufacturing in
the town dates from 1612, when the son of a
Haarlem potter, Pieter Hermansz Valckenhoff,
started a factory. By 1642 there were eleven factories in Rotterdam. This mark belongs to a tile
painter called Cornelius Boumeester (b.1652,
d.1733),.who was active c.1675-1700.

CD

Limoges, Haute-Vienne, France
Hard-paste porcelain was made at Limoges
from 1771 when a factory was established by
the brothers Grellet, under the protection of the
Comte d'Artois. In 1784 it was acquired by the
King to make blanks for decoration at Sèvres.
The factory closed in 1796. The usual mark "C.
D." which stands for "Comte d'Artois" is most
often incised, but sometimes appears in red or
underglaze blue.

**c ∙ G
w**

Johann Caspar Geyer, Würzburg, Lower Franconia,
Germany
See p.36. This mark includes the initials of the
founder of the porcelain factory at Würzburg,
Johann Caspar Geyer (d.1780).

C.H

Henri-Florentin Chanou, Barrière de Reuilly, Paris
A hard-paste porcelain factory was run here by
Henri-Florentin Chanou of Sèvres, 1779-85. This
mark appears in red.

C∙∙K.

G. Frederick Cook, Ambleside, Cumbria, UK
Studio-type pottery and stonewares were
produced at the Potter's Wheel Studio in
Ambleside from 1948. Cook used this personal
mark on individual pieces.

Chelsea Keramic Art Works/Dedham Pottery, Chelsea and Dedham, Massachusetts, USA

Robertson brothers Alexander, Hugh and George had been making redware flower pots in Chelsea since the late 1860s, but changed the company's name and improved their product line in the late 1870s to include fine terracotta in Grecian shapes and art wares with faience glazes. Decorative tiles were also made, designed by John G. Low who later established the Low Art Tile Works in Chelsea. The firm was active in Chelsea 1875-95, and in Dedham 1895-1943. Hugh's experiments to revive ancient Chinese glazes led to the creation of a white crackle glaze that was hand-painted with charming animal and plant figures in cobalt blue. This was the primary product line of the pottery after it was moved to Dedham in 1895; the climate in Chelsea proved too damp to make this type of ware.

C. Newbold, Skipton-on-Swale, North Yorkshire, UK

Studio-type stonewares produced at Arncliffe from 1961, with this incised or painted mark.

Denver China and Pottery Company, Denver, Colorado, USA

William Long started this pottery (active 1900-1905) with many of the same decorators who had been with him at Lonhuda in Steubenville (see p.87), and at Weller. They made the original Lonhuda ware, and a line called "Denaura", that was modelled with relief designs of Colorado flowers and covered with matt green glaze. They also produced flint blue ware which included tableware such as bowls and mugs.

Kloster-Veilsdorf, Thuringia, Germany

See p.74. This initial mark is less common than the "CV" monogram.

Cornelia van Schoonhoven (or Cornelius van Schagen), Delft, Holland

This mark appears on pieces from *De porceleyn Klaeuw* (The Porcelain Claw). It is not clear whether the initials seen here stand for Cornelia van Schoonhoven (proprietor 1668-71), or Cornelius van Schagen (proprietor 1695-c.1702).

Delan Cookson, West Bridgford, Nottinghamshire, UK

From 1958 Studio-type pottery was produced; this impressed seal mark appears on wares after 1961 (marks are rare before this date).

D. H
$$\frac{}{2}$$

Christiane Hörisch, Dresden, Saxony, Germany
A faience factory was first established here in 1708
by Johann Friedrich Böttger (who went on to
establish the porcelain manufactory at Meissen).
Between 1710 and 1718, the factory was run by
Peter Eggebrecht (who held the lease after 1712).
After his death in 1738 the factory was continued
by his widow, and from 1756 by his daughter. In
1768 it passed into the hands of Christiane
Hörisch, who was succeeded by her son Karl
Gottlieb Hörisch in 1782. The factory closed in
1784. This mark was used during the Hörisch
period (1708-84).

DKW

Denis K. Wren, Oxshott, Surrey, UK
Studio-type ceramics were produced at the
Oxshott Pottery from 1919. These intials belong
to Denise K. Wren.

DO·Pi.

Don Pino Bettisii, Faenza, Emilia, Italy
This mark is thought to belong to Don Pino
Bettisii, a potter in Faenza who died c.1589.

D:P.

Proskau, Silesia, Germany
See p.32. This mark was used during the period
when Johann Carl von Dietrichstein was proprietor, 1770-83.

D S
10

Daniel and James Franklin Seagle, Vale, N.
Carolina, USA
Daniel Seagle worked first as a redware potter in
Vale, Lincoln County, North Carolina, and about
1840 he began producing ash or alkaline-glazed
stonewares. When Daniel Seagle died in 1867 his
son, James Franklin Seagle, maintained his own
pottery on the site. They were active 1828-c.1888.

DSK

De dobbelde Schenckan, Delft, Holland
Founded in 1659, this mark for *De dobbelde
Schenckan* (The Double Tankard) was registered
in 1764.

D·V·

Mennecy-Villeroy, Ile-de-France, France
This porcelain and faience concern protected by
Louis-François de Neufville, duc de Villeroy, was
established first in Paris in 1734. It was transferred
to Mennecy in 1748, and then in 1773 to Bourg-la-
Reine. The first manager was François Barbin,
who with his son (from 1751) ran the factory until
1765. The factory was bought in 1766 by Joseph
Jullien and Symphorien Jacques, who had also
taken a lease on the concern at Sceaux in 1763.

They ran both factories until 1772 when they sold the Sceaux factory, and in 1773 transferred the factory at Mennecy to Bourg-la-Reine. The factory continued until 1806. Early porcelain is milky-white with a brilliant, clear glaze. Later porcelain has a yellow tone, and is often painted with Japanese-style decoration; others feature floral designs. Distinctive colours are rose pink and bright blue. This mark, and many variations of the initials "DV" (which stand for "de Villeroy") were used.

Deiderich & Wilhelm Terhellen, Aumund, Hanover, Germany

Two brothers named Deiderich and Wilhelm Terhellen (together with Johann Christoph Mülhausen), were the owners of the faience factory at Aumund between 1751 and 1757. They used this mark. See also p.39.

Eileen Lewenstein, London, UK

Studio-type pottery was produced from 1959 with this seal-type mark or painted initials. She was previously in partnership with Donald Mills at the Briglin Pottery from 1948-59.

Eileen Stevens, Crawley, West Sussex, UK

From 1952 Studio-type ceramics were made, first with this incised or painted mark (1952-55), and with a revised version after 1955.

Aveiro, Portugal

A faience factory was established here c.1785. It used this mark which denotes "Fabrica Aveiro". Tablewares and figures were produced.

Frauenberg, Nr. Sarreguemines, France

In 1760 a factory producing faience and glazed earthenware was established; this mark appears in blue.

Franz Bustelli, Nymphenburg, Bavaria, Germany

See p.71. Franz Anton Bustelli (b.1723, d.1763) was appointed to the position of master-modeller at the Nymphenburg factory in 1754, and remained there until his death in 1763. He made a wide variety of figures which were made in an essentially rococo style. The models are frequently left uncoloured, but where colours have been used they include tomato-red, yellow, brown, strong green and deep pink. His figures are impressed with this mark.

F & B

Worcester Porcelains, Hereford and Worcester, UK
See p.23. Used during the third historical period
of Worcester Porcelains (c.1792-1807), this incised
initial mark only rarely appears.

f.c

Francis Glanville Cooper, Sheffield, South
Yorkshire, UK
Studio-type pottery was produced from 1945, with
this painted, incised or impressed seal-type mark.

fCP
FP

Walter J. Fletcher, Evesham, Hereford and
Worcester, UK
These impressed seal marks appear on Studio-
type pottery from 1960, and stand for "Frogland
Cottage Pottery" and "Frogland Pottery".

FD.

Fulda, Hesse, Germany
Two factories were established here with the
patronage of the Prince-Bishops of Fulda. The
faience concern ran from c.1741-58, while hard-
paste porcelain was produced between 1764 and
1789. The faience factory was set up with the help
of Adam Friedrich von Löwenfinck of Bayreuth,
and his brother Karl Heinrich. "FD" for "Fulda"
was the usual form of factory mark, perhaps also
with a painter's mark or date. Chinese-style,
famille verte decorations appear in muffle colours,
and blue and manganese designs were also used.
Output includes figures and tablewares.

F^d

Jean-Gaspard Féraud, Moustiers, Basse-Alpes,
France
Dating from the late 18thC, a group of wares were
made at Moustiers, featuring high-temperature
painted subjects, that are associated with Jean-
Gaspard Féraud (1779-92), who was part of a
family of potters and painters. Subjects include
figures, mythological and pastoral scenes, and
realistic floral designs. Colours are smooth and
glossy. The style was continued by his descendants
until 1874. This mark appears, with either an
upper-case or a lower-case "F".

Fr. Erlemann, Wiesbaden, Nassau, Germany
Erlemann made earthenware at Wiesbaden from
1893 which featured this mark.

E·F·O

Flaminio Fontano, Faenza, Italy
This mark which has been attributed to Flaminio
Fontano, also of Urbino (see p.27), has been found
on maiolica with blue decoration on the reverse, a
style that is characteristic of Faentine maiolica.

Karl Heinrich, Frankfurt-an-der-Oder, Brandenburg, Germany

In 1763 a faience factory was established here by Karl Heinrich. After his death the factory was continued by his widow and children until the 18thC. Tankards comprised the main proportion of the output, decorated in the style of Berlin or Thuringia. Heinrich's wares feature this mark.

F. M.
Bäyreith
1744

Johann Friedrich Metzsch, Bayreuth, Germany

A Hausmaler in Bayreuth c.1735-51, Metzsch ran a painting school, where painters worked on undecorated pieces from Bayreuth or Meissen. Painted subjects include continuous landscapes, figures, ships and obelisks set within baroque cartouches surrounded by garlands of small flowers. This mark appears in gold.

F·R·

Rato, Nr. Lisbon, Portgual

See p.70. This mark denoting "Fabrica Rato", appeared while the Royal factory was directed by Thomaz Brunetto (1767-71).

FSH

Frederick Harrop, Finchley, London, UK

From 1952 Studio-type pottery and stonewares were produced with these incised or painted initials, often with the date of potting.

·f·X·A·R·
·f·Urbino·

Francesco Xanto Avelli di Rovigo, Urbino, Italy

This potter is known by signed and dated works between 1529-42. His signatures range from his full name, these initials, and the letter "X". His *istoriato* wares are characterized by emphatic outlines and strong figures; his palette usually includes a bright orange-yellow, brown and azure blue. Lustring was sometimes added to his work by craftsmen at Gubbio.

Jean-Baptiste Guillibaud, Rouen, Seine-Inférieure, France

Associated with the decorative period of Rouen where the output featured Chinese and baroque-influenced designs, Jean-Baptiste Guillibaud (d.1739) and his widow operated between c.1720-50. The polychrome palette was derived from Chinese *famille verte*; flowers and landscapes are popular motifs. A service was made for François II, Duke of Montmorency-Luxembourg, and the style is marked by borders in red and green, or red and black, and Chinese-style figures, plants and birds in the middle panels. This mark and also the name "Guillibaud" are found.

G·B·S

Widow Van der Strale, Delft, Holland
This mark was registered by widow Van der
Strale for *'t Jonge Moriaenshooft* (The Young
Moor's Head) in 1764.

G·C·P

Johann Georg Christoph Popp, Ansbach,
Bavaria, Germany
See p.39. This is one of the marks used by Popp
while he was a painter at the faience factory at
Ansbach.

·: G.K·:

Georg Friedrich Kordenbusch, Nuremberg,
Germany
Kordenbusch (d.1763) worked as a faience
painter (and possibly a potter) in Nuremberg.
The best work by Kordenbusch includes figures
on tankards, and floral and landscape decoration.
He signed his pieces "GK" with three dots.

G. M. Creyke & Sons, Hanley, Staffordshire, UK
See p.79. This initial mark was used by this firm
1930-48.

g°g·

Göggingen, Nr. Augsburg, Germany
Prince-Bishop Joseph, Langrave of Hesse-
Darmstadt, granted a privilege to Georg Michael
Hofmann of Oettingen to set up a faience factory
here in 1748. It was continued by a modeller called
Joseph Hackl from 1749-52. Faience was marked
with the name of the town in full, or abbreviated
as seen here. Wares include figures, stove tiles,
narrow-necked jugs and plates. Painting was
executed in European or Chinese style.

HC

Hans Coper, Welwyn Garden City, Hertfordshire, UK
A respected Studio-potter who worked for a
time with Lucy Rie at her studio in London,
Coper (1920-81) produced wares in characteristic
machine-age forms, with textured surfaces and
monochrome colour schemes. He used this
impressed or incised seal mark from 1947.

HC

Hilary Carruthers, Malvern, Hereford and
Worcester, UK
Studio-type pottery was produced from 1960, with
this incised or painted initial mark.

H·C·

Cassel, Hesse-Nassau, Germany
A branch of the faience factory sponsored by
Landgrave Friedrich II, this concern began
producing porcelain in 1766. Production mainly
comprised blue-and-white wares, but some

Japanese Kakiemon-style wares were also made. The factory continued until 1788. This mark denoting "Hesse-Cassel" was used.

Hans Gottlieb von Bressler, Breslau, Germany
A *Hausmaler* in Breslau 1732-40, Bressler signed and dated a number of pieces with marks similar to the one shown here. His work is characterized by delicately-painted flowers and figures with decorative panels.

HM

Heber Mathews, Woolwich, London, UK
Studio-type stonewares and porcelains were produced 1931-58 by Mathews (d.1959), who also held a number of teaching posts. This incised mark was used.

HT

Linthorpe Pottery, Middlesbrough, Cleveland, UK
See p.83. This initial mark was used by Henry Tooth, manager up to 1883.

HVH
2

Hendrik van Hoorn, Delft, Holland
This mark was used by Hendrik van Hoorn, manager of *De 3 vergulde Astonne* (The Three Golden Ash Barrels) from 1759 until at least 1764, when he is known to have registered another factory mark. The factory was established c.1655 by J. P. van Kessel.

HVMD

Hendrick van Middeldijk, Delft, Holland
Proprietor of *'t Hart* (The Heart, established in 1661 by Joris Mes) from 1760, Hendrick van Middeldijk registered this mark in 1764.

HW

Henry Wren, Oxshott, Surrey, UK
See p.45. These initials (in upper or lower case) belong to Henry Wren, and appear with and without the name "Oxshott" c.1919-47.

HW
63.

Helen Walters, Hornsey, London, UK
Working from Stroud Green, Helen Walters produced Studio-type wares from 1953 (and also Doulton wares 1945-53). They feature this painted or incised initial mark.

·I·P·

Siena, Tuscany, Italy
The best maiolica made at Siena is characterized by fine, intricate work produced from c.1500, such as small, geometric, repeating patterns, and figures enclosed within scrolling borders. This mark appears on two plates painted with religious subjects.

IVP & C | **J. van Putten**, Delft, Holland
Potters at *De porceleyn Klaeuw* (The Porcelain Claw), J. van Putten and Co. (also of *De 3 Klokken*) worked here 1830-50, and registered this mark.

J·A·F | **Johann Andreas Fiechthorn**, Bayreuth, Germany
See p.40. This mark belongs to Johann Andreas Fiechthorn, a chief painter at Bayreuth c.1745.

JB | **Joan A. Biggs**, London, UK
Previously based at the Princedale Pottery, Joan Biggs worked in London from 1961, and her Studio-type wares featured this painted or incised initial mark.

IDA | **Johannes den Appel**, Delft, Holland
Owner of *De vergulde Boot* (The Golden Boat, founded in 1634) in the mid-18thC, den Appel registered this mark in 1764.

IDM | **Jacobus de Milde**, Delft, Holland
See p.75. This mark was registered in 1764 by Jacobus de Milde while he was owner of *De Paauw* (The Peacock) c.1740-64 or later.

J.F.S. | **Daniel and James Franklin Seagle**,
Vale, N. Carolina, USA
See p.45. This mark was used by James Franklin Seagle.

J·J·P | **Johann Julius Popp**, Ansbach, Bavaria, Germany
See p.39. Johann Julius Popp (d.1792) and his brother Georg Ludwig became proprietors of the factory at Ansbach after the death of their father Johann Georg Christoph in 1791. Prior to this date, J. Julius was a painter at the factory, and this mark appears with the date 1749.

Bayeux
J.L. | **Joachim Langlois**, Bayeux, Calvados, France
See p.42. This mark together with the word "Bayeux" was used on hard-paste porcelain by Joachim Langlois (d.1830).

JP. | **Jacob Petit**, Fontainebleau, Seine-et-Marne, France
A porcelain factory was founded here in 1795 by Benjamin Jacob and Aaron Smoll. They were succeeded by Baruch Weil in 1830, who sold an offshoot of his factory to Jacob and Mardochée Petit in that year. They produced decorative pieces and their concern was commercially successful. This mark was used by Jacob Petit.

Jacques Jarry, Aprey, Haute-Marne, France
A well-known painter at Aprey (1772-81) and later at Sceaux, Jarry was famous for designs featuring flowers and birds. This mark appears in black or other enamel colours.

J. W. G. Wanderer, Bayreuth, Germany
A member of a family of painters that included Adam Clemens Wanderer (see p.39), who worked on brown and yellow wares made at Bayreuth in the 18thC. This mark appears with the date 1774.

J.S.T. & CO.
KEENE.NH.

Hampshire Pottery Company/James S. Taft & Company, Keene, New Hampshire, USA
Active 1871-1923, the original redware flower pots and stoneware vessels made by this firm were supplanted by the early 1880s by white earthenware art lines decorated with bright majolica and dark matt glazes. All types of jugs, jars, baskets, candlesticks, rose bowls, cuspidors, tea sets, dressing table accessories and souvenir items were made. This mark appears impressed.

K
KB:

Künersberg, Nr. Memmingen, Bavaria, Germany
Faience was made in Künersberg from 1745 when a factory was built by Jakob Küner (b.1692, d.1764), a banker and merchant from Memmingen, who had founded a new town named after himself. In 1752 his son Johann Jakob Küner and his brother-in-law Sigmund Friedrich Wogau became partners. Künersberg is renowned for faience painted in muffle colours with a palette that includes greens tinted with yellow and black, and a nut brown. Gilding was also common. These factory marks were sometimes used, and may be accompanied by the initials of the painter. The name of the town also appears in full. A small amount of porcelain was also made at Künersberg, either by Johann Benckgraff, or by C. D. Busch. Two pieces exist, one featuring the arms of the city, and the other marked "Künersberg".

KB

Katharine Pleydell-Bouverie, Kilmington Manor, Wiltshire, UK
Based at various addresses between 1925 and 1985, Katharine Pleydell-Bouverie worked from Kilmington Manor from 1946. She was one of Bernard Leach's first pupils at his St Ives Pottery in 1924. She made Studio-type pottery and stonewares with this incised initial mark and also a "KB" monogram.

Buchwald and Koch, Buchwald and Leihamer, Kiel, Holstein, Germany

J. S. F. Tännich (b.1728) of Strasburg was the first person successfully to establish a faience factory in Kiel in 1763, following three failed attempts (in 1758, 1759-60 and 1762-63). The factory was first owned by the Duke of Holstein, but was sold to a company in 1766. Tännich left in 1768-69 and was replaced by Johann Buchwald of Eckernförde who was accompanied by painter Abraham Leihamer. Fine wares were made during this time painted in clean, strong muffle colours (such a copper-green and a crimson red), and include decorative bowls, pierced plates, flower pots and vases. The mark above denotes "Kiel Buchwald and Koch (a painter)", while the "JL" within the mark below refers to Johann Leihamer, the father of Abraham Leihamer who joined Tännich before his son arrived in Keil with Buchwald.

Carsten Behren, Kellinghusen, Holstein, Germany

Several faience factories were established here in the 18thC. Carsten Behren's factory operated between 1763-c.1830. After his death in 1782 it passed to his heirs, and then to different owners until production ended. This was the mark of the factory while under Behren's ownership.

Joachim Moeller, Kellinghusen, Holstein, Germany

In 1785, the Kellinghusen faience factory founded by Carsten Behren (see above), was sold to Joachim Moeller who owned it until 1795. He used this mark.

Meissen, Nr. Dresden, Saxony, Germany

Johann Friedrich Böttger (1682-1719) experimented with the production of hard-paste porcelain in Saxony in the early 18thC, the first hard-paste to be made on the Continent. Progress was made, and in 1710 a porcelain manufactory was officially established by the King at the Albrechtsburg Fortress in Meissen. Red stonewares and porcelain were made during this early period. After Böttger's death in 1719, Johann Gregor Herold succeeded him as manager, and techniques of both production and decoration developed significantly over the next 25 years. Johann Gottlob Kirchner, a sculptor, was engaged in 1727, and he was joined by Johann Joachim Kaendler in 1731. After Kirchner was discharged in 1733, Kaendler worked with a number of assistants to model the porcelain figures for which

Meissen is renowned. In c.1723 the first factory mark was used to act as a guarantee of origin. This mark denoting "Königliche Pozellan Fabrik" was used around this time.

K / T / C

Tännich and Christopherson, Kiel, Holstein, Germany
See p.53. This is the mark of Johann Samuel Tännich, who ran the faience factory at Keil between 1763 and and 1768-69, together with the initial of the painter Christoph Christopherson.

L. B.

Jacques-Louis Broillet, Gros Caillou, Paris, France
A hard-paste porcelain factory was set up at this address (also known as Vaugirard-Lès-Paris) in 1765, and this mark was registered in 1762.

L.F.M.

Leonhard Friedrich Marx, Nuremberg, Bavaria, Germany
The 18thC faience factory in Nuremberg produced pieces in a baroque style, owing little to contemporary Delft and Chinese-style decoration. The concern was founded in 1712 by two merchants, Christoph Marx and Heinrich Gottfried Hemmon, in association with the guardians of Johann Conrad Romedi. Johann Caspar Ripp (also of Hanau, Ansbach, Bayreuth, Brunswick and Zerbst), was employed as the first manager, but he left in 1713. In 1715, Hemmon sold his share to his partner's son Johann Andreas Marx (a painter). Romedi's share was sold on his death to Johann Jakob Mayer. Christoph Marx died in 1731, but his position was taken up by his widow until 1751, when her son and Mayer operated the factory. In 1760 Mayer died, and Marx died in 1770. This mark belongs to Leonhard Friedrich Marx, a partner of the factory after 1770 when it was in decline.

·LFM·

Leo F. Matthews, Walford Heath, Shropshire, UK
Studio-type pottery was produced from 1954 with this painted or incised intial mark.

L·m·

Leopold Malériat, Sinceny, Aisne, France
See p.34. Malériat succeeded the previous manager Pellevé in 1737, and continued the Rouen styles produced by Pellevé until 1775.

L P K

De Lampetkan, Delft, Holland
Established in 1637 by Cornelius Harmansz Valckenhoven, *De Lampetkan* (The Ewer) used this factory mark. The factory closed in 1806-10.

'L·S·'

Lorenz Speckner, Kreussen, Nr. Bayreuth, Germany
An important stoneware-producing area,
Kreussen is noted for its brownglazed wares,
often detailed in enamel colours. The best known
figures are a family of modellers called Vest
from Austria. They were succeeded by Lorenz
Speckner (b.1598, d.after 1669) who married the
widow of Georg Vest the Elder. He introduced
the production of faience to the Vest's pottery. His
son and grandson were also potters at Kreussen.
This mark appears on a piece dated 1618.

L S

La Seinie, Saint-Yrieux, Haute-Vienne, France
See p.95. This initial mark also appears on
porcelain made at La Seinie.

L S

Vendrenne, Vendée, France
Marc-Lozelet founded a hard-paste porcelain
factory here c.1800. The mark is the same as La
Seinie (see above).

M C S

Meissen, saxony, Nr. Dresden, Germany
See p.53. Gilding found on wares produced at
Meissen during the early Herold period is now
known to have been carried out at Augsburg by
Bartholomäus Seuter (see p.42) and his associates.
Designs in gilt with black and red monochrome
include Chinoiseries and European figure subjects
often in Watteau's style. This mark (and other
types) appears on Augsburg-decorated pieces
c.1730-35.

M&E

Mayer & Elliot, Longport, Staffordshire, UK
Based at Fountain Place and Dale Hall, and
formerly known as Mayer Bros. & Elliot (1855-58),
this company produced earthenwares 1858-61,
with this initial mark, and other marks that
incorporate these distinguishing initials. Impressed month and year numbers also occur.
Subsequently, the name of the firm changed to
Liddle, Elliot & Son, which continued at the
Dale Hall Pottery 1862-71.

M G H

M̶G̶

Buckfast Abbey Pottery, Devon, UK
Operated by Miss M. Gibson-Horrocks from 1952,
this pottery produced Studio-type wares. These
were her incised or impressed personal marks,
and appear from 1952.

MJ

Mervyn Jude, Glyn Ceiriog, Clwyd, Wales, UK
See p.89. This is Mervyn Jude's intial mark, and
was used from c.1948.

M·J·T

Johann Christoph Mülhausen, Wilhelm and Diederich Terhellen, Aumund, Hanover, Germany
A faience factory existed here between 1751 and 1761. The Terhellens, together with J. Christoph Mülhausen, used this mark while they owned the concern 1751-57. See also p.46.

M:OL.

Oude Loosdrecht, Holland
The Weesp porcelain factory was transferred here in 1771 when it was purchased by a pastor called Johannes de Mol. It flourished until 1782 when it was taken over by a company and moved to Amstel. Wares include openwork vases, and egg-shaped tea and coffee pots. Variations of this mark appear during de Mol's ownership, incised or in enamel colours.

M.P.M

Meissen, Nr. Dresden, Saxony, Germany
See p.53. Also an early factory mark standing for "Meissner Porzellan Manufaktur", this example is relatively rare and was used 1723-24.

M·V

Rouen, Seine-Inférieure, France
The second phase of faience production began in Rouen in 1644 when a privilege was obtained by Nicolas Poirel, and then transferred to Edme Poterat who actually started the concern in 1647. Together with his son and heir, Poterat ran the factory until 1720. This is a painter's mark that has been found on pieces made at Rouen in the late 17thC.

Michel-Mathieu and Michel Vallet, Rouen, Seine-Inférieure, France
General potters in Rouen from 1757; pieces are found with this mark.

NJ

Nerys Jude, Glyn Ceiriog, Clwyd, Wales, UK
See p.89. Nerys Jude used this initial mark from c.1948.

.N S.

Ottweiler, Rhineland, Germany
A faience and porcelain factory was established at Ottweiler in 1763, with the patronage of Prince Wilhelm Heinrich of Nassau, by Etienne-Dominique Pellevé of Sinceny and others. Hard-paste porcelain and faience were made 1763-94, and glazed earthenware from 1784-94. Porcelain wares include tablewares in a rococo style with high quality painting. Porcelain made at the factory features this mark which represents "Nassau-Sarrbrucken".

nx **Hirschvogel-Nickel-Reinhard Factory**, Nuremberg, Bavaria, Germany
See p.34. This mark appears on an armorial dish made at Nuremberg and probably represents the Hirschvogel-Nickel-Reinhard Factory in the second quarter of the 16thC.

O FF **Offenbach**, Nr. Frankfurt-am-Main, Germany
In 1739 a faience factory was established in Offenbach by Philipp Friedrich Lay in 1739, who transferred it to his son Georg Heinrich in 1762. It was sold by the latter in 1765 to Johann Christoph Puschel. Under various owners the factory continued until the early 19thC. Output comprised mainly tablewares decorated with flowers, birds and figures in high temperature colours. The factory probably ceased in the 19thC. This factory mark was used.

OP **Sceaux**, Seine, France
Faience was first produced at Sceaux c.1735 by de Bey and Jacques Chapelle; the latter became sole proprietor in 1759. The material was fine quality with good quality painting in muffle colours. Decorative, tablewares and figures were made. This mark appears on faience.

O.V. **Ohio Valley China Company**, Wheeling, West Virginia, USA
The pottery (active 1887-93) produced good quality hard-paste porcelain tableware as well as some remarkable art wares with figures and elaborate piercing. A shield mark was used on heavy goods, while a "leafy" mark appears on artistic wares.

PA **Rouen**, Seine-Inférieure, France
See p.56. This is a painter's mark found on pieces from made at Rouen in the late 17thC.

P **Peggy Cherniavsky**, London, UK
Pottery figures were produced from 1951. This impressed or printed mark was used 1951-54.

PC **Paul Caussy**, Rouen, Seine-Inférieure, France
Paul Caussy (d.1731), together with his son Pierre-Paul (d.1759) and grandson Pierre-Clement, were potters at Rouen from 1707. This mark appears.

P.F. **Joseph Fouque**, Moustiers, Basse-Alpes, France
See p.26. This mark, together with a number of others, was used by Fouque.

P&H
CHOISY

V. Paillart and N. Hautin, Chiosy-le-Roi, Seine, France

A factory producing white earthenware and porcelain was established here by the brothers Paillart in 1804, and from 1824-36 the firm was V. Paillart and N. Hautin (Hautin and Boulenger from 1936). This mark was used 1824-36.

PH
PH
F

Paul Hannong, Frankenthal, Palatinate, Germany

In 1755 Paul-Antoine Hannong of Strasburg was forced to give up porcelain production by the Vincennes authorities, and he moved to Frankenthal where he obtained a privilege from the Elector Karl (or Carl) Theodor to begin a factory. His son Charles-François-Paul was manager until Paul Antoine's death in 1757, when another son Charles-Adam took over as manager, and then as owner from 1759. Financial problems led to the factory being purchased by Karl Theodor in 1762. Production in this period was similar to the style used at Strasburg, with rococo forms and distictive red-toned decoration. These marks denoting "Paul Hannong" (above) and "Paul Hannong Frankenthal" (below) were used 1755-59. "PH" was previously used at Strasburg 1753-54.

PK

Philip Knight, Lancing, West Sussex, UK

Studio-type wares, animals and portrait busts were produced from 1950. This impressed seal-type mark with initials in relief was used from 1962.

Count Leopold von Proskau, Silesia, Germany

See p.32. This mark was used by Count Leopold 1763-69.

PO:

Johann Georg Christoph Popp, Ansbach, Bavaria, Germany

See p.39. This mark was used from 1715.

PP

Joan A. Biggs, London, UK

See p.51. This painted or incised Princedale Pottery mark was used 1958-61.

P.R.P

Paul Revere Pottery/Saturday Evening Girls, Boston and Brighton, Massachusetts, USA

Daughters of immigrant families, who were members of a club that met weekly in the local public library, decided to take the librarian's advice to make and decorate pottery in order to occupy themselves, earn some money and learn a trade. Books were read to them as they decorated children's dishes and vases in charming conventionalized floral, faunal and landscape patterns. They employed a professional potter and kilnman.

Francisco de Aponte and Pickman & Co., Seville, Andalusia, Spain
Porcelain was produced by this firm at the "La Cartuja" factory in 1867. This is one of the marks used.

R & C
2

Rabe & Co., Brunswick, Germany
See p.83. In 1773 Johann Benjamin Heinrich Rabe and partner Johann Heinrich Christoph Hillecke leased the faience factory in Brunswick. Rabe bought the factory in 1776 and ran it until his death in 1803. Rabe was ordered to use the ducal mark "B" after being granted a privilege in 1781 (see p.40); this mark also appears.

R.
/C

Rudolstadt, Thuringia, Germany
A faience factory was established here in 1720 by Johann Philipp Frantz and D.C. Freischhauer of Dorotheenthal. The factory continued until c.1791. This mark appears; the letter "C" is probably a painter's initial.

Richard Freeman, Bath, Avon, UK
From 1956 Richard Freeman produced Studio-type wares at the Bath Pottery with this impressed seal mark.

Rh

François Dumetz, Aire, Pas-de-Calais, France
See p.33. This mark was used on faience made at Aire under the direction of François Dumetz, 1755-c.1790.

RL.

Robert's Factory, Marseilles, Bouches-du-Rhône, France
See p.33. This mark was also used by this factory which operated from c.1750 until at least 1793. Marks appear in a number of different forms.

(R&L)

Robinson & Leadbeater (Ltd.), Stoke, Staffordshire, UK
Between 1864 and 1924 this factory produced parian figures. This impressed initial mark was found on the back of parian and bone china figures and groups from c.1885. The firm was taken over by J. A. Robinson & Sons Ltd. and then by Cauldon Potteries Ltd.

Rauenstein, Thuringia, Germany
In 1783 Duke Georg von Saxony-Meiningen granted a licence for porcelain production to Johann Georg, Johann Friedrich and Christian Daniel Greiner who founded a factory. To begin with, services were made in the Meissen style. Underglaze designs in blue and purple are characteristic of the concern; rustic overglaze decoration was also used. The factory continued until the late 19thC. This mark appears.

RS

Raymon Silverman, Dulwich, London, UK
This impressed seal mark appears on Studio-type ceramics from 1962.

Ruth Duckworth, Kew, London, UK
Studio-type pottery and sculpture were produced with this painted or incised mark from 1956.

R.X.

Robert's Factory, Marseilles, Bouches-du-Rhône, France
See p.33. This mark was also used. Marks appear in a number of different forms.

Saint-Cloud, Seine-et-Oise, France
Porcelain was made in Saint-Cloud from 1693 by the family of Pierre Chicaneau, who had earlier discovered the process. After his death in 1678, Chicaneau's widow married Henri-Charles Trou, who obtained for the factory the protection of the Duke of Orleans, and letters patent were awarded to the Chicaneau family in 1702. Porcelain production remained their exclusive right until c.1722, when the patent was renewed by Henri and Gabriel Trou. The factory remained in the hands of the Trou factory until it closed in 1766. Saint Cloud porcelain has a creamy or ivory tone, and early pieces are often decorated with lambrequins based on textile ornament. Variations of this mark are found in underglaze blue, red enamel or as an incised mark. The "T" denotes Henri Trou, who was able to produce porcelain after 1722.

S·c·ÿ

Sinceny, Aisne, France
See p.34. These marks were used during the "second period" of the factory 1775-95.

S/L

Johann Leihamer, Schleswig, Germany
A faience factory was established in Schleswig by Johann Christoph Ludwig Lücke in 1755. From 1756 Adriani, Schmattau and two brothers called Otte were proprietors, and in 1758 Johann

Ramsbusch bought the factory. His son was forced to sell in 1801 and the factory was finally closed in 1841. This mark belongs to painter Johann Leihamer (b.1721) from c.1758.

·S·P

Sceaux, Seine, France
See p.57. In 1753 the Duc de Penthièvre succeeded his aunt, the Duchess de Maine, as patron of the factory at Sceaux. This painted mark appears on faience and stands for "Sceaux Penthièvre".

SR

Stanislas Reychan, London, UK
Based at the Garden Studio, Stanilas Reychan produced pottery sculpture and ornaments from 1950 with this impressed seal mark.

S·X

Sceaux, Seine, France
See p.57. The first attempt to produce porcelain at Sceaux in 1749-52, was suppressed in the interest of the concern at Vincennes (Sèvres), and little was produced before 1763, when Joseph Jullien and Charles-Symphorien Jacques took over the factory, and the Sèvres monopoly had become more relaxed. The Duc de Penthièvre (see above) provided powerful support for the factory at Sceaux. In 1772 the factory was sold to Richard Glot. This incised mark appears on soft-paste porcelain from c.1763, and in 1773 Glot submitted it to the police authorities.

t hart

't Hart, Delft, Holland
This factory (The Heart) was established in 1661 by Joris Mes; this mark appears.

THOM PSON

C. C. Thompson Pottery Company, East Liverpool, Ohio, USA
Created originally to make Rockingham and yellow ware, the company (1868-1938) continued to produce these products until 1917. In 1883, they expanded their product line to include decorated earthenware in miscellaneous table and toilet forms, such as diapers, pitchers, teapots, covered dishes, cuspidors, bedpans and toilet sets. About 1890, they added white ironstone toilet and dinner ware to the line, and by 1917 semi-vitreous products were made.

T°

Bristol, Avon, UK
Sophisticated tin-glazed earthenwares were made in Bristol from c.1660. In 1748 Lund's factory in Bristol began to make soft-paste porcelain. In 1751 this concern was relocated to Worcester. Hard-

paste porcelain was made from c.1770 when a Plymouth porcelain manufacture was taken over by Richard Campion and moved to Bristol in 1774. This impressed or moulded "repairer's" mark appears on some pieces of hard-paste. This mark also appears on some pieces made at Bow and Worcester (c.1760-69).

Plymouth Porcelain Works, Devon, UK

A porcelain factory was established here by a man called William Cookworthy, and operated between 1768 and 1770. He discovered the porcelain-production process independently, and found the materials necessary to begin production in Cornwall after a search which took many years. He took out a patent in 1768, and began a factory with the help of Thomas Pitt and a group of Quakers from the Plymouth and Bristol areas. The usual mark was the alchemist's sign for tin, and this may appear in underglaze blue, blue enamel, red or gold. Painting in underglaze blue has a blackish tone. His pieces feature Oriental designs and occasionally bird designs. In 1770 Cookworthy transferred to Bristol, and in 1774 the factory was taken over by Richard Champion. This "repairer's" mark appears on Plymouth porcelain, as well as pieces made at Bow, Worcester (c.1760-69) and Bristol (see above).

"Tebo" Toulouse, Location unknown, UK

Believed to be the mark of a ceramic modeller or "repairer", this impressed or relief-moulded mark appears on porcelain from Bow (c.1750-60), Worcester (c.1760-69), Bristol (c.1770-74) and Plymouth (c.1769-70). The letter "T" was very occasionally used by the same craftsman.

Thomas Plant, Lane End, Staffordshire, UK

This painted mark was used on earthenware figures made 1825-50.

Trenton Potteries Company, Trenton, New Jersey, USA

This company (1892-1960) was created out of five potteries that specialized in sanitary ware, although artistic pieces were sometimes produced like the four mammoth urns elaborately decorated in the style of Sèvres for the company's display at the St Louis world's fair of 1904. During the 1930s, when construction had come to a virtual halt in the US, the company made florists' crockery to fill the kilns and keep the workers busy. These wares with their bright monochromatic glazes are very collectable today. The company made hotel ware at the turn of the century.

Y & Y

Turner & Tomkinson, Tunstall, Staffordshire
Earthenwares were made by this firm 1860-72; it subsequently became G. W. Turner & Sons. The initials "T. T." were used in a variety of marks, and also in a fancy form as seen here.

U- S -E -T- W
INDIANAPOLIS
IND.

United States Encaustic Tile Company,
Indianapolis, Indiana, USA
Colourful floor tiles and standard glossy wall and fireplace tiles decorated with heads and conventional ornament were made in large quantities by this company (1877-1939), which became the U.S. Tile Corporation in 1932. This incised mark appears.

.VA

Vista Alegre, Nr. Oporto, Portugal
A porcelain factory was founded here in 1824 by José Ferreira Pinto Basso, with Royal patronage until 1840. This mark was used after 1840; before 1840 the initials appear beneath a crown. High quality services and luxury porcelain are made at this factory, which is the only one in Portugal to produce these types of wares. The concern is still operated by the family of the founder.

Vᵉ**L.**

Veuve Langlois, Bayeux, Calvados, France
See p.42. After the death of Joachim Langlois in 1830, the porcelain factory at Bayeux was continued by his daughters until 1849. This mark appears. The letter "G" was added after the factory was bought by François Gosse who owned it until 1878.

Veuve Arnoux, Apt, Vaucluse, France
The widow of Apt potter, Antoine Arnoux, who was also a sister of Joseph-Jacques Fouque, continued production of faience and English-style earthenware in the late 18thC until 1802. This impressed mark appears.

WB

Friedrich Thomin, Würzburg, Lower Franconia, Germany
In the 19thC, a *Hausmaler* at Würzburg called Friedrich Thomin, decorated porcelain from Nymphenburg and Thuringia with views of Würzburg. The pieces date from the early 19thC and bear this mark in black.

W D.C.   **Derby Porcelain Works**, Derbyshire, UK
See p.25. This early incised mark from c.1750-55 is rare.

WE   **Wrisbergholzen**, Hanover, Germany
A faience factory was founded 1735-37 by Baron von Wrisberg, and was run by a number of managers until 1804. Production was influenced by Dutch Delft wares. This factory mark appears, often with a painter's mark.

W.E. PCO.
CHINA   **West End Pottery Company**, East Liverpool, Ohio, USA
This pottery (active 1893-1938) made ironstone (or white granite) dinner, toilet and hotel wares and some speciality items. Semi-vitreous dinner, hotel, tea and toilet wares were offered by 1927, along with premium assortments and hospital and druggists' ware.

W.M.   **William Moorcroft**, Burslem, Staffordshire, UK
After working as Art Director at Macintyre and Co., William Moorcroft (1872-1945) set up his own factory in 1913. As well as his famous "Florian" wares designed for Macintyre, Moorcroft produced a wide range richly-glazed, floral-decorated earthenwares. Moorcroft signed all Florian Wares with "W. M. des." or "W. Moorcroft des.". Sometimes pieces were marked "Florian Ware Jas. Macintyre & Co. Ltd. Burslem, England". Florian wares were sold at Liberty's in London, and Tiffany's in New York. These painted initials are found.

WN
53   **William Newland**, Prestwood, Buckinghamshire, UK
Studio-type pottery, ceramic sculpture and architectural wares were produced by Newland from 1948. This painted or incised initial mark appears with year numbers.

H. M. Williamson & Sons, Longton, Staffordshire, UK
Based at the Bridge Pottery, this firm produced porcelain c.1879-1941. Many variations of this mark appear; this example was used from c.1903; a plainer version of the same mark was used from c.1879.

W : V : B   **Willem van Beek**, Delft, Holland
Founded 1661-62 by Sebastian M. van Kuyck, and others, *De twee Wildemannen* (The Two Wild Men) was owned by Willem van Beek between 1760 and 1780. He used this mark.

Reginald Wells, Storrington, West Sussex, UK
Previously based at Wrotham, Kent (c.1909) and
Chelsea in London (c.1910-24), Reginald Wells
(b.1877, d.1951) worked from Storrington from
c.1925. He produced Studio-type pottery, stonewares and figures. This incised or impressed
initial mark was used from 1910.

Zacharias Dextra, Delft, Holland
See p.50. This mark was used by Zacharias Dextra
while he was manager of *De 3 vergulde Astonne*
(The Three Golden Ash Barrels) from 1712-
c.1759.

Monograms

Alan Brough, London, UK
Based in Brixham, Devon from 1946, Alan
Brough moved to London in 1956. His Studio-
type pottery features this painted mark.

Akron China Company, Akron, Ohio, USA
This was a large pottery (1894-1908) making
decorated dinner and toilet wares in white granite
(ironstone) as well as a line of hotel ware called
"Revere".

Elgersburg, Thuringia, Germany
C. E. & F. Arnoldi produced hard-paste porcelain
from 1808. This mark was used together with a
circular stamp with the words "Fabrik Arnoldi
Elgersburg".

Alan Caiger-Smith, Berkshire, UK
Since establishing the Aldermaston Pottery in
1955, Alan Caiger-Smith has become recognized
interna-tionally, not only as one of the most
influential potters of his day but also as a leading
authority on tin-glazed and lustred earthenwares.
His published works are essential reading to
potters and ceramic historians alike. His own
output is of Studio ceramics. While Alan Caiger-
Smith's mark is a combination of his initials, the
example seen here is that of A. Partridge, one of
the several potters who have worked with him at
the Aldermaston Pottery over the years. Marks on
his pottery are incised or painted. Other potters
working at Aldermaston also used monograms,
each featuring the letter "A".

Arthur J. Griffiths, Long Whatton, Leicestershire, UK
This impressed mark used on Studio-type wares
from 1948. Griffiths also worked at the Crowan
and Leach Potteries.

Anna Hagen, London, UK
Anna Hagen produced hand-thrown, moulded
and pressed wares from 1956. The mark above
was incised, and appeared on hand-thrown pots,
and the mark below, an impressed seal mark,
appears on moulded and pressed wares.

Adriaenus Koeks, Delft, Holland
This mark was used by Dutch potter Adriaenus
Koeks (or Kocks), while he was working at *De
Grieksche A* (The Greek A) factory in Delft (1687-
1701). Some of Koeks' accounts are preserved at
Hampton Court Palace. The mark appears on all

types of Dutch Delft wares, and has been extensively faked.

Andreas Kordenbusch, Nuremberg, Germany
Kordenbusch (d.1754) was a faience painter in Nuremberg from c.1726, who produced high quality work, including an armorial tankard painted in blue with a figure, dated 1738.

Alfred Pocock, Slinfold, West Sussex, UK
A. L. Pocock made Studio-type pottery c.1920-35, and used an incised or painted monogram mark with the year of production.

Tenby Pottery, Tenby, Dyfed, Wales, UK
Owned by Anthony Markes, the Tenby Pottery produced Studio-type wares from 1959. Pieces made and decorated by Markes himself bore these initial marks.

Alfred and Louise Powell, Staffordshire and London, UK
The Powells worked as pottery designers and decorators for Wedgwood who supplied them with earthenware blanks. Their painted earthenwares usually bear impressed Wedgwood marks. They also worked independently in London. This personal painted mark was used by Alfred Powell (d.1960) c.1904-39. Louise Powell used a similar mark with the initials "LP".

Albert Potteries Ltd., Burslem, Staffordshire, UK
The Albert Potteries produced earthenwares 1946-54. This printed or impressed mark was used. Also used was a printed mark, "Albert Potteries Ltd., Burslem, Made in England".

Aylesford Priory Pottery, Aylesford, Kent, UK
This impressed seal mark was used on stonewares from 1955. It also appears with the word "Aylesford" written underneath.

Aprey, Haute-Marne, France
A faience factory was established in Aprey c.1744 by Jacques Lallemant, Baron d'Aprey, and his brother Joseph Lallemant de Villehaut. After the former retired, Joseph engaged François Ollivier, a potter from Nevers, and fine wares were made at the factory. Ollivier was director until 1792. The monogram "APR" was not always used; where it does appear it is often accompanied by the initial of the painter.

Anne H. Thalmessinger, Camberley, Surrey, UK
From 1961 Thalmessinger made Studio-type
pottery using this mark or variations.

American Encaustic Tiling Company, Zanesville,
Ohio, USA
The American businessmen who founded the
company brought English tile maker Gilbert
Elliott to Zanesville in 1876 to supervise
production. Encaustic, relief, glazed, plastic
sketches, imitation mosaic, damask, portrait,
unglazed floor, and faience tiles were all made
between 1875 and 1935. In addition, plaques,
plates, figurines, vases, fountains and bathroom
fixtures were also produced. The company was
very successful and had a second plant in California by 1920. Half the tiles in New York's
Holland Tunnel were made by this company.

Antoine Bonnefoy, Marseilles, Bouches-du-Rhône,
France
Personal mark of Antoine Bonnefoy (d.1793), who
ran a successful factory in Marseilles from 1762.
(See p.22.)

Britannia China Company, Longton,
Staffordshire, UK
Porcelain was produced by this factory 1895-1906.
This printed or impressed mark was used
1904-06. The impressed initial mark "B. C. Co."
was used 1895-1906.

Burmantofts, Leeds, West Yorkshire, UK
Owned by a company called Messrs. Wilcox & Co.
(Ltd.), this firm produced Art Pottery 1882-1904.
This impressed mark was used, sometimes with
the words "Burmantofts Faience" also impressed.

Hugo Brouwer, Delft, Holland
Mark of potter Hugo Brouwer registered in 1764,
at *De 3 porceleyne Flessies* (The Three Porcelain
Scent-Bottles), where he worked 1748-77. Brouwer also worked at *Het Bijltje* (The Hatchet).

C. J. C. Bailey (or Bailey & Co.), London, UK
Operating between 1864 and 1889, this pottery
produced stonewares, terracotta and porcelain
(from c.1873). The name subsequently changed
to Fulham Pottery & Cheavin Filter Co. Ltd. This
incised monogram mark comprising the initials
"C. J. C. B." often appears with the words
"Fulham Pottery" and the date.

Jean Bertin, Rouen, Seine-Inférieure, France
Between c.1700 and 1750, Jean Bertin, his father
Henri, and his family, made faience in Rouen.
This mark appears.

Joseph-François Boussemaert, Lille, France
Boussemaert (b.1729, d.1773) took over the factory
established by his father-in-law, Jacques Féburier
(see p.22), after the death of the latter in 1729.
Boussemaert remained as proprietor until his
death.

Hamburg, Germany
See p.25. This mark is one of those probably used
by a painter, c.1625-30.

Baron Jean-Louis de Beyerlé, Niderviller, Lorraine,
France
See p.31. Although pieces were often unmarked
during the ownership of Baron de Beyerlé, this
mark occasionally appears on faience and
porcelain (which was made from 1765).

B

Burgess & Leigh (Ltd.), Burslem, Staffordshire, UK
Active from 1862 and based at the Hill Pottery
c.1867-89, and Middleport Pottery from c.1889,
this firm produced earthenwares. Pieces made
from 1862 feature this monogram mark.

T̃B

Thomaz Brunetto, Rato, Portugal
A royal faience factory was established in 1767,
directed by Thomaz Brunetto from Turin until
1771. This mark was used during Brunetto's
period, with the initials "F. R."

Faenza, Emilia, Italy
Maiolica was made in Faenza (the origin of the
term "faience") from the 14thC, and some of the
finest Italian tin-glazed earthenware was made
there between 1500 and 1530. This "BT" or "TB"
monogram appears on a number of different
pieces which also feature painter's marks, and
probably was probably used by a particular
workshop.

Vodrey Pottery Company, East Liverpool,
Ohio, USA
Created by three brothers after their father had
disastrous results with earlier partnerships in
several cities, Vodrey and Brother Pottery
Company produced Rockingham and yellow
ware in its Palissy Works beginning in 1858.

Following the Civil War, the company prospered
and added white ironstone as a product beginning
in 1876. Semi-porcelain was added to the ironstone line in 1896, and the company continued to
produce dinner, toilet and hotel wares until it
closed in 1928.

J. B. Owens Pottery Company, Zanesville, Ohio, USA

Owens built and operated several potteries during
his life, but this one featured art wares that were
designed, made and decorated by leading potters,
chemists and decorators during the brief time that
the pottery was in production (1896-1907). Overall
the work was derivative, with many references to
the pottery produced at Rookwood (see p.92), but
Owens' ware won gold medals in at least one
international fair.

Joseph Clérissy, Saint-Jean-du-Désert, France

In 1679 Joseph Clérissy, the son of the elder
Antoine Clérissy of Moustiers, took over an
existing faience factory located at Saint-Jean-du-
Désert (a suburb of Marseilles). Clérissy died in
poverty in 1685, and the factory was subsequently
managed by his widow, Anne Roux, and her new
husband, a faience painter at the factory. Joseph
Clérissy's son Antoine took over the factory on his
mother's death in 1694, and conducted the factory
successfully until 1733 when it was moved to
Marseilles itself. This mark was used by Joseph
Clérissy.

Nymphenburg, Bavaria, Germany

One of the main German porcelain-producing
centres of the 18thC, Ignaz Niedermeyer founded
the factory at Nymphenburg with the sponsorship
of Elector Max III Joseph of Bavaria, and the help
of porcelain painter and arcanist Joseph Jakob
Ringler. Pieces made were high in quality and
artistic value, but the concern ran into financial
difficulties and the Elector was forced to increase
his subsidy. He died in 1770, and the factory
passed into the hands of Karl Theodor of the
Palatinate, who already had interests in the
factory at Frankenthal. The Nymphenburg
factory took second place until the Frankenthal
works closed in 1799. In the mid-18thC the
factory at Nymphenburg employed some talented
painters and modellers such as Franz Anton
Bustelli (active 1754-63), and J. P. Melchior (from
1797). The factory remained a State possession

until 1862, and was then leased into private ownership. The factory still exists today. Output includes figures and tablewares in the rococo style. This mark appears on a group of coffee cups made for the Turkish market.

Coalport Porcelain Works, Coalport, Shropshire, UK

This factory was established by John Rose in the late 18thC making table and decorative wares. Now housed at Stoke-on-Trent, the factory is still in production. Early pre-1805 porcelains were unmarked, and marks were rarely used before 1820. The painted or gilt monogram mark (above) was used c.1851-61. The mark below was one of those used on Coalport's decorative floral-encrusted porcelains made during the 1810-25 period. It appears painted in underglaze blue.

Ludwigsburg, Württemberg, Germany

Faience was made in Ludwigsburg from 1757 by Häckher, but in 1758 his privilege was transferred by Duke Charles Eugene to Johann Jakob Mergenthaler and Anton Joachim. (Porcelain was also made, see p.143.) The Duke took over the factory himself in 1763, and it was managed by Frau de Becke (Maria Löwenfinck). Cream-coloured earthenware was made by Gottfried Markt after 1776. Charles Eugene died in 1793, and production went into decline until there was a revival under King Friedrich. Cream-coloured earthenware was the main product during the final years of operation. Pieces feature flower decoration on a white ground and also moulded decoration similar to Niderviller. The mark above appears on faience 1757-1824; the centre mark was used on cream-coloured earthenware 1776-1824; the mark below appears on porcelain during the time of Duke Charkes Eugene, 1758-93. The factory closed in 1824.

Sèvres, France

Originally established at Vincennes, this porcelain factory was moved to Sèvres in 1756, still under the ownership of a joint stock company (25 per cent Royal shares) which was founded in 1753. The eight leaseholders received a Royal privilege for 30 years, but disagreements led to the King taking control of the factory in 1759. Soft-paste porcelain was made up to c.1800, hard-paste after c.1770. The factory was elevated to an Imperial establishment in 1804 and received financial support. Particular marks were used during the time of each reigning monarch. This mark was used during the time of Charles X (1824-30) and appears in blue. The number 25 refers to 1825. The mark may also appear beneath a crown.

Daphne Corke, Colchester, Essex, UK
Daphne Corke worked at the Chelsea pottery from 1951-56, and later independently. This incised or painted monogram mark was used from 1951 on Studio-type wares; name and initial marks appear after 1959.

Charles Ford, Hanley, Staffordshire, UK
Based in Cannon Street 1874-1904 (previously C. & T. Ford and Thomas Ford), this factory produced porcelain. The works were sold to J. A. Robinson & Sons Ltd. in 1904. This impressed or printed monogram mark was used, and also appears on a swan.

Christine Hall, Henley-on-Thames, Oxfordshire, UK
This painted mark was used on porcelain and pottery figures and groups from 1960.

Cornelius Keiser, Delft, Holland
The son of Aelbrecht Cornelisz Keiser who established *De twee Scheepjes* (The Two Little Ships) in 1642, Cornelius Keiser worked at the factory from 1668. This is believed to be his mark.

Coldstone Kiln, Ascott-under-Whychwood, Oxfordshire, UK
Run by Chris Harries, this pottery produced slip-decorated earthenwares from 1953. This impressed seal mark was used.

Lambertus Cleffius, Delft, Holland
Proprietor of *De metale Pot* (The Metal Pot) (established 1638 by Dirck Hieronymusz van Kessel) 1666-91, Cleffius was also proprietor of *De witte Starre* (The White Star) from 1687-89. He used this mark.

Michael Cardew, Cornwall, UK
Cardew (b.1901, d.1982), a Studio-potter, was based at Winchcombe c.1926-39, and at Wenford Bridge c.1939-42; he then moved to Africa. An early pupil of Bernard Leach, Cardew began potting in 1923. He made slip-decorated earthenwares inspired by old English pottery traditions. This impressed seal mark was used by Cardew from c.1926.

Carlo Manzoni, Ashby-de-la-Zouch, Leicestershire, UK

Studio ceramics were produced at the Granville Pottery, Hanley, Staffordshire (1895-98), and then at the Coleorton Pottery, Ashby-de-la-Zouch. This incised monogram was used, accompanied by numerals indicating the year of manufacture.

Caen, Calvados, France

A factory producing hard-paste porcelain existed here 1793-1806, managed by d'Aigmont-Desmares and then Duchevai. Resembling Paris porcelain, they were sometimes sent to be decorated by Parisian enamellers Helley and Dastin. This mark appears in red-brown on wares made after 1799.

Newcomb Pottery, New Orleans, Louisiana, USA

Founded to employ women who had been trained in the art program of H. Sophie Newcomb Memorial College, this pottery (1895-1940) developed a signature style that presented southern flora conventionally in a palette limited to green, blue, yellow and black. Matt glazes were used exclusively after 1911.

Crowan Pottery, Praze, Cornwall, UK

Harry and May Davis, the owners of the Crowan Pottery operated in Cornwall producing Studio-type pottery from 1946. In July 1962 they emigrated to New Zealand. This mark was used from 1946-62.

Carter, Stabler & Adams (Ltd.), Poole Pottery, Dorset, UK

Formerly Carter & Co., this pottery was established in 1921, and continues to the present day. This impressed "C. S. A." monogram mark is rare, and was used from c.1921.

Kloster-Veilsdorf, Thuringia, Germany

The most important Thuringian porcelain factory was established here in 1760 by Prince Friedrich Wilhelm Eugen von Hildburghausen. After his death in 1795, it was sold to the sons of Gotthelf Greiner of Limbach, and Friedrich Greiner of Rauenstein, and remained in the hands of their family until 1822. This mark, which stands for "Closter-Veilsdorf" and appears more rarely as individual letters, appears in underglaze blue. Another "CV" monogram used at Klostert-Veilsdorf was drawn in such a way as to imitate the crossed swords of Meissen.

Vera Cheeseman, Marlow, Buckinghamshire, UK
From 1947, Vera Cheeseman produced Studio-type pottery figures in media such as terracotta. Her monogram mark, which on her pieces appears with the year of production, is similar to one used by Studio-potter Charles Vyse (see below), but Vyse did not produce figures during the same period as Mrs Cheeseman.

Charles Vyse, Chelsea, London, UK
Charles Vyse produced earthenware figures and groups in the 1920s and 1930s, and Chinese glaze-effect stonewares to 1963. This painted mark was used, and features the year of production together with the name "Chelsea". He also used incised or impressed initial marks from 1919.

Dorothy Annan, London, UK
From 1949, Dorothy Annan produced Studio-type pottery, murals and mosaics. She used this incised or painted mark.

De Paauw (The Peacock), Delft, Holland
Established in 1652 by Dirck Hieronymusz van Kessel (also of *De metale Pot*, *De Romein* and *De porceleyn Schotel*), *De Paauw* used this factory mark (and other variations) in the late 17th and early 18thC.

Dora Barrett, Harpenden, Hertfordshire, UK
This incised mark was used on Dora Barrett's terracotta and stoneware models of animals from 1938.

Derek Clarkson, Bacup, Lancashire, UK
This impressed seal-type mark was used on Studio-type wares from January 1961.

Derek Emms, Longton, Staffordshire, UK
Studio-type wares with this impressed seal mark (some were unmarked) from 1955.

Roegina Pottery, Rainham, Kent, UK
Owned by O. C. Davies, this pottery produced earthenwares and operated between 1938 and 1939. Reopened in 1948 by Alfred Wilson Ltd. This monogram "GBD" was used on wares decorated by Mrs Davies c.1938-39.

Daphne Henson, Whitton, Middlesex, UK
This incised mark, often with the date, appears on Studio-type pottery from 1951.

Dorothy Kemp, Felixstowe, Suffolk, UK
Trained by Bernard Leach, Dorothy Kemp made
Studio pottery, slipwares and stonewares from
1939. She used this incised or impressed mark
from c.1939.

Newlyn Harbour Pottery, Cornwall, UK
Run by Dennis Lane, this pottery produced
Studio-type wares from 1956. Pieces made by
Lane feature this incised or impressed mark. The
standard impressed mark is "Newlyn Harbour
Pottery".

 N. Dickinson, Worthing, West Sussex, UK
Dickinson made Studio-type pottery from 1948,
and used this initial mark.

 Deacon Pottery, London, UK
Studio-type pottery was made here from 1952-58.
This impressed, circular seal mark was used.

 Sally Dawson, London, UK
Having previously potted in Canada, Sally Dawson worked at the Canonbury Studio in north
London from 1962. She used this impressed seal-
type mark from 1963, that may also feature the
name "Canonbury Studio".

DVD **Dirck van der Does**, Delft, Holland
Proprietor of *De Roos* (The Rose) 1755-79 (see
p.33), van der Does registered this mark in 1764.

 Eric Barber, Newcastle-upon-Tyne and Sunderland,
Tyne and Wear, UK
From 1951, this company produced non-
commercial, Studio-type earthenwares. This
incised or painted initial mark appeared with
the year of production.

 E. J. D. Bodley, Burslem, Staffordshire, UK
Based at the Hill Pottery and then Crown
Works from 1882, the firm (formerly Bodley &
Son) operated between 1875 and 1892, producing
general ceramics. The distinguishing initials are
found on several printed or impressed marks of
differing design. The initials "J" and "B" are often
joined.

E. Duncombe, Wimbledon, London, UK
Miss E. Duncombe made Studio-type pottery
from 1953, with stonewares from 1962. This
incised or painted mark was used.

Eila Henderson, Eastbourne, East Sussex, UK

Based in London before 1954, Eila Henderson was at the Theda Pottery c.1948-54. She produced Studio-type pottery, one of her marks was this painted or incised mark.

Lambertus van Eenhorn, Delft, Holland

Proprietor of *De metale Pot* (The Metal Pot) (see p.73) 1691-1721, Lambertus van Eenhorn used this monogram mark. The initials below possibly belonged to the painter.

East Liverpool Pottery Company, East Liverpool, Ohio, USA

Organized by John and Robert Hall and Monroe Patterson, this company (1894-1901) made plain and decorated ironstone until 1896 and then semi-vitreous porcelain tableware, toilet ware and souvenir pieces. In 1901, it was one of six firms that merged as the East Liverpool Potteries Company, but two years later the Halls left the merger to form Hall China Company (see p.117). In addition to the company initials, the firm also designated its ware as "Waco China". Other marks featuring these initials were also used.

Raymond Everett, Rye, East Sussex, UK

Studio ceramics were produced by this potter from 1963, with this painted monogram appearing on selected pieces.

Samuel van Eenhorn, Delft, Holland

Manager of the *De Grieksche A* (The Greek A) factory (established by his father, Wouter van Eenhorn (also of *De 3 vergulde Astonne*, *De porceleyn Schotel* and *Het hooge Huys*) and Q.A. van Cleynoven in 1658) from 1674-78, then proprietor from 1678-87. Various combinations of the "SVE" monogram painted in blue on blue and white Delftware. His pieces are generally of high quality, with particular emphasis on Chinese "Transitional" style wares.

Arnoux Fouque & Cie, Valentine, Haute-Garonne, France

Between 1832 and 1860, Joseph-Jacques and Arnoux Fouque produced white earthenware and hard-paste porcelain. This mark appears in red. The Fouques also made creamwares at Toulouse from 1797; a similar mark to this one was used by Antoine and François Fouque with Arnoux from 1829.

H. M. French, Peckham, London, UK

An assistant to Charles Vyse (see p.75) before World War II, Miss French produced Studio-type pottery from 1945. This incised initial mark appears on some pieces made at Vyse's Chelsea pottery in the 1930s.

Faience Manufacturing Company, Brooklyn, New York, USA

The company (1880-92) made a variety of highly decorative earthenware vases, jardinières and baskets, including lines with faience glazes and modelled and applied flowers, as well as a fine creamware with elaborate piercing and gilding. English decorator Edward Lycett directed the factory from 1884 and developed deep cobalt blue and iridescent Persian glazes.

F. S. Robinson, Thundridge, Hertfordshire, UK

Based at the Duckett Wood Pottery from 1959, F. S. Robinson first worked with A. G. Shelley, but produced Studio-types wares featuring this impressed seal mark, independently from 1961.

Sybil Finnemore, Bembridge, Isle of Wight, UK

Sybil Finnemore and her husband T. R. Parsons owned the Bembridge pottery producing Studio-type wares 1949-61. This is her personal mark which she also used during her time at the Yellowsands Pottery (also at Bembridge) c.1927-39.

Anne Gordon, Quick's Green, Pangbourne, Berkshire, UK

Producing Studio-type pottery, figures and bird models, Mrs Gordon used this incised or painted mark, often with the year added from 1958.

Gater, Hall & Co., Burslem, Staffordshire, UK

Formerly Thomas Gater & Co. (established 1895), the firm was based at New Gordon Pottery, Tunstall c.1899-1907, and subsequently at the Royal Overhouse Pottery 1907-43. This mark was used 1914-43. The company became Barratt's of Staffordshire Ltd. in 1943.

Griffen, Smith and Hill, Phoenixville, Pennsylvania, USA

This company (1879-94) was one of a succession of several companies making many different products in the same pottery under different names. During the Griffen, Smith & Hill period the product was majolica, that is cream-coloured earthenware in naturalistic shapes covered with brightly-coloured glossy glazes. Uncoloured ware was called "Ivory". Marks featured the impressed words "Etruscan Majolica", or sometimes only "Etruscan".

Isabel Goudie, Edinburgh, Scotland, UK
Potting between 1920 and 1930 producing Studio-type wares, Isabel Goudie used this monogram mark.

Margaret J. Galbraith, Sydenham, London, UK
From 1961, Studio-type wares were produced with this impressed seal-type mark.

Agnes Benson, Ruislip, London, UK
Based at King's College Road from 1951, Agnes Benson produced Studio-type pottery with this monogram mark from 1959.

Gerald Makin, Bilston, Staffordshire, UK
This impressed, incised or painted monogram mark appears on Studio-type pottery from 1958.

Geoffrey Maund, Croydon, Surrey, UK
Hand-made earthenwares were produced at Geoffrey Maund Pottery Ltd. from 1952. This impressed mark was used from c.1953.

G. M. Creyke & Sons, Hanley, Staffordshire, UK
Between 1920 and 1948 earthenwares were produced by this firm at Bell Works. Pieces are found bearing the initials "GMC".

Grove & Stark, Longton, Staffordshire, UK
Previously called R. H. Grove, this firm was based at the Palissy Works 1871-85, making earthenwares. This monogram appears within a circle on plates in the early 1880s.

Avoncroft Pottery, Hampton Lovett, Nr. Droitwich, Hereford and Worcester, UK
See p.21. This mark is the personal seal mark of owner Geoffrey Whiting used from 1952.

Oldswinford Pottery, Oldswinford, Stourbridge, West Midlands, UK
Operating between 1955 and 1960, this mark comprising the initials of owner Howard Bissell appears on Studio-type wares. The name of the firm was changed to Swincraft Productions c.1960. This impressed seal-type mark was used

up to 1962. Incised initials in a flowing style were used after 1962. The basic mark "Oldswinford Pottery" was also used with the name of the individual potter.

Antoine de la Hubaudière, Quimper, Finistère, France

In c.1690 a faience factory was founded near Quimper by Jean-Baptiste Bousquet. In 1743 it was taken over by Pierre-Paul Caussy of Rouen, and similar wares to those made at Rouen were produced. In 1782 the factory was taken over by Antoine de la Hubaudière (d.1794), the husband of Pierre-Paul Caussy's grand-daughter. In 1872 the factory's director, Fougeray, began to produce imitations of 18thC faience using this mark.

Kelsterbach, Hesse Darmstadt, Germany

Originally a faience-producing factory (see p.29), in 1761 it was taken over by the Landgrave Ludwig VIII, and hard-paste porcelain began to be made under the direction of C. D. Busch of Meissen, who stayed there until 1764. Porcelain continued to be made until the death of Ludwig VIII in 1768, and was not resumed until 1789 with help from J. M. Höckel of Höchst while Johann Jakob Lay was director. Lay bought the factory from the Landgrave in 1799, and in 1802 the Landgrave withdrew his support and the production of porcelain was discontinued. The factory continued, and cream-coloured earthenware was made until c.1823. This mark appears on faience in manganese (more rarely in blue), and on porcelain (during the two periods of production) in underglaze blue usually below a crown from 1766-1802.

Joseph Hannong, Strasburg, France and Frankenthal, Germany

Joseph Hannong (b.1734, d. early 19thC) was the son of Paul Hannong (d.1760), who had been the proprietor of the factory at Strasburg. Joseph was forced to sell his porcelain manufactory at Frankenthal in 1760. He returned to Strasburg two years later to run the factory. In an attempt to make porcelain as well as faience he speculated rashly and as a result bankrupted the concern in 1780. His mark can appear confusing as it appears as an "H" with a dot over the first upright. This is in fact a combination of "J" and "H". In the 18thC the letter "I" was often used as a "J". His mark appears on wares produced at both Strasburg (above), and Frankenthal (below), but the mark used at Frankenthal may be incised, as well as written in blue.

T. S. Haile, Shinners Bridge, Darlington, Devon (and other locations), UK

Samuel Haile was active from c. 1936 until his death in 1948 (apart from a two year gap during World War I, from 1943-45) he produced Studio ceramics using this impressed monogram.

Joseph Holdcroft, Sutherland Pottery, Longton, Staffordshire, UK

From 1865-1940 produced general ceramics as well as more decorative wares, including parian and lead-glazed majolica.

Joyce Haynes, Tuxford, Nr. Newark-on-Trent, Nottinghamshire, UK

Studio pottery, including stoneware and wood-ash glazed wares, was produced c.1940-60. This impressed monogram was used from about 1947.

Johann Heinrich Koch, Cassel, Hesse-Nassau, Germany

A faience factory was founded here c.1680 by the Landgrave of Hesse-Cassel, run by a succession of managers. Johann Heinrich Koch was the manager 1719-24, and the mark above was probably used by him. From 1924 the factory was bought by Johann Christoph Gilze of Brunswick and his son Ludwig, and turned into a successful concern, producing mainly blue-and-white faience. The "HL" in monogram below stands for "Hessen-Land"; this mark may appear with the letter "G" for "Gilze".

Homer Laughlin China Company, East Liverpool, Ohio, and Newell, West Virginia, USA

Prior to 1877, Homer Laughlin was in business with his brother Shakespeare, first in the distribution of pottery made in East Liverpool and then, beginning in 1874, in the production of whiteware. Semi-vitreous porcelain was added during the 1890s. The company, which is still in operation, has made a wide variety of dinner, hotel and toilet wares over the years, although it may be most famous for its Fiesta line, which has been made periodically since 1936. The company expanded to Newell by 1914 and moved its entire operation there in 1929. Today, it is one of the largest potteries in the world.

Paul Hannong, Strasburg, France

From the second generation of the Hannong family who ran the faience factory during its greatest period from 1739-60. He was responsible for the introduction of the full *petit-feu* palette into France and for the employment of some of the finest and most experienced decorators, modellers and arcanists. For example, he employed Adam von Löwenfinck, the Meissen porcelain painter, Johann-Wilhelm Lanz, the modeller who later worked at Frankenthal, and Joseph-Jacob Ringler, the arcanist from Vienna who had gained the secrets of hard-paste porcelain by using his charms on the daughter of the director of the State factory. The marks are generally painted in blue, brown or black, although a few are incised or impressed.

Pierre-Antoine Hannong, Strasburg, France

Son of Paul Hannong, Pierre-Antoine (1739-94) was manager of the factory at Strasburg and Haguenau (1760-62), founder of porcelain factories at Vincennes (1765), Paris (1771) and Vinovo (1776). He revived the production of porcelain at Haguenau 1783-84 using this mark.

Haverfordwest Pottery, T. & A. Whalley, Haverfordwest, Dyfed, Wales, UK

From 1962 producers of Studio-type ceramics including low-fired earthenwares and stonewares. Marks are all impressed.

Seth (or James) Pennington, Liverpool, Mersey, UK

A potter and painter at Liverpool, c.1760-80. Liverpool porcelains made with this mark probably relate to the Penningtons, rather than the Herculaneum Pottery of Liverpool (c.1793-1841). This mark is painted.

Helen Pincombe, Oxshott, Surrey, UK

Operating at The Forge in Oxshott from 1950, this impressed mark appears on Studio-type pottery.

Lorenz Hutschenreuther, Selb, Bavaria, Germany

This hard-paste porcelain factory was founded in 1856 and production began in 1859. Both utility and artistic wares were made. The company expanded taking over other premises and became one of Germany's leading porcelain manufacturers, producing tea and coffee services, household, hotel and restaurant ware, oven-proof

pieces and gift items. This monogram mark was
used, sometimes together with the words
"Hutschenreuther, Selb".

Linthorpe Pottery, Middlesbrough, Cleveland, UK
Founded in 1879 by John Harrison and Henry
Tooth, one of the foremost late Victorian potters
(later, in 1882 proprietor of the Bretby pottery
where a similar monogram was used). Especially
noted for its somewhat unusual forms designed by
Christopher Dresser after pre-Columbian and
Japanese types. The factory closed in 1889.

Tooth & Co., Woodville, Derbyshire, UK
The Bretby Art Pottery was established in 1883
by Henry Tooth and William Ault (who was later
to run his own concern from 1887). Production
was similar to the Linthorpe Pottery (see above)
with coloured, lead-glazed, and ornamental
earthenwares, as well as everyday wares, some
after designs by Christopher Dresser. Large-
scale pieces, such as jardinières with plinths and
umbrella stands, are characteristic of Bretby.
Marks were printed.

Brunswick, Germany
Although established as a small concern in 1707
by Duke Anton Ulrich, this mark refers to the
period between 1710 and 1749 when the factory
at Brunswick was leased to Heinrich Christoph
von Horn and Werner von Hantelmann
(although the substance of the partnership
changed many times). At first production
followed Dutch Delftware but towards the end
of this period more sophisticated and innovative
wares appeared. Production included everyday
wares such as dishes and cylindrical tankards
but somewhat unusually for a faience factory a
relatively wide range of figures and animals in
the rococo style. Marks were painted.

Helen Walters, Stroud Green, Hornsey, London, UK
Studio pottery was produced from 1945. Painted
or incised monograms appear, usually with the
last two numbers denoting the year of
manufacture.

Hawley, Webberley & Co., Garfield Works, Longton,
Staffordshire, UK
Operated from 1895-1902 producing general
earthenwares, including majolica. This printed
mark was used.

Ian Auld, Wimbish, Saffron Walden, Essex, UK
From 1959 Studio ceramics, stoneware and
earthenware were produced. Marks are either
impressed or painted.

Odney Pottery, Grove Farm, Cookham, Berkshire, UK
John Bew of the Odney Pottery (1937-56), used
these painted initials on earthenwares between
1950 and 1954.

Joanna Connell, Great Baddow, Chelmsford, Essex, UK
Joanna Connell produced Studio ceramics,
mainly high-fired wares including stoneware
and porcelain with impressed seal marks.

George Jones & Sons, Burslem, Staffordshire, UK
This concern, based at the Trent Pottery (c.1864-
1907) and then the Crescent Pottery (1907-57),
produced high quality wares for the domestic and
especially for the export markets of North and
South America, Africa, and the Colonies. While
a wide range of wares (including porcelain after
1872) was produced, the factory is probably best
known for its mainly decorative majolica lead-
glazed earthenwares such as centrepieces, vases
and baskets. The mark originally "GJ" from 1861
to 1873 has the words "& Sons" added after this
date together with a crescent. The mark is usually
printed or impressed, but some of the early
monograms used by the firm, appear in slight
relief.

Joan Crawford., Isle of Mull, and Dalkeith, Lothian,
Scotland, UK
From 1951 this potter made Studio-type ceramics.
The marks may be painted or incised with the
initials "J. C." The name "Mull" appears on
specimens made in the Isle of Mull. After her
marriage in 1958 the initials change to a combined
"J. F." (Mrs. J. Faithfull).

John Fisher, Rowlands Gill, Tyne and Wear, UK
From 1950 John Fisher produced Studio ceramics
in association with Denis Rock. As well as his
monogram, which may be either painted or
incised, Fisher also used the kingfisher as his
rebus.

Christopher D. Warham, New Malden, Surrey, UK
Studio pottery was produced from 1949. The
mark "JG" is impressed from 1959. Warham's
incised initial mark was also used 1949-56.

James Hadley & Sons, Worcester, Hereford and Worcester, UK
Operated 1895-1905. Employed as a modeller (and later as chief modeller) during the proprietorship of Kerr and Binns at Worcester (c.1852-62), James Hadley continued to produce models for Royal Worcester even after he became independent in 1875. He established his own company in 1895 producing a wide range of porcelain and pottery. The mark is printed or impressed.

Judith Partridge, Lewes, East Sussex, UK
From 1954 this potter produced Studio pottery and majolica wares. Her monogram appears painted, with or without the word "Lewes".

June Sarene, Pinner, London, UK
From 1954, Studio-type ceramics were produced. An incised or painted monogram may appear, or simply the initials "J. S.".

John Shelly, Bath, Avon, UK
The Bath Pottery also operated in Dorset and Devon from 1949-c.1960, producing Studio pottery. The marks are for the periods 1949-56, and at Littlehempston from 1957.

Kenneth Clark Pottery, London, UK
Tiles and Studio ceramics were produced from 1952, with painted marks.

De Porceleyn Schotel, Delft, Holland
According to some authorities there has been a factory of this name (The Porcelain Dish) in Delft from 1612 until 1777. Over this period it passed through a considerable number of owners including those of Ghisbrecht Cruyck (or Kruyck) who ran it from 1663 to 1671. This individual was also involved if not actually the sole proprietor of *De witte Starre* (The White Star), *De Paauw* (The Peacock) and *De Dissel* (The Pole). This and most of the 30 or so Delft factories produced blue and white tin-glazed pottery i.e. Delftware in the 17thC. This monogram mark is written in cobalt blue.

Kenneth Quick, St Ives, Cornwall, UK
Apart from five years from 1955-60, Kenneth Quick spent all his working life as a potter at the Bernard Leach Pottery making Studio ceramics. Marks are incised. He also worked at the Tregenna Hill Pottery.

Looe Pottery (K. and M. Webb), Barbican, Looe, Cornwall, UK
Stonewares were produced 1932-1962 by K. and M. Webb. Initials appear impressed, printed or incised.

Amédée Lambert, Rouen, Seine-Inférieure, France
Faience was produced by this manufacturer from c.1827. This impressed mark appears on faience wares from c.1827.

Laszlo Bruckner, London, UK
From 1949 Bruckner produced pottery animals and ceramic jewellery. The mark is an impressed monogram but his initials in Roman type are also used.

Bernard Leach, St Ives, Cornwall, UK
See p.41. This personal mark was used by Bernard Leach, 1921-79.

David Leach, Bovey Tracey, Devon, UK
Between 1932 and 1956, David Leach worked with his father, Bernard Leach, at the St Ives Pottery. Pieces made by David Leach at the St Ives Pottery feature his initials "D. A. L." as an incised or seal mark. After 1956, David Leach was based at the Lowerdowne Pottery at Bovey Tracey in Devon. He used this impressed seal mark from 1956.

Eileen Stevens, Ifield, Crawley, West Sussex, UK
Studio ceramics with incised or painted marks were made from 1952 onwards. This monogram was used 1955-60; a similar mark after 1960.

Louis H. H. Glover, Barnsley, South Yorkshire, UK
From 1930 Glover made Studio-type ceramics. Incised or painted marks appear, sometimes with the year of manufacture.

John Leach, Muchelny Pottery, Somerset, UK
Grandson of Bernard Leach (see p.41), John Leach worked at the St Ives Pottery between 1950 and 1963 (where his pots bore the Leach Pottery mark). His individual pieces made before 1958 bear this mark.

Lawrence Keen, Moat House, Stanmore, London, UK
From 1953, Lawrence Keen produced Studio-type ceramics, with these impressed seal marks or painted initials.

Michael Leach, Yelland Manor Pottery, Fremington, Devon, UK
See p.37. Michael Leach trained at his father's St Ives Pottery in Cornwall, but from 1956 worked at the Yelland Manor Pottery. This is his personal seal mark.

Max Läuger, Baden, Germany
This architect, engineer, sculptor and Art Nouveau ceramicist (b.1864, d.1952), is known for pieces with French-style floral or organic forms.

Lahens and Rateau, Bordeaux, Gironde, France
Lahens and Rateau conducted a short-lived porcelain factory here in 1819, and used this mark.

Lonhuda Pottery Company, Steubenville, Ohio, USA
William Long formed a pottery company with W. H. Hunter and Alfred Day, which they named by using the first two or three letters of each name. The earthenware art vases were covered with a mahogany-coloured slip ground and slip-decorated with flowers. The company operated between 1892 and 1894. Long went to work for Weller (see p.226), in 1895 and moved to Denver, Colorado, in 1900, where he founded the Denver China and Pottery Company (see p.44).

Masseot Abaquesne, Rouen, France
Active 1526-57, Abaquesne was the director of an important faience pottery supplying drug pots, tile pavements and interiors for grand chateaux. His work is distinctive, employing the style of decoration associated with the Fontainebleau School of Mannerist ornament. The present monogram appears to combine the letters "MAB".

Molly Coryn, Gomshall, Surrey, UK
From c.1939 Studio pottery was produced, and was marked with this monogram. In 1953 she opened the Gomshall Pottery.

Dorothy B. Martin, Brighton, East Sussex, UK
Studio ceramics were produced from c.1920-35. This "DBM" monogram is incised or painted.

Green Dene Pottery, East Horsley, Surrey, UK
Studio ceramics made at the Green Dene Pottery from 1953 feature the impressed monogram of the proprietor Denis Moore (above). The "MB" monogram (below) was used by Moore's associate Michael Buckland.

Erna Manners, Ealing, London, UK
From c.1920 to 1935, Studio ceramics were
produced with either the initials "E. M.", or a
painted or incised signature.

M. E. Bulmer, Burrill, Yorkshire, UK
Studio ceramics and figurines were produced
c.1956-60, with this incised or painted monogram.

Joris Mes (or Mesch), Delft, Holland
Mes (d.1691) potted at *'t Fortuyn* (The Fortune)
and also at *'t Hart* (The Hart) factories in Delft.
This mark is from 1661.

Fortuné de Monestrol, Rungis, Nr. Paris, France
Historismus pieces, i.e. historical revivals of classic
wares, mainly Italian maiolica, especially Gubbio
lustreware, were made during the second half of
the 19thC. This painted monogram appears in
black.

Maureen Cooper, Roehampton Village, London, UK
From 1955 Studio ceramics and panels were made
with this incised signature, or incised or painted
monogram.

Muriel Harris, Washington, Tyne and Wear, UK
Operating from Old Hall Smithy, Muriel Hall
produced Studio-type pottery 1953-59. From 1961
she worked from St Margarets-at-Cliffe, Dover,
and used this monogram mark.

Milton Head Pottery, Brixham, Devon, UK
From 1951 the Milton Head Pottery produced
earthenware with an incised or painted "MHP"
monogram.

Cricklade Pottery, Cricklade, Wiltshire, UK
This pottery was established 1951 to produce
Studio pottery. Impressed seal marks were used
comprising the initials of the proprietors Ivan and
Kay Martin.

James Macintyre & Co., Washington Works,
Burslem, Staffordshire, UK
Manufacturers of earthenwares from 1860-
1928 (after this date only electrical wares were
produced). Of especial note are the black-glazed
wares, including door furniture and the fine,
cream-coloured body sold under the name "Ivory
China". This impressed or printed monogram
appears in a number of forms.

M. J. Lamb, Kensington, London, UK
Studio ceramics were made from 1951 with this impressed or printed monogram, which appears within a circle.

Joan Motley, Much Wenlock, Shropshire, UK
Based in Chelsea, London (1946-57), Joan Motley moved to Shropshire in 1957. She made Studio pottery and figures, with her incised or painted monogram.

Mervyn Jude, Glyn Ceiriog, Clwyd, Wales, UK
Previously based in Oxshott, Surrey (1948-54), and Cranleigh, Surrey (1954-63), Mervyn and Nerys Jude moved to North Wales in 1963. Studio ceramics are produced; Mervyn Jude used this individual monogram.

Ray Marshall, Stedham, Nr. Midhurst, West Sussex, UK
Based at the Milland Pottery at Liphook, Hampshire prior to establishing his own pottery at Bridgfoot Cottages in 1957, from 1945 Marshall produced Studio-type stonewares. This impressed seal mark was used throughout this period.

Mildred Lockyer, Various locations, UK
Based at a number of addresses in England during her career, Mildred Lockyer produced Studio ceramics between 1928 and 1939, with this incised or painted mark.

Maestro Giorgio Andreoli, Gubbio, Italy
Born at Intra in Lombardy, Giorgio Andreoli established a pottery in Gubbio with his brother Salimbene (d.c.1523) in 1492. In 1498 Giorgio became a citizen of Gubbio. From surviving documents it is apparent that he was making lustreware before 1500, although no piece from this date can be attributed to him. His marked specimens which bear similar devices to the one illustrated here, date from 1518 to 1541. Maestro Giorgio's workshop not only produced both plain and lustred pottery but also lustred pieces made by other Urbino potters. Pieces signed by him are among the most sought-after by modern collectors.

Pierre Mouchard & Family, Rouen, France
These Rouen-based potters operated at Rouen from c.1740 onwards. Pieces have this painted "MP" monogram.

Reginald Marlow, Various locations, UK
Working at a number of addresses in England, and also holding a number of teaching posts, Marlow produced Studio-type pottery from c.1930, with this impressed or relief monogram mark.

Marjorie Scott-Pitcher, Rye, East Sussex, UK
Studio ceramics and figurines were produced in Rye from 1954 onwards. They feature this painted or incised monogram.

Mosbach, Baden, Germany
See p.35. The "MB" monogram under the Palatinate crown is generally accepted as Mosbach. The monogram "MT" probably stands for "Mosbach-Tännich", used while Tännich was the manager and proprietor of the factory.

Morris and Willmore, Columbian Art Pottery, Trenton, New Jersey, USA
English potters founded this pottery (1893-1905), that made decorated ironstone table and toilet wares as well as belleek art wares.

Norah Braden, Coleshill, Wiltshire, UK
Based at The Leach Potter at St. Ives, Cornwall c. 1924-28, Nora Braden moved to Wiltshire in 1928. She produced Studio pottery until 1936 with this impressed and incised monogram.

Nuremberg, Bavaria, Germany
See p.34. This factory mark was used on faience made at Nuremberg after 1750.

Nicola da Urbino, Urbino, Italy
Full name was probably Nicola di Gabriele Sbraga (or Sbraghe). Arguably the most accomplished painted in the *istoriato* or narrative style of maiolica painting. He was active in Urbino from c.1520 until his death in 1537-38, and his work has been identified, starting with five pieces bearing signatures or monograms such as the present mark. Among his greatest work are the two services commissioned firstly by Isabella d'Este of Mantua and secondly by the Calini family of Brescia.

St Agnes Pottery (A. & N. Homer), St Agnes, Cornwall, UK
See p.22. This impressed monogram and seal mark was used.

Nerys Jude, Glyn Ceiriog, Clwyd, Wales, UK
See p.89. Nerys Jude used this monogram mark
from 1948.

Nora Kay, Gerrards Cross, Buckinghamshire, UK
Studio ceramics were made by Nora Kay from
1951, with this impressed monogram.

Nicholas Vergette, London, UK
Also working from other addresses around
England, Vergette produced tiles and Studio
ceramics from 1946-58. This incised or painted
monogram was used.

Joseph Olerys, Moustiers, Basse-Alpes, France
Established in 1738-39 by Joseph Olerys (d.1749)
and his brother-in-law Joseph Laugier, this
pottery was one of several in Moustiers. After
spending over ten years with the Alcora factory in
Spain, Olerys introduced polychrome decoration
to Moustiers using the *style Berain* at first, but this
was soon replaced by medallions and festoons, and
also with a fantasy style of exotic vegetation and
strange creatures. Although Moustiers is associated with the *grand-feu* palette, *petit-feu* was used
to a limited extent after c.1770.

Orchard Pottery, Addiscombe, Surrey, UK
The workshop of B. J. Cotes (later with the
Hastings Pottery), the Orchard Pottery produced
Studio ceramics from 1954-56 with this mark.

Peter Ainslie, Leicester, Leicestershire and Chester,
Chester, UK
Studio ceramics with impressed seal marks as
initials or in the form of a monogram were
produced from 1948.

Percy Brown, Twickenham, London, UK
Featuring either initials or the monogram seen
here, Brown made Studio-type pottery 1930-47.

Pijnacker and Keiser, Delft, Holland
This monogram incorporates the initials of
Adriaen and Jacobus Pijnacker with Albrecht
Keiser. These three potters were involved with
several potteries in Delft from c.1680 including
De vergulde Blompot, *De porceleyn Schotel*, *De
twee Scheepes* and *De twee Wildemannen*. These
factories produced mainly blue and white tin-
glazed ware. This monogram appears painted in
cobalt blue.

Patty Elwood, Meon Pottery, West Meon, Hampshire, UK
Initially based in Newlyn, Cornwall (from 1953-62), Patty Elwood operated from Sussex from 1962, producing Studio ceramics and tablewares. This impressed monogram was used.

Gordon Plahn, Langton Pottery, Nr. Langton Green, Kent, UK
Potter Gordon Plahn made Studio-type pottery at Langton Green from 1961 with this impressed seal comprising his monogram. The mark was previously used by Plahn at the Sevenoaks Pottery, Kent, 1958-61.

Peter Holdsworth, Ramsbury, Wiltshire, UK
Earthenwares and stonewares were made at the Holdsworth Potteries from 1945. This is one of the marks used.

Peter Lane, Andover, Hampshire, UK
Peter Lane made Studio ceramics at The Pottery from 1961, with this impressed monogram, and also with painted and incised marks.

Rookwood Pottery, Cincinnati, Ohio, USA
Founded by Cincinnati socialite ceramics decorator, Maria Longworth Nichols, this factory (1880-1967) was considered the quintessential art pottery at the turn of the century. Decorators trained in art academies painted a variety of subjects in naturally coloured slips on damp earthenware forms that were bisque fired and then glazed. Although hand-decorated pieces continued to be made well into the 20thC, the company's later work was largely moulded and covered with a monochromatic glaze. Work can be dated by the number of flames in combination with Roman numerals that appear in the mark. Many pieces are artist-signed, and contemporary collecting is largely focused on individual artists's work.

Robineau Pottery, Syracuse, New York, USA
Adelaide Alsop Robineau was a ceramics painter when she began publication of *Keramic Studio*, a monthly magazine from New York City and Syracuse. During the early 1900s, she studied pottery making with Charles Fergus Binns (see p.166), and by 1905 was producing her own work regularly. From 1909 to 1911, she worked at the University City Pottery (see p.167), returning to Syracuse after it closed. By 1920, she was on the

faculty at Syracuse University. Her work, almost all ornamental, is characterized by exquisite detail in form, surface modelling and glazing. The company was active c.1905-28.

Pierre Roussencq, Marans-la-Rochelle, Charente-Inférieure, France

Founded in 1740, this factory was one of several large concerns operating in the general area around La Rochelle. These factories being at a cultural crossroads absorbed influences from Moustiers and Marseilles in the south and from Nevers and Rouen in the north, making certain attribution difficult in most cases. It appears that this factory may have ceased production in the early to mid-1750s when Henri Brevet, one of the partners, opened a new factory at La Rochelle. The monogram of Pierre Roussencq is painted.

Paula Schneider, London, UK

Based in London, Paula Schneider produced Studio pottery marked with her incised or painted monogram, from 1956.

Bryan Rochford, Willowdene, Cheshunt, Hertfordshire, UK

Studio ceramics were produced from 1960. This personal seal mark was used by Bryan Rochford.

Robert and Sheila Fournier, Greenwich Studios, London, UK

Previously based at Ducketts Wood in Hertfordshire c.1946-61, and London from 1962, Robert and Sheila Fournier produced Studio ceramics. This "RF" impressed monogram was used by Robert Fournier.

Frances E. Richards, Highgate, London, UK

Studio ceramics were made from 1922-31, marked with an incised monogram and the date. Examples of this potter's work exist in the Victoria & Albert Museum, London.

Richard Franz Bayer, Shipley, West Yorkshire, UK

Bayer's Studio ceramics dating from 1939-c.1960 were marked with impressed or painted initials.

Ronald G. Cooper, London, UK

Working from Hornsey College of Art and other addresses in England, Cooper made Studio ceramics from 1946. His mark consists of his painted or incised initials (sometimes with date).

Lucie Rie, London, UK
Active 1938-95, Lucie Rie was one of the most important and influential Studio potters of the 20thC. Her work was executed mainly in stoneware and porcelain, and are classic in their simplicity, including some highly abstracted Chinese forms. She used this impressed monogram.

Lowe, Ratcliffe & Co., Longton, Staffordshire, UK
General earthenwares were made at the Gold Street Works 1882-92. The mark was impressed or printed.

Renee Mendel, London, UK
Studio ceramics and terracotta figures were produced from 1942 onwards with this incised or painted initial mark.

R. M. Greenwood, London, UK
A ceramic decorator from 1948 onwards, Miss Greenwood used this painted monogram.

Bryan Rochford, Willowdene, Cheshunt, Hertfordshire, UK
See p.93. This is the Rochford Pottery monogram, which was used from July 1960, and appears on Studio-type wares.

Eric & Meira Stockl, Stroud Green, London, UK
Studio-type pottery and stoneware were made from 1956. Initially the couple used a joint initial mark "M. E. S.", but after 1961 they used this painted, incised or impressed mark.

Samuel E. Saunders, East Cowes, Isle of Wight, UK
The monogram of Samuel E. Saunders was first registered as a trademark in 1927. After 1930 Saunders was at the Isle of Wight Pottery (1930-40) and the Carisbrooke Pottery (1930-32). Both potteries used printed or impressed marks which comprised his initials.

Robert and Sheila Fournier, Greenwich Studios, London, UK
See p.93. This "SF" impressed seal mark was used by Sheila Fournier.

Hilda M. Snowden, Thackley, Bradford, West Yorkshire, UK
Studio ceramics were produced from 1950, some featuring this incised or impressed monogram.

La Seinie, Saint-Yrieix, Haute-Vienne, France
Hard-paste porcelain was made here between
1774 and 1856, with the monogram "LS" in red
enamel. St Yrieix is where the first deposits of clay
suitable for producing hard-paste were discovered
in France in 1768.

Mildred Slatter, High Wycombe, Buckinghamshire, UK
Studio ceramics produced from 1956 onwards.
Her monogram painted, incised or impressed.

Cafaggiolo, Nr. Florence, Tuscany, Italy
One of the foremost maiolica potteries in
Renaissance Italy. In 1498 the Medici drafted in
two potters, Stefano and Piero di Filippo, from
Montelupo to oversee production in an outhouse
of the Medici villa. From this date pottery was
produced here until well into the 18thC. However
it is the output of brilliant wares from the first 30
or 40 years of the 16thC that guarantees its place
in the front rank of Renaissance maiolica. The
mark of Cafaggiolo is "SPR" or "SF", as well as a
trident and occasionally the place name. There are
a considerable number of fakes bearing the marks
of this pottery.

Taylor, Smith and Taylor, East Liverpool, Ohio (with a
plant in Chester, West Virginia), USA
Originally organized in 1899 as Taylor, Lee
and Smith, the firm was reconfigured in 1901
when Lee withdrew, and continued until 1972.
After several poor years at the beginning, the
firm was reorganized in 1906 and production
commenced in earnest. Although a wide range
of semi-vitreous dinner and toilet wares as well
as products for hotels and restaurants were
produced, the pottery's most popular lines were
Lu-Ray and Vistosa, both solid-colour dinner-
wares. Another type of ware was "Pebbleford",
which was plain coloured with speckles in light
and dark blue-green, yellow, grey and tan.
Anchor Hocking Corporation's ceramic products
division operated the factory from its purchase in
1972, until its closure in 1981.

Mosbach, Baden, Germany
See p.35. Also thought to be the mark of
Frankenthal, this "CT" monogram was derived
from the initials of the Elector Palatine Carl
Theodor, who was patron or protector of the
ceramics concerns in both Mosbach and
Frankenthal.

LONGTON

Thomas Cone Ltd., Longton, Staffordshire, UK
From 1892–c.1935, Thomas Cone Ltd. were makers of general earthenwares. This printed monogram was used 1912-35.

C. C. Thompson Pottery Company, East Liverpool, Ohio, USA
See p.61. This monogram mark also appears on earthenwares, stonewares and other wares made by this firm 1868-1938.

Marianne de Trey, Shinner's Bridge, Dartington, Devon, UK
Formerly a potter in the United States, de Trey produced Studio ceramics in Devon from 1947. This painted or incised mark was used.

Tiffany Studios, Corona, New York, USA
Although Louis Comfort Tiffany, famous for glass and metal work, began experimenting with pottery as early as 1898, the official introduction of the ware was at the St Louis Exposition in 1904. Vases and lamp bases (to hold his famous leaded-glass shades) were the principal products, many formed by making the master models from natural plant materials, such as ferns, Queen Anne's lace, jack-in-the-pulpits, etc. Green, brown, ivory and blue glazes predominate, although crystalline and iridescent effects are known. The Studio operated 1902-1919.

Tregenna Hill Pottery, Cornwall, UK
Studio pottery was made here by Kenneth Quick c.1955-60 (see p.85). The "TH" monogram is incised or impressed.

Ruskin Pottery, Smethwick, Nr Birmingham, West Midlands, UK
Highly refined earthenwares with innovative monochromatic glazes (e.g. copper-red flambé, orange or mottled), were produced in this pottery owned by W. Howson Taylor. The forms are often derived from classic Chinese ceramics. The factory was established in 1898 and closed in 1935. This painted or incised monogram was used from c.1898.

MADE IN ENGLAND

Thomas Mayer (Elton Pottery) Ltd, Hanley, Staffordshire, UK
General earthenwares were produced from 1956. This monogram mark was used 1956-60. An Elton Pottery name mark was also used.

Mosaic Tile Company, Zanesville, Ohio, USA
Karl Langenbeck, a chemist, and Herman
Mueller, a modeller, had worked together for
American Encaustic Tiling Company (see p.69),
before establishing Mosaic Tile Company (1894-
1967) which they operated until 1903. Many
different kinds of plain and ornamental tiles were
made for floors, walls and fireplaces. Faience tiles
were added in 1918. The company's tiles were
used in a number of important buildings in the
U.S., including some New York subway stations.
A variety of miscellaneous forms was made when
the Depression slowed the construction business,
including boxes, bookends, souvenirs, hot plates
and the like.

T. Ristori, Marzy, Nièvre, France
From 1854, tin-glazed reproductions of classic
French faience including Nevers and Rouen were
made by T. Ristori.

William Tudor, High Wycombe, Buckinghamshire, UK
Studio ceramics made from 1947 feature this
impressed monogram seal mark.

**Union Co-operative Pottery Company/Union
Potteries Company**, East Liverpool, Ohio, USA
Organized by a group of potters during a general
strike, the pottery (1894-1905) produced ironstone
and semi-porcelain table and toilet wares and
railroad sanitary ware. The financial management
of the firm changed in 1900, but the products
remained the same.

Veuve Perrin, Marseilles, France
Operating between c.1740 and c.1795, the Veuve
Perrin factory was one of the leading Marseilles
faience makers, noted for painterly use of the
petit-feu enamels. Chinoiserie subjects, fish and
landscapes typical. The painted "VP" monogram
has been faked extensively within the past 100
years.

Anne Wedd, Brixton, London
See p.37. Anne Wedd used also used this incised
monogram mark, which may feature the year
numbers 1955-57.

William Barnes, Swinton, Greater Manchester, UK
Studio-type pottery was produced both before
World War II, and from 1945, featuring this
incised or painted initial mark. Between 1948 and

1957, Barnes worked at the Royal Lancastrian Pottery, (Pilkingtons), whose pieces are marked with a "P".

William B. Dalton, London, UK
Studio-type stonewares and porcelain were produced from 1900 with this incised or painted monogram mark. Dalton emigrated to the United States in 1941.

Wiesbaden, Nassau, Germany
A small faience concern was established here in 1770, under the patronage of Prince Karl of Nassau-Usingen, by Johann Jacob Kaisin of Poppelsdorf. Kaisin's work was deemed to be unsatisfactory and the work was taken over by Strupler and Hagemann. Poor quality faience was made. In 1774 Caspar Dreste of Flörsheim was employed to improve the production. The factory was continued by his widow after his death in 1787, until its closure in 1795. Output includes figures, stoves, mirror frames etc. Wares are characterized by a strong, copper-green enamel. This mark stands for "Wiesbaden-Dreste".

Edward R. Wilkes, Various locations, Staffordshire, UK
A decorator of earthenwares 1900-30, Edward Wilke's signature mark has been found on vases made by A. G. Richardson of Cobridge. This monogram has been found on pieces decorated for Bernard Moore. Wilkes also decorated for other Staffordshire manufacturers.

William Gill & Son(s), Castleford, West Yorkshire, UK
Formerly G. Gill, this company worked from the Providence Pottery from 1880-1932. This printed "WGS" mark was used from 1880, with "England" added from 1891.

Willets Manufacturing Company, Trenton, New Jersey, USA
The factory purchased by the Willets brothers in 1879 was one of the largest in the United States. The pottery (1879-1908) produced large quantities of decorated ironstone table and sanitary wares. Beginning in 1886, they also made belleek porcelain having hired the Bromley potters and Walter Lenox from Ott and Brewer (see p.149). Their early belleek ware is often factory decorated, but by the mid-1890s they were selling much of their belleek in the white for independent decorators.

Helen Wickham, London, UK
Earthenware figures were made from c.1920-35.
This painted mark appears; an incised or painted
signature mark is also used.

Tom W. Howard, Loughton, Essex, UK
From 1956, Tom Howard produced a variety of
Studio-type pottery and earthenwares from
c.1956-60, and "Semi-Stoneware" from c.1960.
This incised mark was used, with the number
relating to the year of production.

Monkton Combe Pottery, Bath, Avon, UK
Studio ceramics were produced at the Monkton
Combe Pottery by Rachael Warner between 1946
and 1953; she used this incised monogram. The
pottery was subsequently operated by Peter
Wright, who used a painted or incised "PW"
mark, and also a written name mark.

Winifred Rawsthrone, Bramcote, Nottinghamshire, UK
Studio-type pottery was produced by Winifred
Rawsthorne at the Winthorn Pottery from 1958.
Some pieces feature this incised or painted
monogram mark.

William Ruscoe, Exeter, Devon, UK
Ceramic sculptures and figures were made
at Stoke, Staffordshire, from c.1920-44, and
subsequently at Exeter, with this incised or
painted monogram, sometimes accompanied
by the year of manufacture.

Peters and Reed/Zane Pottery Company,
Zanesville, Ohio, USA
Founded by John D. Peters and Adam Reed,
who had been working at Weller (see p.226),
the pottery (1898-1941) started with flowerpots,
added cuspidors and jardinieres, and by 1903
was making cooking ware. In 1905, Frank Ferrel
designed several ornamental lines, including Moss
Aztec, for florists' crockery and garden wares.
Like the utilitarian pieces, these latter wares were
made of red clay. From 1921 to 1941, the firm was
called Zane Pottery Company, and after 1926
white clay was used rather than red.

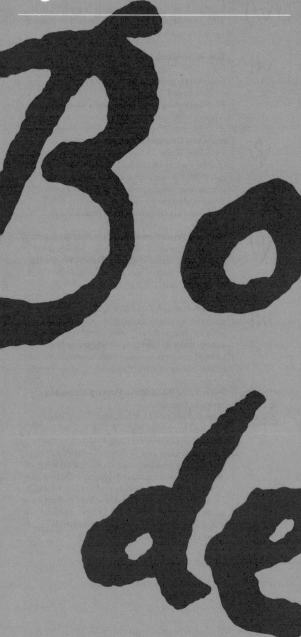

Many firms and potters use name, signature or trade name marks that are (or appear to have been) written, painted or incised by hand. This section has been ordered alphabetically according to the surname of the individual potter or the title of the firm. Where the firm or potter's name is unclear, the entry has been placed under the first letter that appears.

Abselon yarm

William Absolon, Great Yarmouth, Norfolk, UK
See p.37. This painted name mark was used 1784-1815. "N 25" was added to some pieces made after 1790 and refers to the address, 25 Market Row.

Alpha

Alpha Potteries, Sidcup, Kent, UK
This pottery made individually-designed Studio wares 1954-58. This written mark was used. The Greek symbol for "alpha" appears as an incised mark.

D. & J. Henderson/American Pottery Company, Jersey City, New Jersey, USA
This is the earliest of the large production potteries to be successful in the United States, and was active 1828-c.1850. Methods, moulds and skills brought from England and Scotland were translated into an array of high quality brown-glazed, Rockingham and yellow ware products for kitchens, tables and taverns. The pottery was incorporated as American Pottery Company in 1833, but the corporate structure changed several times after the death of David Henderson in 1845. By 1855, English potters John O. Rouse and Nathaniel Turner owned the pottery and the Jersey City Pottery (see p.168).

Amstel
Amstel

Amstel, Nr. Amsterdam, Holland
This concern was transferred here from Oude Loosdrecht in 1784. The factory produced hard-paste porcelain not unlike Meissen. The wares are conventional and in keeping with contemporary neo-classical, or a somewhat old-fashioned rococo style, echoing Meissen and Sèvres. The decoration is generally of high quality, in which a mid-brown is used extensively in landscapes or natural settings. The script mark is rendered in various colours sometimes incorporating the letters "MOL" which denote "Mol Oude Loosdrecht", Johannes de Mol (d.1782) being the name of the proprietor.

Ansbach, Bavaria, Germany
One of the most important faience factories in Germany which made some of the finest wares, especially in the first half of the 18thC. The earlier wares copy Delft, Rouen and Strasburg but the factory is noted more for the brilliant 'green-family' of enamelled wares loosely based on Chinese exportware and a curious group of Imari-type wares in which fired cobalt blue is employed together with unfired red and gold. Factory marks are rare and are mostly initials, but a few marks include an abbreviated town mark.

Aprey, Haute Marne, France
See p.68. This rare mark sometimes appears.

Ashby Potters' Guild, Burton-on-Trent, Staffordshire, UK
Based at Woodville near Burton-on-Trent, this firm produced earthenwares 1909-22. The company became Ault & Tunnicliffe Ltd. This mark appears.

De 3 Astonne, Delft, Holland
See p.50. This mark was registered by the proprietors in 1764.

Avon Art Pottery Ltd., Longton, Staffordshire, UK
Earthenwares were made by this firm from 1930, first at the Jubilee Works (to 1961), and then at Edensor Road. The printed mark above was used 1939-47, the mark below, also printed, from 1947.

Aylesford Priory Pottery, Aylesford, Kent, UK
See p.68. This impressed mark was used from 1955.

I. E. Baron, Moustiers, Basses Alpes, France
The painted mark I. E. Baron is that of a decorator apparently employed at the Olerys' factory in Moustiers c.1750.

Jean Baron, Rennes, Ille-et-Vilaine, France
Jean Baron was faience decorator in Rennes in the second half 18thC. He used this mark.

Bartolomeo Terchi, Rome, Italy
Bartolomeo Terchi, probably born in Rome, was active as a maiolica decorator from c.1714 until the 1730s. In terms of palette, the sombre,

brown-dominated tones resemble Castelli maiolica but his subjects, which include large-scale biblical and classical figures, are perhaps more vigorously treated. A small number of pieces signed by Terchi (and in some cases dated) are extant. He worked at San Quirico, Siena and Bassano in the first half of the 18thC.

Bassano, Nr. Venice, Italy
Maiolica was produced in this area from the 16thC but such early pieces have never been clearly identified. As well as drug-jars and other utilitarian vessels, output included dishes painted with architectural ruins. A number of different potters are known to have worked in this area including Antonio and Bartolomeo Terchi.

Bayeux, Calvados, Normandy, France
See p.42. The mark (above) was used during the time of Joachim Langlois (d.1830). The mark (below) was used by Jules Morlent in the 19thC.

Bayreuth, Bavaria, Germany
See p.40. This town mark appears on faience from c.1713.

D. Beckley, Seaview, Isle of Wight, UK
Formerly the Island Pottery Studio Ltd. (1956-58), this printed or impressed mark appears on earthenwares from 1959.

Edwin Bennett Pottery, Baltimore, Maryland, USA
Bennett of Derbyshire, England, worked first in Jersey City, New Jersey, in 1834, and later founded potteries in East Liverpool, Ohio, and Pittsburgh, Pennsylvania, before settling permanently in Baltimore. His pottery in Baltimore (1845-1936) made a variety of popular wares including Rockingham, majolica, parian, porcelain, and white ware. The company was incorporated in 1890. Bennett died in 1908.

John Beswick (Ltd.), Longton, Staffordshire, UK
Earthenwares were made by this firm (formerly called J. W. Beswick) at Gold Street, Longton from 1936. This mark was used from 1936.

Biltons (1912) Ltd., Stoke, Staffordshire, UK
Known as Biltons Ltd. c.1900-1912, this firm
produced earthenwares. This mark is the
standard post-war mark; pattern names may
also appear.

De vergulde Blompot, Delft, Holland
See p.41. The mark (above) appeared from
1654; the mark (below) was registered by the
proprietor in 1764.

Blue John Pottery Ltd., Hanley, Staffordshire, UK
From 1939 the Blue John Pottery produced
earthenwares. This mark was used from 1939.

Johann Valentin Bontemps, Ansbach, Bavaria,
Germany
See p.39. This is the full signature of Johann
Valentin Bontemps, a faience painter at
Ansbach (c.1716 to 1729).

Giacomo Boselli (or Boselly), Savona, Italy
A potter and painter in Savona in the last
quarter of the 18thC, this is the painted
signature of Giacomo Boselli.

Ignaz Bottengruber, Breslau, Silesia, Germany
An independent decorator or *Hausmaler*,
Ignaz Bottengruber was active in the 1720s
and 1730s, and painted mainly on Meissen
blanks and occasionally Chinese exportware,
and after c.1730 on Vienna porcelain. One of
the most accomplished *Hausmalerei*, Bottengruber painted battle and hunting scenes,
putti and *bacchic* subjects, flowers and ornate
strapwork. He sometimes worked in monochrome, especially purple and black.

Lester & Barbara Breininger, Robesonia,
Pennsylvania, USA
Perhaps the finest of the contemporary American colonial revival potteries is that established
in Robesonia, Berks County, Pennsylvania by
Lester and Barbara Breininger in 1965, and is
still in production today. While production is
limited by the labour-intensive process of
reproducing or adapting early Pennsylvania
German red-ware, many signed examples of
their modelled or moulded figures and slip-
decorated or *sgraffiato*-decorated pottery may
be found. The couple have collected fine early
local wares for inspiration, as well as old

potters' tools that they then use to produce their new examples. All wares are clearly marked with incised inscriptions and dates in order to discourage confusion with antique pieces.

Bristol
Est. 1683
Pountney & Co Ltd
England.

Pountney & Co. (Ltd.), Bristol, Avon, UK
Formerly Carter & Pountney, Pountney & Allies (c.1816-35) and Pountney & Goldney (1836-49), this pottery produced earthenwares 1849-1969. It is now Cauldon Bristol Potteries Ltd. The mark above appeared c.1816-35. The words "Pountney" and "Bristol" appear as distinguishing details on a variety of marks used from 1889.

J.BURGER JR.
ROCHESTER.N.Y.

John Burger, Rochester, New York, USA
In 1839 John (or Jean) Burger, from Alsace-Lorraine, operated a stoneware factory with partners that included Nathan Clark of Lyons, New York. By 1854, Burger owned and opera-ted the pottery himself and moved to a Mount Hope Avenue site in Rochester in 1860. The usual wide variety of forms were made that included beer bottles, preserve jars, jugs, water fountains, butter pots, pitchers, and churns. Other members of the family joined Burger after 1861 and the pottery maintained production until 1890.

caen
CAEN

Caen, Calvados, Normandy, France
See p.74. These written marks appear in the early 19thC.

Caribe
PUERTO RICO
U.S.A.

Sterling China Company, East Liverpool, Ohio, USA
Although the firm has always used East Liverpool as its address, the pottery is actually located in Wellsville, Ohio. Founded by a group of investors that refitted an old yellow ware factory in 1917, the pottery has long produced vitreous hotel china. Indeed, by 1949 the company was one of the three largest hotel ware producers in the world, although it is probably best known among collectors for its line designed by Russel Wright about 1945. Caribe China was produced by Sterling at a plant in Vega Baja, Puerto Rico, established to manufacture hotel ware, between 1951 and 1976. In 1954, the firm absorbed Scammell China Company, Trenton, and continues to produce its Lamberton China.

Carlton Ware Ltd., Stoke, Staffordshire
Previously called Wiltshaw & Robinson (Ltd.)
(1890-1957), the firm was retitled Carlton
Ware Ltd. from 1958. This style of mark was
used by both companies.

Carter & Co. (Ltd.), Poole, Dorset
This company produced earthenwares, art
pottery and tiles 1873-1921. The firm was
subsequently renamed Carter, Stabler &
Adams. This mark was used 1873-1921.

Charles Cazin, Fulham, London
Cazin, a Frenchman, worked in England at
C. J. C. Bailey's works in Fulham designing
stonewares 1871-74. He returned to France
c.1874. Pieces bearing his signature are rare.

Chantilly

Chantilly, Oise, France
See p.190. This written mark featuring the full
town name is rare.

Christian Friedrich Clar, Rendsburg, Holstein,
Germany
Clar established a factory in Holstein (formerly Denmark) in c.1765, producing tin-
glazed earthenware, lead-glazed pottery, creamware,
redware and a type of black-basaltes. The
concern under different proprietors survived
until 1818. The full name mark although "C.
R." initials are also used.

Nathan Clark Pottery, Athens, New York, USA
Nathan Clark, Sr. founded the stoneware and
redware pottery at Athens, New York, with
Captain Thomas Howe, an Englishman, in
1805, and it was operated by the family and
employees including his son until c.1899.
Branches of the pottery were also operated at
Lyons, Mt. Morris, and Rochester, New York.

Clement-Massier
Golfe-Juan.A M

Clement & Jerome Massier, Vallauris, France
Clement and Jerome Massier produced high
quality Studio-type pottery from c.1870 in Art
Nouveau style. This mark is one of those used.

Clermont fd
m

Clermond-Ferrand, Puy-de-Dôme, France
A small number of factories were established
here in the 18thC making, with a few notable
exceptions, mostly mundane faience in the
manner of Moustiers. In the late 18thC robust
and somewhat crude "faience patriotiques"

was made here. The full town mark is generally associated with the early factory of Perrot and Sèves, active from 1730 to 1743.

Clarice Cliff, Burslem, UK

Clarice Cliff (1899-1972) joined A. J. Wilkinson's Royal Staffordshire Pottery in 1916 where she was taught modelling, firing, gilding and pottery design. After 1927 with a group of assistants, she began hand-decorating whitewares (mainly tablewares) with bold, geometric designs in vivid colours. Most of her pieces are marked with this signature.

Clinton Pottery Company, Clinton, Missouri, USA

The Clinton Pottery Company opened in 1889, and quickly became a dominant force in the stoneware industry of the Midwest. Indeed, in 1891, one million gallons of pottery were shipped, which amounted to one-third of all Missouri pottery manufactures in that calendar year. A large, steam-operated pottery, the firm produced mainly utilitarian brown-wares with a slip glaze, such as crocks and jugs. By 1906, the Clinton Stoneware Company (as it had been reorganized), was merged into the Western Stoneware Company (see p.252).

Coalport Porcelain Works, Coalport, Shropshire, UK

See p.72. The mark above is a rare early mark from c.1805-15. The mark below is from another early period 1810-25, and appears painted in underglaze blue, and usually appears on colourful, encrusted floral wares.

Colclough China Ltd., Longton, Staffordshire, UK

Formerly H. J. Colclough (1897-1937), and subsequently Booths & Colcloughs Ltd. (1948-54), Colclough China Ltd. produced porcelain 1937-48. This style of mark was used in a number of forms from 1939, and was also used by Booths & Colcloughs Ltd. The company now forms part of the Ridgway group of potteries.

Morris and Willmore, Columbian Art Pottery, Trenton, New Jersey, USA

See p.90. This mark also appears on wares produced by this firm.

COMMERAW:2
STONEWARE
NEW YORK

Thomas H. Commereau, Manhattan, New York, USA

Near Corlear's Hook on the East River in Manhattan, Thomas H. Commereau established a stoneware pottery in 1797, which operated sporadically (1797-98, 1802-19), sometimes with David Morgan, until 1819. Numbers of salt-glazed stoneware vessels survive from this manufactory, and the best of them feature impressed swags and tassels highlighted in cobalt blue.

CROWN WORKS
BURSLEM
ENGLAND

Susie Cooper, Burslem, Staffordshire, UK

Susie Cooper worked for A. E. Gray & Co. c.1922-29, decorating a variety of wares in floral, abstract, or, more rarely, geometric designs. From 1929 she decorated blanks bought in from other manufacturers, and in 1931 she set up her own pottery producing vases, jugs, tea and dinner sets. The company became Susie Cooper Ltd. from c.1961, and from 1966 formed part of the Wedgwood group. This signature appears in many forms, and was used from c.1922-80; "Crown Works" does not appear before 1932. She also used a leaping deer mark 1932-64.

*Agostino Corado
a Nevers*

Agostino Corrado, Nevers, Nievres, France

The Corrado or Conrade family emigrated to France and helped establish the faience factory at Nevers under the patronage of Lodovico Gonzaga. At first the Italian style predominated, but by the second quarter of the 17thC the influence of Chinese porcelain is evident. From about 1650 the native baroque style, following Poussin and Vouet, emerged. Nevers was the foremost faience factory in France until superseded by Rouen at the end of the 17thC. The full signature marks appear mainly in the late 16th and early 17thC.

COWAN

Cowan Pottery, Cleveland and Rocky River, Ohio, USA

Begun as a backyard studio pottery by R. Guy Cowan in Cleveland 1913, the firm was expanded and moved in 1920 to nearby Rocky River. The product also changed from a lead-glazed redware to a high-fired porcelain body that was covered with brilliant coloured faience glazes. Although Cowan created most of the designs for the vases and figures that were made, several artists provided models for limited editions, including Waylande Gregory, Viktor Schreckengost, Paul Bogatay, Alexander Blazys, and others. The firm continued until 1931.

JD·CRAVEN

Jacob Dorris Craven, Randolph and Moore Counties, North Carolina, USA
Many members of the Craven family were active as potters in North Carolina during the 18th and 19thC. Jacob Dorris Craven worked in Randolph and then in the Browers Mill vicinity of neighboring Moore County. In 1860 he was manufacturing over 60,000 gallons of alkaline-glazed stoneware annually, and continued until 1890. Some other Craven potters remained in business in Randolph County until 1917.

Creilsheim
1749

Crailsheim, Wurtemberg, Germany
A faience factory was established here in c.1714 and continued in production until the early 19thC. A considerable portion of the output consisted of tankards painted in manganese and blue with detailing in green and yellow. The subject matter includes figures, animals, heraldic devices and flowers.

crepy

Crepy-en-Valois, Oise, France
Louis-Francois Gaignepain, a former employee of the Mennecy factory, established a soft-paste porcelain manufactory here in 1762 which closed in 1770. Production appears to have been snuff-boxes and figures in the manner of Mennecy. It is most likely that a considerable body of such *bijouterie* has been mistakenly attributed to Mennecy. This rare name mark, or the initials "C. P." have so far only been found on porcelain figures.

C.CROLIUS
MANUFACTURER
NEW YORK

Clarkson Crolius, Manhattan, New York, USA
Clarkson Crolius (b.1773) was born into a family of New York potters in 1773 and took over his father, John Crolius Jr.'s, stoneware pottery in 1800 and continued until 1838. His extensive production was marketed as far as New England and the Carolinas, and, for advertising purposes, he marked a large number of pieces. An early price list dated March 28, 1809 includes jugs, jars, pots, pitchers, mugs, oyster pots, chamber pots, inkstands, and churns. Most wares were plain, although fine cobalt-blue decorated

incised examples may be found. Crolius' son, Clarkson Jr., operated the pottery until 1849. A number of different marks in this style were used, all featuring the name "C. Crolius".

Pierre Custode, Nevers, Nivernais, France
Pierre Custode is recorded as a master potter in 1632, and as a merchant dealing in faience in 1652. His family remained in the business until the late 18thC.

Darte Freres, Paris, France
Prominent manufacturers and decorators of hard-paste porcelain from 1795 until c.1840. The mark is usually stencilled in red.

Dastin, Rue de Bondy, Paris, France
A decorator and retailer of hard-paste porcelain, these marks appear in red and gold.

T. H. Deck, Various locations, France
Theodore Deck (1823-91) was one of the foremost ceramists in 19thC France. Writer, historian, designer and potter, he was one of the earliest Studio potters producingpieces with Islamic or Oriental influence from c.1860.

Dlles Delemer, Arras, Pas-de-Calais, France
See p.39. This mark was used by the Dlles Delemer 1771-90.

William De Morgan, London, UK
From 1863 William De Morgan (1839-1917) designed tiles and glass for the William Morris workshops. He began to decorate pottery with Islamic-style designs in 1869 and set up his own kiln. In 1873 he established a workshop in Chelsea, but was subsequently based at Merton Abbey (1882-88) and Sand's End in Fulham (1888-1907). He produced decorative Islamic-style and lustre wares. This name mark appears after 1882 in various forms. "& Co." was added to most marks after 1888.

De Villeroy, Mennecy, Ile-de-France, France
See p.45. This is the incised mark of the Duc de Villeroy, patron of the Mennecy factory.

Dihl, Rue de Bondy, Paris, France
From 1780-1829 Dihl manufactured hard-paste porcelain, with this mark in red or underglaze blue.

A.P. Donaghho
Parkersburg W. Va.

A. P. Donaghho, Parkersburg, West Virginia, USA
The most prolific stoneware production in the state of West Virginia was that of Pennsylvania-born A. P. Donaghho, active 1874-1900. Most common salt-glazed stoneware forms were made, and preserve jars and pans are frequently found with stenciled cobalt blue geometric designs.

Doulton & Co. (Ltd.), Lambeth, London, UK
A stoneware works was established at Vauxhall in 1815 by John Doulton. John Watts became his partner, and in c.1826 the works moved to Lambeth. Watts died in 1858 and the factory was continued by Doulton in partnership with his sons, and was retitled Henry Doulton & Co. The company produced decorative, domestic, architectural and industrial wares in stoneware and terracotta. Another works was opened at Burslem in 1882, and has continued to the present day. Production ceased at the Lambeth factory in 1956. A large number of marks were used, characterized by the words "Doulton Lambeth" or "Doulton Burslem". This impressed mark was used c.1869-77; the year of production was used in the centre from 1872.

Duban, Rue Coquilliere, Paris, France
A potter active c.1800; this script mark appears in red.

Duhamel, Quai de la Cité, Paris, France
A dealer and perhaps manufacturer of hard-paste porcelain from 1790-1827. This script mark appears in gold.

BARNABAS EDMUNDS
& CO.
CHARLESTOWN

Edmands & Co., Charlestown, Massachusetts, USA
Barnabas Edmands was a well-to-do brass founder in Charlestown, Massachusetts, who owned a pottery run first by Frederick Carpenter (see p.290), but later wares were marked with Edmands' name. In 1852 he passed along ownership of the stoneware pottery (1827-1905) to his two sons, Thomas and Edward. They ran the factory until 1868, when a third generation, John B. Edmands, took over and managed the company into the 20thC. This is an example of one of the signatures that appear; another mark features just the name "Edmands & Co."

Sir Edmund Elton, Clevedon, Somerset, UK
Earthenwares were made by Elton (d.1930)
from 1879, and by 1882 his Sunflower Pottery
was in production. Decoration on pieces of
Elton Wares, as it became known, was created
using coloured slips covered with transparent
glaze. This painted or incised mark was used
1879-1920, sometimes with the date.

Etoilles, Seine-et-Oise, France
From c.1768 Jean Baptiste Monier and
Dominique Pelleve were manufacturers of
hard-paste porcelain. The name of the towm
appears in script, together with initials "P"
and "M. P." and the name "Pelleve".

Michel Derrennes, Rennes, Ille-et-Vilaine, France
Michel Derrennes faience decorator at Tutrel's
factory (est. 1748).This mark appears.

William H. Farrar, Geddes, New York, USA
William H. Farrar of Vermont established a
redware pottery at Geddes (later part of
Syracuse, New York) about 1840 and later
produced stoneware and Rockingham ware,
including spaniel and lion figures based upon
Staffordshire, England, prototypes until 1872.
William Farrar also appears to have been an
investor in the United States Pottery Company
(see p.135) in Bennington, Vermont, and by
1856 had established a pottery in Kaolin,
South Carolina, where Rockingham and
fine whitewares, including porcelain were
manufactured.

Fauchier

Joseph Fauchier, Marseilles, Bouches-du-Rhône,
France
See p.26. This rare script mark is sometimes
found.

Fayence d'Auxerre

Auxerre, Yonne, France
Claude Boutet established a pottery here in
1799 apparently concentrating on popular
wares including "faiences patriotiques" in the
manner of Nevers mainly employing cobalt
and manganese colours. This mark appears.

ferrat moustier

Jean-Baptiste Ferrat, Moustiers, Basses Alpes,
France
Jean-Baptiste Ferrat established a factory here
in 1718 and until about 1770, or slightly later,
most of its production is similar to other

Moustiers wares. After this date, and to the end of production in 1791, the most notable products are those painted in *petit-feu* enamels (developed at Strasburg) in the Aprey or Marseilles style with birds and flowers, landscapes or chinoiserie subjects. The relatively rare marks are either hand-written or stencilled in overglaze enamels.

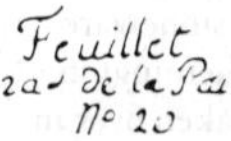

Feuillet, Paris, France
A decorator of hard-paste neo-rococo porcelain from about 1820 to 1850. The full and the single "F" marks are generally written in gilding or green enamel. This workshop also used a mark that imitated the interlaced "L"s of Sèvres (see p.163).

Homer Laughlin China Company, East Liverpool, Ohio, and Newell, West Virginia, USA
See p.81. This tradename was used.

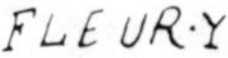

Fleury, Rue de Faubourg Saint Denis, Paris, France
From 1803 probably until 1835, this factory made good hard-paste porcelain.

Worcester Porcelains, Hereford and Worcester, UK
See p.23. Used during the Flight Period (1783-92), the painted "Flight" mark appears in various forms (with a crescent c.1783-88, with a crown c.1788-92). This mark was used c.1788-92.

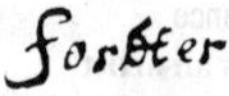

Johann Leonhard Forster, Ansbach, Bavaria, Germany
Johann Leonhard Forster (b.1714, d.1744), a faience painter at Ansbach used this mark.

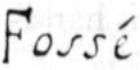

Fossé (or Fossey), Rouen, Seine-Inferieure, France
Gabriel Fosse and widow were potters from c.1740-c.1760. This script mark was used.

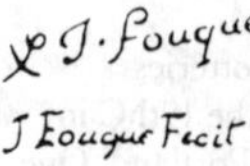

Joseph Fouque, Moustiers, Basses Alpes, France
In 1774 Joseph Fouque and Jean-Francois Pelloquin took over the factory established by Pierre Clerissy. It remained in production until 1852. The wares of this concern are barely to be distinguished from the other Moustiers factories. On the later wares the hand-written mark is abandoned in favour of a stencilled mark. A number of different marks incorporating this name are found.

Fownhope Pottery, Fownhope, Hereford and Worcester, UK

Dennis Lacey produced Studio-type wares at the Fownhope Pottery from 1956. This painted mark appears from 1958. The impressed name "Herefordshire" was used 1956-58.

Fulper Pottery, Flemington, New Jersey, USA

A pottery for making utilitarian stoneware and drainage tile was begun in Flemington about 1815 by Samuel Hill and taken over in 1858 by Abraham Fulper, who had been a potter for Hill during the 1820s and continued to make stoneware and tile. In 1909 the firm replaced its utilitarian product with Vasekraft, an art pottery line that featured elaborate crystalline and flambé glazes over the traditional stoneware body. J. Martin Stangl acquired the company in 1929 and eventually changed the name and product.

Treviso, Venetia, Italy

Guiseppe and Andrea Fratelli, Fontebasso, manufacturers of soft-paste porcelain probably from c.1790 to 1840. "G. A. F. F. Treviso" is the full factory mark.

Gailliard, Passage de l'Opéra, Paris, France

This decorator of hard-paste porcelain, who operated in Paris c.1840, used this script mark that appears in gold.

GALLE NANCY

Galle, Nancy, Meuthe-et-Moselle, France

Emile Galle (b.1846, d.1904) was an artist potter who is better known for his acid-etched Studio glass, but was also a manufacturer of contemporary style faience including the celebrated glass-eyed cats. This is his handwritten mark.

Gardiner Stoneware Manufactory, Gardiner, Maine, USA

Several substantial stoneware potteries were located through much of the 19thC in Gardiner, Maine, north-east of Portland. One of the more successful ones was owned by Charles Swift and William M. Wood. Often decorated with cobalt-blue impressed or stamped motifs of eagles, cows, or swans, their work was attractive and competitive with the more commonly employed blue brushed or trailed designs. The firm was active between 1876 and c.1892.

George Fishley Holland, Dunster, Somerset, UK
Previously based at The Pottery, Clevedon (1955-59), Holland moved to Dunster in 1959. His earthenwares bear this printed, painted or impressed mark, with "Dunster" added after 1959.

Agnes Benson, Ruislip, London, UK
See p.79. This painted or incised mark was used from 1951.

Michele Giordano, Naples, Italy
Michele Giordano and his son Guiseppe were modellers at Naples in the late 18th and early 19thC. They used this incised mark.

Giovine, Naples, Italy
A decorator of imported ceramics 1826-30, Giovine's wares feature this mark inscribed in red enamel.

Justus Alex Ernst Gluer, Nuremberg, Bavaria, Germany
Justus Alex Ernst Gluer, faience decorator at Nuremberg and at Oettingen-Schrattenhofen (active 1719 to 1740). He specialized in biblical subjects rendered in polychrome. His signature is very small and is invariably incorporated into the design rather than inscribed on the base.

Goldscheider (Staffordshire) Pottery Ltd., Hanley, Staffordshire, UK
Formerly Goldscheider Art Pottery, this firm produced earthenware and porcelain figures 1946-59. This printed signature of Marcel Goldscheider was used.

G. F. Grebner, Nuremberg, Bavaria, Germany
Georg Friedrich Grebner (active between 1717 and 1741), faience painter at Nuremberg, Bayreuth, Oettingen-Schrattenhofen and Donauworth. A versatile painter, capable of working in many styles including landscape, biblical, floral subjects. A considerable number of his signed and dated pieces exist. As well as his signature Grebner also added the day, month and year to many of his possibly independently-decorated (*Hausmaler*) pieces.

Gross-Stieten, Mecklenburg, Germany
Christoph Rudolph Chely and other members
of his family were faience potters at Brunswick, Wismar, as well as Gross-Steiten from
c.1753.

Lavender Groves, Chelsea, London
From 1952 Studio-type pottery was produced
here. This incised or painted mark appears.

GRUEBY POTTERY
BOSTON.U.S.A.

**Grueby Faience Company/Grueby Pottery
/Grueby Faience and Tile Company**, Boston,
Massachusetts, USA
Founded to make glazed brick and architectural tile in 1894, the company added an art
pottery line during the late 1890s, producing
vases with low relief floral decoration made
with rolled fillets of clay and covered with a
green flowing matt glaze that was sometimes
accented with yellow, ochre, rose or white.
The art pottery was discontinued in 1910, but
tiles were made until 1920, when the firm was
purchased by the C. Pardee Works of Perth
Amboy, New Jersey.

E Guignet

F. Guignet, Giey-sur-Aujon, Haute Marne, France
F. Guignet, manufacturer of hard paste
porcelain 1809-40, used this mark.

Guillibaud

Jean-Baptiste Guillibaud, Rouen, Seine
Inférieure, France
Jean-Baptiste Guillibaud (d.1739) and his
widow, succeeded Edme Poterat at Rouen.
They were active between 1720 and 1740
making good quality blue and white and polychrome faience, often using a combination of
formalized Chinese motifs and indigenous
"textile" or embroidery designs within trellis
diaper borders.

Rouen, Seine Inférieure, France
Inscribed script mark "gun" associated with
the second (Poirel-Poterat) phase of faience
production at Rouen from the mid-17thC
until c.1720 or beyond.

James Hadley & Sons (Ltd.), Worcester,
Hereford and Worcester , UK
See p.85. This incised or impressed signature
appears on figures, groups, vases and other
decorative pieces made by James Hadley for
the Worcester Royal Porcelain Co. c.1875-94.

Haeger Potteries, Inc., Dundee, Illinois, USA
In 1912, flower pots were added to brick and tile, which had been the primary products of this pottery since 1871. In 1914, they started glazing the pots, and what started as florists crockery expanded to include ornamental, garden and table wares in a variety of solid glossy glazes. This firm is still in operation.

Hall China Company, East Liverpool, Ohio, USA
Robert Hall created this firm in 1903, from his portion of the East Liverpool Potteries Company's assets, at first making bed pans, cuspidors, combinets and some dinnerware. In 1911, the company developed the first successful leadless glaze, which allowed them to produce ware in a single fire. This breakthrough, coming just before US markets were closed to foreign products used in food preparation and service during World War I, gave the firm a decided advantage with its institutional line. The firm also became famous for its range of gold-decorated teapots which were produced from 1919. Specialty items for domestic kitchens, refrigerators and tea service as well as some dinnerware have also been made. These marks are among those used.

HAly
1762

Pierre or Philippe Haly, Nevers, Nivernais, France
Pierre or Philippe Haly came from a family of potters active in Nevers in the 18thC. Recorded as painters, they produced a number of signed pieces dated in the 1760s and 1770s. This family is associated with figures and *tromp-l'oeil* dishes of fruit.

Hampshire
Pottery

Hampshire Pottery Company/James S. Taft & Company, Keene, New Hampshire, USA
See p.52. This mark was also used.

Hanau, Nr. Frankfurt-am-Main, Germany
See p.170. The two marks (above) appear during the Hieronymus von Alphen period (1740-86); the mark (below) is a later mark. Hieronymus von Alphen became the owner of the faience factory in Hanau on the death of his father, Heinrich Simons von Alphen, in 1740. Hieronymus von Alphen died in 1775, and his daughters continued the factory until 1787.

R. Hancock facit

Robert Hancock, Various locations, UK
Hancock was an engraver who worked at a
number of factories c.1755-65 (Battersea, Bow,
Worcester, Caughley). He is best known for
his work on first-period Worcester porcelains
(see p.23). This signature mark in various
forms occurs on pieces with fine quality
printed patterns.

*WM. HARE
WILMINGTON, DEL.*

William Hare Pottery, Wilmington, Delaware, USA
The most productive pottery in the state
of Delaware, was that established by
Pennsylvania-born William Hare in
Wilmington on French Street, c.1838. In the
earliest years, redware and stoneware were
made, but, later, stoneware utilitarian forms
were made exclusively. "Air-Tight Stone Jars"
were featured from the mid-1850s on for their
superior (to glass) strength and cheapness.
Virtually all stoneware was plain and salt-
glazed; blue decoration is infrequently found.
The firm continued until 1882.

Harker Pottery Company, East Liverpool, Ohio,
and Chester, West Virginia, USA
Founded by Benjamin Harker, Sr. in 1840 and
operated by his sons, Benjamin and George,
the Harkers joined with James Taylor in 1847
and after 1851 continued as George S. Harker
and Company until 1890 through several
changes in management. Before 1879, the
pottery made yellow ware and Rockingham
kitchenware and jugs, after which time it
specialized in white granite table and toilet
ware. Incorporated in 1890 as the Harker
Pottery Company, the firm soon changed its
product to semi-porcelain dinner, kitchen,
toilet and hotel ware and advertising novelties.
In 1931, the pottery moved into the old Edwin
M. Knowles factory in Chester, West Virginia.
The firm continued until 1972.

*C. HART & SON
SHERBURNE*

James and Charles Hart, Sherburne,
New York, USA
James Hart and his brother, Samuel, were
potters trained by their father in High Holden,
Kent, England, before settling in New York
State in the 1820s. By 1841, James and his son
Charles established a stoneware pottery at
Sherburne, New York, that remained in
operation until 1885; after 1866, Charles was in
partnership with his son, Nahum. The Hart

family members also maintained potteries in Fulton and Ogdensburgh, which were extremely successful.

Hastings Pottery, Sussex, UK

Studio-type pottery was produced by Bernard J. Cotes at the Hastings Pottery between 1956 and 1959. This incised mark was used.

Manufactured by Jos Hemphill Philad—

William Ellis Tucker/Tucker and Hulme/Tucker and Hemphill, Philadelphia, Pennsylvania, USA

Tucker started his career in ceramics by decorating French blanks for his father's ceramics and glass store. By 1825, his experiments to make hard-paste porcelain were successful. Thomas Hulme was a partner briefly in 1828; Joseph Hemphill joined the firm about 1832 and continued operating the pottery after Tucker's death in that year, until 1838. Tucker's brother, Thomas, managed the workers. Sometimes called the American China Manufactory, they made porcelain table and ornamental wares in the style of French porcelain painted mostly with flowers and landscapes. This is Hemphill's mark.

D.& J. Henderson/American Pottery Company, Jersey City, New Jersey, USA

See p.101. This mark was also used. Other marks in a similar style appear featuring the company name and "Jersey City".

William Fishley Holland, Clevedon, Somerset, UK

Formerly at Fremington, W. F. Holland produced earthenwares from c.1921. He used this incised signature mark as well as an initial mark.

HOWE & CLARK
ATHENS

Nathan Clark Pottery, Athens, New York, USA

See p.106. This mark was also used by this company.

Hünger. F.
. 2 .

Christoph Conrad Hunger, Various locations, Europe

One of the most important German enamellers and gilders in the first half of the 18thC. At Meissen c.1715-17 and later at Du Paquier's factory in Vienna (1717-19), Vezzi's factory in Venice (1719-24), Rostrand (1729), Copenhagen (1730 and 37), Stockholm (1741) and St Petersburg (1744-48).

⊗. Ign Heſs

Ignatz Hess, Hochst, Mainz, Germany
Ignaz Hess, faience painter c.1750, specialized in landscape and flower subjects often enclosed in elaborate rococo cartouches. Son of Georg Friedrich Hess, also a notable faience painter. This mark appears c.1750.

ID FAENCIA
>VR Æ‹

Faenza, Emilia, Italy
Faenza was one of the most important maiolica centres in Renaissance and post-Renaissance Italy. A large quantity of wares were exported, and this probably gave the name "faience" to tin-glazed wares later produced in other European centres. Noted for very high quality wares, especially the blue-ground *berettino* type and the celebrated and influential *bianco-di-Faenza* of the Mannerist period at the end of the 16thC. The work "Faenza" in its various guises rarely, if ever, appears alone, but is generally accompanied by initials such as the present examples, which are probably those of the workshop of Maestro Virgiliotto Calamelli (d. c.1570). Faenza is still active as a centre for the manufacture of tin-glazed ware.

Iſigny

Frederic Langlois, Calvados, Normandy, France
Frederic Langlois was a manufacturer of hard-paste porcelain in Isigny 1839-45.

ISIS

Isis Pottery, Oxford, Oxfordshire, UK
Studio-type pottery bearing this mark was produced at the Isis Pottery c.1947-53.

Jeanne

Jeanne, Paris, France
This decorator of hard-paste porcelain from 1827 used this gold mark.

Jever

Jever, Oldenburg, Germany
A faience factory was established here in 1760 by Johann Friedrich Tannich (later to move to Kiel in 1763). Barely viable for most of its short life, the factory closed in 1776 but did make some fine quality faience, especially in the first few years. The full or abbreviated place name rarely occurs alone and is usually accompanied by the one of the following letters or initials: "K", "J. C. K.", "K. O.", or "R".

Jill S.

Jill Salaman, Selsey, Sussex, UK
Jill Salaman's signature mark appears on Studio-type pottery and tiles made 1929-50.

Kiel, Holstein, Germany

A number of mainly short-lived faience factories were active here from 1758 until 1788 employing good craftsmen such as Johann Tannich (of Jever) and Abraham Leihamer (also of Eckernförde and Stockelsdorf). Johann Tobias Kleffel is the name of the proprietor of one factory which appears to have survived only a year or so in 1762-3. The other mark shown is the town mark.

Halley-Lebon, Paris, France

A decorator of hard-paste porcelain 1800-1812, Halley-Lebon used this script mark in gold.

Lagrenee le jeune, Paris, France

Decorator of Paris porcelain 1793-1800. This script mark appears in russet.

Peter Lane, Andover, Hampshire, UK

Studio-type ceramics were produced at The Pottery in Andover from 1961. Important pieces bear this signature mark.

Leplé, Rue de Bacq, Paris, France

Leplé directed a porcelain-decorating studio in Paris c.1808. Pieces signed by his son (Leplé jeune) are also found.

Jean-Marie Levavasseur, Rouen, Seine Inférieure, France

Jean-Marie Levavasseur and family potters in Rouen in the 18thC. A group of polychrome *petit-feu* enamelled wares was done at this factory from c.1770 onwards. This script mark appears.

Leveille, Rue Thiroux, Paris, France

Manufacturers of hard-paste porcelain in Paris 1832-1850. This mark was used.

L. Levy, Vallauris, Eastern France

Lucien Levy was an artist and designer at Clément & Jérome Massier in the late 19thC.

Lille, France

Lille was an important ceramic centre producing common pottery, faience and both hard and soft-paste porcelain in the 18thC. The faience was strongly influenced by Rouen and Delft in the first half of the 18thC and by Strasburg in the latter half. The mark illustrated appears on an original piece but is one of the most faked marks in French ceramics. It is frequently found on small metal-mounted snuff-boxes painted in *petit-feu* colours with Watteauesque figure subjects, landscapes or flowers. This mark appears in blue.

Limoges, Haute-Vienne, France
Although faience was produced here in the 18thC, Limoges is probably best known for its later hard-paste porcelain of which there were (and still are) a considerable number of factories in the area. Mostly the word Limoges appears on porcelain from the second half of the 19th and 20thC. While the majority of the marks are stencilled or printed, earlier wares tend to be hand-written. This mark appears on faience.

Lewis Miles, Horse Creek, South Carolina, USA
John Landrum established a pottery at Horse Creek (about 15 miles (24km) south east of Edgefield), South Carolina in 1817. In 1847 his son, Benjamin F. Landrum, and his son-in-law, Lewis Miles, took over the management of this pottery The "L. M." seen in the mark here, is for Lewis Miles. Dave (d.c.1863), an African-American slave potter, worked for Landrum and Miles, and his large alkaline-glazed storage jars, sometimes inscribed with poems, dates, and his name, are among the most sought-after pieces of American southern pottery. The firm continued until c.1865.

Jean Louis, Orleans, Loiret, France
Jean Louis was a modeller employed from 1756 to 1760 by the factory established by Jacques-Etienne Dessaux de Romilly in 1753. As well as faience the factory produced a soft-paste porcelain of Mennecy type. The factory probably closed in 1812. This mark appears on a figure.

De Lampetkan, Delft, Holland
Over 30 tin-glazed (delftware) factories were active in Delft in the 17thC onwards. *De Lampetkan* (The Jug or Ewer) appears to have had a large output judging by the number of marked specimens extant. Most bearing the script marks date from the middle of the 18thC. This mark was registered in 1764.

Lyman Fenton & Co., Bennington, Vermont, USA
Though a short-lived partnership (1848-52),
the principals, Christopher Webber Fenton
and Alanson Potter Lyman, working with
Calvin Park in 1848 and 1849, and Oliver
Gager after 1852, produced a wonderful
assortment of parian, Rockingham, and porcelain. Coloured metal oxides were frequently
used to decorate the fine Rockingham pitchers
and wash basins, picture frames, animal
figurines, etc., and the impressed oval "1849"
mark is probably the most frequently
encountered on all American Rockingham
ware. This firm evolved into the United States
Pottery Company.

Maestro Giorgio Andreoli, Gubbio, Urbino, Italy
Gubbio has been a pottery centre since the
14thC but its fame rests with the lustred wares
decorated by Maestro Giorgio Andreoli in the
first half of the 16thC. While painted maiolica
was probably first made towards the end of the
15thC, it is difficult to say when lustre appears.
The Maestro's script marks and monograms
bear dates which range from 1519 until 1541
on wares which, in many cases, were painted
in polychrome elsewhere, prior to their arrival
at Gubbio for the final addition of lustre
decoration.

Manteau, Paris, France
Manteau was a decorator of hard-paste
porcelain 1807-1811. This mark appears.

Martin Brothers, Fulham and Southall, London, UK
The four Martin brothers (Robert Wallace,
Walter, Edwin and Charles) designed, made
and decorated individual stonewares, c.1873-
1914. They are regarded by many as the first
of the Studio potters, and notable wares
include their models of birds with human-
type expressions, decorated with cream and
brown salt glaze. Their incised signature mark
with the address "Fulham" was used 1873-74;
"London" 1874-78; "Southall" c.1878-79;
"London & Southall" from 1879. "Bros" or
"Brothers" was added from 1882. Most pieces
feature a date near the signature mark.

Clement & Jerome Massier, Vallauris, France
See p.106. This mark appears on Studio-type
wares produced by these potters.

William Moorcroft, Burslem, Staffordshire, UK
See p.64. William Moorcroft's signature was
registered as a trade mark in 1919, but it was
previously used on pieces decorated by
Moorcroft while at Macintyre & Co.

Matt Morgan Art Pottery, Cincinnati, Ohio,
United States
An English cartoonist, Morgan settled in Cincinnati in the 1870s, where he worked for
a lithography company and briefly operated
a pottery as a sideline in partnership with
George Ligowsky, the inventor of the clay
pigeon, 1883-84. The art wares have a Moorish
look that combined low relief, moulded
decoration with gold or painted coloured slip.

**McNicol, Burton and Company/D. E.
McNicol Pottery Company**, East Liverpool, Ohio,
and Clarksburg, West Virginia, USA
This pottery (active 1869-1954) produced good
quality Rockingham and yellow ware. White
ironstone table and toilet wares were added
sometime in the 1880s. In 1892, the firm was
incorporated as D. E. McNicol and Company
and continued to make the same products.
Indeed, yellow ware was produced as late as
1927, although the firm was most famous for
its calendar and souvenir plates. The company
built a large additional plant in Clarksburg, in
1914, which specialized in hotel ware for a
wide variety of institutions, and concentrated
production there after 1927. Marks usually
appear on dinner and oven wares, and on
food dishes.

C. H. Menard, Rue de Popincourt, Paris, France
C. H. Menard was a manufacturer of hard-
paste porcelain in the mid-19thC.

Johann Friedrich Metzsch, Various locations,
Germany
A leading independent decorator or *Hausmaler*
and arcanist (active 1731-51 in Bayreuth, Dresden and at Furstenberg), Johann Friedrich
Metzsch (d.1766). His work which employs a
sophisticated colour scheme includes landscapes and shipping scenes after engravings by
Melchior Kysell, as well as birds on table tops.
All his signed pieces date from 1744-48. He
decorated Chinese, Meissen and other German
porcelains.

Donald Mills, London
Studio-type pottery and stonewares were
produced 1946-55. This signature was
registered as a trade mark in 1948 and was
used until c.1955, often with the year added.
A painted initial mark was also used.

Minton, Stoke, Staffordshire
Thomas Minton (1765-1836), who trained as
an engraver at the Caughley China Works,
established his own pottery in 1793, that has
continued under various titles and ownership
until the present day. The company produced
tiles, porcelain (some in the Sèvres style),
stoneware (domestic and decorative wares),
china (services and ornaments), earthenware,
parian and majolica. A large number of marks
were used including year marks; this painted
mark appeared on earthenwares c.1900-08.
(For further details of year marks, see p.362 in
Additional Information.)

Bernard Moore, Stoke, Staffordshire, UK
See p.41. This painted or impressed mark
appears 1905-15; the year may be added to
these marks.

Morley & Company, Wellsville, Ohio, USA
This is one of the few American potteries that
made majolica, and its wares were of very high
quality. It operated 1879-85. The pottery also
produced good white ironstone tableware.

a moulins

Moulins, Allier, France
Faience has been produced here probably from
the early 18thC until the beginning of the
19thC. Although rarely marked, several types
can be attributed to this town. The best wares
date from the third quarter of the 18thC.

Keith Murray, Staffordshire, UK
A New Zealander, Murray (b.1892, d.1981)
produced modernist ceramic wares in the
1930s and 1940s. From 1933, Murray worked
part-time for Wedgwood, designing hand-
thrown and hand-turned tablewares, and
other functional, but ornamental items. His
initials also appear within a Wedgwood mark.

Nast, Rue Popincourt, Paris, France
Manufacturers of porcelain 1793-mid-19thC.
The mark is usually stencilled in red.

New York Stoneware Company, Fort Edward, New York, USA

George A. Satterlee and Michael Mory operated a successful stoneware and Rockingham manufactory, the New York Stoneware Company, at Fort Edward, New York, on the upper Hudson River. Even before their partnership, this enterprise (known as the Fort Edward Pottery Company and so marked) was a thriving one, producing 75,000 pieces of ware in 1860. The New York Stoneware Company was active 1861-91.

Nicola da Urbino, Urbino, Italy

See p.90. These marks have also been attributed to Nicola di Gabriele Sbraga (or Sbraghe), a pottery decorator in Urbino from c.1520 until his death in 1537-38.

Niloak Pottery, Benton, Arkansas, USA

Various naturally-coloured clays were combined, but not mixed, to make the variegated agate ware in simple wheel-thrown forms of bowls, vases, smoking sets, candlesticks, punch sets, fern dishes, clock cases, and other items, were produced by this firm 1909-46. The basic line was called "Mission Ware", a swirled, hand-thrown type of art pottery.

Niderviller, Lorraine, France

See p.31. The town name can be impressed or may appear written in script, either in full or abbreviated.

Nove, Venezia, Italy

An important faience and porcelain centre in the 18thC. A number of painted, impressed and incised name marks appear.

Osterbro, Copenhagen, Denmark

A faience factory was established here in 1763 by Peter Hofnagel but was forced out of business after a law-suit in 1769. Osterbro wares are usually lower quality than the fine faience made at Store Kongensgade, but their wares are sometimes confused.

Offenbach, Nr. Frankfurt-am-Main, Germany

A factory was set up here by Philipp Friedrich Lay in 1739 and passed through several owners; the last recorded owner was Johannes

Klepper (1775-79) although a number of dated pieces with the town marks indicate that production continued into the early 19thC. "Offenbach", "Offenbak" and simply "Off", are all recorded marks of this town.

G. E. OHR, BILOXI.

George E. Ohr's Biloxi Art Pottery, Biloxi, Mississippi, USA

Ohr described himself as the "Greatest Art Potter on Earth" because of his ability to wheel-turn red earthenware into exquisitely thin vase and teapot forms and then alter them with twists and pinches to resemble ornamental art glass and frilly Belleek china. The murky, pitted glazes that are highly prized today were secondary to the forms, many of which were left unglazed. He was active 1883-1906.

OLLIVIER A PARIS

ollivier a paris

Ollivier, Rue de la Roquette, Paris, France

One of a number of Paris faienciers, the Ollivier factory specialized in the manufacture of stoves of which a number of dated and documentary specimens survive. These marks, both impressed and painted, are typical.

OWENS

J. B. Owens Pottery Company, Zanesville, Ohio, USA

See p.71. This mark was also used.

paauw
1740

De Paauw, Delft, Holland

See p.75. This mark appears. The proprietor of this factory 1729-40 was Jan Verhagen. He was succeeded by Jacobus de Milde.

X
1563
a pridoa

Padua, Italy

A centre for maiolica and *sgraffiato* earthenware from the late 15th-18thC. As well as conventional style maiolica, Padua is noted for Isnik (Turkish) influenced designs. This script mark is known.

PATENT ART TILE WORKS CHELSEA MASS. USA

Low Art Tile Works, Chelsea, Massachusetts, USA

Although a factory building was started in 1877 by John Gardner Low and his father, John, production did not begin until 1879 under the direction of George W. Robertson from Chelsea Keramic Art Works (see p.44), and continued until 1902. Tiles were made by the pressed dust, and plastic or wet process: both covered with glossy, coloured glazes. Subjects included heads, ornamental patterns, realistic and conventional flowers, figures and scenes. English artist Arthur Osborne, produced a large series of "plastic sketches", hand-worked low-relief pictures in clay.

P. Dam

Potsdam, Nr. Berlin, Germany
The principal factory in Potsdam was started by Christian Friedrich Rewend in 1739, producing conventional Delft style faience as well as unglazed and lacquered pottery (probably similar to the chinoiserie lacquered vases of Berlin).

PEWABIC DETROIT

Pewabic Pottery, Detroit, Michigan, USA
Ceramic painter Mary Chase Perry joined with her neighbour Horace Caulkins, who was in the dental supply business, to make vases and tiles with a variety of decorative glazes, including flambé, crystalline, volcanic and lustre from 1903. The pottery was most famous for its iridescent lustre effects. Many important churches throughout the United States are paved with tiles from this pottery. From 1966 to 1981, Michigan State University operated the pottery as a ceramic centre, museum and studio. Since 1981, the non-profit making Pewabic Society has been making tiles and continuing the educational program.

Pierre Renault (or Renard), Orleans, Loiret, France
Repairer and modeller, Renault was engaged at the faience manufactory at Orleans c.1760. He used this incised mark.

Pinxton.

Pinxton Works, Derbyshire, UK
The Pinxton Works was established by John Coke in c.1796. He employed William Billingsley of the Derby China Works, who produced high quality porcelain, and a famous group of wares painted with views of Derbyshire. Billingsley left in 1799, and landscape painter John Cutts was then appointed manager. He became a partner, and in the final years of the works ran the concern alone. Cutts left to work for Wedgwood in 1813, and Pinxton closed.

De Rosly, Pontenx-les-Forges, Landes, France
De Rosly was a small-scale manufacturer of hard-paste porcelain 1779-90, and used this script mark.

·P·O·P·
∂785

Johann Georg Christoph Popp, Ansbach, Bavaria, Germany
See p.39. This mark was one of those used by Johann Georg Christoph Popp (1697-1786), faience painter, manager and latterly proprietor of the Ansbach factory.

N. Poſsinger

N. Possinger, Nuremberg, Bavaria, Germany
N. Possinger was a faience painter of bibical subjects in strong high-fired colours. He is recorded at Nuremberg between 1725 and 1730.

Potter
Paris
86

Christopher Potter, Rue de Crussol, Paris, and Chantilly, France
Christopher Potter, an Englishman who established a hard-paste factory in 1789 which continued in production in the early 19thC, used this painted mark in underglaze blue.

THE PROVIDENTIAL
TILE WORKS
TRENTON, N.J.

Providential Tile Works, Trenton, New Jersey, USA
The company made plain or relief glazed tiles using glossy coloured glazes, underglaze decoration, gilding and cloisonné-like effects 1885-1913. Isaac Broome was the company's first designer and modeller.

J.M.PRUDEN
ELIZABETH, N.J.

Pruden Pottery, Elizabeth, New Jersey, USA
Keen Pruden bought an existing pottery and made brown glazed redware and blue-decorated stoneware. His son, John Mills Pruden, continued the business beginning about 1835. He made utilitarian stoneware, Rockingham and yellow ware for domestic use as well as drainage tile and other industrial stoneware products, c.1820-79.

Red Wing Stoneware, Red Wing, Minnesota, United States
In the southwestern corner of Minnesota, below Minneapolis, a number of stoneware potteries were established at or near Red Wing, Goodhue County. The Red Wing Stoneware Company was organized in 1877 and prospered, in spite of competition from the Minnesota Stoneware Co. (1883-94), North Star Stoneware Co. (1892-97), and Union Stoneware Co. (1894-1906). Eventually, in 1906 the Red Wing Union Stoneware Co. was formed from the remaining potters and they continued to 1930, when the name was

changed to Red Wing Potteries Inc. A variety
of different name and tradenames were used;
most incorporate "Red Wing".

Rennes, Ille-et-Vilaine, Brittany, France
A number of minor potteries have existed here
from the 16thC on, and apart from a small
handful of documentary pieces little can be
readily ascribed to Rennes. Apart from
conventional northern French faience, the
output included figures of saints. Marks are
rare but this example is characteristic of
Rennes.

REVIL
Rue Neuve
das
Capucines

Renou, Paris, France
Decorator of hard-paste porcelain from late
18thC to 1820. This mark was gilded.

*Bursley-Ware
Charlotte Rhead
England*

H. J. Wood (Ltd.), Burslem, Staffordshire, UK
Now part of Wood & Sons Ltd., H. J. Wood
(Ltd.) produced earthenwares from 1884.
During the 1920s Charlotte Rhead produced
wares for the company which bear this mark.

RH *Worcester*

Worcester Porcelains, Hereford and
Worcester, UK
See p.23. Signature marks sometimes appear in
the design of some printed wares. The initials
"R. H" are those of Robert Hancock, an
engraver at Worcester c.1756-65 (see p.118).
This mark appears in various forms.

Rihouet

J. Rihouet, Paris, France
J. Rihouet was a decorator of Paris hard-paste
porcelain from 1820. This mark appears.

J&R.Riley

John & Richard Riley, Burslem, Staffordshire, UK
Based first at Nile Street (c.1802-14) and subsequently at the Hill Works (c.1814-28), this
factory produced general ceramics. Several
different painted, printed or impressed marks
appear featuring the name "Riley" between
1802 and 1828. The works were later taken
over by Samuel Alcock.

R.F
Sèvres

Sèvres, France
See p.72. This mark in blue was used at Sèvres
during the First Republic (1793-1804).

Rookwood Pottery, Cincinnati, Ohio, USA
See p.92. This impressed mark was used,
and may appear with the monogram mark.

Roos

De Roos, Delft, Holland
See p.33. This mark was used during the late 17thC and early 18thC.

Rossi 1785

Rossi, Coimbra, Portugal
A faience factory was established here by Rossi in the latter 18thC, and survived into the 19thC. This mark appears.

Rousseau 43 Rue Coquillere

Rousseau, Rue Coquillere, Paris, France
F. Rousseau from 1837-1870, manufactured and decorated hard-paste porcelain in Paris. Pieces bear this mark.

Salamander Works, Woodbridge, New Jersey, USA
Operated by Michel Lefoulon and Henry DeCasse 1836-42, this pottery made high-quality, brown-glazed yellow wares for domestic and public use, especially as pitchers and coolers. Some designs were patterned after the successful ware made by the American Pottery Company. While some pieces identify Woodbridge as the location of manufacture, others mention New York. The firm had a shop in nearby New York City and some speculate this site was also a second pottery works. Fire brick and drainage tile were made in the same Woodbridge pottery both before and after the operation of Lefoulon and DeCasse.

Samadet 1732

Samadet, Landes, France
In 1732 a faience factory was founded here by the Abbé de Roquepine. The factory passed through several hands, finally closing in 1836. The pre-Revolutionary wares are eclectic borrowing from Rouen, Moustiers and nearby Bordeaux with whom it was in competition. This mark was used.

SARGADELOS

Sargadelos, Spain
See p.32. This mark appears during the mid-19thC. There are a number of variations of this mark.

Sarreguemines

Sarreguemines, Lorraine, France
In 1770 Paul Utzschneider established a faience and pottery factory which remained in production throughout the 19thC making a variety of fine wares including *faience fine*, Wedgwood-style stonewares, and lead-glazed

pottery such as majolica. This mark was used together with a straightforward mark "Majolica Sarreguemines".

Sceaux

Sceaux, Seine, France
See p.216. This late stencilled mark appears on faience made at Sceaux.

Schleswig, Germany
A faience factory was founded here in 1755 by arcanist Johann Christoph Ludwig Lücke (Ludwig von Lück). Between 1756 and 1758 the factory was owned by Adriani, Schmattau and the Otte Brothers, before it was bought by Johann Rambusch in 1758. The factory produced typical Danish type wares including table-tops, centre-pieces, baskets and punchbowls in the form of a bishop's mitre. The factory passed through a number of different owners before closing in 1814, unable to keep pace with competition from British cream-coloured earthenware. The script marks (seen here) are relatively rare; various letter and initial marks are more frequently found.

Schrattenhofen Kohler

Oettingen-Schrattenhofen, Bavaria, Germany
A faience factory was established here in 1735 on the initative of Jeremias Pitsch from Ansbach. The factory was taken over in 1748 by Albrecht Kohler and Johann Sperl who relocated the concern in newly-built premises. Output in the earlier years seems to have included tankards of standard German form and decoration in high-fired colours. During the 19thC, the factory concentrated on the production of cream-coloured earthenware. This mark was used.

Schoelcher

Marc Schoelcher, Paris, France
Marc Schoelcher was a hard-paste porcelain decorator in Paris c.1800 to 1810. This script mark appears in red, and occasionally in other colours.

Seligmann, Nuremberg, Bavaria, Germany
This faience painter worked at Nuremberg from c.1760-80. He used this script mark.

devres,

Sèvres, France
See p.72. This impressed mark was used c.1810-20 on cameo-relief wares made in the Wedgwood style.

Sincheny
à Sinceny
'S'pellevé

Sinceny, Aisne, France
See p.34. The mark (top) was used at Sinceny
during the early period 1733-75. The mark
(centre) appears during the "second period"
1775-95. The mark (below) was used by Denis-
Pierre Pellevé, who was director of the factory
1733-37.

à s.ᵗ jean.
au desert

Joseph Clérissy, Saint-Jean-du-Desert, Marseilles,
Bouches-du-Rhône, France
In 1679 Joseph Clerissy, son of Antoine
Clerissy of Moustiers, took over an existing
factory in this suburb of Marseilles. The
factory was continued by his family after his
death in 1685, and was relocated to Marseilles
in 1743. The best period was probably from
about 1700-20 when blue and white with
purple manganese detailing was chiefly used.
Subjects were typical baroque with classical
figures, hunting scenes or biblical themes. This
factory has been much faked. A number of
other minor factories also operated in this area
at the time. This script mark appears.

Johann
Henrich
Steinbach

Johann Heinrich Steinbach, Bayreuth, Bavaria,
Germany
Steinbach (d.1761) was a painter of faience at
Bayreuth. This name mark was used.

Stockelsdorff, Nr. Lübeck, Germany
A faience factory was started here in 1771,
principally making stoves and tablewares,
cisterns, jardinières and vases painted in
petit-feu enamels in rococo, Chinoiserie or
Neo-classical style. The factory closed in 1811.
Abraham Leihamer formerly from Kiel was a
decorator here for a brief period. This mark
appears.

SIPE & SON
WMSPORT.PA.

William Sipe & Sons, Williamsport,
Pennsylvania, USA
William Sipe was born in 1826, the son of
the potter Phillip Sipe, and he built his first
pottery in 1869 at Williamsport. He worked in
partnerships – Sipe, Nichols & Co. from 1875-
77, and Moore, Nichols & Co. from 1877-79 –
and later worked with his sons Luther and
Oscar until 1893. Their blue-decorated
stonewares were thrown by male potters but
were decorated on the second floor of the
pottery by women. Wares were shipped all
over Pennsylvania and Maryland.

Asa E. Smith Pottery, Norwalk, Connecticut, USA
On October 31, 1825, Asa E. Smith established
a stoneware factory "at the foot of Mill Hill a
few rods east of the Bridge" in Norwalk,
Connecticut. In 1843, Asa's cousin Noah S.
Day joined the firm and they remained
together until 1849. Smith's several sons also
joined the company and ran it after the father's
retirement in the early 1860s until 1887.

Smith, Fife and Company, Philadelphia,
Pennsylvania, USA
Little is known about this short-lived company, active 1830, since few pieces survive,
and all of them are flower-painted Grecian
pitchers like those produced by William Ellis
Tucker (see p.119), at the same time.

Rorstrand, Nr. Stockholm, Sweden
Founded in 1752 this faience factory produced
wares similar to Copenhagen, Rouen and
Delft with table-tops, dinner wares and stoves
similar to other Scandinavian/Danish/North
German factories. Wares were decorated in
high-fired and low-fired colours. A novelty of
this factory was the use of *bianco-sopra-bianco*
decoration similar to that at Bristol delftware.
In 1773 the factory began to make English
style creamware, and in the middle of the
19thC bone-china. The factory still exists,
producing high-quality ceramics. Many marks
exist, such as the example seen here.

C. Tharaud, Limoges, Limousin, France
C. Tharaud established a hard-paste porcelain
factory in 1919. The monogram "CT" together
with the name Limoges, was also used by
Tharaud.

Teco Gates, Terra Cotta, Illinois, USA
William Gates, a maker of tiles since 1881,
officially introduced the art pottery line
TECO in 1902, although experimental pieces
had been made since 1895. Many modellers,
designers and architects furnished designs for
the ornamental ware decorated almost entirely
in a matt green crystalline glaze, including
Fernand Moreau, Kristian Schneider, Hugh
Garden, William Le Baron Jenney, Howard
Van Doren Shaw and Frank Lloyd Wright.
The company closed in 1929. These impressed
marks were used.

Tomaszów, Poland
Michael Mezer produced hard-paste porcelain
here between 1805 and 1810. This script mark
appears in black and other colours.

Trenton Potteries Company, Trenton, New
Jersey, USA
See p.62. This mark also appears.

**William Ellis Tucker/Tucker and
Hulme/Tucker and Hemphill**, Philadelphia,
Pennsylvania, United States
See p.119. This mark was used by William
Ellis Tucker.

United States Pottery Company, Bennington,
Vermont, USA
After the firm of Lyman, Fenton & Co.
disbanded (see p.123), the financial backer,
Oliver A. Gager, reopened the factory as the
United States Pottery Company in 1852.
Daniel Greatbach of England modelled a
number of new shapes for the company,
including a fine hound-handled pitcher, and
John Harrison, a modeller from Copeland's
works in Stoke-on-Trent, England, assisted
C. W. Fenton with developing new shapes in
parian. The pottery was one of only seven
American potteries to exhibit at the New York
Crystal Palace Exhibition, 1853. In 1858, the
factory shut down but was vainly reopened for
one additional year. Porcelain, parian, and
Rockingham were the principal lines.

Varsovie, Warsaw, Poland
Seen here is the written mark of the Belvedere
factory established in 1774 by Elector King
Stanislas Poniatowski. Wares including the
famous Poniatowski service intended for
the Sultan of Turkey were based on Japanese
Imari porcelain or more commonly on
Chinese exportware. Single letters "B" or
"W" are also used. Some fakes of the afore-
mentioned Turkish service are known.

M^{RE} DE
VALOGNES
M^{tt} de Valognes

Valognes, Manche, France
A factory was founded here in 1793 by Le
Tellier de la Bertinière. By 1795 it belonged
to Le Masson. In 1802 it was taken over by
Joachim Langlois who transferred the concern
to Bayeux in 1812. A number of marks occur,
including those seen here.

Johannes Van Duyn, Delft, Holland
Johannes Van Duyn was proprietor of *De porceleyn Schotel* (The Porcelain Dish) factory in Delft from 1763-77, making mainly blue and white wares. This mark was registered in 1764.

Venezia, Veneto, Italy
Various tin-glazed and porcelain factories were established here from the 16thC. These marks belong the the Vezzi factory which produced hard-paste porcelain from c.1719-40. The full town name may appear in blue, with abbreviations in red, green or blue.

Josiah Wedgwood (& Sons Ltd.), Various locations, Staffordshire, UK
From c.1759 to the present day, this celebrated company has produced earthenwares and porcelain at Burslem, Etruria and Barlaston. Founded in 1759 by Josiah Wedgwood (d.1795). Wares include creamware, jasper, basaltes, majolica, lustre, agate, red and other wares. This basic impressed name mark appears on earthenwares from c.1759. Early examples have individually impressed upper and lower case letters. A "Wedgwood & Bentley" circular mark was used c.1769-80 on ornamental basalt, jasper and marbled wares. (For further details of year marks, see p.373 in Additional Information.)

Noah, Nicholas A., and Charles N. White, Utica, New York, USA
Noah White of Vermont began one of the most successful family dynasties of potters in the United States. Born in 1793, he was working as a potter by 1831 and owned his own stoneware manufactory in 1838 at Utica, New York with his son Nicholas. Through time there were many changes as family came and went. When Noah died in 1865, Nicholas and his son controlled the firm as N. A. White and Son (later the Central New York Pottery). Nicholas died in 1886, and his son Charles N. White ran the pottery until 1910. Under the direction of Hugo Bilhardt, a German designer, moulded stoneware pitchers, mugs, water coolers, steins, and other wares, were introduced in 1894, and these proved to be as profitable then as they are popular now with collectors.

Willoughby Smith
Womelsdorf

Willoughby Smith, Womelsdorf, Pennsylvania, USA
Though most American redware potters did
not sign their products, one exception stands
out – Willoughby Smith of Womelsdorf,
Pennsylvania. Traditional wares included milk
pots, pitchers, jugs, jars, dishes, pie plates,
spitoons, and chamber pots, made for a local,
rural eastern Pennsylvania clientele. The
quality of the work is excellent, and a good
many slip-decorated pie plates survive to
tempt collectors. He was active 1864-1905.

STERLING CHINA
BY
Russel
Wright
MADE U.S.A.

Sterling China Company, East Liverpool,
Ohio, USA
See p.105. This company is probably best
known among collectors for its line designed
by Russel Wright shortly after World War II.
This mark was used.

⊕*Zeschinger*·

Zeschinger, Höchst, Mainz, Germany
Johannes Zeschinger (b.1723) was employed as
a painter of faience from c.1750, Furstenberg
(1753) and Poppelsdorf (1756). He appears to
have specialized in fine quality bird painting.

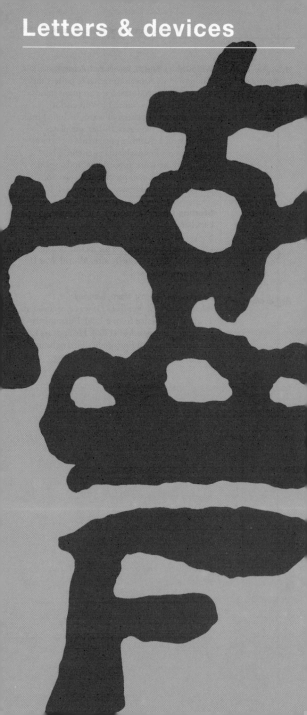

In this section, devices are featured in the order listed on the contents page, together with one or more initial (in alphabetical order), that may refer to an individual potter, firm, centre of production, or patron of a factory.

Crowns

St Petersburg, Russia
See p.29. The marks used on porcelain made at the Imperial factory in St Petersburg during the reigns of Alexander I (above) 1801-25, II (below left) 1855-81, and III (below right) 1881-94; all three emperors used the letter "A" together with a crown.

Rue Thiroux, Paris, France
See p.21. This mark appears on porcelain by André Marie Leboeuf in gold. The "A" mark was originally registered in 1776.

Fulda, Hesse, Germany
The Fürstlich Fuldaische Feine porcelain factory was founded in 1764 by the Prince Bishop of Fulda, Heinrich von Bibra (1759-88). The factory produced figures (similar in style to those made at Frankenthal) and other wares, characterized by a pure white body and a shiny glaze. This mark was used on porcelain made at Fulda. The mark represents Adalbert III von Harstall, Prince Bishop 1788-1803. Production came ended in 1789.

Wagner & Apel, Lippelsdorf, Thuringia, Germany
A porcelain factory was founded here in 1877, producing figures of animals and children, boxes, vases, ornaments and technical porcelain.

Beyer & Bock, Rudolstadt Volkstedt, Thuringia, Germany
Utility porcelain was produced at this factory from 1890, but it is thought that it existed as a decorating workshop from 1853. These marks appear; the mark below often includes the date 1853 as the year of foundation. The factory became known as VEB (K) Porzellanfabrik Rudolstadt-Volkstedt.

J. S. Vaume, Schaerbeek, Brussels, Belgium
A porcelain factory was founded at Schaerbeek near Brussels in 1786 by J. S. Vaume. Pieces were made in the style of contemporary Parisian wares. Dominant colours include sepia and green.

Bremer & Schmidt, Eisenberg, Thuringia, Germany
Founded in 1895, this porcelain factory produced
household wares, mocha services and mocha cups
for export to the Balkans and for China and the
Far East. The company still exists under the name
VEB Spezialporzellan Eisenberg. This mark was
used.

Worcester Porcelains, Hereford and Worcester, UK
See p.23. This standard impressed mark was used
on all wares during the Barr, Flight & Barr Period
c.1807-13. Many written marks featuring the full
name of this period in various forms, appear
beneath a crown.

Naples/Savona, Italy
Large maiolica vases with this mark and dated
1684 were recorded at Naples. It is possible that
they were made locally, but it is more likely that
they were made in Savona.

Burroughs and Mountford, Trenton,
New Jersey, USA
Although this pottery made the general line
of decorated hotel ware and domestic table and
toilet ware characteristic of late 19thC American
potteries, the quality of their decal work and
printed and filled decorations was exceptional.
They also produced an art ware having raised
gold decorations on a royal blue ground, and
some tiles. They were active 1879-c.1900.

Schomberg & Söhne, Teltow, Prussia, Germany
Founded in 1853, this factory produced good
utilitarian porcelain wares. It became a subsidiary
of the royal factory in Berlin from 1866, but was
independent by 1904. At different periods the
factory produced ordinary and art porcelain, and
technical wares. Marks of this form were registered in the early 20thC, denoting "Berliner
Porzellan-Manufaktur".

Robert Wilson, Hanley, Staffordshire, UK
Originally founded as Neale & Wilson (c.1784-95),
and subsequently called David Wilson (c.1802-18),
this firm based at the Church Works in Hanley,
produced earthenwares and creamwares in the
Wedgwood style. Robert Wilson died in 1801, his
sons Daniel and then David continued the Church
Works to c.1815; the firm was David Wilson &
Sons to 1818. This mark was one of those used by
Robert Wilson 1795-c.1802.

Pauline Pottery, Chicago, Illinois, and Edgerton, Wisconsin, USA

Pauline Jacobus started as a ceramic painter, but became interested in making pottery during the early 1800s. In 1883 she established her first small pottery in Chicago, but wanted to expand and in 1888 moved to Edgerton where good clay was found. The art wares were decorated under the glaze by a small group of artists. A battery cup factory on the first floor made the art pottery viable, but the operation failed in 1902.

Carl Alberti, Uhlstädt, Thuringia, Germany

Utility porcelain was produced at this factory from 1837. Various forms of this mark were used.

Charles Amison & Co. Ltd., Longton, Staffordshire, UK

Porcelains wares were made at the Stanley China Works by this firm 1889-1962. These impressed initials were used from 1889 (the "L" stands for Longton). This printed mark was used 1906-30.

Cartwright & Edwards (Ltd.), Fenton, Staffordshire, UK

See p.167. This mark was used on wares made at the Victoria Works from c.1912. Most other marks include the initials "C. & E."

Limoges, Haute-Vienne, France

See p.43. Wares made at Limoges for decoration at Sèvres sometimes feature the Sèvres mark and a painter's mark together with the mark of the Comte d'Artois as seen here. This mark appears incised and in blue enamel.

Collingwood & Greatbatch, Longton, Staffordshire, UK

Based at the Crown Works, this pottery produced porcelain 1870-87. The mark used was the crown mark (above) which appeared with or without the initials "C. & G." The company subsequently became known as Collingwood Bros. (Ltd.) and operated between 1887 and 1957. After 1957 the Crown Works were taken over by Clayton Bone China Co. The printed mark (below) was used 1900-12; a crown mark was also used up to 1930.

Fauborg Saint-Denis (or Saint-Lazare), Paris, France

See p.28. The factory at Fauborg Saint-Denis was taken over by Stahn, who registered the mark

"CP" in 1779, indicating the protection of Charles-Philippe, Comte d'Artois. Various forms of this mark appear in red, underglaze blue and gold.

Carl Theodor, Frankenthal, Palatinate, Germany
See p.58. Elector Karl Theodor owned the porcelain factory at Frankenthal between 1762 and 1795, when successive military occupations forced the factory to change hands a number of times. It was closed in 1800. During the "Carl Theodor" period this mark appears in blue in various forms. From 1762-70 the crowned monogram occasionally appears with the initials of Adam Bergdoll the manager. c.1770-88 the mark appears with the last two digits of the year of production. The late mark (below) (c.1780-93) features a row of dots under the monogram. This mark has also been recorded on some Derby pieces that were probably made as replacements for Frankenthal services.

Charles Waine (& Co.) (Ltd.), Longton, Staffordshire, UK
Formerly Waine & Bates, this company produced porcelain 1891-1920. This printed mark appeared c.1913-20.

Derby Porcelain Works, Derbyshire, UK
See p.25. This painted Derby porcelain mark was used c.1770-82. This mark appeared with dotted crossed swords c.1782-1825 (puce, blue and black c.1782-1800; red c.1800-25).

Thomas Dimmock (Junr.) & Co., Shelton, Staffordshire, UK
Based at Albion Street (c.1828-59) and Tontine Street (c.1830-50), this pottery produced earthenware 1828-59. The distinguishing initial "D" appears in many marks including this crown. Marks such as this may also be dated.

Helena Wolfsohn, Dresden, Germany
Helena Wolfsohn ran a studio for porcelain decoration in Dresden from 1843, decorating pieces in the Meissen style. The studio was taken over by Leopold Elb and W. E. Stephan. This mark appears.

Dahl-Jensens, Copenhagen, Denmark
Founded in 1925, this porcelain factory produced Art Nouveau and other decorative porcelain bearing this mark.

Mennecy-Villeroy, Ile-de-France, France
See p.45. This crowned mark appears in red on
early wares in Japanese style.

B. Bloch, Eichwald, Bohemia, Czech Republic
This factory owned by Bloch founded in 1871 was
granted a licence to produce porcelain by Meissen,
and pieces were made with the onion pattern.
This mark was used.

Edwin Bennett Pottery, Baltimore, Maryland, USA
See p.103. The mark shown above appears on
cream-coloured earthenware in 1897; the mark
below, was used in 1896. Many different marks
were used by this company: most incorporate the
name mark "Bennett", or the initials "E. B. P. Co."
Decorator's marks, usually in the form of a
monogram may also appear.

Ackermann & Fritze, Rudolstadt Volkstedt,
Thuringia, Germany
Fine porcelain figures and luxury goods were
produced here from 1908. This is one of the
factory marks.

Ludwigsburg, Württemberg, Germany
The porcelain works at Ludwigsburg was
founded by decree of Duke Charles Eugene von
Württemberg (1737-93) in 1758; Johann Gottlieb
Trothe was appointed the first director, and was
succeeded by Joseph Jakob Ringler in 1759. The
palace at Ludwigsburg housed the court between
1762 and 1775, and this period represents some of
the best production. The court returned to Stutt-
gart in 1775. King Friedrich of Württemberg
assumed the administration of the factory in 1802,
and there was a period of revival 1806-16. The
factory closed in 1824 following an order by King
Wilhelm I. Fine figures were made, with quality
declining after 1793. This "F" mark representing
King Friedrich was used 1806-16.

Fürstenberg, Brunswick, Germany
See p.25. This mark used on 19th and 20thC
wares made at Fürstenberg, and appears in
underglaze blue.

Worcester Porcelains, Hereford and Worcester, UK
See p.23. This standard impressed mark which
may appear with or without the crown, was used
at Worcester during the Flight, Barr & Barr
period, c.1813-40.

FBB

Emil Fischer, Budapest, Hungary
Hard-paste porcelain (utility wares, vases and
bonbonnières) was produced at this factory
founded in 1866. This is one of the marks used.

Fulda, Hesse, Germany
See p.139. This mark found on porcelain made at
Fulda appears 1780-88, and denotes "Fürstlich-
Fuldaisch".

Fraureuth, Saxony, Germany
Utility porcelain was produced in Fraureuth
from 1866, with a branch factory at Wallendorf
from 1919-26. This mark appears on wares
from both factories; the monograms stands for
"Porzellanfabrik Fraureuth". The factory closed
in 1935.

Ludwigsburg, Württemberg, Germany
See p.143. This mark appears 1806-16; the
monogram denotes "Friedrich Rex".

Royal Factory, Naples, Italy
Ferdinand IV of Naples established a porcelain
factory in 1771, which was moved to the Royal
palace in 1773. From 1806-34 the factory operated
under various owners. Copies of antique marble
and bronze were made in biscuit, and also
figures in the Empire and Neo-classical style.
This monogram stands for "Fabbrica Reale
Ferdinandea", and appears 1773-87 in purple,
red or blue.

(James) Neale & Co., Hanley, Staffordshire, UK
This firm produced Wedgwood-type earthenwares such as creamware, basalt and jasper ware
c.1776-84. The partnership was previously called
Neale & Palmer (c.1769-76). This impressed mark
comprising a crown and the letter "G" or "C" was
used c.1776-86

Greiner & Herda, Oberkotzau, Bavaria, Germany
Founded in 1898, this porcelain factory producing
utility wares became the "Neuerer porcelain
factory KG" in 1943. This mark was used.

Metzel Brothers, Könitz, Thuringia, Germany
A porcelain factory was founded here in 1909, and
was taken over by a company based at Hermsdorf
in 1950. Items produced include porcelain services
with the onion pattern. Various forms of this
mark appear.

George Procter & Co. Ltd., Longton, Staffordshire, UK

Operating from the Gladstone Pottery, and formerly known as Procter, Mayer & Woolley, this firm made porcelain 1891-1940. This printed mark was used 1924-40.

George Warrilow (& Sons) (Ltd.), Longton, Staffordshire, UK

Based at the Queen's Pottery, this firm (formerly Warrilow & Cope) made porcelain 1887-1940. The initials "G. W." were included in many marks used by this company. "& S." or "& Sons" was added after 1892, and "Ltd." after 1928. The company later became Rosina China Co. Ltd.

Harvey Adams & Co., Longton, Staffordshire, UK

Between 1870 and 1885, this company made porcelain and earthenwares. Many pieces feature floral relief patterns in the style of Dresden. Formerly Adams and Scrivener and subsequently Hammersley & Co. (see below), the firm used this printed mark.

Hibbert & Boughley, Longton, Staffordshire, UK

This printed mark was registered by a firm operating under this name in 1889 producing earthenware and porcelain.

Hammersley & Co., Longton, Staffordshire, UK

Based at the Alsager Pottery in Longton, this firm produced porcelain 1887-1932. It continued as Hammersley & Co. (Longton) Ltd. from 1932. This crown mark appears with various marks, including the initials "H. & Co."

Heber & Co., Neustadt, Gotha, Germany

A porcelain factory producing utility items, figures and other wares, was established in 1900. This mark was used.

Kelsterbach, Hesse Darmstadt, Germany

See p.80. This mark is rare on porcelain before 1789 and appears in blue; it is impressed on cream-coloured earthenware.

Hilditch & Son, Lane End, Staffordshire, UK

Formerly Hilditch & Martin (and subsequently Hilditch & Hopwood), this pottery produced porcelain and earthenwares from 1822-30. The initials "H. & S." appear in a variety of marks, including this crowned version.

J. H. Cope & Co. Ltd., Longton, Staffordshire, UK
Between 1887 and 1947 this company produced porcelain. This printed mark was used from c.1906. Other marks were also used.

J. H. Walton, Longton, Staffordshire, UK
Formerly Walton & Co., this firm based at the Albion China Works produced porcelain 1912-21. These initials appear on their marks.

J. H. Weatherby & Sons (Ltd.), Hanley, Staffordshire, UK
From 1891 this pottery made earthenwares at the Falcon Pottery. Many marks were used; this printed example was used from 1928.

J. Wilson & Sons, Fenton, Staffordshire, UK
Operating at the Park Works 1898-1926, this company (formerly Wilson & Co.) used this printed mark.

Carl Knoll, Karlsbad, Bohemia, Czech Republic
Pottery was made by Knoll from 1844. One of his marks features this "KC" monogram with a crown.

Keller & Guerin, Lunéville, Meuthe-et-Moselle, France
In 1731 a faience factory was established at two premises by Jacques Chambrette. The factories were conducted by his heirs after his death in 1758, but by 1788 had run into financial problems and were sold to Keller & Cuny, later Keller & Guérin (from 1788), whose descendants continued the concerns into the 19thC. Characteristic wares are models of lions and dogs. This mark was used from 1788-19thC.

Carl Krister, Waldenburg, Silesia, Germany
Krister (1802-67) came to Waldenburg from Thuringia, initially working as a decorator for Rausch. He founded a porcelain factory in 1829, and in 1833 he purchased Rausch's factory. After his death the factory changed hands. This mark denotes "Krister Porzellan Manufaktur".

Philipp Dietrich, Passau, Bavaria, Germany
Founded in 1840, and formerly known as Dressel, Kister & Co., this factory belonged to the Lenck family until 1937, when it was taken over by the Philipp Dietrich porcelain factory of Passau. At some point the factory began to call itself Aelteste (the oldest) Volkstedter Porzellan-Fabrik AG. It

closed in 1942. Wares include artistic porcelain
and pieces made from Höchst moulds. This is one
of the marks known, 1937-42.

Ludwigsburg, Württemberg, Germany
See p.143. This mark appears in blue and appears
on porcelain made at the time of Duke Ludwig of
Württemberg, 1793-95.

Rue Amelot, Paris, France
Porcelain was made from 1784 by Louis Honoré
de la Marre de Villiers and Montarcy, at rue
Amelot, and later at rue Pont-aux-Choux. In
1786 Montarcy together with Outrequin and
Edme-Alexis Toulouse secured the protection
of Louis-Philippe-Joseph, duc d'Orléans, and
registered this mark. Wares are painted in monochrome with no gilded decoration; at this time the
use of gilding and polychrome were exclusive to
Sèvres. This mark appears in underglaze blue.

Maddock Pottery Company, Trenton, New Jersey,
USA
There were three potteries in Trenton operated by
Maddock family members. In this pottery (1893-
1923) they made vitreous hotel ware with and
without decoration under the name Lamberton
China (Lamberton is the section of Trenton in
which the pottery stands).

Sèvres, France
See p.72. This "LP" monogram beneath a crown
was one of the marks used at Sèvres during the
reign of Louis-Philippe (1830-48) and appears in
blue or gold. This particular mark is frequently
faked.

Moore (Bros.), Longton, Staffordshire, UK
Samuel Moore's porcelain-producing business
(Samuel Moore (& Son), established 1859) was
continued by his sons Bernard and Samuel from
1870, and was renamed Moore (Bros.) in 1872.
Good quality porcelain services and ornamental
pieces were produced. The firm also developed
some new glazes and produced some original
gilded and enamelled designs. Notable are richly-
decorated "pilgrim's" bottles. Painted decoration
was also high quality. Majolica and *pâte-sur-pâte*
wares, and mirror frames were also made. After
1905 Bernard Moore moved to Stoke and ran his
own business (see p.41). This printed mark was
used 1902-05.

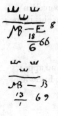

Marieberg, Nr. Stockholm, Sweden

The founder of the faience factory at Marieberg in 1760 was Johann Eberhard Ludwig Ehrenreich, who engaged Johann Buchwald as his manager in 1758. Porcelain was not produced at the factory until 1766 when Pierre Berthevin of Mennecy and Copenhagen succeeded Ehrenreich as manager. Wares include modelled pieces, figures, and items featuring delicate flower painting. This mark comprising three crowns appeared with the initials denoting the respective managers: "MB-E" (for Ehrenreich) 1760-66, "MB-B" (for Berthevin) 1766-69 (Heinrich Sten was manager 1769-88). Painters' marks sometimes also appear.

Buen Retiro, Madrid, Spain

Carlos III of Spain (previously Karl IV of the two Sicilies) moved his porcelain and maiolica factory to Buen Retiro from Capodimonte (Naples) in 1759, when he inherited the Spanish throne. Soft-paste porcelain was made 1760-1804. Hard-paste porcelain was made after 1804 under the direction of Bartolome Sureda who had studied at Sèvres. This mark was used during the "Sureda period" at Buen Retiro, 1804-08, and afterwards at La Moncloa 1817-50.

Metzler Brothers & Ortloff, Ilmenau, Thuringia, Germany

Founded in 1875, this porcelain factory produced artistic porcelain, ornaments, and small useful wares. This crowned monogram is one of the marks used.

Myott, Son & Co. (Ltd.), Hanley, Staffordshire, UK

Based first in Stoke (1898-1902), and then at Cobridge (1902-46), this firm moved to Hanley in c.1947. Earthenwares were produced with various marks including this one used from c.1900. The word "Stoke" indicates a date prior to 1903.

Mayer & Sherratt, Longton, Staffordshire, UK

Porcelain was produced by this firm at the Clifton Works 1906-41. This printed mark was one of those used. The firm also used the tradename "Melba".

Müller & Co., Rudolstadt Volkstedt, Thuringia, Germany

This factory, founded in 1907, produced all kinds of luxury wares. Destroyed during World War II, it was in operation again by 1949. This mark was used.

Ernst Bohne & Söhne, Rudolstadt Volkstedt, Thuringia, Germany

See p.160. This was another mark used by this factory.

Royal Factory, Naples, Italy

See p.144. In 1806 production came to a halt owing to French occupation, and in 1807 the factory was taken over by the French firm Giovanni Poulard Prad in Doccia who sold the concern in two halves. After changing hands again, the factory closed in 1834. Various forms of this mark were used in the 19thC, and appear incised or in underglaze blue.

Sèvres, France

See p.72. This mark was used during the Second Empire (1852-70) under Napoleon III, a period in which the production of soft-paste was revived. This mark appears in red, and may feature numerals that denote the date of decoration.

Ginori Factory, Doccia, Nr. Florence, Italy

See p.25. General pottery and porcelain was produced by the Ginori factory at Doccia from 1848. This mark appears on pieces made using moulds and models bought from Capodimonte and Naples. In the late 19thC the Ginori family went into partnership with Giulio Richard of the Milan factory.

Ott and Brewer/Etruria Pottery, Trenton, New Jersey, USA

The Etruria Pottery was operated by changing partnerships from 1865 until John Hart Brewer and Joseph Ott offered a stable combination (1871-93). This large pottery produced a wide variety of table and sanitary wares in ironstone as well as the earliest ornamental eggshell-thin belleek wares made in America. English potters of the Bromley family that had worked for Goss and Belleek developed the body in Trenton using American materials. Walter Scott Lenox was their designer from 1881 to 1884.

Krummennaab, Bavaria, Germany

A porcelain factory was founded in 1897 making coffee and table services, gifts and useful wares. Known under a number of different names, including W. Mannl (from 1892), Illinger & Co. (from 1931) and Hermann Lange (1934-39), this is one of the marks used.

Lubau, Bohemia, Czech Republic
A porcelain factory was first founded in by the
Martin brothers in 1874. It became known as
"Porzellan Fabrik and Kaolinschlämmerei Alp
GmbH". This mark was one of those used.

Pfeiffer & Löwenstein, Schlaggenwald, Bohemia,
Czech Republic
See p.158. This mark was used on wares by
Pfeiffer & Löwenstein.

J. & H. Procter (& Co.), Longton, Staffordshire, UK
Based at a number of potteries (Heathcote
Pottery c.1857-59, New Town Pottery c.1859-75,
Heathcore Road Pottery c.1876-84), this firm
made earthenwares 1857-84. This printed or
impressed mark was used.

Winterling Brothers, Röslau, Bavaria, Germany
A hard-paste porcelain factory was founded by the
Winterling Brothers in Röslau in 1906. This mark
is found on their wares.

Joseph Rieber & Co., Mitterteich, Bavaria, Germany
From 1868 this firm produced hard-paste
porcelain, and has operated under a number of
different names. Output includes utility wares
and tea and coffee services. This mark appears.

Scäfer & Vater, Rudolstadt Volkstedt, Thuringia,
Germany
This porcelain factory and decorating studio was
established in 1890, producing utility and luxury
articles and doll's heads with this mark.

C. & E. Carstens, Reichenbach, Thuringia, Germany
Founded in 1900, producing good quality utility
porcelain, this company was still operating in
1977. This mark is currently used. Older pieces
do not include the words "Carstens Porzellan"
that appear on the example seen here.

Grünlas, Bohemia, Czech Republic
A porcelain factory was founded here 1908-11 and
produced tableware. This mark is one of those
used.

Roper & Meredith, Longton, Staffordshire
Earthenwares were produced by this firm at the
Garfield Pottery 1913-24. This mark appears. A
crown device which appears with the pattern
name was also used.

Richard Vernon Wildblood, Longton, Staffordshire, UK
Operating from the Peel Works, this firm produced porcelain 1887-88. Also working from the Peel Works at this time was a firm called Massey & Wildblood, which operated 1887-89.

P. Donath, Tiefenfurt, Silesia, Germany
This mark was one of those used by this factory on table services made here from 1883.

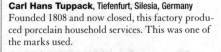

Carl Hans Tuppack, Tiefenfurt, Silesia, Germany
Founded 1808 and now closed, this factory produced porcelain household services. This was one of the marks used.

Alfred Voigt, Sitzendorf, Thuringia, Germany
Good quality copies of Meissen porcelain were made at the factory owned by the Voigt brothers, founded in 1850 and still in operation in 1977.

Christian Seltmann, Weiden, Palatinate, Germany
From 1911 this factory made utility porcelain, gift items, ovenproof cooking vessels and hotel porcelain. This is one of the marks used by the firm.

Shore, Coggins & Holt, Longton, Staffordshire, UK
Based at the Edensor Works, this pottery produced porcelain and earthenware 1905-10. It was formerly known as J. Shore & Co. 1887-1905, and subsequently became Shore & Coggins (1911-66). This printed mark was used c.1905-10.

Fielding & Co. (Ltd.), Stoke, Staffordshire, UK
Operating from the Railway Pottery and the Devon Pottery from 1911, this pottery produced earthenwares, majolica and other wares from c.1879. The mark (above) was used c.1891-1913, and also appears with a lion above the crown. The mark (below) was used from c.1913. Other crown marks appear with the "Fielding's".

Derby Porcelain Works, Derbyshire, UK
See p.25. Following the closure of the original Derby factory in 1848, a group of former employees started a new works at King Street in Derby. This mark (the old basic Derby mark with the initials "S" and "H" added for "Stevenson & Hancock") was used 1861-1935, when the King Street factory was taken over by the Royal Crown Derby Co. Ltd.

Paul Meyer, Bayreuth, Bavaria, Germany
Founded at the turn of the century, this porcelain factory produced household, hotel and restaurant ware. Various forms of this mark appear.

Samuel Radford (Ltd.), Fenton, Staffordshire, UK
Originally based in Longton (1879-85), Samuel Radford established a pottery in Fenton that produced good quality china that appeared under the trade name "Radfordian". The concern continued until 1957. Marks in the style of the one above were used c.1880-c.1913. A monogram such as the one seen in the mark below was used after c.1924.

E. & A. Müller, Schwarza-Saalbahn, Thuringia, Germany
Luxury hard-paste porcelain wares were produced at this factory from 1890. Some pieces bear this mark; other marks were used. The factory is now closed.

Thomas Bevington, Hanley, Staffordshire, UK
The Bevington family ran a pottery at the Burton Place Works from 1862, making useful and ornamental wares, ivory earthenware, gold thread ware and "Victorian Ware" which was designed to resemble quartz. This is the usual factory mark used by the firm.

Thomas C. Wild & Co., Longton, Staffordshire, UK
Porcelain was produced by this firm at the Albert Works 1896-1904; marks such as this one with these initials were used. The business continued as Thomas C. Wild at St Mary's Works in Longton (1905-17).

Klosterle, Bohemia, Czech Republic
See p.29. This mark, painted in chrome-green underglaze, was used from 1895. A variety of other marks appear.

Taylor & Kent (Ltd.), Longton, Staffordshire, UK
From 1867, this pottery produced a wide range of porcelain and majolica ware at the Florence Works. Printed marks with the initials "T. K. L." appear, such as this one used from 1880.

Taylor, Tunnicliffe & Co., Hanley, Staffordshire, UK
Earthenwares and porcelain were made by this firm from 1868, with useful wares only made after c.1898. Marks with a monogram such as this example beneath a crown were used c.1875-98.

Vista Alegre, Nr. Oporto, Portugal
See p.63. This mark was used on porcelain made here 1824-40.

William Lowe, Longton, Staffordshire, UK
See p.166. This mark was used from c.1912. Other marks featuring crown devices were used by this firm; these feature the name "W. Lowe" or the initials ""W. L. L." (the final "L" stands for Longton).

Ludwigsburg, Württemberg, Germany
See p.143. This mark which comprises two interlaced "Cs" under a ducal coronet for Charles Eugene, Duke of Württemberg, was used in various forms 1758-93, and also appears without the crown during this period. The modern factory at Ludwigsburg also used a similar mark (among others) from 1948.

Wildblood & Heath, Longton, Staffordshire, UK
See p.151. Based at the Peel Works from 1889, this firm produced porcelain until 1899, when it became known as Wildblood, Heath & Sons (Ltd.) (1899-1927). The mark above was used by Wildblood & Heath c.1889-99; the mark below was one of those used by Wildblood, Heath & Sons (Ltd.) from 1899.

Fasolt & Staunch, Bock-Wallendorf, Thuringia, Germany
From 1903 ornamental porcelain was produced by this firm. This mark was one of those used.

Comte de Custine, Niderviller, Lorraine, France
See p.31. These marks were used during the time of Comte Philibert de Custine 1770-93. Painter and chemist François-Antoine Anstett was director until 1779.

Rome, Italy
Filippo Cuccumos and Samuel Hirtz founded a porcelain factory in 1761 that continued until 1784. This mark has been attributed to this factory. A piece inscribed "Roma 1° Maggio 1769" bears this mark.

M. Bauer & Pfeiffer, Schorndorf, Württemburg, Germany
Now closed, this factory founded in 1904, produced table, coffee and tea services, and household porcelain. This mark was one of those used; the

letters "WPM" that appear beneath the mark stand for the factory name Württembergische Porzellan-Manufaktur. Other marks used by this factory are based on those used on 19thC porcelain made at Ludwigsburg.

Royal devices

Agostino Levantino, Savona, Liguria, Italy
See p.155. Possibly the son of another known Italian potter, Luigi Levantino, to whom the orb mark seen here is attributed, Agostino Levantino worked in Savona in the late 17th and early 18thC.

Luigi Levantino, Savona, Liguria, Italy
See above. This mark is found on late 17th and early 18thC faience from Savona.

Berlin, Prussia, Germany
See p.27. The printed orb mark (top) appears in blue or red, and has been added at the decorating stage to porcelain made at Berlin from 1832. A similar mark in red is used as a painters' mark today. The mark (below left) was used 1837-44. Towards the end of World War II the models, library and porcelain collection were moved to Selb to escape destruction. Some porcelain was also produced in a factory leased in that area. Production continued independently at Selb and Berlin after the end of the War due to occupation, until c.1957, when the factories were united. The mark (below right) was used on pieces made at Selb.

C. Tielsch & Co., Altwasser, Silesia, Germany
See p.175. This is one of a number of different marks used by this firm. After Tielsch's death, the factory was taken over by his son, Egmont, in 1882.

Joseph Schachtel, Charlottenbrunn, Silesia, Germany
See p.176. This mark was used. A cross may also appear beneath the mark

Shields

Ansbach, Bavaria, Germany
See p.21 This mark on Ansbach porcelain appears in underglaze blue.

A. B. Jones & Sons (Ltd.), Longton, Staffordshire, UK
Formerly A. B. Jones, this company based at the
Grafton Works and other addresses in Longton,
produced porcelain and earthenwares 1900-72. In
its latter years the firm became known as Royal
Grafton Bone China Ltd. Many different marks
were used, including several in the style of this
example used 1900-13. The same mark appears
with the word "England" after 1930.

Savona, Liguria, Italy
Faience was made in and around the three cities
on the Ligurian coast (Savona, Albissola and
Genoa) in the 17th and 18thC. This mark features
the arms of Savona.

Benedict Hasslacher, Alt-Rohlau, Bohemia, Czech
Republic
See p.29. This mark was one of those used by this
firm 1813-23.

Brown-Westhead, Moore & Co., Hanley ,
Staffordshire, UK
This firm was based at Cauldon Place, a works
originally established in c.1802 by Job Ridgway
and subsequently run by his sons, John and
William together with various partners. The
trading name became Brown-Westhead, Moore
& Co. in 1862. All types of ceramics were made,
including services and ornamental articles with
high quality decoration. Also notable are the
firm's floral-encrusted wares. This printed mark
was one of those used from c.1895 until 1904,
when the company became Cauldon Ltd.
(1905-20).

Kloster-Veilsdorf, Thuringia, Germany
See p.74. This rare and early mark, which incorporates the arms of Saxony, was used before
1765.Many other forms of these initials were used.

**McNicol, Burton and Company/D.E. McNicol
Pottery Company,** East Liverpool, Ohio, and
Clarksburg, West Virginia, USA
See p.124. A number of different marks were used
by this firm. Most feature the name "Mc.Nicol".

Fulda, Hesse, Germany
See p.47. This mark used on faience made
at Fulda features the arms of the city, and the
signature of Adam Friedrich von Löwenfinck
of Bayreuth.

George Grainger (& Co.), Worcester, Hereford and Worcester, UK

These works were originally established in 1801 by Thomas Grainger, who worked with different partners (Grainger & Wood, Grainger & Lee) until his death in 1839, when the business was carried on by his son George Grainger. Up to 1848 only porcelain was made, but after this date hard-wearing "Semi-Porcelain" was invented and produced commercially at the works. Parian vases, figures and ornaments were also made. In 1889 the Grainger company was taken over by the Worcester Royal Porcelain Co. Ltd., and production continued until 1902. The mark above was used c.1870-89. The mark below was used 1889-1902; the letter that appears under the word "England" represents the year of production: A (1891)-L(1902).

Godwin & Hewitt, Hereford, Hereford and Worcester, UK

Tiles were produced by this firm at the Victoria Tile Works (subsequently known as Godwin & Thynne) 1889-1910. This impressed or printed mark was registered in 1889 and used in 1910.

Gareis, Kühnl & Cie, Walssassen, Bavaria, Germany

This porcelain factory was founded in 1889, and made household porcelain, vases and other basic wares. The company became a joint stock concern in 1950. This mark was one of those used.

Savona, Liguria, Italy

See p.155. This mark features the arms of Savona; the initials "G. S." may refer to Girolamo Salomini, a potter at Savona in the late 18th and 19thC.

Josef Strnact Jnr., Turn, Bohemia, Czech Republic

This mark appears on earthenwares made at Turn from 1881.

Worcester Porcelains, Hereford and Worcester, UK

See p.23. Used during the Kerr & Binns Period (c.1852-62), this printed shield mark appears on fine-quality specimens. The last two numerals of the year of production occur in the central bar. An artist's monogram may also appear. The "TB" monogram seen here, was used by Thomas Bott, an artist who specialized in painting in enamels. Bott died in 1870, and his work is especially collectable.

Lancaster & Sons (Ltd.), Hanley, Staffordshire, UK

Previously known as W. Harrop & Co., this firm based at the Dresden Works in Hanley produced earthenwares 1900-44. The mark (top) was used from 1906 ("Ltd." was added to marks used after 1906); the mark (centre) was used after 1920. In 1944 the company became Lancaster & Sandland Ltd. The mark (below) was among the marks used, and appears from 1944. Many other marks were used featuring the firm's initials or the trade name "British Crown Ware" or "Crown Dresden Ware", which were both continued by Lancaster & Sandland.

Morley and Company, Wellsville, Ohio, USA

See p.125. This mark was also used. A number of different marks appear: most feature the name "Wellsville". Some of the marks were also used by the Sterling China Co., which owned this firm 1959-69.

Mueller Mosaic Tile Company, Trenton, New Jersey, USA

Herman Mueller (active 1909-41), from the Mosaic Tile Company (see p.97), organized this firm. In Trenton he made matt glazed conventionalized pictorial tiles and mosaics for interior and exterior decoration as well as fountains and architectural ornament.

Zacharias Pfalzer, Baden-Baden, Germany

See p.22. These marks appear on faience in black or in colour. Pfalzer had worked at Strasburg, and founded this concern with financial help from J. G. Wörscheler and J. G. Geyer.

Ansbach, Bavaria, Germany

The faience factory at Ansbach was established 1708-10 with the support of the Margrave Frederick William of Brandenburg by a Nuremberg merchant, Mathias Bauer, with the help of arcanists Johann Bernard Westernacher and Johann Caspar Ripp. Bauer was succeeded after his death in 1725 by his son-in-law Georg Christian Oswald who had worked as a painter in the factory since 1711. Johann Georg Köhnlein became manager in 1734, and remained there until 1747, when the factory came under the management of the Popp family (see p.39). The coat of arms seen here, appears together with an abbreviation for "Onolzbach", the 18thC name for Ansbach.

Onondaga Pottery, Syracuse, New York, USA
The large, long-lived company (1871-1966) was
organized to make white granite table and toilet
ware. In 1890, they added "Imperial Geddo," the
earliest vitreous ware made by the company. After
1897, this line was called "Syracuse China". A
cream-coloured earthenware line was added in
1893. An extensive line of hotel ware was made
for many years.

Ollivant Potteries Ltd., Stoke, Staffordshire, UK
Based at the Etruscan works, Ollivant Potteries
Ltd. (formerly H. J. Ollivant) produced earthenwares 1948-54. This mark appears c.1948-54,
together with a similar mark that features the
initials "O. P." only.

Ohio Valley China Company, Wheeling, West
Virginia, USA
See p.57. This mark was also used.

Ferdinand Selle, Burgau-Göschwitz, Thuringia,
Germany
Established in 1900 but no longer in operation,
this porcelain works produced luxury and Art
Nouveau porcelain as well as useful wares. The
initials on this marks stand for "Porzellan-
Manufaktur-Burgau".

Pfeiffer & Löwenstein, Schlaggenwald, Bohemia,
Czech Republic
This porcelain factory operated between 1873 and
1945, and produced coffee and tea services, hotel
and domestic wares. This mark appears.

Retsch & Co., Wunsiedel, Bavaria, Germany
Founded in 1885, this factory produced utility
and other services, together with vases, bowls
and boxes. This was one of the marks used.

Savona, Liguria, Italy
See p.155. This mark is based on the arms of
Savona.

Gotha, Thuringia, Germany
Wilhelm Theodor von Rotberg founded a porce-
lain factory here in 1757. In 1782 the factory was
leased to its workers, and named Schultz & Co.
In 1802 von Rotberg's widow sold the factory to
Prince August von Sachsen-Gotha, whose heirs
sold the concern to the Simson brothers in 1833.
Wares were made with Meissen floral-type

decoration in the rococo style, and include dinner, coffee and tea services, memorial cups, solitaires and tête-à-têtes. This mark was used from 1883.

Scammell China Company, Trenton, New Jersey, USA

This company was created by five Scammell brothers and occupied the old Lamberton works of the Maddock Pottery Company (see p.147). D. William Scammell had been in business with the Maddocks since 1901, and in 1923 completed the purchase of Maddock's remaining stock. The company produced a wide variety of patterns on a high-quality vitreous china body made lightweight for domestic use and heavier for institutional use 1924-54. The company's work is probably best known among collectors of railroad memorabilia who treasure the cobalt blue patterns made for the Baltimore and Ohio Railroad. This firm was taken over by the Sterling China Company (see p.105) in 1954, who continued to use this mark. This mark appears withwording in a number of different forms: "Lamberton China" is usually accompanied by the name "Scammell", and "Ivory" occurs in some marks, such as here.

Wardle & Co. (Ltd.), Hanley, Staffordshire, UK

Formerly James Wardle, this firm made earthenware, parian, majolica and other wares 1871-1935. The company went by the name of Wardle Art Pottery Co. Ltd. after 1910, and was a branch of A. J. Robinson c.1910-24, and Cauldon Potteries Ltd. 1924-35. This printed mark was one of those used c.1890-1935.

Anchors

British Anchor Pottery Co. Ltd., Longton, Staffordshire, UK

Earthenwares were produced at this pottery from 1884. The company has been known as Hostess Tableware Ltd. from 1971. This printed or impressed mark was used 1884-1913; the word "England" was added from 1891.

Coalport Porcelain Works, Coalport, Shropshire, UK

See p.72. This anchor mark with the letter "C" appears in blue on a Coalport copy of a Chelsea vase. Other Coalport copies of Chelsea feature a gold anchor which is larger than the mark that appears on original Chelsea wares, c.1845-55.

Chelsea Porcelain Works, London, UK

This 18thC soft-paste porcelain factory was established c.1745 by Nicholas Sprimont, a Huguenot silversmith from Liège. The production of the factory is divided into periods according to the marks used (incised triangle, raised anchor, red, anchor, gold anchor). In 1769 the Chelsea works were bought by William Duesbury, the proprietor of the Derby Porcelain Works. Porcelain continued to be made here until 1784; this period of the factories at Chelsea and Derby is known as the "Chelsea-Derby" period. The Chelsea gold anchor mark was continued, and this new mark incorporating the letter "D" was introduced, and is painted in gold.

Ernst Bohne & Söhne, Rudolstadt Volkstedt, Thuringia, Germany

From 1854 Bohne made hard-paste porcelain, marked with an anchor bearing the initials "E. B." (as here) or simply "B". After 1945, the company became known as Albert Stahl & Co. Luxury and fancy items were produced.

Thomas Fell (& Co.) (Ltd.), Newcastle-upon-Tyne, UK

All the usual earthenwares and creamwares were made by this firm at St. Peter's Pottery c.1817-90. This impressed mark occasionally appears 1817-30. Other marks were used incorporating the name "Fell" or the initials "T. F. & Co."

Boulogne, Pas-de-Calais, France

A porcelain factory was founded here c.1817 by Haffringue. In the year 1857 the owners were Clarté and Dunand. High quality hard-paste was made here; Haffringue employed Italian modellers. The factory closed in 1859. This mark appears in red.

Britannia Porcelain Works, Meierhöfen, Bohemia, Czech Republic

This works producing luxury and useful wares was founded by the Moser brothers in 1890; it was formerly known as Eberhard & Co. In 1884 the factory was acquired by the Benedikt brothers who ran another porcelain concern in the same locality. This mark was used before 1884.

Möller & Dippe, Unterköditz, Thuringia, Germany

An earthenware and porcelain factory was established in 1846 producing dolls and luxury porcelain figures. The works is now closed.

Middlesbrough Pottery Co., Yorkshire, UK
Established c.1834, this pottery produced
creamwares and general earthenwares until
1844 when the company became known as the
Middlesbrough Earthenware Co. (1844-52). This
mark was used c.1834-44. The anchor device
continued to be used 1844-52 with the initials
"M. E. & Co.", and occasionally with the words
"Middlesbro Pottery". (The firm was renamed
Isaac Wilson & Co in 1852, and operated until
1857.)

Porsgrunn, Norway
The Porsgrunn porcelain factory was established
in 1887, and produced porcelain services. This
mark appears, sometimes with the words
"Porsgrund Norge".

Andrea Fontebasso, Treviso, Veneto, Italy
Initially working with his brother Giuseppe
producing soft-paste porcelain from the end of
the 18thC, Andrea Fontebasso made earthenware
from the mid-19thC. This mark with letters
denoting "Royal Fabrique, Fontebasso", was
used from 1873.

Sampson Bridgwood & Son (Ltd.), Longton,
Staffordshire, UK
Established c.1805, this factory was based at the
Anchor pottery. Output included services for the
home and export markets (particularly Canada
and the United States). White graniteware was
also made for export to the United States, Australia and Canada. Their speciality was "Parisian
Granite" (stamped "Limoges") which had a fine
durable body and an excellent glaze. Many
printed marks were used, including a number
featuring anchors. This one was used 1885. Other
20thC anchor marks feature the name of the
company.

Thomas Morris, Longton, Staffordshire, UK
Based at the anchor works, this pottery produced
porcelain c.1897-1901, when it became the Anchor
Porcelain Co. Ltd. This impressed or printed
anchor was used as a trademark, often with the
letters "TM".

Vernon, Fismes, Marnes, France
English-style, soft-paste porcelain was produced
by Vernon at Fismes from 1840. This mark, and a
more elaborate version were both used.

Swords

John Bevington, Hanley, Staffordshire, UK
Operating from the Kensington Works in Hanley, Dresden-style porcelain was made here c.1872-92. This blue painted mark was used, and often appears on floral-encrusted porcelains or figures.

Baehr & Proeschild, Ohrdruf, Thuringia, Germany
This porcelain factory established in 1871 produced utility porcelain, religious pieces, dolls and dolls' heads. This hallmark was used.

Dornheim, Koch & Fischer, Gräfenroda, Thuringia, Germany
Founded in 1860, this porcelain factory produced luxury and fancy goods, dolls and dolls' heads. The factory is now closed.

Fontainebleau, Seine-et-Marne, France
A porcelain factory was founded in 1795 by Benjamin Jacob and Aaron Smoll. In c.1830 the factory was sold to Jacob and Mardochée Petit, who used the mark below 1830-62. Records show that the initials of E. Jacquemin, a decorator, appear within a similar mark, above 1863.

Meissen, Nr. Dresden, Saxony, Germany
See p.53. Another early Meissen factory mark denoting "Königliche Porzellan Manufaktur", this was used on teapots and sugar basins 1723-24. Here it appears in combination with the crossed swords mark which was proposed by manager Steinbruck c.1722, but not adopted until 1724.

Rauenstein, Thuringia, Germany
See p.60. This mark was used by the factory at Rauenstein in the 19thC.

Scroll marks

Sèvres, France
See p.72. Scroll marks (in fact crossed "L"s for Louis XV and XVI) were used at Sèvres, from 1749 without date letters, and from 1753 with date letters. Date letters were used to indicate the year of manufacture, such as these seen here. Any letter that appears below the mark, usually denotes the painter. These marks generally appear in blue enamel. (For further details of date letters, see p.363 in Additional information.)

Burford Brothers, East Liverpool, Ohio, USA
Organized originally by three brothers to make floor and wall tiles, the factory was converted a few years later to make ironstone and earthenware, and was active 1879-1904. They made semi-porcelain table, tea and toilet sets as well as miscellaneous speciality items, such as cuspidors and punch bowls. Hotel ware was also produced here. The factory was sold in 1904 to Standard Pottery Company, which occupied the plant until 1920.

Coalport Porcelain Works, Coalport, Shropshire, UK
See p.72. The painted mock Sèvres mark (above) was used on ornate pieces made at Coalport c.1845-55. The "ampersand" mark (below) appeared painted or in gilt c.1861-75; the gold anchor mark of Chelsea (which represents the Chelsea period c.1756-69) was also copied.

Carl Thieme, Potschappel, Dresden, Germany
See p.181. This mark was one of those used by this firm from 1875.

Sèvres, France
See p.72 and p.162. This Sèvres mark which appeared in blue or red enamel bears the date letter for 1781. The crown seen here, was usually used on hard-paste porcelain c.1770-93. (For further details of date letters, see p.363 in Additional information.)

Derby Porcelain Works, Derbyshire, UK
See p.25. This painted imitation Sèvres mark was one of those used on wares made during the Bloor period, c.1825-48.

Rue de la Paix, Paris, France
Feuillet established a porcelain decorating studio here c.1820. His work appears primarily on hard-paste porcelain in the Sèvres style. This mark appears on green or gold.

Ludwig Wessel, Poppelsdorf, Bonn, Germany
A faience and general ceramics factory was founded here in 1755, producing utility and luxury porcelain, artistic faience, services, vases and flowerpots. This mark was one of those used in the late 19thC. A similar mark appears on modern wares. As well as featuring the name of the town in full, this mark also appears with the letter "P" below the mark.

Minton, Stoke, Staffordshire, UK

Founded by Thomas Minton in 1793, this factory produced earthenwares, parian, majolica, stoneware, china, pâte-sur-pâte. Minton's sons Herbert and Thomas were admitted into the partnership in 1817, but the latter left the business in 1828. After Thomas Minton's death in 1836, Herbert took over the company, entering into a partnership with John Boyle c.1836-41, and subsequently with Michael Hollins and Colin Minton Campbell (a nephew). Hollins and Campbell continued the firm after Herbert's death in 1858. The trading name after 1873 became simply "Minton". Up to the end of the 18thC only white, blue and white, and creamwares were made, porcelain was made 1797-1816, and from 1824 onwards. Highly skilled painters were employed. Minton's celebrated majolica was produced from 1850. All types of items were produced, ranging from ornamental vases and ewers, to mass-produced tiles after 1844. The first mark shown here (above) appears on early porcelains c.1800-30, and may occur with or without the pattern number. The second mark (below), is one of those used c.1822-36. A number of different marks in this decorative, scrolling style were used.

Pierre-Joseph Fauquez, Saint-Amand-les-Eaux, Nord, France

Fauquez founded a faience factory here in 1718 as a branch of his works at Tournai. Fauquez's son (Pierre-François-Joseph) and grandson (Jean-Baptiste-Joseph) succeeded him in turn, and the factory was given up by the family following the Revolution c.1793. Soft-paste porcelain was made 1771-78, but was stopped due to competition with Tournai. This mark was used on cream-coloured earthenware.

United States Pottery Company, Bennington, Vermont, USA

See p.135. This mark was one of those used.

Shapes: Triangles

Noel Brannan, Burbage, Leicestershire, UK

From 1947 Studio-type pottery was produced with this incised or painted mark. In some cases the name "Noel" may replace the letter "N" beneath the mark.

Bridge Products Co., Winscombe, Somerset, UK
Earthenwares were produced by this company, owned by H.C. Swann, between 1954 and 1963. This printed or impressed mark was used.

C. T. Maling, Newcastle-upon-Tyne, Tyne and Wear, UK
Christopher T. Maling originally worked for his father, William Maling at the North Hylton Pottery in Sunderland, Tyne and Wear (established 1762), which made patterned earthenwares. This factory continued until 1815 when William Maling's other son Robert founded the Ouseburn Pottery in Newcastle, where he produced marmalade, jam and other types of pots. Christopher Maling took over the business in 1859 and built the Ford Potteries. Called C. T. Maling c.1859-90, the company became known as C. T. Maling & Sons (Ltd.) (1890-1963). Government measure jugs and mugs and a wide range of other wares were made. This impressed or printed mark was used 1875-c.1908.

Antoine de la Hubaudière, Quimper, Finistère, France
See p.80. This mark was also used by Hubaudière in the 19thC.

Schoenau Brothers, Hüttensteinach, Thuringia, Germany
Founded in 1865 this factory made utility ware. This marks was used. The firm was later known as Porzellan-Fabriken Gebr. Schoenau, Swaine & Co.

Janet Leach, St Ives, Cornwall, UK
The seal mark found on Studio-type wares made by Janet Leach (wife of Bernard Leach, see p.41) at the Leach Pottery appears from 1956.

J. Tiélès, Paris, France
Hard-paste porcelain was produced by this Parisian factory probably in the 19thC. This mark appears.

Lonhuda Pottery Company, Steubenville, Ohio, USA
See p.87. This mark was also used. Pieces made at Lonhuda may also feature the initials and monograms of the decorator.

Diana Myer, London, UK
This painted mark appears on Diana Myer's Studio-type wares from 1958.

Sèvres, France
See p.72. After the capture of Napoleon III at
Sedan in 1870, the Third Republic (1871-1940)
was established in France. The mark above in
chrome green, was used on porcelain made at
Sèvres from 1900; the mark below was used on
stoneware.

William Lowe, Longton, Staffordshire, UK
Previously known as Tams & Loew, this company
operated between 1874 and 1930 producing china.
This printed or impressed mark was used 1874-
1912; sometimes it appears beneath a crown.

Shapes: Circles

Adam Ludwig, Höchst, Nr. Mainz, Germany
See p.24. Adam Ludwig was a painter at Höchst
(c.1749-58). This mark is not to be confused with
Adam Friedrich von Löwenfinck, founder of the
factory.

Charles Fergus Binns, Alfred, New York, USA
Though born and trained in Worcester, England,
where his father was director of the Royal
Porcelain Works, Binns (b.1857-d.1934) made his
reputation as the first director of the School of
Ceramic Art at Alfred University from 1900 to
1931, where many important American studio
potters were later trained. Binns's mature work in
stoneware was characterized by disciplined forms
based on classic Asian models and finely textured
matt and crystalline glazes developed in his
research.

Georg Friedrich Hess, Höchst, Nr. Mainz, Germany
See p.24. Hess was employed at Höchst from the
beginning, from 1746-50 as an arcanist and later as
a painter and probably a modeller. His son Ignatz
also worked at the factory.

Johannes Zeschinger, Höchst, Nr. Mainz, Germany
See p.24. Johannes Zeschinger was a painter at the
Höchst porcelain factory from 1750; he used this
mark.

Casa Pirota, Faenza, Emilia, Italy
A workshop was believed to have existed in
Faenza during the 16thC, the name "Casa Pirota"
is mentioned in a number of inscriptions found on
Faentine maiolica. Two pieces are known to bear

the name of the workshop in full. This device featuring a fire-ball (*pyros rota*), was believed to be associated with the factory. This mark, with the fire-ball in the centre, with the date 1525 has been found on a plaque. A number of variations of this style of mark occur.

University City Pottery, University City, Missouri, USA
E. G. Lewis, a magazine publisher, founded the American Woman's League in 1907 to provide mail-order instruction in a variety of subjects, including the arts. In 1909, the famous French potter Taxile Doat headed the ceramic department; English potter Frederick H. Rhead wrote the educational materials; and Adelaide A. Robineau (see p.92), Edward Dahlquist and Kathryn Cherry were instructors. The project ended in 1914, when the legitimacy of Lewis's publishing empire was questioned by the federal postal authorities. Artists produced the wares for which they were famous: Doat and Robineau carved porcelain and glazed with crystalline effects; Rhead concentrated on slip-decorated earthenware; Cherry was a china painter.

Maximilien-Joseph Bettignies, Saint-Amand-les-Eaux, Nord, France
Production of porcelain was originally begun by Jean-Baptiste-Joseph Fauquez, but competition from Tournai forced production to stop in 1778. The manufacture of porcelain was resumed c.1800 by Maximilien-Joseph Bettignies. Reproductions of Sèvres and other early porcelain were produced with this mark in underglaze blue, c.1800-82.

Shapes: Diamonds

Cartwright & Edwards (Ltd.), Fenton, Staffordshire, UK
Based at a number of different potteries in Fenton (Borough Pottery from 1896, Victoria Works from 1912, Longton and Heron Cross from 1916), Cartwright & Edwards produced general ceramics from c.1857. The initials "C. & E." appear in many marks, and appear in this form from c.1900.

Heath & Greatbatch, Burslem, Staffordshire, UK
Based at the Union Pottery 1891-93, this company was previously known as Buckley Heath & Co. (1885-90). Produced earthenwares with this printed or impressed mark.

E. Hughes & Co., Fenton, Staffordshire
This firm operated 1889-1953 at the Opal China
Works in Fenton producing porcelain. This
impressed or printed mark was used 1898-1905.

Jersey City Pottery, Jersey City, New Jersey, USA
English potters John Owen Rouse and Nathaniel
Turner acquired the pottery works of the
American Pottery Company, about 1850. This
firm was active c.1850-92. Although they
continued to make Rockingham and yellow
ware, perhaps until the pottery closed, they also
made earthenware blanks for the amateur and
professional decorating trade and telegraphic
insulators. This printed mark was one of those
used.

R. Floyd & Sons, Stoke, Staffordshire
Earthenwares were produced by this company
(formerly R. Floyd & Co.) 1907-30. This printed or
impressed mark was used.

New England Pottery Company, East Boston,
Massachusetts, USA
Founded for making Rockingham and yellow
ware, the pottery added white granite and cream-
colored earthenware dinnerware to its repertoire
in the early 1870s. In addition, the pottery also
made toilet sets and short sets of odd dishes. The
firm was active 1854-1914.

Peter Ainslie, Leicester, Leicestershire, and Chester,
Cheshire, UK
See p.91. Peter Ainslie also used this impressed
initial mark.

Shapes: Hearts

Baehr & Proeschild, Ohrdruf, Thuringia, Germany
See p.162. This mark was used; the initials may
appear within the heart.

Stars

Albertus Kiehl, Delft, Holland
De witte Starre (The White Star) was founded in
1660 by Wilhelm Cleffius (also proprietor of *De
Paauw*, and *Het hooge Huys*) and Gisbrecht
Cruyck (also of *De Dissel* and *De Paauw*) and
changed hands a number of times before 1761,

when it was taken over by Albertus Kiehl until 1772. Delft wares produced during the time of Kiehl may bear this or a similar mark.

Deruta, Umbria, Italy
See p.32. This mark appears on a piece in the "petal-back" class, c.1500-10.

A. Farini, Faenza, Emilia, Italy
Urbino and Patanazzi-style maiolica was made at Faenza in the 19thC. This mark was used from 1878.

Nymphenburg, Bavaria, Germany
See p.71. This "hexagram mark" in blue underglaze was used 1763-67. The letters and numbers seen here also appear as a mark without the hexagram.

Johannes van den Bergh, Delft, Holland
Together with his brother Dirk, Johannes van den Bergh ran *De witte Starre* (The White Star) factory (see p.168), 1772-89. This mark has been ascribed to him.

Joseph Hackl, Göggingen, Nr. Augsburg, Germany
See p.49. This mark is one of those used by Joseph Hackl probably after the factory at Göggingen was closed in 1752.

Ilmenauer Porzellanfabrik Graf von Henneberg AG, Ilmenau, Thuringia, Germany
A factory was established in Ilmenau in 1777 by Gräbner. It was taken over by Duke Karl August von Sachsen-Weimer in 1782. In 1784 he appointed Franz Joseph Weber as director. The factory was leased to Gotthelf Greiner in 1786, and to Christian Nonne in 1792. In 1808 Nonne bought the factory together with his son-in-law Roesch. In 1871 it was taken over by a limited liability company, and until 1945 was known under the name Ilmenauer Porzellanfabrik Graf von Henneberg AG. The factory is now known as VEB Henneberg Porzellan Ilmenau. Notable wares are Meissen copies, produced during the early years of the factory, and Wedgwood-style jasper wares. These are later marks.

Lettin, Saxony, Germany
Utility and ornamental porcelain was made at this factory from 1858. This is one of the marks used. The letter also appears with a crown device.

Deruta, Umbria, Italy
See p.32. The letter "M" is the most common letter that appears on pieces in the "petal-back" class of maiolica made at Deruta in the late 15thC.

Price Brothers, Burslem, Staffordshire, UK
Based at the Crown Works in Burslem 1896-1903, this firm producing earthenwares continued at other premises after 1903 under different titles. This printed mark was used 1896-1910 (use was continued by successors Price Bros. (Burslem) Ltd. 1903-61).

Arno Fischer, Ilmenau, Thuringia, Germany
Fancywares were made at this porcelain factory from 1907. This is one of the marks used.

Rauenstein, Thuringia, Germany
See p.60. This is an early mark used on porcelain made by the Greiner brothers at Rauenstein.

Girolamo Salomini, Savona, Liguria, Italy
This "pentagram" or "Solomon's seal" is found on all classes of faience from Savona, and was probably used by Salomini who was a potter in Savona, together with his family, in the 17th and 18thC. It has also been ascribed to Siccardi who worked in Savona at around the same time.

Seville, Andalusia, Spain
Faience was made in Seville in the 19thC. This mark appears.

Schoenau & Hoffmeister, Burggrub, Bavaria, Germany
Porcelain dolls and doll's heads were made at this factory from 1901 with this mark.

Crescents

Bembridge Pottery, Bembridge, Isle of Wight, UK
See p.78. This seal or painted mark was used by T. R. Parsons and his wife Sybil Finnemore at their Bembridge Pottery 1949-61.

Hanau, Frankfurt-am-Main, Germany
Established in 1661 by Dutchmen Daniel Behaghel and Jacobus van de Walle, the faience factory at Hanau was one of the earliest and most productive in Germany. The factory's first manager Johannes Bailly took over in 1671. After

his death in 1688 the factory was continued by his widow, who was joined by Behagel and van de Walle's widow. In 1727 it became the property of Heinrich Simons von Alphen, and then in 1740 that of his son Hieronymus. Early wares are similar to Delft, painted with Chinese-style motifs including "Dotted" grass in the manner of Transitional wares. European motifs are also used. Wares include the characteristic *Enghalskrug*, inkstands, salt-cellars and pear-shaped jugs. The crescent mark appears on early wares with the incised marks of throwers and painters, such as the "H" seen here.

George Jones (& Sons Ltd.), Burslem, Staffordshire, UK
See p.84. A crescent appears under the "GJ" monogram from 1874, and the word "crescent" was also used c.1924-51.

Ott and Brewer/Etruria Pottery, Trenton, New Jersey, USA
See p.149. This mark is one of the many used by this firm.

William H. Lockitt, Hanley, Staffordshire, UK
Formerly Bednall & Heath (1879-99), and Wellington Pottery Co. (1899-1901), this company produced earthenwares 1901-19. This printed mark was used 1901-13.

Crosses

Carl Schumann, Arzberg, Bavaria, Germany
Founded in 1881, this factory produced porcelain table and coffee ware, vases, bowls and gift articles. These distinguishing initials appear in a number of marks including this one.

Estella Campavias, London, UK
While most pieces made by this potter are unmarked, this incised or painted mark is found on pieces 1954-56. Studio-type earthenwares were made c.1954-56, and stonewares with glaze effects from c.1957

Miss P. Shillinglow, Ringmore, Shaldon, Devon, UK
Formerly working at the Kenn Pottery near Exeter (1945-59), and subsequently at Ringmore, Miss P. Shillinglow produced hand-made pottery from 1945. This mark appears.

Hanau, Frankfurt-am-Main, Germany
See p.170. Hieronymus von Alphen was proprietor of the faience factory at Hanau from 1740 until his death in 1775; his daughters carried the factory on in a diminished form until 1787 when it passed into other hands. Marks such as this "F", with a double cross on one end of the Hanau crescent device, appear 1740-87.

F. Hirsch, Dresden, Germany
This company painted wares in the Meissen style from the late 19thC until c.1930. This mark was used until legal action by Meissen 1896-98 succeeded in it being struck from the register.

H. Bühl & Söhne, Groszbreitenbach, Thuringia, Germany
This porcelain factory was founded in 1780, and output included pipe bowls, dolls and doll's heads. This was one of the marks used. The factory is no longer in operation.

Henry Dreydel & Co., London, UK
Retailers and importers of ceramics in the late 19thC, this company used this mark on the foreign and English wares that it distributed.

Raeren, Rhineland, Germany
Stonewares were made at Raeren from the 15thC, but the best wares were not produced until the late 16thC. Intricate, architectural-style, moulded vessels were made from greyish stoneware, covered in an iron-brown or sometimes paler salt glaze. The potteries declined in the late 17thC, and simple, tavern wares were produced after this date until the late 19thC. This is the mark of Jan Emens, a potter at Raeren (active c.1566-94).

Hanau, Frankfurt-am-Main, Germany
See p.170. This mark was also used during the Hieronymus von Alphen period.

K.P.M.

A. W. F. Kister, Scheibe, Thuringia, Germany
This award-winning factory produced high quality porcelain figures in the Meissen style, busts, tomb ornaments, dolls and doll's heads 1836-1914. This is one of the marks used.

M4

Giovanni Brame, Faenza, Emilia, Italy
This mark appears on a plaque from Faenza dated 1546, and signed by Giovanni Brame "in Faenza".

Karl Friedrich Lüdicke, Rheinsberg, Brandenburg, Germany

A faience factory was founded here in 1762 by Baron von Reisewitz, and continued by others on a small scale until 1770 when the factory was bought by Karl Friedrich Lüdicke of Berlin. After this date the factory flourished, with English-style cream-coloured earthenware as the principal output from 1786. After Lüdicke's death in 1797, the factory was continued by his family until 1866. This "RL" mark appears on polychrome wares in the Thuringian style, but pierced wares were also made.

F. A. Reinecke, Eisenberg, Thuringia, Germany

This factory founded in 1796 produced porcelain utility ware and pieces decorated with the Meissen onion pattern. This mark was originally used.

E. Liebmann, Schney, Bavaria, Germany

This porcelain factory operated from 1780 and produced utility wares bearing this mark. The factory no longer exists.

A. W. F. Kister, Scheibe, Thuringia, Germany

See p.172. Variations of this mark were also used by this firm.

Swaine & Co., Hüttensteinach, Thuringia, Germany

This mark was used on porcelain made by this factory from 1854. Swaine & Co. merged with Schoenau Bros. at some point. Luxury and utility porcelain were made.

Rye Pottery, Rye, Sussex, UK

Based at the Bellvue Pottery, this firm operated from 1869. The mark above denoting "Sussex Art Ware" was used c.1920-39; the mark below denoting "Sussex Rustic Ware" was used c.1869-c.1920. The factory was closed 1939-45, and was reopened by John C. Cole and Water V. Cole in 1947.

Carl Thieme, Potschappel, Dresden, Germany

See p.181. This manufacturer also used this mark on its porcelain.

Vinovo, Nr. Turin, Italy

In 1776 Giovanni Vittorio Brodel founded a porcelain factory at Vische with Paul-Antoine Hannong, but this was forced to close in 1780. A workshop run by Dr. Gionetti moved to Vinovo, where it flourished and continued until 1820. The owner for the last five years was Lomello. This mark appears in blue, and may also feature the initials of Dr. Gioanetti. At the time of Lomello, the mark appears in conjunction with the letter "L".

Arrows

Carl Schneidig, Gräfenthal, Thuringia, Germany
Decorative and electroporcelain was produced from 1906. The company is now known as VEB Gräfenthaler Porzellan-Figuren, and is the factory of the ornamental porcelain works, Lichte. This mark appears.

Unger, Schneider & Hutschenreuther,
Gräfenthal, Thuringia, Germany
A porcelain factory was founded here in 1861. Schneider was a businessman and Unger was a modeller. After 1885 the firm became Schneider & Hutschenreuther; Hutschenreuther left the firm in 1886. Wares include figures, groups and animals, and some fancy pieces. This mark was used in various forms.

Christian Nonne, Giesshübel, Bohemia, Czech Republic
Christian Nonne (also of Rudolstadt Volkstedt and Ilmenau) founded a porcelain factory here in 1803 called Nonne & Roesch. It was sold in 1810 to Johann Anton Hladik. Subsequently, ownership changed a number of times. Output included figures, vases and export wares. This is an early mark used 1803-28.

Schrezheim, Württemberg, Germany
A faience factory was founded here in 1752 by Johann Baptist Bux (or Buchs) who also hoped to produce porcelain but no pieces have been identified. Bux died in 1800, and the factory was continued by his heirs until 1862. Modelled wares such as melon, cabbage and boars-head tureens (as made at Strasburg) are characteristic, as well as traditional German items decorated in blue and later in muffle colours. This factory mark appears with additional, unidentified marks.

Harker Pottery Company, East Liverpool, Ohio, and Chester, West Virginia, USA
See p.118. This mark was also used by this firm, and appears in a variety of forms.

C. Gebrauer, Bürgel, Thuringia, Germany
"Majolika" wares were made at this factory with
this mark from 1892.

Birds

Charles Ford, Hanley, Staffordshire, UK
See p.73. This impressed or printed swan mark
featuring the Charles Ford monogram was used
c.1900-04.

C. Tielsch & Co., Altwasser, Silesia, Germany
A porcelain factory was founded in 1845 by C.
Tielsch and a partner. The company expanded
and continued under different ownership into
the 20thC. This mark was one of those used.

Walter Crane, Various locations, UK
An independent designer, Crane worked for
Wedgwood, Mintons and Pilkingtons. This
personal mark was used by him c.1865-1915.

Erdmann Schlegelmilch, Suhl, Prussia, Germany
A porcelain factory was founded by Erdmann
Schlegelmilch in 1861 producing utility porcelain
and luxury wares. These bird marks each with the
initials "E. S." are both found. Other marks may
feature these initials, the name "Suhl", or the
names "Prussia" or Germany".

Sebastian Folco, Savona, Liguria, Italy
A potter in Savona called Folco used this mark
and variations in the 18th and 19thC.

Count Ferniani, Faenza, Emilia, Italy
See p.26 This mark was used by the descendants
of Count Annibale Carlo Ferniani during the
18thC.

Ford & Pointon Ltd., Hanley, Staffordshire, UK
Based at the Norfolk works, this firm (formerly
known as Pointon & Co. Ltd. 1883-1916) produced porcelain 1917-36. It was amalgamated with
the Cauldon group c.1921. This printed mark was
used.

Hulme & Christie, Fenton, Staffordshire, UK
Formerly Forester & Hulme (1887-93) and
subsequently Christie & Beardmore (1902-03) and
then Frank Beardmore & Co. (1903-14), this firm
produced earthenwares 1893-1902. This mark was

used in various forms from 1903-14, and appears with the initials of the relevant company.

This mark with the initials "C. P. P. Co." was also used by the Crystal Porcelain Co. Ltd. based in Cobridge, Staffordshire 1882-86. This company produced pottery and porcelain tiles and plaques.

New York City Pottery, New York, New York, USA
First known as Morrison and Carr, this pottery made a variety of bodies from American materials, including Rockingham and yellow ware, majolica, parian, ironstone and porcelain in forms for kitchen and table 1853-88. The parian busts for the 1876 Centennial Exhibition in Philadelphia included George Washington, Jesus Christ and Ulysses S. Grant modelled by W. H. Edge.

Glasgow Pottery, Trenton, New Jersey, USA
Founded by John Moses, the pottery (1863-1900) produced decorated white granite, hotel and steamboat china in table and toilet sets as well as souvenir wares. They made much institutional ware for various U.S. government agencies. Between 1900 and 1905 the company was known as John Moses and Sons Company.

Joseph Schachtel, Charlottenbrunn, Silesia, Germany
Joseph Schachtel bought a porcelain factory in 1859. To begin with only pipe bowls were produced, in an attempt to curb the need for the area to buy supplies of these expensive products from neighbouring Thuringia. Simple white utility wares were produced after 1866. Painted decoration appears after 1875. The factory closed c.1920.

Johann Seltmann, Vohenstrauss, Bavaria, Germany
Founded 1901, this porcelain factory made table, coffee and mocha services and gift items. This mark appears on some of the pieces produced.

Knowles, Taylor and Knowles, East Liverpool, Ohio, USA
Isaac Knowles began making Rockingham and yellow ware as early as 1853 in East Liverpool, and in 1870 he was joined by his son, Homer, and son-in-law, John N. Taylor. The firm was active 1870-1929. The company began making white ironstone in 1872 and has specialized primarily in tableware for home and hotel use throughout its

history. Lotus ware, a fine white porcelain body cast in elaborate ornamental shapes, was made between 1890 and 1897.

Moritz Zdekauer, Alt-Rohlau, Bohemia, Czech Republic
See p.29. In 1823 the founder of the porcelain factory at Alt-Rohlau sold the concern to August Nowotny who continued until 1884. In this year the factory was bought by banker Moritz Zdekauer. C. M. Hutschenreuther from Hohenberg acquired the business in 1909. The mark above was used c.1900; the mark below 1938-45.

New Milford Pottery Company/Wannopee Pottery, New Milford, Connecticut, USA
Active 1886-1903, during the earliest years of operation, the company made white granite, cream-coloured and semi-porcelain table and toilet wares. In 1890, the name was changed to Wannopee and the pottery produced a variety of novelty table wares, such as a luncheon set to look like lettuce leaves, and art wares with muddy brown glazes.

Peter Holdsworth, Ramsbury, Wiltshire, UK
See p.92. This mark appears on Peter Holds-worth's wares from 1945.

Shorter & Son (Ltd.), Stoke, Staffordshire, UK
Formerly Shorter & Boulton, this company produced earthenwares from 1905. This printed mark was used from 1940.

Stiegauer Porzellanfabrik, Stanowitz, Silesia, Germany
Formerly C. Walter & Co., this firm was founded in 1873, and made table, coffee and washing services. This mark appears.

Union Porcelain Works, Greenpoint (Long Island), New York, USA
C. H. L. and Thomas Smith purchased the Boch factory, and continued to make porcelain, made from a true hard-paste body, as table and orna-mental wares, such as pitchers, coffee and tea cups, bowls, mustard cups, shaving mugs, oyster plates, miscellaneous serving dishes and the like 1863-c.1922. Their work for the 1876 Centennial Exhibition in Philadelphia included important parian exhibition pieces designed by German sculptor Karl Muller. They also produced

decorated house hardware such as door knobs and escutcheons. They later produced electrical porcelain insulators c.1900.

Thomas Forrester & Sons (Ltd.), Longton, Staffordshire, UK

Based at the Phoenix Works, this firm (formerly Thomas Forrester) made china and earthenwares 1883-1959. This printed mark was used 1891-1912 ("LD" or "LTD" did not appear in marks before 1891). "Phoenix China" is used in later marks.

Touze, Lemaitre Frères & Blancher, Limoges, Haute-Vienne, France

Originally founded by Soudana & Touze in 1863, this porcelain-decorating studio operated under a variety of names including Touze, Lemaitre Frères & Blancher (1920-42). This mark appears.

T. Rathbone & Co., Tunstall, Staffordshire, UK

Earthenwares were made by this firm at the Newfield Pottery 1898-1923. The mark above was used from 1912, the one below c.1919-23. Other marks also appear.

The same initials were used by Thomas Rathbone & Co. of Portobello near Edinburgh. This firm produced earthenwares c.1810-45.

Animals

E. Brain & Co. Ltd., Fenton, Staffordshire, UK

Porcelain was produced by this factory (formerly Robinson & Son (1881-1903)) at the Foley China Works, 1903-63. This printed mark was used 1948-63. In 1958 this company took over the business of Coalport China Ltd., and since 1963 production has continued under the Coalport name.

C. C. Thompson Pottery Company, East Liverpool, Ohio, USA

See p.61. This mark appears. A variety of marks were used, and may feature the company name or the pattern name.

Hudson & Middleton, Longton, Staffordshire, UK

Previously known as Middleton & Hudson and William Hudson (c.1889-92), and based at the Sutherland Pottery in Longton, this firm produced porcelain from 1941. This printed mark was from 1947.

Lorenz Hutschenreuther, Selb, Bavaria, Germany
See p.82. This is one of the marks used. The
modern mark features the date 1814 (the year
Lorenz's father founded his original porcelain
factory at Hohenberg-upon-Eger), and the name
"Hutschenreuther".

Redfern & Drakeford (Ltd.), Longton,
Staffordshire, UK
Based at the Chatfield Works (c.1892-1902) and
the Balmoral Works (c.1902-33), this company
made porcelain 1892-1933, when it was taken over
by the Royal Albion China Co., which continued
at Albion Street in Longton until 1948. This
printed or impressed mark appears c.1892-1909;
the same mark appears painted 1909-33 with the
tradename "Balmoral China" and "England".

Tettau, Franconia, Germany
See p.35. This 20thC mark appears in a number of
variations.

Wood & Clarke, Burslem, Staffordshire, UK
Formerly E. Clarke, this firm made earthenwares
c.1871-72. The company subsequently became
W. E. Withinshaw (1873-78). This printed mark
with lion rampant appears c.1871-72.

Holinshed & Kirkham (Ltd.), Tunstall,
Staffordshire, UK
Based at the Unicorn Pottery in Tunstall from
1876 (previously at Burslem 1870-76), this
company produced earthenwares 1870-1956, when
it was bought up by Johnson Bros. (Hanley) Ltd.
Printed marks featuring unicorns such as this one
were used 1900-56. Johnson Bros. continued at the
Hanley Pottery and other Hanley Potteries.

Yvonne Hudson, Chichester, Sussex, UK
Studio-type pottery and sculpture were made at
Earnley near Chichester 1947-48 and from 1957.
One of the marks used was this seal mark based
on a Greco-Roman intaglio. The numbers seen in
this mark represent the last two digits of the year
of manufacture.

Edge Malkin & Co. (Ltd.), Burslem, Staffordshire, UK
This firm produced earthenwares at the Newport
and Middleport Potteries in Burslem between
1871 and 1903. The company had existed under
a number of different names since 1846, and continued with more title changes until 1919. This

trademark was registered in 1873, but slight
variations occur. A variety of name and initial
marks were also used.

Thomas Forrester & Co., Longton, Staffordshire
Based at the Melbourne Works (previously
known as Leigh & Forrester), this factory made
earthenwares from c.1888 with this printed mark.

Knowles, Taylor and Knowles, East Liverpool, Ohio,
USA
See p.176. This mark was also used. A large
number of different marks appear, most of which
incorporate the company initials.

C. K. Weithase, Rudostaldt Volkstedt, Thuringia,
Germany
This decorating studio founded in the late 19thC
specialized in views, armorials and lettering on
individual orders. This was one of the marks
used.

Forrester & Hulme, Fenton, Staffordshire, UK
This earthenware factory operated between
1887 and 1893 and used this printed mark,
with "England" added from c.1891. The firm
subsequently became Hulme & Christie (see
p.175).

Ford & Riley, Burslem, Staffordshire, UK
Formerly Whittingham, Ford & Riley (1876-82)
and later Ford & Sons (Ltd.) (1893-1938) and then
Ford & Sons (Crownford) Ltd., this firm made
earthenwares from 1882-93. Many different
designs of mark appear, often with the name of
the pattern. This is one example.

Fish

Julius Hering & Söhn, Köppelsdorf, Thuringia,
Germany
Founded in 1893, among other items this factory
produced coffee and tea services, and figures.
Variations of this mark appear.

Pfluger Bros. & Co., Nyon, Switzerland
Originally founded in 1781, this factory was
started by Fränkenthal decorator Ferdinand
Müller and Johann Jakob of Berlin. Porcelain was
produced until 1813, and after this date general
pottery including pipeclay was produced. Many

artists worked here on Empire-style and Louis XVI tablewares. This mark appears on general pottery.

John Dan, Wivenhoe, Essex, UK
Studio-type pottery was produced at the Wivenhoe pottery from 1953. This factory mark was used.

Peter Wright, Bath, Avon, UK
See p.99. This mark was used on repeat items made at the Monkton Combe pottery after 1953.

Plants, Flowers & Trees

Birks, Rawlins & Co. Ltd., Stoke, Staffordshire, UK
Previously L.A. Birks & Co. (1896-1900) this company produced bone-china and earthenwares 1900-33. This mark was one of those used from 1900, and was also used 1896-1900 with the letters "B & Co."

Burroughs and Mountford, Trenton, New Jersey, USA
Although this pottery (active 1879-c.1900) made the general line of decorated hotel ware and domestic table and toilet ware characteristic of late 19th-century American potteries, the quality of their decal work and printed and filled decorations was exceptional. They also produced an art ware having raised gold decorations on a royal blue ground and some tiles. The initials "B. M. " or "B. & M. Co." appear with a variety of different marks.

Carl Thieme, Potschappel, Dresden, Germany
A porcelain factory was founded here from 1872, making hand-painted fancy wares and luxury porcelain. This mark is one of those used. The factory was still in operation in 1977.

R. F. Dixon & Co., Longton, Staffordshire, UK
This company were London firm of importers and retailers who used this mark on porcelain and earthenwares made for them at the Ruby Porcelain Works 1916-29.

Dressel Kister & Co., Passau, Bavaria, Germany
See p.147. This mark appears on artistic porcelain wares made at this factory, which was founded in 1840.

William De Morgan, London, UK

See p.110. This impressed or printed mark was used from 1882, the year in which the pottery was relocated to Merton Abbey in south London.

Wade (Ulster) Ltd., Portadown, Co. Armagh, Northern Ireland, UK

From 1953 earthenwares with the trade name "Irish Porcelain" have been made at the Ulster Pottery in Portadown. This printed or impressed mark was used from 1953; "made in Ireland" was added from 1954. Later "Wade Co. Armagh" was also added. The mark appears with or without a painter's initial, such as the letter "E" seen on this example.

New England Pottery Company, East Boston, Massachusetts, USA

Originally founded by Frederick Meagher in 1854 for making Rockingham and yellow ware, by 1875 the plant was owned by Thomas Gray and W. L. Clark and became the New England Pottery Company. The pottery added white granite and cream-coloured earthenware dinner-ware to its repertoire in the early 1870s. Around 1886 they made "Reiti" ware, a semi-porcelain decorated ware, and they also made porcelain with old ivory and mazarine blue finish. No more "Reiti" wares were made after 1889. Many pieces were decorated with old designs which were engraved and printed by J. W. Phillips. Output included chocolate jugs, vases, jarinières, biscuit jars, rose jars and other items. In addition, the pottery also produced toilet sets and sets of odd dishes. The firm was active 1854-1914.

Haas & Czjzek, Chodau, Bohemia, Czech Republic

A porcelain factory was originally opened here in 1811 by coalmine owner Franz Miessl. The factory changed hands a number of times before it was purchased by Haas & Czjzek of Schlaggenwald in 1872. The business became successful, with output principally consisting of utility porcelain for households, restaurants and hotels. This is one of the marks used by Haas & Czjzek.

Jaeger & Co., Marktredwitz, Bavaria, Germany

This company made porcelain table, coffee and tea services and gift items from 1872. This is one of the marks used, and is also incorporated into other marks.

Lenox China/Ceramic Art Company, Trenton and Lawrenceville, New Jersey, USA

Walter Scott Lenox, who had worked for Ott & Brewer and Willets (see p.105), founded the Ceramic Art Company in 1889 to make only ornamental belleek wares, dainty tea sets and luxury souvenir items, mostly hand-painted by a small staff of immigrant artists. The name was changed to Lenox in 1906. Bone china tableware was added about 1905 and belleek tableware about 1910. The firm began making dinner services for the White House in 1918. The company still exists today. These marks appear.

Ohio Valley China Company, Wheeling, West Virginia, USA

The pottery (1887-93) produced good quality hard-paste porcelain tableware as well as some remarkable art wares with figures and elaborate piercing. The shield mark was used on heavy goods, while the other "leafy" mark appears on artistic wares.

Pilkington's Tile & Pottery Co. Ltd., Manchester, Greater Manchester, UK

This factory made tiles, and ornamental wares with decorative lustre effects, from c.1897-1938. Early wares were generally unmarked, but some pieces feature an incised "P". The trademark above, was registered in 1904; it appears printed c.1904-05, and printed to 1914. This stylized "P" appeared within a Lancastrian rose c.1914-38, with "England" until c.1920, and "Made in England" c.1920-38. The initials or monogram of the designer or artist also appears on most pieces. The mark below was used when the factory reopened their pottery department, 1948-57.

Portishead Studio Potteries, Portishead, Bristol, UK

Studio-type wares were made here by Gwen Horlick, 1950-61, bearing this mark. She died in March 1961.

Retsch & Co., Wunsiedel, Bavaria, Germany

See p.158. This mark is one of those used. Other marks may feature a shield or crown device, usually including the initial "R".

Rousset & Guillerot, Limoges, Haute-Vienne, France

Founded in 1923 and formerly known as Rousset & Co., this concern was a porcelain-decorating studio. This mark was used.

Reinhold Schlegelmilch, Tillowitz, Silesia, Germany
Utility and luxury porcelain was produced at this factory from 1869. Various forms of this mark appear, and may also feature the words "Prussia" or "Germany".

Steubenville Pottery Company, Steubenville, Ohio, USA
This pottery (1879-1960) made dinner and toilet sets throughout its history of a variety of bodies, including ironstone, earthenware and semi-porcelain. Russel Wright designed American Modern in 1939. This is one of many marks used by this firm.

Sebastian Schmidt, Schmiedefeld, Thuringia, Germany
Founded in 1857, this porcelain factory made luxury porcelain and figures with this mark.

Union Céramique, Limoges, Haute-Viennes, France
This porcelain factory was founded in 1900. This mark appears, also without the wreath. Other firms based in Limoges used this style of mark, featuring different initials in the centre of the wreath.

August Schweig, Weisswasser, Silesia, Germany
Founded in 1895, this factory produces utility porcelain and still operates today under the name VEB-branch factory Weisswasser. This mark was used.

Count Wrtby, Teinitz, Bohemia, Czech Republic
In 1801 a factory producing English-style lead glazed earthenware was founded by Count Wrtby. This impressed mark was used 1801-39.

Buildings

A. Bauer, Magdeburg, Hanover, Germany
Magdeburg had been a faience-producing centre since c.1754. Bauer ran a pottery manufacturing earthenwares in Magdeburg from 1865. His pieces bear this mark.

Bing & Grøndhal, Copenhagen, Denmark
See p.40. Marks such as this were used by Bing & Grøndhal from 1853. Marks may feature the words "Danish China Works", "Made in Denmark" or "Copenhagen".

C. T. Maling & Sons (Ltd.), Newcastle-upon-Tyne, Tyne and Wear, UK

See p.165. This printed mark was one of those used by this firm (Formerly C. T. Maling c.1859-90) at the A. & B. Ford Potteries between 1890 and 1963.

Florence, Tuscany, Italy

A type of soft-paste porcelain was made here during the time of the Medici c.1575-87, with the majority being made 1581-86. The slightly yellowish paste was covered in a white tin glaze. This mark in blue appears in a number of different variations.

Josef Kratzer & Son, Haindorf, Bohemia, Czech Republic

A porcelain-decorating workshop using this mark operated here in the late 19th and 20thC. Output included domestic goods, children's and dolls' services. The factory closed c.1941.

Joseph Boussemaert, Liège, Belgium

The first successful faience factory in Liège was established by Jacques Lefèbvre and Nicolas Gauron of Tournay (a previous venture by Baron von Bülow started in 1752 was unsuccessful). In c.1770 Lefèbvre and Gauron sold the factory to Joseph Boussemaert, said to be a son of Joseph-François Boussemaert of Lille. The concern continued until 1811. The mark is taken from the arms of Liège. Wares were painted in the Rouen and Strasburg styles, and with Chinese-style figures.

Pfaltzgraff Pottery, York, Pennsylvania, USA

This long-lived pottery established in 1811 and still in existence today, has made nearly every kind of ceramic, including utilitarian redware and stoneware for house and barnyard, kitchenware, stoneware dinnerware and serving dishes and some ornamental wares. A line of bone china was added during the late 1980s.

Porzellanfabrik Königszelt, Königszelt, Silesia, Germany

Founded in 1860, this porcelain factory made tablewares, hotel ware and gift articles. Early wares were painted with the onion and straw-flower patterns. The factory has been known by various titles and is now in Polish possession. This is one of the marks used.

Porzellanfabrik Kloster Vessra, Kloster Vessra, Saxony, Germany

All types of utility porcelain were made at this factory from 1892 with this mark. The factory no longer exists.

Sampson, Bridgwood & Son (Ltd.), Longton, Staffordshire, UK

See p.161. This printed mark was used from c.1853, and a variation of this crest mark was used from 1884. Other marks feature the name "Bridgwood & Son" or the initials "S. B. & Son".

David Eeles, London and Dorset, UK

A Studio-potter, first at the Shepherd's Well Pottery, London from 1955, and then at Mosterton in Dorset. This impressed mark of the Shepherd's Well Pottery was used from 1955.

Boats

C. & E. Carstens, Neuhaldensleben, Saxony, Germany

This company produced earthenware from 1904 with this mark. A number of other manufacturers operated in this area.

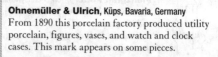

Della Robbia Company Ltd., Birkenhead, Mersey, UK

Owned by Harold Rathbone, this firm was established in 1894 and produced earthenwares, tiles and plaques until 1901. Pieces made here were based on Italian maiolica, and were very popular. This incised mark was used during this period. The initials above relate to the decorator.

Ohnemüller & Ulrich, Küps, Bavaria, Germany

From 1890 this porcelain factory produced utility porcelain, figures, vases, and watch and clock cases. This mark appears on some pieces.

Marblehead Pottery, Marblehead, Massachusetts, USA

Established originally to benefit patients in the sanatorium of Dr. Herbert J. Hall, the pottery (1904-36) was separated from that institution about 1908 and acquired in 1915 by Arthur Baggs, who had been managing the pottery since its inception. Throughout its production, the pottery maintained its characteristic simple forms and stylized decoration rendered in speckled matt glazes.

Wilhelm Dienst, Wiesbaden, Nassau, Germany
This area was known for its faience and cream-coloured earthenware. General pottery was produced by Wilhelm Dienst from 1770.

Pots

Johannes and Dirk Harlees, Delft, Holland
Proprietors of *De porceleyn Fles* (The Porcelain Bottle) c.1795-1800, these two potters used these marks. *De porceleyn Fles* was founded in 1655 by Wouter van Eenhorn and Quirinus Aldersz van Cleynoven (also of *De Griekſche A*).

Gibson & Sons (Ltd.), Burslem, Staffordshire, UK
Formerly Gibson, Sudlow & Co., this firm made earthenwares at the Albany (and Harvey) Pottery from 1885. A large number of marks were used, this is an early example which appeared c.1904-09.

Morley Fox & Co. Ltd., Fenton, Staffordshire, UK
Previously known as William Morley, this company produced earthenwares at the Salopian Works 1906-44. A number of different marks were used, many incorporating the initials "M. F. & Co.". This one appeared c.1906. The company then became William Morley & Co. Ltd (1944-57).

Moritz Zdekauer, Alt-Rohlau, Bohemia, Czech Republic
See p.177. This mark was one of those used by this manufacturer c.1900.

Paul Revere Pottery/Saturday Evening Girls,
Boston and Brighton, Massachusetts, USA
See p.58. This mark was one of those used by this firm.

Henry Watson Potteries Ltd., Wattisfield,
Suffolk, UK
Earthenwares and stonewares were made here from c.1808. Early wares were unmarked; this printed or impressed mark was used from c.1948.

Figures

Abicht & Co., Ilmenau, Thuringia, Germany
Both faience and porcelain were produced in Ilmenau in the characteristic Thuringian style. This company produced earthenwares from 1875 with this mark.

Mount Saint Bernard Abbey, Nr. Coalville, Leicestershire, UK

Situated in Charnwood Forest, this pottery produced earthenwares from 1949; this trademark was registered in 1951.

J. H. Cope & Co. Ltd., Longton, Staffordshire, UK

See p.159. This printed mark appears c.1924-47. Other marks also feature the name "Wellington China", the initials "J. H. & Co." and "Longton, England".

W. & J. A. Bailey, Alloa, Scotland, UK

Formerly Anderson & Gardner, this pottery made earthenwares 1855-1908. This late printed mark was used 1890-1908. Earlier marks feature the name "Bailey".

Globes

Barkers & Kent, Fenton, Staffordshire, UK

Based at the Foley Pottery in Fenton, this firm produced earthenwares 1889-1941. Other marks incorporate the initials "B. & K." or "B. & K. L."

Globe Pottery Company, East Liverpool, Ohio, USA

This company (active 1881-1912) started as Frederick, Shenkle, Allen and Company, but reorganized in 1888 as Globe. Beginning in 1901, the company joined East Liverpool Potteries Company and then returned to independent status in 1907. The pottery's business declined steadily and it finally closed due to extensive damage from the flood of 1912. Their earliest wares were Rockingham and yellow ware. By the 1890s they had added cream-coloured ware, decorated jet ware, teapots and speciality items. During the last phase of operation they made semi-porcelain dinner and toilet wares as well as vases, plaques, tankards, jugs, trays and other speciality items. This is one of the many marks used, although most feature the name "Globe" or the initials "G. P. Co.".

Joseph Holdcroft, Sutherland Pottery, Longton, Staffordshire, UK

See p.81. This printed mark was used 1890-1939 and continued when the company was renamed Holdcrofts Ltd. in 1906, and subsequently by Cartwright & Edwards who continued the works until 1940.

H. J. Colclough, Longton, Staffordshire, UK
Based at the Vale Works 1897-1937, this company
made general ceramics. The company became
Colclough China Ltd. after 1937. These initials
were used with many marks, including this
example which appears on ware produced
1908-28.

J. Goodwin Stoddard & Co., Longton, Staffordshire,
UK
Based at King Street in Foley, Longton, this
company made bone-china 1898-1940. This mark
was used 1898-1936; the words "Foley Bone
China" and "England" were added 1936-40.

Green & Clay, Longton, Staffordshire, UK
Between 1888 and 1991 this firm (formerly Green,
Clark & Clay) made earthenwares at a works in
Stafford Street. This printed or impressed mark
was used during this period.
  Another mark incorporating a compass device,
was used by the Campbell Tile Co. (Ltd.) from
1882.

Bells

C. F. Kling & Co., Ohrdruf, Thuringia, Germany
This porcelain factory operated between 1836 and
1941, making fancy wares, gift articles, dolls and
dolls' heads. This mark was used.

Franz Manka, Alt-Rohlau, Bohemia, Czech Republic
A porcelain factory was originally founded in
1926. In 1936 it was taken over by Franz Manka
and expanded into a master workshop. Output
consists of utility ware with this mark.

Flags

Harrop & Burgess, Hanley, Staffordshire, UK
Based at the Mount Pleasant Works, this company
produced earthenwares 1894-1903. The firm
subsequently became Thomas Burgess and
continued until 1917. This mark was used 1894-
1917.

Julius Hering & Söhn, Köppelsdorf, Thuringia,
Germany
See p.180. A number of different marks were used
incorporating the initials "J. H. & S.".

J. H. Weatherby & Sons (Ltd.), Hanley, Staffordshire, UK
See p.146. This printed mark was used by this firm from 1892. Other marks feature the initials "J. H. W." and the name "Falcon Ware".

C. K. Weithase, Rudostaldt Volkstedt, Thuringia, Germany
See p.180. This mark was used.

Wings

F. Hirsch, Dresden, Germany
See p.172. This mark was used on pieces painted in the Meissen style from the late 19thC until 1930.

Hoffmann Brothers, Erkersreuth, Oberfranken, Germany
This modern factory produces hard-paste porcelain bearing this mark.

Ignaz Bottengruber, Breslau, Silesia, Germany
A celebrated porcelain *Hausmaler*, Bottengruber (or Pottengruber) worked in Breslau and Vienna 1720-30. This mark appears on a piece decorated at Breslau.

Louis Lourioux, Foecy, Cher, France
Founded in 1898, this porcelain factory made luxury and utility wares. This is one of the marks used.

Miscellaneous

Hilda Burn, Edinburgh, Scotland, UK
In the 1920s and 1930s earthenwares were made by Hilda Burn that feature this incised or painted mark.

Chantilly, Oise, France
A soft-paste porcelain factory was founded here by Louis de Bourbon, Prince de Condé, in 1725, and run by a succession of directors until 1792. In this year the factory was bought by an Englishman, Christopher Potter, who also owned a factory in Paris. Potter gave up the works c.1800. A high quality, smooth white tin glaze was used on early wares; good pieces were also made 1755-80. Notable wares decorated with Japanese

Kakiemon-style designs, and many of the
forms are Japanese-inspired. Figures were also
produced. The hunting horn of Chantilly appears
in many variations, often with incised letters – the
marks of throwers and other workmen – such as
the ones seen here. The marks are found in red
(and sometimes black) in the early period, and
blue (and occasionally crimson) during the later
period.

Pigory, Chantilly, Oise, France
The mayor of Chantilly, Pigory, founded a
porcelain factory in the town in 1803 which
specialized in utility wares and tea services.
This mark in underglaze blue was used.

Johann Seltmann, Vohenstrauss, Bavaria, Germany
See p.176. This mark also appears on porcelain
made here from 1901.

Samuel Ford & Co., Burslem, Staffordshire, UK
Based at the Lincoln Pottery and the Crown
Pottery (from c.1913), this firm produced
earthenwares 1898-1939. The company was
previously known as Smith & Ford (1895-98).
This mark was used 1895-1936. Between 1898
and 1936 the initials "F. & Co." may appear
instead of "S. & F.".

Jo Lester, Freshwater, Isle of Wight, UK
Based in London c.1951-52, and at Freshwater
from 1953, Jo Lester produced Studio-type earthenwares. This printed Isle-of-Wight outline
mark was used from 1953. The same mark was
used by J. H. Manning at Cowes, Isle of Wight,
with the initial "M" added c.1956-61.

William Ratcliffe, Hanley, Staffordshire, UK
Based at the New Hall Works in Hanley,
earthenwares with this printed mark in
underglaze blue were produced c.1831-40.

New Milford Pottery Company/Wannopee Pottery, New Milford, Connecticut, USA
Established 1886, during the earliest years of
operation, the company made white granite,
cream-coloured and semi-porcelain table and
toilet wares. In 1890, the name was changed to
Wannopee, and the pottery produced a variety of
novelty table wares, such as a luncheon set to look
like lettuce leaves, and art wares with muddy
brown glazes. It continued until 1903.

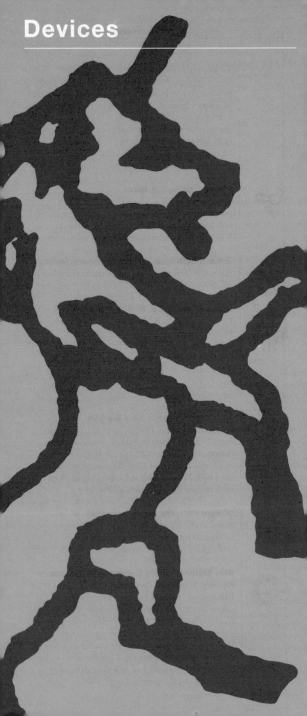

Devices

In this section, devices that appear on their own are featured first, followed by those that appear with the name of the individual potter or firm (in alphabetical order). Devices of a similar form or style within each category appear together. See p.192 for devices which appear with one or more initial.

Crowns

Thomas Poole, Longton, Staffordshire, UK
Based at the Cobden Works 1880-1952, this pottery (formerly Johnson & Poole) produced general ceramics, including majolica useful ware, for the domestic and export markets. The firm continued as Thomas Poole until c.1925 when it was retitled Thomas Poole (Longton) Ltd. This company merged with Gladstone China Ltd. in 1948, and after 1952 continued under Royal Staffordshire China. This impressed or printed crown mark was also used by Enoch Plant of the Crown Pottery, Burslem 1898-1905.

Pauline Pottery, Chicago, Illinois, and Edgerton, Wisconsin, USA
See p.141. As well as using marks featuring a crown device, this firm also used a written name mark which appears in various forms.

Hicks, Meigh & Johnson, Shelton, Staffordshire, UK
Formerly John & Edward Babbeley (1784-1806) and Hicks & Meigh (1806-22), this successful Staffordshire firm (active 1822-35) made earthenwares and high quality ironstone in the tradition of Masons (see p.200). They used the name "Stone China". They also made more ordinary parts of porcelain. This printed mark appears on wares 1822-30.

Höchst, Nr. Mainz, Germany
See p.24. This mark appears on pieces made at Höchst c.1765-74.

Worcester Porcelains, Hereford and Worcester, UK
See p.23. From 1862 the firm was known as Worcester Royal Porcelain Co. Ltd. This standard Royal Worcester printed mark was used c.1862-75. From c.1876-91 the crown was closed in, and a year letter appeared below the mark. From 1891 the mark featured "Royal Worcester England", with a series of dots. "Made in England" was added in the 20thC. (For further details of year marks, see p.374 in Additional information.)

William Adams & Sons (Potters) Ltd., Tunstall and Stoke, Staffordshire, UK

Founded in 1769, this family company known under a number of different versions of the name given above, produced earthenwares, basaltes, jasper-type ware, parian etc. Earthenwares were noted for richness of colour and variety of patterns. Among other items, output consisted of tea, toilet and table services. An impressed mark on earthenwares (above) featuring a crown was used 1810-25. The printed mark (centre) appears 1914-40. The mark (below) was used after 1945.

Adderleys Ltd., Longton, Staffordshire, UK

Originally known as William Alsager Adderley (& Co.) (1876-1905), from 1906 this company produced good quality general ceramics. The name "Adderley" was used in many marks, including this one used 1950-62. The company was taken over by Ridgway Potteries Ltd. in 1947, but a similar mark continued to be used.

Charles Allerton & Sons, Longton, Staffordshire, UK

Based at the Park Works in Longton, this company (1859-1942) produced general ceramics, including lustre wares. The firm was taken over in 1912 by the Cauldon Potteries Ltd. Various printed marks appear, including the one above from 1890, and the one below c.1903-12.

Coopers Art Pottery Co., Hanley, Staffordshire, UK

Formerly the Art Pottery Co. (1900-11), this company, which operated under various titles, produced earthenwares c.1912-58. This printed mark was used by both firms.

G. L. Ashworth & Bros. (Ltd.), Hanley, Staffordshire, UK

Between 1862 and 1968, this company produced earthenwares, ironstone and other wares at the Broad Street Works. This firm produced Mason's "Patent Ironstone" using the mark originally used by Mason's (see p.200). This printed mark was used from c.1880 onwards with slight variation in the wording.

John Aynsley & Sons (Ltd.), Longton, Staffordshire, UK

Porcelain was made by this firm at the Portland Works from 1864. Early wares were unmarked, but printed marks such as this one were used from 1891.

P. E. Bairstow & Co., Shelton and Stoke, Staffordshire, UK
Formerly Fancies Fayre Pottery (see p.27), this company used this mark on its earthenware and porcelain from 1954.

Barker Bros., Lane End, Staffordshire, UK
From 1867, this pottery produced general ceramics. Many marks were used; this one appears in variations from 1937.

Booths (Limited), Tunstall, Staffordshire, UK
See p.23. Many marks used. The printed mark (above) was used 1891-1906. The mark (below) appears from c.1906, with or without the word "England". The company subsequently became Booths and Colcloughs Ltd. and became part of the Ridway group in 1955.

Arthur Bowker, Fenton, Staffordshire, UK
Porcelain figures and other items were produced by Arthur Bowker at King Street, Fenton, 1948-58 with this printed mark (used 1950-58) with slight variations.

Bradley's (Longton) Ltd., Longton, Staffordshire, UK
Operating between 1922 and 1941, this firm manufactured porcelain at the Crown Clarence Works. This printed mark was used 1922-28, with a variation c.1928-41.

E. Baggerley Ltd., Bournemouth, Dorset, UK
Formerly Branksome Ceramics Ltd. (1945-56), this firm produced earthenwares from 1957. Variations on this mark were used by both companies.

British Anchor Pottery Co. Ltd., Longton, Staffordshire, UK
See p.159. This mark was used from 1954. Many marks appear, usually comprising name marks on their own, or an anchor device.

Lancaster & Sons (Ltd.), Hanley, Staffordshire, UK
Between 1900 and 1944, this pottery produced earthenwares at the Dresden Works in Hanley. These marks were used from c.1935. The company became Lancaster & Sandland Ltd. after 1944, and the two marks seen here continued to be used. Many other written name marks and marks featuring devices such as shields were used by Lancaster & Sandland.

Brown-Westhead, Moore & Co., Hanley, Staffordshire, UK
See p.155. This printed or impressed mark was one of those used after 1891. The company became known as Cauldon Ltd. (1905-20) and then Cauldon Potteries Ltd. (1920-62). Variations of the mark seen here were used by both of these firms.

Clementson Bros. (Ltd.), Hanley, Staffordshire, UK
Started by Joseph Clementson in c.1839, this company was based at the Phoenix Works from 1865, and produced earthenwares until 1916. This printed mark was used 1913-16.

James & Ralph Clews, Cobridge, Staffordshire, UK
Earthenwares were made by this firm 1818-34, and porcelain was produced c.1821-25. This impressed mark is found on good quality blue-printed earthenwares. Many other marks were also used incorporating the name "Clews".

J. Dimmock & Co., Hanley, Staffordshire, UK
Formerly Thomas Dimmock (Junr.) & Co. (see p.142), this company produced earthenwares 1862-1904. From c.1878 the firm was owned by W. D. Cliff, and his name occurs in most marks, such as this one used c.1878-1904.

Coalport Porcelain Works, Coalport, Shropshire, UK
See p.72. Printed crown marks were used by Coalport c.1881-1939, such as this one, with "England" added after 1891, and "Made in England" from c.1920. Crown marks were also used after World War II. Since 1967 this company has formed part of the Wedgwood Group.

Ridgway Potteries Ltd., Hanley, Staffordshire, UK
See p.202. This mark was one of those used after 1962 by one of Ridgway's associate potteries. This name was formerly used by H. J. Colclough (1897-1937), in a mark that appeared 1935-37.

Collingwood Bros. (Ltd.), Longton, Staffordshire, UK
See p.141. This printed mark was one of those used 1912-24. Other marks feature a crown device or just the name of the firm.

Alfred Colley & Co. Ltd., Tunstall, Staffordshire, UK
Based at the Gordon Pottery, this firm produced earthenwares 1909-14 with this printed or impressed mark.

Barratt's of Staffordshire Ltd., Burslem, Staffordshire, UK

Formerly Gater, Hall & Co. (see p.78), this company operated from 1943. As well as using marks that featured the new company name, this mark used by the previous company (from 1914) was also continued by Barratt's from 1943.

T. W. Barlow & Son Ltd., Longton, Staffordshire, UK

Established in 1882, this pottery produced all types of earthenwares until 1940. This printed or impressed mark was used 1928-36. A variation of this mark appeared without a surrounding circle 1936-40.

Co-operative Wholesale Society Ltd., Longton, Staffordshire, UK

Based at the Crown Clarence Pottery, this company produced earthenwares from 1946. Porcelain was also produced by this company at the Windsor Pottery in Longton from 1911. A number of marks were used on earthenwares, including this one from 1950, which all featured the name "Crown Clarence".

S. Fielding & Co. (Ltd.), Stoke, Staffordshire, UK

This company founded the Railway Pottery in 1870, and produced majolica and good quality earthenwares. They produced a ware which they called "Majolica argenta". Hand-modelled flowers and foliage appeared on the finest pieces of majolica. Many different patterns were produced, and ouput included all types of services and other useful and ornamental wares. The 20thC trade name is "Crown Devon" and many marks exist such as the ones shown here: the mark (above) c.1917-30, the mark (below) from c.1930. Variations do occur.

A. G. Richardson & Co. Ltd., Cobridge, Staffordshire, UK

Based at Tunstall 1915-c.1924, this pottery then moved to the Britannia Pottery in Cobridge. The firm used the trade name "Crown Ducal" in many of its marks, such as this one used from 1925.

Crown Staffordshire Porcelain Co. Ltd., Fenton, Staffordshire, UK

Based at the Minerva Works from 1889, this company made all types of porcelain goods. Marks of this type were used from 1906; prior to 1906 it appears within a wreath.

Davenport, Longport, Staffordshire, UK
See p.216. A crown mark was used on porcelains produced by Davenport c.1870-86. An earlier printed mark used from 1815 features the words "Davenport Longport".

Derby Porcelain Works, Derbyshire, UK
See p.25. Used during the Bloor Period (c.1820-48), the mark (top) appeared printed or was transferred by thumb c.1820-40. The mark (centre) was printed in red c.1830-48. A later example, the mark (below) is impressed on "Crown" earthenware made by Derby Crown Porcelain Company Ltd. after 1876. Potting dates may occur under this last mark, and include the month represented by a digit (March=3), and the last two digits of the year (99=1899). "Derby" on its own, appears on porcelains.

Doulton & Co. (Ltd.), Burslem, Staffordshire, UK
See p.111. These marks were among those used by the Burslem works c.1882-1902. "England" appears from 1891. A lion was added above the crown from c.1902, and many variations of the mark occur. The production of porcelain was added to that of earthenware in 1884. "Made in England" was added from c.1930. The names of different effects also appear with the mark.

Dresden, Germany
In 1883 this mark was registered by four different decorating studios in Dresden, including Donath & Co. (est. 1872) and Adolf Hamann (see p.246).

A. T. Finney & Sons (Ltd.), Longton, Staffordshire, UK
A. T. Finney originally took over Blythe Porcelain Co. Ltd. based at the Duchess China Works in 1935, and the company was renamed in 1947. The tradename "Duchess" was used in many marks including this one used c.1947-60.

Empire Porcelain Co. Ltd., Stoke, Staffordshire, UK
Established c.1896 at the Empire Works, this company produced a wide range of pottery and porcelain. This mark used 1928-39, is one of those that appears. The company closed in 1967.

Worcester Porcelain Works, Hereford and Worcester, UK
See p.23. This mark was used on porcelains made at Worcester during the Barr and Flight & Barr Period c.1792-1807. Flight & Barr marks are rare.

Thomas Forester Son & Co., Fenton, Staffordshire, UK
Operating between 1884 and 1888, this firm produced general ceramics at the Sutherland Pottery with this printed mark. The firm subsequently became Forester & Hulme (see p.180).

Gibson & Sons (Ltd.), Burslem, Staffordshire, UK
See p.187. The printed mark (above) used from c.1930, is one of wide range of marks that appear c.1909-40. The mark (below) was used from c.1950. The tradename changed to "Gibsons" from c.1940.

Ginori Factory, Doccia, Nr. Florence, Italy
See p.25. Marks such as this one were used on general pottery made at the Ginori Factory 1847-1903.

Gladstone China, Longton, Staffordshire, UK
Formerly Gladstone China (Longton) Ltd. (1939-52), this firm made porcelain 1952-70. This printed mark was used in variations by both firms.

Thomas Goode & Co. Ltd., London, UK
A retailing firm that has operated since the 19thC, this mark was one of those used. The word "Ltd." appears after 1918.

W. H. Grindley & Co. (Ltd.), Tunstall, Staffordshire, UK
Based at the New Field Pottery (c.1880-91) and the Woodland Pottery (from 1891), this pottery made earthenwares and ironstones. Many marks featuring the name of the factory were used with this one appearing from 1925.

Jackson & Gosling (Ltd.), Longton, Staffordshire, UK
Originally established at Fenton where it operated until 1908, the firm moved to Longton c.1909. Output comprised porcelain tea, breakfast and dessert services. The firm continued until 1961. This mark was one of those used, and appeared from c.1912.

Sampson & Hancock (& Sons), Stoke, Staffordshire, UK
Earthenwares were made by this firm 1858-1937. Many marks were used, with this one appearing 1912-37.

Herculaneum Pottery, Liverpool, Mersey
This pottery was established in 1796 in a works
originally founded c.1793. The first owner was
Richard Abbey, and he sold the concern to
Humble & Holland. The first wares produced
were blue and white printed wares of all types.
Cream-coloured wares were made later. Subse-
quent owners continued the works until 1841.
This impressed or printed mark was one of those
used c.1796-1833.

Carl Magnus Hutschenreuther, Arzberg, Bavaria,
Germany
A porcelain factory in Arzberg founded by Äcker
in 1839 was incorporated into Hutschenreuther's
company in 1918. This example is among the
marks used. C.M. Hutschenreuther later merged
with Lorenz Hutschenreuther of Selb.

Johnson Bros. (Hanley) Ltd., Hanley,
Staffordshire, UK
Established in 1883, this pottery produced
earthenwares and ironstone. The printed mark
shown here appears from c.1900. Other marks
also appear.

Worcester Porcelains, Hereford and Worcester, UK
See p.23. This rare printed mark appears during
the Kerr and Binns Period (c.1852-62), and was
used c.1856-62.

Hermann Lange, Krummennaab, Bavaria, Germany
This company made hard-paste porcelain utility
ware from 1934. In 1939 the firm was taken over
by Christian Seltmann.

John Maddock & Sons (Ltd.), Burslem,
Staffordshire, UK
See p.253. Many crown marks were used by this
firm. This example appears c.1880-96. Many
marks feature the name "John Maddock & Sons".

Charles James Mason, Lane Delph, Staffordshire, UK
The inventor of the famous Mason's Patent
Ironstone China, Charles James Mason took out
a patent for his invention in 1813. The original
name of the firm was G. M. & C. J. Mason, which
operated 1813-29. The firm was carried on under
many titles until c.1845-48, when the name
Charles James Mason was used. In 1848 the firm
went bankrupt and Francis Morley bought the
business. The mark was continued by Francis

Morley and subsequently by G. L. Ashworth & Bros. (Ltd.) (see p.194). Many versions of the mark exist.

Alfred Meakin (Ltd.), Tunstall, Staffordshire, UK
Working from a number of works in Tunstall (Royal Albert, Victoria and Highgate Potteries), this firm produced earthenwares and good ironstone wares from 1875. The firm was renamed Alfred Meakin (Tunstall) Ltd. from c.1913. Many marks feature the name of the company, such as the one illustrated here that was used from c.1907, as well as marks used after World War II. Other marks appear.

Mellor, Taylor & Co., Burslem, Staffordshire, UK
Earthenwares were produced by this firm 1880-1904. This printed or impressed mark was one of those used.

W. R. Midwinter (Ltd.), Burslem, Staffordshire, UK
Established c.1910, this company produced earthenwares. A number of post-World War II marks featured crowns, such as this one used from c.1946.

Francis Morley (& Co.), Shelton, Hanley, Staffordshire, UK
Based at the Broad Street Works 1845-58, this company produced earthenwares and Mason's Patent Ironstone China (see p.200). This is one of the marks used.

Myott, Son & Co. (Ltd.), Hanley, Staffordshire, UK
See p.148. This mark was used from c.1936. The firm was renamed Myott-Meakin Ltd. from 1977. Many other printed marks were used. Most incorporate the name of the firm or simply "Myott".

British Anchor Pottery Co. Ltd., Longton, Staffordshire, UK
See p.159. This mark was used from 1952. Other tradenames were used by this firm, but most marks feature the name of the company.

Reid & Co., Longton, Staffordshire, UK
Based at the Park Place Works, this pottery made porcelain 1913-46. Pieces made from 1913 feature this mark. The trade name "Roslyn" was used from c.1914. The company became Roslyn China in 1946.

Crown Pottery Company, Evansville, Indiana, USA
This pottery (active 1891–c.1955) made decorated ironstone and semi-porcelain dinner and toilet ware, and sets of odd dishes. In the firm's later years, their ware was sold in the white, and their business declined when they could not expand from their original building. This mark was one of those used.

British Anchor Pottery Co. Ltd., Longton, Staffordshire, UK
See p.159. This mark appears on wares from 1958 onwards.

Ridgway Potteries Ltd., Stoke, Staffordshire, UK
This firm was originally founded in 1866 at the Bedford Works in Shelton, built by Edward John Ridgway, son of William Ridgway. E. J. Ridgway had previously been in partnership at the Church Works with a Mr. Abington 1848-60. In 1870 Ridgway took his sons into the business, and on his retirement they formed a partnership with Joseph Sparks, and the firm continued as Ridgway, Sparks & Ridgway until 1879. The firm produced all types of fine and utility earthenware for the home and export market. This firm continued under various titles into the 20thC (Ridgways 1879-1920, Ridgways (Bedford Works) Ltd. 1920-52, Ridgway & Adderley with Booths & Colcloughs 1952-55, Ridgway, Adderley, Booths & Colcloughs Ltd. January-February 1955, Ridgway Potteries Ltd. February 1955-64). By 1955 the business comprised eight different works in Staffordshire. Many marks include the name of the pottery concerned. The mark (above) is the basic Ridgway mark, several variations occur. The mark (below) is an example of those used by Ridgway Potteries Ltd. c.1962.

Rosina China Co. Ltd., Longton, Staffordshire, UK
See p.145. Various forms of this mark were used from 1941, together with those previously used by George Warrilow (& Sons) (Ltd.).

Thomas C. Wild & Sons (Ltd.), Longton, Staffordshire, UK
See p.152. Previously Thomas C. Wild & Co. (1896-1904) and Thomas C. Wild (1905-17), this firm operated from St Mary's Works, Longton, from 1917. The Royal Albert trade name was incorporated into all printed marks, such as this one.

Royal Albion China Co., Longton, Staffordshire, UK
This company produced china at Albion Street,
Longton 1921-48. Marks used include this one
that appeared from c.1921.

Thomas Cone Ltd., Longton, Staffordshire, UK
See p.96. The name "Alma Ware" was incorporated into many printed marks, such as this
one used from 1946.

Clough's Royal Art Pottery, Longton, Staffordshire,
UK
Previously Alfred Clough (Ltd.) (c.1913-61), the
parent company to Barker Bros., Cartwight &
Edwards, W. H. Grindley, Royal Art Pottery and
Sampson Smith, Clough's Royal Art Pottery made
earthenwares from 1961. This mark was also used
by Alfred Clough Ltd. from 1951.

Cauldon Potteries Ltd., Stoke, Staffordshire, UK
See p.196. Marks such as this one were used 1920-
62 on porcelain and earthenwares. In 1962 the
firm was taken over by Bristol-based Pountney &
Co. Ltd.

The Royal Factory, Copenhagen, Denmark
After attempts to begin production of porcelain
in 1731 and 1754, the first successful factory was
established in 1755, directed by Johann Gottlieb
Mehlhorn. This concern merged with the faience
factory of Jakob Fortling at Kastrup in 1760. The
factory was taken over by the state in 1779, and
became known as the Royal Danish Porcelain
Factory. Highly skilled painters were employed
and pieces are of good quality. Many marks were
used with the original "wave-mark" adopted in
1775, such as the one (above) used from 1889, and
the example (below) from 1884. Many variations
exist.

Norfolk Pottery Co. Ltd., Shelton, Staffordshire, UK
From 1958, this pottery made earthenwares
with printed marks such as this one. Marks may
include "Staffordshire, England" as seen here, or
"Made in England".

Royal Stafford China, Longton, Staffordshire, UK
Formerly Thomas Poole (see p.193) and
Gladstone China Ltd., this pottery made porcelain
from 1952. A number of marks featuring the
name Royal Stafford including this one were used,
by this firm and previously by Thomas Poole.

Colclough & Co., Longton, Staffordshire, UK
Based at the Stanley Pottery from 1887, this firm
produced porcelain and earthenwares. The
company became known as Stanley Pottery Ltd.
in 1928 and continued until 1931. The trade name
Royal Stanley Ware was used during both periods.

William Lowe, Longton, Staffordshire, UK
See p.166. This printed mark featuring the name
of the works at which the firm was based was
used from c.1915.

Royal Tara, Galway, Eire
From 1942 this company based at Tara Hall in
Galway, has produced bone-china wares with this
mark, or others that feature the name "Royal
Tara" or "Regina".

James Sadler & Sons (Ltd.), Burslem,
Staffordshire, UK
Based at the Wellington and Central Potteries in
Burslem, this company (previously Sadler & Co.)
produced earthenwares (mainly teapots) from
c.1899. This printed mark was used from c.1947.

Salisbury Crown China Co., Longton,
Staffordshire, UK
Bone-china was made at the Salisbury Works by
this firm c.1927-61, when it was taken over by
Thomas Poole. Many marks featuring the name
Salisbury were used, including this one c.1927-37.

Soho Pottery (Ltd.), Tunstall and Cobridge,
Staffordshire, UK
Based at the Soho Pottery in Tunstall 1901-06, and
then at the Elder Works in Cobridge, this firm
produced earthenwares 1901-44. Marks before
1906 feature the name "Tunstall"; after this
date "Cobridge" appears. This mark was used
c.1906-22.

The Staffs Teapot Co. Ltd., Burslem,
Staffordshire, UK
Teapots were made by this firm 1929-48 with this
printed mark. The firm became the Hanover
Pottery in 1948, continuing until 1956.

Chapmans Longton, Ltd., Longton, Staffordshire, UK
Based at the Albert Works from 1916, this company produced poorcelain with the tradename
"Royal Standard" appearing on a number of
marks. This printed mark was used 1916-30.

Charles Amison & Co. Ltd., Longton, Staffordshire, UK
See p.141. This printed mark was used 1930-41. A similar mark was used with "Made in England" added 1946-49. The factory was closed 1941-45.

Andrew Stevenson, Cobridge, Staffordshire, UK
Formerly known as Bucknall & Stevenson, this firm was founded c.1816 and continued to 1830. Earthenwares were produced, some with this impressed mark.

John Steventon & Sons Ltd., Burslem, Staffordshire, UK
Formerly Brown & Steventon (1900-23), this firm produced earthenwares at the Royal Pottery in Burslem from 1923. This printed mark was used c.1923-36. After 1936 production was mainly concerned with tiles and sanitary wares.

Grimwades Ltd., Stoke, Staffordshire, UK
Previously known as Grimwade Bros. (1886-1900), this firm made a variety of decorative and useful earthenwares at the Winton and Stoke Potteries. This early mark (c.1900) was one of those used. The trade name Royal Winton appears in many marks after 1930. This mark was also used by J. Plant & Co. at the Stoke Pottery (1893-1900) before it was taken over by Grimwade Bros. c.1900. It may also have been used by previous firms operating at the Stoke Pottery.

William Hudson, Longton, Staffordshire, UK
Based at the Alma Works (c.1889-92) and the Sutherland Pottery (c.1892-1941), this concern produced porcelain. This printed mark was used 1912-41. In 1941 the firm became Hudson & Middleton Ltd. (see p.178). This firm should not be confused with William Hudson & Son of Longton, active c.1875-94.

Porzellanfabrik Viktoria, Alt-Rohau, Bohemia, Czech Republic
Formerly Schmidt & Co., this porcelain company was founded in 1883, producing keepsakes and utility ware. Various marks were used, including this one.

Chesapeake Pottery/D. F. Haynes and Son, Baltimore, Maryland, USA
Though founded by three Englishmen in 1880, the firm flourished after its purchase by noted

ceramics dealer David F. Haynes. The company made a variety of ornamental earthenwares, artistically decorated with transfer prints that were filled with colour and gilded by hand, as well as parian plaques and figures. Many of the shapes and decorations were designed by Haynes himself, his daughter Fannie, or his staff. It continued until 1924.

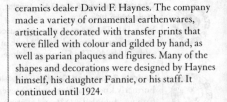

Wedgwood & Co. (Ltd.), Tunstall, Staffordshire, UK
Between 1860 and 1965 this firm, headed by Enoch Wedgwood, made earthenware and stone china at the Unicorn Pottery and Pinnox Works. Earthenware items included dinner, breakfast, toilet and other services for the Colonial, Continental and American markets. The primary product "Imperial Ironstone China" was made to a very high standard, and was designed to be artistic as well as durable and practical. One of the most successful designs was known as "Asiatic Pheasants", and this was extensively copied. The marks used by this firm are not to be confused with those of Josiah Wedgwood & Sons Ltd. This mark was one of those used and appears from c.1908. A similar crown was used to mark the firm's "Imperial Porcelain".

Westminster Pottery Ltd., Hanley, Staffordshire, UK
Earthenwares were produced 1948-56. This printed mark was one of those used. This firm also used the tradename "Castlecliffe Ware" which was registered in 1952.

Arthur J. Wilkinson (Ltd.), Burslem, Staffordshire, UK
Based at the Royal Staffordshire Pottery (and formerly at Central Pottery), this firm made earthenwares and ironstones (particularly with gold lustres) from 1885. Clarice Cliff was based here from 1916 (see p.107). This printed mark was among those used, and appears from c.1930.

Winterton Pottery (Longton) Ltd., Longton, Staffordshire, UK
Earthenwares were produced by this firm 1927-54. This mark used c.1927-41 is characteristic. "Bluestone ware" was a trade name.

Wood & Son(s) (Ltd.), Burslem, Staffordshire, UK
Based at the Trent and New Wharf Potteries, this form made earthenwares and ironstones. This printed mark appears 1891-1907. From c.1907 "& Sons" appears. "Ltd." was added from c.1910.

Royal devices

Royal Factory, Berlin, Prussia, Germany
See p.27. After the Berlin porcelain factory became the property of Frederick the Great in 1763, the King took an active role in ensuring its success. The sceptre mark was adopted and appears in many forms, such as those seen here. The mark (above left) was used c.1763-65 and later; the mark (above right) c.1775-1800. The mark (below) was used from 1870. (See also p.154.)

Limoges, Haute-Vienne, France
See p.43. In 1784 the porcelain factory previously owned by the Grellet brothers became the property of the crown. White wares were made here to be painted at Sèvres. This impressed or incised fleur-de-lis was one of the marks used.

Honoré Savy, Marseilles, Bouches-du-Rhône, France
Formerly a partner of Veuve Perrin, Honoré Savy founded a factory in Marseilles from c.1770. This mark has been found.

Buen Retiro, Madrid, Spain
See p.148. The fleur-de-lis was used from 1760-1804 in many forms including the examples shown, and may be impressed, or painted in blue, black or gold.

Duc de Penthièvre, Sceaux, Seine, France
See p.57 and p.216. This painted fleur-de-lis was used.

Pont-aux-Chou, Paris, France
Mignon owned a factory producing soft-paste porcelain in the English style 1774-84. This mark executed in underglaze blue was registered in 1777.

Saint-Cloud, Seine-et-Oise, France
See p.60. This mark appears on soft-paste porcelain from c.1700-66 when production ceased.

Capodimonte, Italy

The factory here was founded in 1743 by King Charles II of the Two Sicilies. Initially pieces were made for the Court. The factory was transferred to Spain in 1759 (see p.152). The mark above is impressed, the mark below was used c.1745 and appears in gold.

Barker Bros., Lane End, Staffordshire, UK
See p.195. This printed mark was one of those used 1912-30; a variation of this mark was also used 1930-37.

Cook Pottery Company, Trenton, New Jersey, USA
This company (active 1894-1929) succeeded to the business of Ott & Brewer, and continued to call the pottery works by the name Etruria as the former owners had done. They made a variety of wares for domestic and institutional consumption, including white granite, semi-porcelain, hotel ware and some belleek. In order to avoid confusion with Cook & Hancock, a dinner-ware company operating at the same time, the designation Mellor & Co. frequently appears in their marks as seen here.

Mintons, Stoke, Staffordshire, UK
See p.164. Mintons used this type of mark to commemorate pieces made for special events, and these usually include the date. Others incorporate the name of the retailer Thomas Goode & Co. Ltd. (see p.199).

Hammersley & Asbury, Longton, Staffordshire, UK
This firm was based at the Prince of Wales Pottery in Longton 1870-75, producing earthen-ware tea, coffee, dessert and trinket services. The pottery was originally established by Benjamin Shirley of Bangor, Wales, on the day of the marriage of the Prince of Wales (who later became King Edward VII) on 10 March 1863. Many of their marks feature the Prince of Wales' crest such as this one. A similar mark was also used by the firm's successor, Edward Asbury & Co. (1875-1925), which appears with the word "Trade Mark" above the crest and also features the motto "Ich Dien".

John Turner, Longton, Staffordshire, UK
Initially based at Stoke and then at Lane End, John Turner was one of Staffordshire's most successful potters. He began potting at Lane End in 1762 and produced earthenwares, creamwares and Wedgwood-type wares until his death in 1787. Collectors should take care not to mistake his wares for those by Wedgwood. The concern was taken over by his sons John and William and continued until 1806. This printed or impressed mark was used after 1784 when John Turner was appointed potter to the Prince of Wales.

Shields

Vienna, Austria

The Vienna porcelain factory was founded in
1718 by Claudius du Paquier, the Austrian War
Commissioner, assisted by the Meissen enameller
and gilder Christoph Konrad Hunger. The factory was sold to the state in 1744, and du Paquier
retired in 1745. Wares followed a baroque style. In
the second period of state ownership (1744-85) the
influence of the rococo and subsequently Sèvres is
evident. The discovery of high quality kaolin
made the factory independent with regard to raw
materials, and these pieces were marked with a
banded shield in underglaze blue. The mark is
based on the State shield, a simple device with
one, two or more cross-bars. Although various
forms appear, it remained in use until the closure
of the concern in 1864. Following financial
difficulties the factory was taken over by Konrad
Sorgenthal in 1784. This third period is characterized by neo-classicism. The factory closed in
1864 and the moulds were sold. The two marks
(top) are from the first period; these generally
appear irregular because they were incised or
impressed by hand. The two next examples were
used during the second period, and appear in blue.
The mark (below) is one of those used during the
Sorgenthal period and also appears in blue. A
small proportion of Vienna marks are scored
through with a shallow groove cut on the wheel.
This indicates that the piece is flawed in some way
and was sold off by the factory as a second. In
addition to the factory marks, thrower's marks
(numerals), year numbers (the last two or three
numerals of the date from 1783 onwards),
modeller's or repairer's marks (initials or signs),
signs indicating the type of paste used, and
painter's or gilder's marks in colour or gold, may
also appear.

Wachtersbach, Schlierbach, Prussia, Germany

Manufacturer of porcelain, stonewares and
pottery from 1832. This mark was registered in
1884. Note the resemblance to the Vienna mark.

Frankenthal, Palatinate, Germany

See p.58 and p.142. A quarter or part shield,
painted with a checked pattern in underglaze blue
was used at Frankenthal, taken from the arms of
Karl Theodor, Elector of the Palatinate. It only
appears on the very earliest wares c.1756.

Nymphenburg, Bavaria, Germany

See p.71. A selection of shields were used by
potters at Nymphenburg in the 18th and 19thC.
While most are impressed using a pre-worked
mould, a few were incised *ad hoc*. The marks
shown here appear (from the top) 1754-65, c.1765-
80, c.1780-90, c,1810-50, mid-19thC. Unlike other
factories the mark is often prominently displayed
as part of a design or on the upper side of the base.
Modern wares made at Nymphenburg can be
marked with both an impressed and an
underglaze blue printed mark.

Ludwigsburg, Württemberg, Germany

See p.143. The shield mark with antlers was used
by the Ludwigsburg factory towards the end of
the 18th and into the early 19thC.

Muriel Harris, Washington, Co. Durham, UK

Studio-type pottery was made at Old Smithy Hall
1953-59 before continuing at St Margarets-at-
Cliffe, Dover, from 1961. This impressed or
printed shield mark appears 1953-59.

Kieler Kunst-Keramik, Kiel, Holstein, Germany

Active during the first quarter of the 20thC, this
company produced general pottery and porcelain
wares featuring this mark.

C. H. Brannam Ltd., Barnstaple, Devon, UK

Based at the Lichdon Pottery from 1879 onwards,
this potter made earthenware jugs and vases
decorated with coloured slip or incised motifs.
This printed or impressed mark was used from
1929.

Greenwood Pottery Company, Trenton, New Jersey, USA

This company (active 1868-1933) made a variety
of good quality domestic and institutional wares,
including vitreous hotel ware, and ironstone and
vitreous dinner and toilet wares, decorated with
prints or decals. From 1883 to 1886 they made a
line of art porcelain, called Ne Plus Ultra, in
imitation of Royal Worcester with a mark that
mimicked the original.

William Morley & Co. Ltd., Fenton, Staffordshire, UK

See p.187. Formerly Morley Fox & Co. Ltd., this
company operated at the Salopian Works 1944-57.
This printed mark was one of those used.

Grossherzogliche Keramische Manufaktur,
Karlsruhe, Baden, Germany
This company made general earthenwares from
c.1901.

Moritz Fischer, Herend, Budapest, Hungary
Moritz Fischer (d.1880), manufacturer of hard-
paste porcelain in Chinese export style as well
conventional wares. Still in production making
high quality wares and decorative animals. This
mark usually appears in blue enamel applied over
the glaze.

Mühlberg, Eisenberg, Thuringia, Germany
Earthenwares were produced by this firm during
the first half of the 19thC. This mark appears on
their wares.

C. G. Schierholz & Sohn, Plaue-on-Havel, Thuringia,
Germany
C. G. Schierholz & Sohn were manufacturers of
hard-paste porcelain from 1819 and for most of
the 19thC. Mainly decorative wares: candlesticks
or flower holders with encrusted flowers. This
mark appears.

Rudolf Eugen Haidinger, Elbogen, Bohemia,
Czech Republlic
See p.299. This manufacturer produced hard-
paste porcelain and earthenwares. This mark was
used in a number of different variations; the
example seen here appears coloured, and also as
an underglaze mark.

Gibson & Sons (Ltd.), Burslem, Staffordshire, UK
See p.187. This printed shield mark appears
on Gibson wares from c.1930. Most marks
incorporate the name of the firm, and many
feature a crown device.

Ernst Wahliss, Turn, Bohemia, Czech Republic
Wahliss, a porcelain retailer, took over a porcelain
factory in Turn in 1897. He bought some original
models from the discontinued Vienna factory. He
died in 1900 but his sons took over the business,
producing artistic porcelain and faience under the
trademark "Alexandra Porzellan Works". In
1902-03 high fire enamelling on white and
coloured porcelain was introduced. Porcelain
flowers were produced. A number of shield and
crown marks in varying sizes were used,
including this one.

The Henry Alcock Pottery, Stoke, Staffordshire, UK
Formerly Henry Alcock & Co. (Ltd.) (1861-1910),
this company moved from the Elder Pottery,
Cobridge, to the Clarence Works in Stoke, and
produced earthenwares 1910-35. This printed
mark appears 1910-35.

Thomas Dean (& Sons) (Ltd.), Tunstall,
Staffordshire, UK
Based at the Black Works, this company made
earthenwares 1789-1947. Between 1947 and 1952
the firm operated from the Adderley Teapot
Works. This printed mark was used by the firm
1896-1947.

Empire Porcelain Co. Ltd., Stoke, Staffordshire, UK
See p.198. This mark is one of those used on
porcelains made during the 1930s. Most marks
used by this firm feature the name of the company, and may also feature a tradename, such as
"Shelton Ivory" or "Empire Ware".

Phillips, London, UK
W. P & G. Phillips (c.1858-97) (later Phillips & Co.
(c.1897-1906), Phillips Ltd. (c.1908-29)), retailers of
porcelain. This mark appears with the address of
the firm which gives an approximate guide to
dating: c.1858-97 Oxford Street; c.1859-89, 155
New Bond Street; c.1897-1906, Mount Street;
c.1908-29, 43 Bond Street.

Lorenz Reichel, Schirnding, Bavaria, Germany
This porcelain factory founded in 1902 produced
utility services. This mark is among those used.
Marks feature the name "Schirnding", sometimes
together with the name "Bavaria".

T. & R. Boote (Ltd.), Burslem, Staffordshire, UK
In 1850 the Waterloo Works in Burslem were
taken over by T. & R. Boote. In 1853 the firm took
out a patent on a style of pottery which involved
coloured relief-moulded designs on different-
coloured grounds. In addition, the company made
vases, groups and jugs among other items in
parian. After 1865 the firm no longer made
decorative wares and concentrated on the
production of white granite ware for the
American market, and pavement tiles. Later the
firm made domestic wares in "Royal Patent
Ironstone". This mark is one of those used and
appears 1890-1906. After 1906 only tiles were
produced.

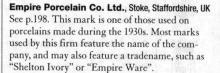

International Pottery/Burgess & Campbell, Trenton, New Jersey, USA

Between 1879 and 1936, this pottery made hotel ware, semi-porcelain, and white granite, dinner and toilet sets, odd sets and novelties. Most of the ware was decorated. Types of decorated wares include "Roysl Blue" and "Rugby Flint" ware. For a few years, this pottery shared owners and products with the New York City Pottery (see p.176), and the Mercer Pottery Co. (see p.309), Consequently they also shared a double-shield mark that was differentiated by the names that appear below it.

Edward Clarke (& Co.), Tunstall and Burslem, Staffordshire, UK

Based at the Phoenix Works Tunstall c.1865-77, and at the Churchyard Works, Burslem c.1878-87, this company produced earthenwares 1865-87. This printed mark was used during the Burslem period c.1880-87. The firm subsequently became A. J. Wilkinson.

East Liverpool Potteries Company, East Liverpool, Ohio, USA

A merger of six potteries in 1901 was made in an effort to compete with the larger potteries making semi-vitreous table and toilet wares. In 1903, four of the companies abandoned the merger and in 1907 the last two returned to independent operations. The name, however, went on for some time, and pieces with the printed marks that only show the name "East Liverpool Potteries Co." were actually made by a former member of the cooperative, the United States Pottery Company, after the merger had finally disbanded.

(W.) Baker & Co. (Ltd.), Fenton, Staffordshire, UK

This firm produced the usual types of printed, sponged and pearl-white graniteware, mainly for export to North America, the West Indies, Africa and India 1839-1932. The printed shield mark denotes a date c.1930-32.

Burgess & Leigh, Burslem, Staffordshire, UK

This company made utilitarian and decorative earthenwares at the Hill Pottery (c.1867-89) and the Middleport Pottery (from c.1889). This printed mark appears 1880-1912. Many different marks were used, including a monogram mark (from 1862) and marks featuring a globe device (used from 1906).

Bovey Pottery Co. Ltd., Bovey Tracey, Devon, UK
In 1842 the Folly Pottery in Bovey Tracey was bought by Messrs Buller and Divett, who made Staffordshire-type wares in all colours and styles under the name Bovey Tracey Pottery Company. The title changed in c.1894 to the Bovey Pottery Co. Ltd. which continued until 1956. The shield mark (above) was used 1949-56, and the example (below) appeared c.1954-57.

Co-operative Wholesale Society Ltd.,
Longton, Staffordshire, UK
This manufacturer of bone china was based at the Windsor Pottery from 1911. Many printed marks appear; this is one of those used in the 1950s and 1960s.

Franz Junkersdorf, Dresden, Germany
Founded in 1897, this company specialized in buttons, belt buckles, hat pins, armorial painting and heraldic articles. This mark was one of those used.

T. G. Green & Co. (Ltd.), Church Gresley, Derbyshire, UK
Situated near near Burton-on-Trent, the pottery at Church Gresley were taken over by T .G. Green in c.1864. The company produced general house-hold earthenwares and stonewares, and was best known for its "Cornish Kitchen Ware". This mark was one of those used by the firm during the 1930s.

Leighton Pottery, Burslem, Staffordshire, UK
Manufacturers of earthenwares at Orme St., Burslem 1940-54. This printed mark appears from 1946-54.

Myott, Son & Co. (Ltd.), Hanley, Staffordshire, UK
See p.148. The mark (above) appeared from c.1930, the mark (below) from c.1961. Other marks incorporate a crown device, and either the firm's name or initials. If the place name "Stoke" appears on a mark, this indicates a date before 1902. The tradename "China-Lyke Ware" was used from c.1959.

Wedgwood & Co. (Ltd.), Tunstall, Staffordshire, UK
See p.206. This mark was used from c.1957, and gives a date of 1835 for the original foundation of the company. A wide range of other marks were also used.

Rustington Pottery, Rustington, Nr. Worthing, West Sussex, UK
Studio pottery was produced from 1947. This impressed or printed trademark was used.

Washington Pottery Ltd., Shelton, Staffordshire, UK
Manufacturers of earthenwares from 1946-73, this company used this printed mark. Other marks include the name in full.

C. & A. Carstens, Blankenhainer, Thuringia, Germany
Originally founded in 1790 by Christian Andreas Speck, this factory made high quality porcelain. Under various owners, table, coffee, tea and mocha ware was produced with a wide variety of decoration. This mark was used by different owners.

Anchors

Chelsea Porcelain Works, London, UK
See p.160. Production at Chelsea can be roughly divided into periods according to the mark used. The raised anchor, a small moulded mark (top), was used c.1749-52, but rarely appears. The small red anchor mark (centre) was used c.1752-56. Chealsea figures made during the raised anchor or red anchore periods are generally held to be the best in England. The gold anchor mark (below) appears c.1756-69. This mark is often used on reproductions of Chelsea porcelains; on genuine pieces the mark should never be more than ¼in (0.6cm) in height. In addition the gold anchor may also appear on Derby porcelain decorated at Chelsea c.1769-75. The anchor mark was also used during the Chelsea-Derby period (1769-c.1784).

Derby Porcelain Works, Derbyshire, UK
See p.25. A small anchor painted in red, brown or gold, sometimes appears on Derby porcelains 1760-80. Usually this is a Chelsea mark (see above). From c.1769-75 William Duesbury was working the Chelsea factory in London, and then at Derby. This is known as the Chelsea-Derby period.

Worcester Porcelains, Hereford and Worcester, UK
See p.23. Rare pieces of Worcester porcelain painted in gilt by independent decorators sometimes bear the Chelsea anchor mark seen here.

Duc de Penthièvre, Sceaux, Seine, France
See p.57. The anchor in these two marks refers to
the Duc de Penthièvre, Grand-Amiral de France,
who was the patron and protector of the factory.
The painted anchor mark above appears on
faience, and the mark below is found on porcelain
made from c.1775.

Ludwig Wessel, Poppelsdorf, Rhineland, Germany
This factory was established in 1755 and made
pottery and porcelain of all kinds. This anchor
mark is one of those used.

Geminiano Cozzi, Venice, Italy
A porcelain factory was founded in Venice by
Geminiano Cozzi in 1765 with help from the
Venetian senate; the concern continued until 1812.
The material was a hybrid soft-paste porcelain
with a greyish colour. Output primarily comprised
tablewares, figures and vases. Good pieces are
distinguished by their fine colours (bright emerald
green and bluish purple), and gilding was finely
executed. An anchor mark in red, or more rarely
gold, was used.

James Woodward (Ltd.), Burton-on-Trent,
Staffordshire, UK
Based at the Swadlincote Pottery 1859-88, this
factory made terracotta and majolica. Output
consisted mainly of sanitary wares after c.1880.
This painted or impressed mark was used.

Davenport, Longport, Staffordshire, UK
Ceramic factories were originally established in
Longport by John Brindley, Edward Bourne and
Robert Williamson. In c.1793 the first factory
passed into the hands of John Davenport. After
his retirement in 1830, the factory was run by his
two younger sons Henry and William. Henry
then bought Robert Williamson's factory and
expanded the business. After Henry's death
William continued the firm, and in turn it was
taken over by his son after his death. In 1881 the
business became a private company. Early output
comprised white, cream-coloured and blue-and-
white earthenwares. Porcelain was subsequently
produced in many forms and styles. All are of
high quality. Other notable styles include richly-
coloured Chinese and Japanese-style wares. The
anchor is the distinguishing characteristic of
Davenport marks; the anchor alone appears on
porcelains and earthenwares made in the 1820s

(top). The anchor frequently appears with the name of the company as in these further examples (from the top: from c.1795; on blue porcelains c.1850-70; printed mark on wares sold in the Liverpool shop c.1860-87).

Anchor Porcelain Co. Ltd., Longton, Staffordshire, UK

See p.161. This company produced porcelain at the Anchor Pottery 1901-18. The impressed or printed anchor mark above, was used 1901-15, and the printed mark below, appears 1915-18. Another mark used comprises the initials "A. P. Co." The tradename "Royal Westminster China" was used.

Bow China Works, Stratford, London, UK

See p.21. The hand-painted anchor and dagger mark was the standard Bow mark from c.1760-76, and is usually found on figures and groups. Pieces produced with this and other later marks are usually made from less high quality paste (which often features black specks) than earlier wares.

Thomas Furnival & Sons, Cobridge, Staffordshire, UK

Based in Elder Road, this company produced earthenwares 1851-90. Output included white granite and vitrified ironstone and decorated sanitary ware for export to the United States, Canada and Europe. For the domestic market they made "patent ironstone" services in a variety of decorative styles. The crest mark (above) was registered in 1878. The firm subsequently became known as Furnivals (Ltd.) and continued until 1968. The trademark (below) was used 1890-1910.

Gustavsberg, Sweden

The Odelberg factory in Gustavsberg existed from the mid-17thC; porcelain was first made here in 1822, and bone china was made from 1866 (the only European factory to produce bone china apart from England). Still in existence today, the factory produces "Modern Swedish" wares. A number of 20thC marks feature an anchor together with the word "Gustavsberg", as here.

Thomas Fell (& Co.) (Ltd.), Newcastle-upon-Tyne, Tyne and Wear, UK

See p.160. This impressed mark appears 1817-30. Several impressed or printed marks were used by this firm, many of which feature the company name or initials.

Anchor Pottery, Trenton, New Jersey, USA
This pottery (1893-1926) made decorated semi-porcelain dinner and toilet sets in its early years and closed its history by making premiums used by the Grand Union Tea Company in its house-to-house sales program. The Fulper Pottery (see p.114), bought the works in 1926.

Herculaneum Pottery, Liverpool, Mersey, UK
See p.200. This impressed mark appears c.1796-1833.

Mafra & Son, Caldas da Rainha, Portugal
A factory here was run by Mafra & Son from 1853, producing imitation Palissy ware. This impressed mark appears.

New Chelsea Porcelain Co. (Ltd.), Longton, Staffordshire, UK
Porcelain was made by this company c.1912-61 (the name changed to the New Chelsea China Co. Ltd. in 1951). A number of anchor marks were used, often featuring the words "New Chelsea" (as here) and later "Royal Chelsea".

Sampson Bridgwood & Son (Ltd.), Longton, Staffordshire, UK
See p.161. Marks such as the example shown here were used on wares by Sampson & Bridgwood from 1912.

Duc de Penthièvre, Sceaux, Seine, France
See p.57. This late mark is another that refers to the Duc de Penthièvre, patron of the factory at Sceaux.

Swords

Meissen was the first factory to employ crossed swords as a mark, and did so from 1724. As in so many cases, particularly in the German-speaking world, factories used a mark based on either the coat-of-arms of the state or principality, or indeed the initials of the patron or proprietor.

Meissen, the most important porcelain factory in Europe until the 1750s, derived its mark from the crossed swords of Saxony. The success of Meissen encouraged lesser factories not only to emulate its wares and figures, but also to copy its famous mark. This mark, and that of Sèvres, are the most copied marks in European porcelain. It is fairly safe to assume that the majority of wares bearing either of these marks are reproductions or outright fakes, but if in doubt always seek expert advice. In Germany alone the following factories used marks imitating the Meissen crossed swords marks: Wallendorf, Nymphenburg and Limbach as well as many minor Thuringian concerns in the 18th or 19thC. Outside Germany, many other European factories followed suit. In France, Choisy-le-Roi, Fontainebleau and Montreuil, in Belgium, Tournai; in Holland, Weesp; and in Britain, Bristol, Coalport, Derby, Longton Hall (and West Pans), Lowestoft and Worcester.

Meissen, Nr. Dresden, Saxony, Germany

See p.53. First used in 1724 the earliest version of the crossed swords mark is relatively small with quite open blades, transecting approximately at right-angles (90°). These are usually drawn in overglaze blue or black enamel.

Prior to c.1745 some crossed swords have tiny blobs at the tip of the handle.

From 1763 to 1774 a dot appears between the hilts of the swords (although the odd piece of c.1740 can be marked in a similar way).

From 1774 until 1814 a star that generally appears above the handles, is used to denote the Marcolini period.

From 1814 to 1818 the Roman numerals I or II accompany the crossed swords, and are known to appear on pieces for which the paste has an individual composition.

From 1818 until 1924 the swords are long with slightly curved blades. "1710" and "1910" appear on marks of important pieces during 1910.

From 1924 the crossed swords marks appear with a dot between the points of the blades. In previous "Dot" periods the dot appears between the handles.

Georg Heinrich Macheleid, Rudolstalt Volkstedt, Thuringia, Germany

Founded in 1762, this factory operated under various owners. From 1760 onwards the crossed pitchforks were used which in some cases can be mistaken for the crossed swords of Meissen. These marks were hand-drawn in the 18th and early 19thC, but later became more formalized. Due to a protest from Meissen, a cross-bar was added at the intersection of the two forks (see mark below) after 1787, but it is not known for how long this was used.

Coalport Porcelain Works, Coalport, Shropshire, UK
See p.72. Crossed swords were used by Coalport on some decorative, flower-encrusted, Dresden-style porcelains during the 1820-30 period.

Bristol, Avon, UK
See p.61. Crossed swords marks were used by Richard Champion's hard-paste porcelain factory between 1770 and 1781.

Derby Porcelain Works, Derby, Derbyshire, UK
See p.25. A rather thin and weak-looking crossed swords mark was used here intermittently between c.1780 and 1830. It was usually painted in blue enamel.

Lowestoft, Suffolk, UK
See p.231. Crossed swords marks were used at Lowestoft between 1775 and 1790.

Worcester Porcelains, Hereford and Worcester, UK
See p.23. Crossed swords were used on various wares between c.1760 and 1770. They are painted in underglaze blue, and may appear with or without numerals..

Longton Hall, Staffordshire, UK
One of the few Staffordshire factories to produce porcelain in the 18thC, Longton Hall survived barely a decade from c.1749-60. The factory produced figures, decorative leaf-shaped wares and blue and white wares. This mark, while clearly attempting to imitate a Meissen crossed-swords mark, is in fact a pair of entwined "L"s, used probably because the owner's name was William Littler.

Wallendorf, Thuringia, Germany
A small hard-paste factory producing standard, mainly Meissen-inspired wares, and some figures. This hand-drawn mark appears in blue and other colours before 1778. Later marks resemble a letter "W".

Fountainebleau, Seine-et-Marne, France
See p.162. This mark appears in the second half of the 19thC.

Ruskin Pottery, Smethwick, Nr. Birmingham, West Midlands, UK
See p.96. This painted or incised scissor mark was used on some wares.

Choisy-le-Roi, Seine, France

A crowned, crossed swords mark appears on some early hard-paste porcelain from c.1785.

Tournai, Belgium

A porcelain factory was founded here in 1751 by F. J. Peterinck under the patronage of the Empress Maria Theresa. In 1800 it was taken over by the de Bettignies family who continued it until 1850. Pieces were made in the style of Sèvres and Meissen. This complicated arrangement of crossed swords and tiny crosses was used on porcelain between 1756 and 1781.

Nymphenburg, Bavaria, Germany

See p.71. Crossed swords in various guises (including a straightforward copy of Meissen) was used on porcelain made for the Turkish market in the mid-1760s.

Weesp, Holland

Established in 1759 by Count Gronsfeldt-Diepenbroek, this short-lived and financially insecure factory produced hard-paste porcelain in the manner of contemporary German porcelain. It was acquired by Johannes de Mol in 1771 who transferred the enterprise to Oude Loosdrecht. The crossed swords mark vaguely resembles Tournai.

Montreuil, Seine, France

This double crossed swords mark was used on hard-paste porcelain made at this factory from 1815-73.

Pountney & Co. (Ltd.), Bristol, Avon, UK

See p.105. Pountney's factory, which made earthenwares, incorporated the crossed swords (they were never used alone) into some of their marks from 1900 until c.1960.

Warwick China Company, Wheeling, West Virginia, USA

This large pottery (active 1884-1951) made a tremendous amount of table and toilet ware over a long period of time in various vitreous and semi-porcelain bodies. Their wares for domestic consumption were nicely decorated with prints, including flow blue, or decals. Hotel ware was added to the firm's production in 1912. Vases, umbrella stands, pitchers, tankards, and the like, were also made.

Scroll marks

Sèvres, France

See p.72 and p.162. The royal porcelain factory in France was first established at Vincennes in 1738 when Louis XV granted a privilege to the brother of his Minister of Finance. Experiments began and porcelain was successfully produced from 1745. After 1751 and under a new proprietor, the concern was retitled "Manufacture Royale de la Porcelaine de France", and adopted the royal crest as a mark. The factory was transferred to Sèvres in 1756. The first two marks shown here are examples of those used before 1953, and appear in underglaze blue. The third mark is one of those used during the reign of Louis XVIII (1814-24). The number 21 refers to 1821, the date of manufacture. The final mark was used during the reign of Charles X (1824-30), and appears in blue; this mark may feature a cross between the interlinked letter "C"s.

Emile Samson,, Paris, France

See p.231. This mark was used by Samson on imitations of Sèvres and terracotta.

Saint-Amand-les-Eaux, Nord, France

See p.164. These marks were used on faience produced at Saint-Amand-les-Eaux during the early years of the factory, in the first part of the 18thC.

De porceleyne Klaeuw, Delft, Holland

Founded in 1662, this factory (The Porcelain Claw), used a number of marks. This example is one of the forms of the mark registered in 1764.

Greenwood Pottery Company, Trenton, New Jersey, USA

See p.210. The number "61" in the centre of the mark represents the year in which the pottery was originally organized.

Worcester Porcelains, Hereford and Worcester, UK

See p.23. The standard Royal Worcester has been used in a number of forms to the present day. This version was used c.1862-75. A similar mark used c.1876-91 differed in two ways: a crescent appeared in the centre rather than the letter "C", and the crown was filled in and fitted the circle. After 1891 the words "Royal Worcester England" were added together with year marks. From 1938 the words "Bone China" appear. (For further details of year marks, see p.374 in Additional information.)

W. T. Copeland (& Sons Ltd.), Stoke, Staffordshire, UK

See p.245. This printed mark was used by Copeland 1851-85. An earlier, less elaborate version appears c.1847-51.

Thomas Dimmock & Co., Hanley, Staffordshire, UK

This firm was based at a number of works in Hanley 1828-59, producing fine quality earthenwares. This mark appears impressed or in conjuction with other printed marks.

Derby Porcelain Works, Derbyshire, UK

See p.25. This printed mark appears c.1878-90; a similar mark was used from c.1890. Both feature year cypher marks printed below. "Bone China" occurs on marks used after World War II. (For further details of cypher marks, see p.361 in Additional information.)

Lille, France

See p.22. This mark commonly found on modern forgeries. When in doubt about the authenticity of a piece, always seek expert advice.

Maddock Pottery Company, Trenton, New Jersey, USA

See p.147. This is one of the marks used; most marks incorporate the company name.

Minton, Stoke, Staffordshire, UK

See p.164. This mark is a typical example of a 19thC Minton mark.

Josiah Spode, Stoke, Staffordshire, UK

The first Josiah Spode was born in 1733 and worked for Thomas Whieldon. His son, also called Josiah, was born in 1754, and took over a works in Stoke in c.1784 and produced earthenwares to begin with, and porcelain after c.1790. A new development "Stone China" was made in 1805. The third Josiah Spode took over the works after his father's death in 1827, but he died only two years later. The business was then carried on until 1833 when the whole concern was bought by Alderman William Taylor Copeland. This printed mark was one of those used on special earthenware bodies c.1805-33.

Shapes: Triangles

Trevor Logan, Leeds, West Yorkshire, UK
Active since 1943, Studio-type pottery and
stonewares with this impressed mark have been
made since 1957.

Chelsea Porcelain Works, London, UK
See p.160. This incised triangle mark, sometimes
with the addition of "Chelsea" and the year was
used c.1745-49. On rare occasions the triangle
appears painted in blue.

Pinder, Bourne & Co., Burslem, Staffordshire, UK
This firm took over the works at Nile Street,
Burslem in 1862 and produced a variety of
printed, enamelled and gilded earthenwares and
redwares. This mark was one of those used by the
firm 1862-82.

Iden Pottery, Rye, East Sussex, UK
From October 1961 Studio-type earthenwares and
stonewares were made by D. Townshend (who
previously worked at the Rye Pottery) and J. H.
Wood. This printed mark was used from 1961.
Originally established at Iden, in 1963 it moved to
Rye but kept its original name.

VAN BRIGGLE

Van Briggle Pottery, Colorado Springs, Colorado, USA
Founded by Artus van Briggle, who had been a
decorator for the Rookwood Pottery (see p.92), the
pottery made ornamental wares with matt glazes
applied over moulded Art Nouveau forms based
almost entirely on native plants. Van Briggle
died in 1904, but the pottery was continued by his
wife for a while and then by others. Many of the
designs from these early years are still made, along
with newer forms.

Shapes: Circles

Colin Pearson, Aylesford, Kent, UK
Studio-type pottery was produced here from 1962
at the Quay Pottery. Colin Pearson previously
worked at the Aylesford Priory Pottery. This
impressed seal mark was used.

Derek M. Davis, Arundel, West Sussex, UK
From 1953 this potter produced Studio-type
earthenwares; stonewares and tiles were made
c.1959-62. This painted or incised mark was
introduced early in 1963.

Walton Pottery Co. Ltd., Old Whittington, Nr. Chesterfield, Derbyshire, UK

William Gordon produced salt-glazed stonewares 1946-56 with this incised or impressed mark.

Höchst, Nr. Mainz, Germany

See p.24. This wheel mark was used by the Höchst factory in many variations . This example was used 1762-96 and appears in underglaze blue. A crowned version was used c.1765-74.

Philipp Dietrich, Passau, Bavaria, Germany

See p.146. This mark was used on wares made from Höchst moulds.

Josiah Spode, Stoke, Staffordshire, UK

See p.223. This impressed was used on early porcelains c.1790-1820.

Margaret Leach, Various locations, UK

Not related to Studio-potter Bernard Leach, although she did work at the Leach Pottery in St Ives between 1943 and 1945, Margaret Leach began potting at the Barnhouse Pottery in Brockweir, Monmouth, in 1946. She continued at various other locations until 1956. This mark was used while she was at the Taena Pottery at Aylburton in Gloucestershire 1951-56.

Humphrey Palmer, Hanley, Staffordshire, UK

Based at the Church Works in Hanley c.1760-78, Palmer made Wedgwood-type earthenwares including basaltes in association with James Neale. A firm (J.) Neale & Co. was formed at Church Works from c.1776. This mark appears.

Roseville Pottery Company, Roseville and Zanesville, Ohio, USA

See p.33. This applied clay mark appears. A foil label with the words "Roseville Pottery" was also used.

Wedgwood & Bentley, Etruria, Staffordshire, UK

Josiah Wedgwood and Thomas Bentley formed a partnership from c.1768-80 with the intention of producing ornamental wares in the Classical style. They established a new factory which they called Etruria, named after a site in Ancient Italy where pottery had been excavated. This impressed or raised mark appears only on ornamental wares c.1769-80; the word "Etruria" is sometimes missing.

Weller Pottery/S. A. Weller Company, Fultonham and Zanesville, Ohio, USA

Active between 1872 and 1948, Weller's earliest potteries made painted flowerpots and stoneware garden ware and umbrella stands. In 1893, the first art wares were produced. During the early years of this century, the pottery produced a wide variety of decorative effects on ornamental wares, including painted underglaze slip in the Rookwood (see p.92) style and unique iridescent effects brought from France by Jacques Sicard, a protégé of Clement Massier. While much of this early art ware was artist decorated, the later work depends on moulds and decorative glazes. The name Weller appears in most marks; a large number of decorator's marks (as signatures or monograms) were also used.

Shapes: Squares & diamonds

Worcester Porcelains, Hereford and Worcester, UK
See p.23. This square or fret mark was used in many variations, hand-painted in underglaze blue c.1755-75. It also appears on hard-paste porcelain and earthenware reproductions.

C. H. Menard, Rue de Popincourt, Paris, France
See p.124. This mark is one of those used by Menard, whose output primarily comprised copies of Chinese porcelain.

Meissen, Nr. Dresden, Saxony, Germany
See p.53. Imitation Chinese marks such as this one were sometimes used, mainly on blue and white wares c.1720-25.

Mayer China Company/Mayer Potteries Company, Ltd., Syracuse, New York, USA
Although this pottery (1881-present) has made a high grade of hotel ware for some time, over the last century their product line has varied a great deal, including white ironstone with lustre sprig (tea leaf), white granite and decorated semi-porcelain dinner and toilet sets and miscellaneous tableware. Originally based at Beaver Falls, Pennsylvania, the company is now based in Syracuse.

Emile Samson, Paris, France
See p.231. This mark was used by Samson on Japanese and Chinese-style wares.

Doulton & Co. (Ltd.), Lambeth, London, UK
See p.111. This impressed mark was used c.1912-56 on slip-cast wares. This motif is incorporated into many other Doulton marks down to the present day. This device appears with a crown and a lion c.1902-22 and c.1927-36, and a lion from c.1922.

William Marshall, St Ives, Cornwall, UK
See p.232. This impressed seal mark was one of those used from 1956.

William Bloor's East Liverpool Porcelain Works, East Liverpool, Ohio, USA
Bloor worked alternately in East Liverpool, Ohio, and Trenton, New Jersey, over many years. During this "brief" stay in Ohio (1861-62), he converted an existing pottery to the production of parian and "double thick hotel ware." But the Civil War created financial and labour problems. This raised diamond-shaped mark is similar to a British Patent Office Registration Mark.

Davenport, Longport, Staffordshire, UK
See p.216. This printed mark was found on Davenport porcelains of registered form or pattern c.1842-83. (For further details of Patent Office Registration Marks, see p.360. in Additional information)

G. & J. Hobson, Burslem, Staffordshire, UK
Formerly C. Hobson (1865-80), this firm produced earthenwares 1883-1901. This printed mark occurs on the firm's advertisements in 1884. Other forms of mark may occur.

Thomas Ford, Hanley, Staffordshire, UK
Originally established in 1854 as T. & C. Ford, this firm operated as Thomas Ford 1871-74. Many marks were used, this example is based on the registration device. (For further details of Patent Office Registration Marks, see p.360 in Additional information.)

J. E. Jeffords and Company/Philadelphia City Pottery, Philadelphia, Pennsylvania, USA
Rockingham and yellow ware were Jeffords' stock-in-trade throughout their years of business, 1868-1915. The pottery made cow creamers, teapots, florists' crockery, table and toilet wares (some in whiteware) and blue-glazed ware. Much of the company's work is not signed.

Shapes: Hearts

Benedikt Brothers, Meierhöfen, Bohemia, Czech Republic

The Benedikt Brothers founded a factory here in 1883 and produced white and decorated porcelain. Various marks featuring a heart were used.

C. H. Menard, Rue de Popincourt, Paris, France

See p.124 and p.226. This mark was also used.

Stars

Florence, Tuscany, Italy

The star (or more correctly aterisk) mark seen here, can be single, or as a group of three, and located below the lower terminal of the strap handle on "oak-leaf" drug jars made in Tuscany. It is tentatively associated with the workshop of Giunta di Tugio in the south of the city. In 1430-31 a large order for about 1,000 drug jars was placed with this workshop by the hospital of the Santa Maria Nuova whose device or emblem was a crutch. A considerable number of "oak-leaf" jars bearing both the emblem of the crutch and the asterisk (or asterisks) have survived in international collections and these are probably the earliest documentary wares in European ceramics.

Nove, Venezia, Italy

It is not surprising that with a name like Nove that the mark adopted by the faience pottery run by the Antonibon family should be a *nova* (literally "new star"). In isolation the star is found on 18thC wares. The comet-like star with a tail (below) is 19th or 20thC.

Ginori Factory, Doccia, Nr. Florence, Tuscany, Italy

See p.25. One of the most important Italian porcelain factories established in 1735 by Carlo Ginori and still in production today. The star mark can be impressed or enamelled in blue, red or purple, and denotes a date of the late 18thC or the first half of the 19thC.

David Hilton, Compton Dundon, Somerton, Somerset, UK

In production from 1956, David Hilton (formerly of Street in Somerset) produced Studio pottery. From 1962 he specialized in stonewares. The mark is impressed.

L. B. Beerbower, Elizabeth, New Jersey, USA
Beerbower, formerly of the Phoenix Pottery in
Phoenixville, Pennsylvania, took over the old
Pruden pottery in Elizabeth, New Jersey. The
new pottery (active 1880-c.1905) made ironstone
china, semi-granite, cream-coloured and print-
decorated goods in druggists' ware, and toilet,
table and kitchen sets.

F. Legrand & Cie, Limoges, France
Known under various names (Betoule & Legrand
(1910), Betoule & Cie (1920)), this firm was known
under this title 1923-26. This is one of the marks
used.

Star China Co., Longton, Staffordshire, UK
Based at the Atlas Works and other addresses, this
porcelain manufacturer operated 1900-19. The
firm became the Paragon China Co. from 1920.
Various printed marks were used including these
examples used c.1912-19. Other marks include a
monogram or the initials of the firm; a crown
device was sometimes used.

Star Pottery, Possil Park, Glasgow, Scotland, UK
Johnstone Wardlaw were manufacturers of
earthenwares and stonewares 1880-1907. This
impressed or printed mark was used.

Star Pottery Works, Elmendorf, Texas, USA
Ernest Richter established a stoneware pottery in
Elmendorf, Bexar County, Texas, in 1888, and he
sold his pottery in 1905 to Newton, Weller, and
Wagner. Their firm became the Star Pottery
Works in 1909 and continued until 1915. White,
Bristol-glazed stoneware in all of the common
utilitarian forms was manufactured, as well as an
unusual type of stoneware and cast-iron patented
churn.

Crescents

Hanau, Nr. Frankfurt-am-Main, Germany
See p.170. This painted mark was used on tin-
glazed earthenwares in the 17th and 18thC.

Bow China Works, Stratford, London, UK
See p.21. Imitating a mark used at Worcester, this
crescent mark appears heavily painted in
underglaze blue, and was used on figures and
wares c.1760-76.

Worcester Porcelains, Hereford and Worcester, UK

See p.23. The crescent mark used by Worcester was taken from a device in the arms of the city of Worcester. The mark (above) was used by Dr Wall's factory from c.1755-90. The open painted crescent appears on blue and white hand-painted porcelains. The crescent mark can also be printed and open or printed and hatched over. The mark (below) was used during the Flight period (1783-92). The open painted crescent continued to be used, but was generally smaller and less grey.

Lowestoft, Suffolk, UK

See p.231. The Lowestoft factory (c.1757-99) had no formal trademark and indeed many of their bone-ash porcelains are unmarked. However a number of pieces carry hand-painted versions of other factory marks such as the crescents seen here.

Pinxton Works, Pinxton, Derbyshire, UK

See p.128. The mark of a crescent and a star was used occasionally c.1799-1806.

Tessa Fuchs, London, UK

A producer of Studio-type ceramics from 1961, Tessa Fuchs used this painted, crescent-like symbol. The mark also appears with her name.

W. Goebel, Oeslau, Bavaria, Germany

Formerly the Oeslau and Wilhelmsfeld porcelain factory founded in 1871, the factory was taken over by W. Goebel from 1879. Ornaments in porcelain, fine earthenware and terracotta were produced. This is one of the marks used.

William Hulme, Cobridge, Staffordshire, UK

Manufacturers of earthenwares 1948-54, this firm operated from the Argyle Works. This printed mark was used, and also appears without the words "Imperial Porcelain".

Crosses

Crosses are frequently used on ceramics as subsidiary marks, mostly identifying a workman or painter. For example, the major blue and white porcelain factories Bow, Bristol, Worcester, Lowestoft and Liverpool all marked their wares with scratched or painted crosses, and as such can rarely be used alone to attribute a piece.

Lowestoft, Suffolk, UK

Established in 1757 Lowestoft manufactured a
phosphatic soft-paste formula similar to Bow. The
main output was Chinese style blue and white, at
least until c.1770 when enamel colours were also
used and some fine quality painting appears.
The factory closed in c.1802, but produced very
little in its last years. There was no factory mark
(although they "borrowed" the crescent mark of
Worcester and the crossed swords of Meissen) but
did inscribe some of their wares with workman's
marks, especially on the inside of the footrim. As
well as numerals and letters the cross shown here
was also used.

Bristol, Avon, UK

See p.61. The Bristol cross marks which are
mostly painted in a pale blue enamel, appear from
1770, until the closure of Champion's factory in
1781. Sometimes the marks are used together with
a number or very rarely a date.

Moustiers, Basses Alpes, France

See p.91. A painted cross mark was used on
faience made at Moustiers from c.1710-40.

Fulda, Hesse, Germany

See p.47. The cross was used as a factory mark on
hard-paste porcelain from c.1765-80.

Emile Samson, Paris, France

Emile Samson (1837-1913) was probably the most
famous manufacturer of porcelain reproductions,
especially of Meissen and Sèvres, although his
factory also made imitations of faience. As well as
using crossed batons recalling the Meissen crossed
swords, Samson employed pseudo-Chinese seal
marks and other devices. However, on copies of
European porcelains and enamels the factory used
an entwined "S" mark resembling a cross, as
shown here.

Helen Walters, Stroud Green, Hornsey, London, UK

This potter made Studio-type pottery from 1945.
As well as her initials, Helen Walters used an
incised cross and dots mark on pottery made for
Doulton between 1945 and 1953.

E. T. Leaper, Newlyn, Nr. Penzance, Cornwall, UK

Hand-made pottery was produced by E. T.
Leaper from 1954. This mark loosely resembles
that of Bernard Leach.

Francesco Xanto Avelli da Rovigo, Urbino, Italy
See p.48. Although he signed many of his pieces
with a full or an abbreviated signature mark,
modern scholarship has subsumed a considerable
body of works by this potter marked merely with
the words "fabula", "nota" or "istoria", or simply
with a character similar to a lazy, cursive "y", or in
his late work of c.1540-42, with an "x" similar to
the example shown.

Cafaggiolo, Nr. Florence, Tuscany, Italy
One of the most important maiolica workshops
or "bottega" in Cafaggiolo, was run by the
Fattorini family. The mark shown here which
dates from a signed piece of 1514 is very close to
that of William Cookworthy's mark on Plymouth
porcelain (1768-70), in that it looks like the combined numerals "2" and "4", the alchemist's
symbol for tin.

William Marshall, St. Ives, Cornwall, UK
William Marshall worked in the pottery of
Bernard Leach from 1954 on. His incised device
involves a series of four connected diagonal crosses
flanked by dots. His mark should be accompanied
by the official Leach pottery mark. Two examples
appear here.

Padua, Italy
The manufacture of lead-glazed pottery and
maiolica has been recorded from the 15thC. In the
former category are *sgraffiato* wares echoing the
technique of Chinese Cizhou type of stonewares
of the Song and Yuan dynasties. Also of note are
the17thC maiolica dishes and wares based on
Isnik pottery. The painted mark shown is a rare
but typical example.

Carlo Norway, London, UK
Studio-type pottery and ceramic sculptures and
figures were produced 1920-35. This incised key-
like cross mark was used.

Worcester Porcelains, Hereford and Worcester, UK
See p.23. Dr. John Wall established the factory ar
Worcester in 1751, utilizing the tools, material and
craftsmen from the Lund's factory in Bristol.
These underglaze blue marks illustrated here
were used by decorators during the early years of
the Worcester factory, and date from between
1751 and c.1765. Similar marks are found on other
early porcelains.

Casa Pirota, Faenza, Emilia, Italy

See p.166. The marks seen here are typical of those found on Faentine maiolica in the first half of the 16thC, although they may well have been used elsewhere. Marks are generally painted in dark, high-fired colours. These marks have been attributed to the so-called "Casa Pirota" workshop whose existence is now in doubt.

Prinknash Benedictines, Prinknash Abbey, Gloucestershire, UK

Earthenwares were made here from 1945. This printed or impressed mark appears.

Arrows

Pinxton Works, Derbyshire, UK

See p.128. Although factory marks are rare on Pinxton wares, some do appear, including the arrow shaped marks illustrated.

Bow China Works, Stratford, London, UK

See p.21. The incised marks shown here are from the early period of the factory c.1750. An incised anchor mark has also been recorded, but this is very rare.

St Petersburg, Russia

See p.29. The Russian Imperial factory was founded in 1744 to produce hard-paste porcelain for the court. The early period up to c.1765 was strongly influenced by Meissen and after this date by Sèvres and Paris porcelain. Among the more successful lines was the series of Russian peasants modelled at the turn of the 18thC. The incised or impressed mark of the arrow and circle was sometimes used.

Thomas Plowman, Stalham, Norfolk, UK

Thomas Plowman founded the Clay Brook Pottery in 1958 and produced Studio-type wares. This impressed mark was used.

Minton, Stoke, Staffordshire, UK

See p.164. The arrow and dots mark (above) appeared on early parian ware figures made by Minton c.1845-50. The painted "ermine" mark (below) indicates a special soft glaze. This mark, which may appear with or without the letter "M", was occasionally used as the factory mark during the 1850s.

Pouyat, Russinger, Russinger-Pouyat,
Rue de la Roquette, Paris, France

The crossed arrows were used by the above
concerns in their Paris factories, probably from
the late 18th and first half of the 19thC, on hard-
paste porcelains. The marks are usually painted
in underglaze blue. Similar marks of crossed
arrows, crossed tridents or even torches were
used in Paris from c.1770–c.1840 by a number of
concerns at La Courtille, rue Fontaine-au-Roy
(or Basse Courtille), and faubourg du Temple.

Porzellanfabrik Kalk, Eisenberg, Thuringia, Germany

These manufacturers of hard-paste porcelain
from 1899 used a number of variations of this
printed mark. They produced patterned coffee
and tablewares.

Ernst Teichert, Meissen, Saxony, Germany

Ernst Teichert manufactured general pottery,
much transfer-printed in blue, with Meissen-style
designs from 1884 onwards. The word "Meissen"
usually appears in the marks. These wares should
not be confused with the hard-paste porcelain
produced at the original Meissen factory, whose
pieces were never marked with the word
"Meissen".

Denver China and Pottery Company, Denver,
Colorado, USA

See p.44. This mark was also used. Marks usually
feature the name "Denver".

Henry Mills, Hanley, Staffordshire, UK

A manufacturer of earthenware from c.1892,
Henry Mills used this printed mark.

Ridgways, Shelton, Hanley, Staffordshire, UK

See p.202. The printed trademark (above) was
registered in 1880. Later versions feature the
words "Stoke-on-Trent". A later version appears
after c.1912 (below).

Birds

Derlwyn Pottery, Betws-y-Coed, Gwynedd, Wales, UK

Studio-type pottery was made by Ms Campion
and Ms Pritchard at the Derlwyn Pottery from
1959, with this incised or painted swallow mark,
the place name, and often with the initial of the
potter.

Van der Straeten, Linton, Nr. Cambridge, UK
This pottery produced individual Studio-type earthenwares from 1948, with this printed or impressed mark.

Cybis Porcelains, Trenton, New Jersey, USA
This company (active 1942-present), was founded by Polish artist Boleslaw Cybis. From 1942-49 tea and coffee pots moulded with porcelain lace, ribbons and flowers. Other elborately-decorated wares were made up until c.1953. The company also produced elaborate figurines that are brightly coloured and have a bisque finish. Their early work was religious in nature, but their current production is more fanciful, including storybook characters, circus subjects and famous women. These marks appear.

Elenor Whittall, London, UK
This potter made Studio-type stonewares from 1944 (and porcelains from 1958). She used this impressed owl device that was originally made up from the initials "E. E. W."

George Wade & Son Ltd., Burslem, Staffordshire, UK
Based at the Manchester Pottery from 1922, this firm made earthenwares. This printed owl trademark was used from c.1947.

Carlton Ware Ltd., Stoke, Staffordshire, UK
See p.106. This style of mark was used by both Wiltshaw & Robinson (1890-1957) and Carlton Ware Ltd. (from 1957).

New England Pottery Company, East Boston, Massachusetts, USA
See p.182. This mark was among those used by this firm.

Crooksville China Company, Crooksville, Ohio, USA
The company (active 1902-late 1950s) made dinnerware, toilet sets and kitchen ware decorated with quaint decals. The kitchenware, called "Pantry Bak-in Ware", was popular. Their best dinnerware line was called Stinthal China, which appears without any Crooksville designation.

Toni Raymond Pottery, Torquay, Devon, UK
This pottery made earthenwares, tablewares and figures from 1961. The pottery is known for its floral-decorated, storage jars. This impressed or printed mark was used.

Watcombe Pottery Co., St Mary Church, Devon, UK

Earthenwares, terracotta, ornamental wares, busts, figures and other items were produced by this firm c.1867-1901. Founded by G. T. Allen, the original company was formed to sell terracotta clay found on his property. Subsequently a pottery was established to produce pots using the clay. Many decorative wares were produced which are similar to Wedgwood's jasper ware; busts and ornamental items were also made. Notable are vases made in various styles with floral decoration which is either pressed, printed or painted. Other items include services, medallions, ewers, candlesticks and flower stands. As well as an impressed name mark, this printed mark featuring a woodpecker was used 1875-1901.

John Fisher, Rowlands Gill, Tyne and Wear, UK

Studio-type pottery was made here from 1950. This is the personal mark of John Fisher which appears from 1950; Fisher also used an incised or painted monogram mark.

OXSHOTT

Oxshott Pottery, Oxshott, Surrey, UK

This wren seal mark was used by Rosemary Wren at the Oxshott Pottery from 1945. The word "Oxshott" appears underneath the mark from 1950.

Swan Hill Pottery, South Amboy, New Jersey, USA

Several owners and a number of potters operated this pottery (1849-89) making earthenware, Rockingham, yellow ware and some white ware for table, kitchen and toilet purposes. Charles Fish owned the pottery for the longest single period; the potters included James Carr, Thomas Locker, Charles Coxon, John L. Rue, and others. The business was reorganized in 1889 as the South Amboy Pottery Company, which made, bought and sold pottery. This raised mark was used.

Arnhem, Holland

Faience was produced here from 1755-73. This mark was used.

ITALIA

Ulysse Cantagalli, Florence, Tuscany, Italy

From 1878 Cantagalli (d.1901) made maiolica reproductions of early Urbino, Faenza, Gubbio, Deruta and della Robbia wares. The mark is a cockerel that appears in various forms, such as the examples seen here. This mark may also appear in a very abstract form.

E. Brain & Co. Ltd., Fenton, Staffordshire, UK
Based at the Foley China Works, this company
produced porcelain 1903-63. This printed mark
appears c.1905. The name "Foley China" was used
in many different marks.

The Hague, Holland
Hard-paste porcelain was made at this factory
founded in 1775, and directed by Anton Leichner
from Vienna until his death in 1781. The factory
continued until 1790. Notable wares feature floral
decoration and monochrome purple designs.
Marks including those shown here were used,
based on the city coat of arms.

Rozenburg, Holland
Active 1883-1916, the Rozenburg Pottery initially
concentrated on simple earthenwares. However,
in the late 1880s and 1890s, the firm led a revival
of Dutch ceramics, and its eggshell earthenware is
now regarded as some of the finest ever made.
Wares were influenced by both Art Nouveau and
Japanese art. The mark seen here was used before
1900; after this date it appears beneath a crown.

Holkham Pottery Ltd., Holkham, Norfolk, UK
Formerly Holkham Studio Pottery (1951-61), this
pottery produced earthenwares from 1961. This
printed or impressed mark was used by both
firms.

Parrott & Co. (Ltd.), Burslem, Staffordshire, UK
Operating from c.1921, this firm made earthenwares at the Albert Street Pottery. This parrot
mark was registered in 1921, with a slightly
different mark appearing after c.1935.

Herculaneum Pottery, Liverpool, Mersey, UK
See p.200. Printed or impressed Liver bird marks
were used by the Herculaneum Pottery in various
forms c.1833-36.

Samuel Barker & Son, Swinton, Yorkshire, UK
Based at the Don Pottery which was purchased by
Samuel Barker in 1834. The company became
known as Samuel Barker & Son in 1851 and
continued until 1893. Fine earthenwares were
made, and pattern books record designs for wares
such as tureens, vegetable dishes, dishes, plates
and all types of other wares. Creamware, caneware, redware and porcelain were also produced.
This rare mark appears c.1850.

Berlin, Prussia, Germany
See p.27. This blue-printed factory mark was used
at Berlin 1844-47, with a similar mark appearing
1849-70.

Chesapeake Pottery/D. F. Haynes and Son,
Baltimore, Maryland, USA
See p.205. A number of marks were used
featuring a monogram, initials ("C. C. P". stood
for "Chesapeake Pottery"; "H. B. H." stood for
"Haynes & Bennett"), or the company name.

William Adams & Sons (Potters) Ltd., Tunstall
and Stoke, Staffordshire, UK
See p.194. This mark appears on blue printed
earthenwares 1804-40.

William Henry Goss (Ltd.), Stoke, Staffordshire, UK
From 1858 Willam Henry Goss produced parian,
porcelain and terracotta. He specialized in ornaments made from jewelled porcelain, such as
scent bottles and items of jewellery including
brooches. Parian wares include busts and statues.
Fine porcelain wares were also made. This printed
mark was used from c.1862 with "England"
added from 1891. The company was taken over by
Cauldon Potteries Ltd. in c.1934 and retitled Goss
China Ltd.

F. Grosvenor (& Son), Glasgow, Scotland, UK
From c.1869-1926 this firm made stonewares and
earthenwares. This printed eagle trademark was
registered by Frederick Grosvenor in 1879 and
was used until 1926.

Enoch Wood & Sons, Burslem, Staffordshire, UK
Originally established as Enoch Wood, who had
been an apprentice under Wedgwood c.1784, this
pottery operated from the Fountain Works and
other addresses in Burslem. A talented modeller,
Wood conducted a partnership with James
Cauldwell 1795-1818, before the title of the firm
changed again to Enoch Wood & Sons and
continued until 1846. Fine earthenwares of all
types were made. Impressed marks such as this
were used 1818-46.

Coxon and Company, Empire Pottery, Trenton,
New Jersey, USA
Charles Coxon and J. F. Thompson established
this pottery (active 1863-84) to make cream-
coloured ware and white granite. Coxon died in

1868, but the pottery continued under the
direction of his widow and four sons. They made
souvenirs for the 1876 Centennial Exhibition. In
1884, the company was sold to Alpaugh and
Magowan (see p.270).

Goodwin Pottery/Goodwin Brothers, East Liverpool, Ohio, USA

The Goodwin family had several potteries in
East Liverpool and Trenton, New Jersey,
beginning as early as 1844. This pottery (1876-
1912) was organized to make whiteware, which
they produced in several variations, including
pearl-white, cream-coloured, ironstone and semi-
porcelain; some was decorated.

Thomas Lawrence (Longton) Ltd., Longton, Staffordshire, UK

Based at the Falcon Works (1897-1957) and the
Sylvan Works (from 1957), this company made
earthenwares from 1892. This mark appears from
1944. Others featuring the name Falcon Ware
were also used.

Animals

J. Leofold, Paris, France

This modern porcelain manufacturer uses this
mark.

Fürstenberg, Brunswick, Germany

See p.25. This mark of a small jumping horse was
impressed or incised on busts and reliefs at the end
of the 18thC. A letter may appear under the mark
and refers to the modeller.

Cassel, Hesse-Nassau, Germany

See p.81. Porcelain was made at the faience factory
at Cassel 1766-88 with the mark (above). Note the
double tail on this Hessian lion. Earthenwares
were produced 1771-1862 with the impressed
mark (below).

Frankenthal, Palatinate, Germany

See p.58. This lion mark from the arms of the
Palatinate was used at Frankenthal c.1756-59.

Hudson & Middleton, Longton, Staffordshire, UK

See p.178. This mark was formerly used by W.
Hudson (from c.1936), and was continued by
Hudson & Middleton.

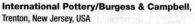

International Pottery/Burgess & Campbell, Trenton, New Jersey, USA
See p.213. This mark was among those used by this firm.

Pickard China, Chicago and Antioch, Illinois, USA
Founded by Wilder Pickard as a ceramic-decorating studio in 1894, the company had a reputation for fine hand-painted and elaborate gold-etch decorations. In 1930 they began to experiment with making their own wares, which they introduced to the market in 1938. Today Pickard makes chinaware for the U.S. embassies around the world.

Wade, Heath & Co. (Ltd.), Burslem, Staffordshire, UK
Based at the High Street Works (1927-38) and the Royal Victoria Pottery (fom 1938), this firm (formerly Wade & Co. 1887-1927) made earthen-wares. This is one of the marks used and appears from c.1927. A similar mark with the words "Wade Heath" above the lion was used from c.1934.

Homer Laughlin China Company, East Liverpool, Ohio, and Newell, West Virginia, USA
See p.81. This mark was among those used. A wide variety of marks appear; most incorporate the name of the company.

(W.) Baker & Co. (Ltd.), Fenton, Staffordshire, UK
See p.213. This mark was used c.1928-30. A number of different marks was used, most ofthem incorporate the company name.

Paul Revere Pottery/Saturday Evening Girls, Boston and Brighton, Massachusetts, USA
See p.58. This mark, an incised impression of Paul Revere on a horse, was one of those used by this group. The mark appears with a dark background as here, and also with a light background.

George Hobson, Burslem, Staffordshire, UK
Formerly Charles Hobson (1865-80), and G. & J. Hobson (1883-1901), this firm produced earthenwares 1901-23. Operating at the Albert Pottery (later the Sneyd Pottery), the firm produced services and other items in many types of earthenware. This printed or impressed mark was used 1901-23.

Edward Marshall Boehm, Inc., Trenton, New Jersey, USA

This company (active 1950-present) specializes in elaborate porcelain figures of birds, animals and flowers, some of the larger pieces being used as gifts of state by the President of the United States. Boehm was one of the world's most renowned sculptors and a keen conservationalist, and this interest is reflected in his work. Boehm died in 1969, and since then his wife has expanded the business. These are some of the marks that appear. Most marks feature a horse's head, together with the name of the firm.

E. Hughes & Co., Fenton, Staffordshire, UK

See p.168. This printed mark was used from c.1908-12. A globe device was used on wares produced after c.1912.

Thomas Hughes & Son Ltd., Burslem, Staffordshire, UK

Thomas Hughes took over this firm, originally established by his grandfather, in 1895. The business was first based at the Waterloo Road Works (c.1860-76), then at the Top Bridge Works (c.1872-94), before being transferred to the Unicorn Pottery in 1895. A unicorn mark was used from 1930, with this version appearing 1935-37. The firm continued until 1957.

Hollinshead & Kirkham (Ltd.), Tunstall, Staffordshire, UK

See p.179. This printed mark was used on earthenwares 1900-24.

Taylor & Kent (Ltd.), Longton, Staffordshire, UK

See p.152. One of the principal printed marks, this example appears from c.1939. The firm's initials or the company name appear on their marks.

Wedgwood & Co. (Ltd.), Tunstall, Staffordshire, UK

See p.206. The printed trademark (top) was used; the words "trade mark" indicate a date after the Act of 1862. The mark (centre) is a new version of the earlier unicorn mark, and was used from c.1908. The mark (below) appears from c.1956. The company name usually appears on marks used by Wedgwood & Co. Occasionally only the tradename or pattern name appears with the mark, such as "Wacol" or "Wacolware" or "Royal Tunstall". These tradenames appear on wares made after c.1950.

William Adams & Sons (Potters) Ltd., Tunstall and Stoke, Staffordshire, UK
See p.194. This printed mark was first introduced in 1879. The word "England" was added after 1891.

George Wade & Son Ltd., Burslem, Staffordshire, UK
See p.235. This mark was used on earthenwares from c.1936.

Donald Brindley Potttery Ltd., Longton, Staffordshire, UK
Based at Chelston Street, this pottery produced earthenware figures and other items from 1961. This printed or impressed mark appears.

Buffalo Pottery Company/Buffalo China Inc., Buffalo, New York, USA
Founded by the Larkin Soap Company in 1901 to make tableware for the company's premium-purchase plan, which supplied porcelain in exchange for purchase certificates collected by the consumer, the firm made a wide variety of transfer-printed and decal decorated earthenware including a line called "Deldare", decorated with traditional English scenes, printed and filled on a contrasting background. Today's production is largely for the food service industry. These marks appear.

A. Lamm, Dresden, Germany
This porcelain decorating studio was founded in 1887. As well as the Meissen style, pieces were decorated in the style of Copenhagen. The studio produced very high quality painting.

Franz Junkersdorf, Dresden, Germany
See p.214. This mark appears on porcelains made by this firm in the style of Dresden, Meissen and Vienna.

Alfred (and Isaac) Baguley, Swinton, Yorkshire, UK
Isaac Baguley (formerly employed at the Derby China Works) took over part of the discontinued Rockingham Works in c.1842, where he decorated white wares which he then sold. After his death in c.1855, the business was carried on by his son Alfred at the Rockingham Works until 1865, and then at Mexborough c.1865-91. Among other techniques, the Baguley's used chocolate or bown, Rockingham-style glazes on services, tea and

coffee pots, drinking horns and jugs. White stonewares, cane-coloured wares, and green-glazed earthenwares were also made. This printed mark appears 1842-65; the wording may vary.

Rockingham Works, Swinton, Yorkshire, UK
The Rockingham Works were established c.1745, and continued under various owners until 1842. Thomas Bingley was the principal proprietor in 1778, with John and William Brameld as his partners. At this time good quality brown, yellow, white, and blue and white wares were produced. From 1787-1800 a type of brown or Rockingham ware was made. The body was covered in a characteristic streaky brown glaze. This style was copied extensively by many other manufacturers. In 1813, the sons of John and William Brameld took over the firm, and increased the quality of the production and the range of wares produced. Due to financial difficulties the Works closed in 1842. The griffin mark in red, was used when porcelain was introduced c.1826-30 (top); on some rare examples the crest appears with no wording. Later versions of the griffin mark after 1830 (centre), were printed in puce with the words "Royal Rock(ingham) Works", and/or "China Manufacturers to the King" c.1830-42. Rare examples of the mark (below) appear with "China Manufacturers to the Queen"; these were probably decorated by Alfred Baguley after 1842.

Bwthyn Pottery, Barmouth, Wales, UK
This pottery, situated on the coast in north-west Wales, produced Studio-type wares from 1956. This mark was used, and may appear printed or impressed.

H. M. Williamson & Sons, Longton, Staffordshire, UK
Based at the Bridge Pottery, this firm produced porcelain c.1879-1941. Many marks were used, including this one from c.1908.

Onondaga Pottery, Syracuse, New York, USA
See p.158. Several different marks were used by this firm; most feature the name "Syracuse China".

Vodrey Pottery Company, East Liverpool, Ohio, USA
See p.70. This is one of the many marks used by this firm. It appears in a number of forms, and may feature the words "Semi-porcelain" rather than "Vodrey China".

Roblin Pottery, San Francisco, California, USA
Linna Irelan worked with Alexander W.
Robertson to create exquisite small vases 1898-
1906. He threw the pots, and she decorated them
with a variety of matt and coloured finishes. The
mark below includes the figure of a bear, the
symbol for California. An incised spider and web
mark may also be found. The pottery was
destroyed in the San Francisco great earthquake
and fire of 1906.

Lavender Groves, Chelsea, London, UK
See p.116. This incised or painted mark appears
from 1952.

Barker Pottery Co., Chesterfield, Derbyshire, UK
Operating between 1887 and 1957, this pottery
produced stonewares. This mark was used
1928-57.

Belleek Pottery, Co. Fermanagh, Northern Ireland, UK
The Belleek Works were established in 1863 by
David McBirney and Robert Williams
Armstrong. High quality, ultra-thin porcelain
was produced. Notable are ornamental items in
marine-type forms were made, with iridescent
glazes. Services and wares of all types were also
produced. Also made was parian, ordinary white
china and white graniteware. The standard trade
mark (above) was used from 1863-91. The second
version (below), with the addition of "Co.
Fermanagh" and "Ireland", is still used.

S. W. Dean, Burslem, Staffordshire, UK
This firm produced earthenwares at the Newport
Pottery 1904-10, before becoming Deans (1910)
Ltd. (1910-19). This mark was used 1904-10.
Other marks occur with the firm's title in full.

Arij de Milde, Delft, Holland
Red stoneware was produced at Delft from c.1675
to the 18thC. Arij de Milde was active in Delft
1680-1708. This was one of the marks used.

T. & R. Boote (Ltd.), Burslem, Staffordshire, UK
See p.212. This printed mark was used 1890-1906.
Other marks usually incorporate the company
name or initials.

William Bailey & Sons, Longton, Staffordshire, UK
Earthenwares were made by this firm at the
Gordon Pottery 1912-14 with this printed mark.

New Devon Pottery Ltd., Newton Abbot, Devon, UK
This pottery on the south coast of Devon
produced earthenwares from 1957 with this
printed mark.

Chelsea Keramic Art Works/Dedham Pottery,
Chelsea and Dedham, Massachusetts, USA
See p.44. These marks were used by the Dedham
Pottery. Their rabbit pattern tablewares (designed
by Joseph Linden Smith) became one of their best-
known styles and was adopted as a trademark.
The word "Registered" may appear under the
mark below.

Mousehole Pottery, Mousehole, Cornwall, UK
Studio-type pottery was produced by Mr. & Mrs.
Picard from 1953. This impressed seal or printed
mark appears from 1953.

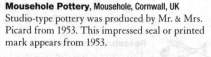

John Tams (& Son) (Ltd.), Longton, Staffordshire, UK
From 1875 John Tams manufactured the usual
types of earthenwares at the Crown Pottery,
specializing in the production of government
measures, jugs and mugs. This mark was used
from c.1952.

Robinson & Leadbeater (Ltd.), Stoke,
Staffordshire, UK
This firm produced high quality parian at a
number of works in Stoke 1864-1924. The firm
made figures, groups, busts, centrepieces, caskets,
flower holders, jugs and other items. This printed
mark appears c.1905-24.

Cromer Pottery, Aylmerton, Nr. Norwich, Norfolk, UK
Earthenwares were produced by this pottery
owned by Rosemary Middleton, from 1952. This
impressed crab mark was used.

Cincinnati Art Pottery, Cincinnati, Ohio, USA
See p.42. Marks are usually impressed, but
decorator's monograms may also appear and these
are generally incised.

W. T. Copeland (& Sons Ltd.), Stoke,
Staffordshire, UK
Formerly Spode (c.1784-1833) and Copeland &
Garrett (1833-47), this firm has operated since
1847. Porcelain, parian and earthenwares of all
types were produced with many different types of
decoration. Many innovations were made,
including the development of an "Ivory body".

Decorative tiles were also produced. Several
marks were used; this example appears on
earthenwares 1867-90.

Fish

Nyon, Nr. Geneva, Switzerland
See p.180. Although the form of the Nyon mark
does vary, these are typical examples. The mark
appears in underglaze blue.

Adolf Hamman, Dresden, Germany
This porcelain-decorating studio began in 1866.
Pieces were decorated in the Dresden, Meissen
and Viennese styles. This mark was used.

Pescetto, Savona, Liguria, Italy
This potter was active in Savona in the late 17thC,
and marked his pieces with a device such as this
one.

Lille, France
A soft-paste porcelain factory existed here during
the first half of the 18thC. In 1784 Leperre-Durot,
under the protection of the Dauphin, founded a
hard-paste porcelain factory. The factory was
called "Manufacture Royale de Monseigneur le
Dauphin" and the dolphin was used as the mark.
Wares were made in the Parisian style. Production
continued until 1817.

Dennis Edward Lucas, Hastings, East Sussex, UK
This potter made Studio-type wares in Hastings
from 1956. This incised mark was used from 1956;
the words "Hastings Pottery" may be added on
wares from 1963.

Merrimac Ceramic Company/Merrimac Pottery Company, Newburyport, Massachusetts, USA
T. S. Nickerson founded Merrimac Ceramic
Company in 1897 to make drainage pipe, florists'
crockery and tiles. In 1902, when the business was
reorganized as Merrimac Pottery, he made
domestic ornamental wares and then decorative
garden pottery. The ornamental wares were
covered with dark dull or metallic glazes of
several different colors. The most famous line
was Etruscan, which copied moulded Roman
Arretine ware seen in the Museum of Fine Arts,
Boston. The factory continued until 1908. These
marks were used.

Carter, Stabler & Adams (Ltd.), Poole, Dorset, UK
See p.106. After 1921, Carter & Co. became Carter,
Stabler & Adams (Ltd.), better known as the
famous Poole Pottery. The firm was retitled Poole
Pottery Ltd. from February 1963. Many printed
marks in the style of this example, appear from
1950-51; the redrawn version seen here was used
from 1956. Another version appears on oven
tablewares produced from c.1961. A more
conventional-style dolphin appears as a special
printed mark on individual "Studio"-type wares
from 1963.

Plants, flowers & trees

De Roos, Delft, Holland
See p.33. The marks (above and centre) were
among those used by this factory (The Rose),
during the early 18thC. The mark (below) was
registered by proprietor Dirck Van der Does in
1764. Van der Does continued as proprietor until
1779, when the factory was run by Hendrick
Janszoon.

Coalport Porcelain Works, Coalport, Shropshire, UK
See p.72. Early wares are mostly unmarked, but
this mark is one of those found on pieces from the
early period c.1805-15.

William De Morgan, London, UK
See p.110. This Sands End address mark appears
on wares produced after 1888 when the factory
relocated to Fulham.

Shaw & Copestake, Longton, Staffordshire, UK
Earthenwares were produced by this firm 1901-
82. Early wares were probably unmarked. This
mark appears c.1925-36.

Adderley Floral China, Longton, Staffordshire, UK
A branch of Ridgway Potteries Ltd., that
continued to operate under this title, this pottery
was founded in 1945, and produced bone china
figures and ornaments. This printed mark was
used from 1945.

Dresden Floral Porcelain Co. Ltd., Longton,
Staffordshire, UK
Between 1945 and 1956 this firm produced
porcelain figures and floral wares with this
printed mark.

Grueby Faience Company/Grueby Pottery/Grueby Faience and Tile Company, Boston, Massachusetts, USA

Founded to make glazed brick and architectural tile in 1894, the company added an art pottery line during the late 1890s, producing vases with low-relief floral decoration made with rolled fillets of clay, and covered with a medium green flowing matt glaze that was sometimes accented with yellow, ochre, rose or white. The art pottery was discontinued in 1910, but tiles were made until 1920, when the firm was purchased by the C. Pardee Works of Perth Amboy, New Jersey. Thisi characteristic marks was used, together with other name marks.

Doulton & Co. (Ltd.), Lambeth, London, UK
See p.111. This printed or impressed mark was used on Persian-style wares made by Doulton c.1920-28.

Lorenz Reichel, Schirnding, Bavaria, Germany
See p.212. This mark is among those used on the porcelain utility services made at this factory from 1902. The name "Schirnding" or "Sch" also appears.

Empire Porcelain Co. Ltd., Stoke, Staffordshire, UK
See p.198. This printed or impressed mark was used during the late 1940s and 1950s, and usually include month and year numbers and the date of manufacture.

Britannia China Company, Longton, Staffordshire, UK
See p.69. This printed mark was used on porcelains 1900-04. Other fully-named marks were used 1904-06.

Crown China Crafts Ltd., Stoke, Staffordshire, UK
Porcelain and earthenware floral wares were made by this firm at the Crown Works 1946-58. This printed mark was used. The full name of the firm appears.

Selb-Plössberg, Bavaria, Germany
The porcelain factory at Selb-Plössberg (formerly Selb-Bahnhof) was founded by Rosenthal of Selb in 1867. Output included table and coffee services, vases, bowls, figures, lamps, candelabra and table decorations. This mark was used.

Co-operative Wholesale Society Ltd., Longton, Staffordshire, UK
See p.214. This printed mark was one of those used in the 1950s and early 1960s.

Longton Pottery Co. Ltd., Longton, Staffordshire, UK
Earthenwares were made by this firm at the Bluebell Works 1946-55. This printed mark is typical of those used.

New Jersey Pottery Company, Trenton, New Jersey, USA
This pottery (active 1869-83) made cream-coloured white graniteware, plain and decorated. During the 1880 Presidential campaign, they made ｜ :s with portraits of the candidates. In 1883, the name was changed to the Union Pottery.

Pope-Gosser China Company, Coshocton, Ohio, USA
Organized by C. F. Gosser from 1902, the company first made an ornamental line in a high quality tranmslucent, highly vtrified body, but quickly changed to another form of tableware with decal decoration as its mainstay. One of the most popular patterns, made from 1935, was "Rosepoint". During its early years the company won a couple of awards at world's fairs. It became part of American China Corp, a cooperative alliance of eight companies that dissolved in 1932. Unlike most other members, which simply went out of business, Pope-Gosser reorganized and continued in operation afterwards until 1958. Marks used feature the company name.

Taylor, Smith and Taylor, East Liverpool, Ohio (with a plant in Chester, West Virginia), USA
See p.95. This mark was among the many used by this firm.

J. Dimmock & Co., Hanley, Staffordshire, UK
See p.196. This printed mark was one of those used c.1878-1904.

Thomas Till & Son(s), Burslem, Staffordshire, UK
Formerly Barker, Sutton & Till (1834-43), this firm produced earthenwares at the Stych Pottery c.1850-1928. Good quality earthenware services and other useful items were made with coloured bodies. They also made stoneware, jet glazed ware, terracotta, and enamelled and lustrewares. This mark was one of those used c.1861.

Wedgwood & Co. (Ltd.), Tunstall, Staffordshire, UK
See p.206. "Asiatic Pheasants" was one of
Wedgwood & Co.'s most successful ordinary
printed designs and was extensively copied by
other manufacturers. This mark appears from
c.1925.

Grossbreitenbach, Thuringia, Germany
A factory was founded here in 1778 by Anton
Friedrich Wilhelm Ernst von Hopfgarten. He
sold the concern to Gotthelf Greiner, the owner of
the Limbach porcelain factory in 1882. Porcelain
decorated with underglaze blue was made. This
clover-leaf mark was used from 1778, but after
1788 it was also used by Limbach and Ilmenau.
Pieces bearing this mark that were produced
after 1788, cannot attributed with certainty to
Grossbreitenbach.

Ilmenau, Thuringia, Germany
See p.169. This mark has been attributed to
Ilmenau while the factory was leased to Gotthelf
Greiner 1788-92.

Sevenoaks Pottery Ltd., Sevenoaks, Kent
Owned by Gordon Plahn (see p.92), this pottery
operated between 1958 and 1961 producing
Studio-type wares. This impressed seal-type mark
was used.

Karlsbader Kaolin-Industry-Gesellschaft,
Merkelsgrün, Bohemia, Czech Republic
Originally founded in 1871, this company began
in 1881, at first producing utulity ware, and later
electro-porcelain. This mark is one of those used.
Others also feature the clover leaf.

Carrigaline Pottery Ltd., Carrigaline, Co. Cork, Eire
Earthenwares are produced by this firm that was
founded in 1928. This mark appears.

A. Bourne Claverdon, London, UK
Operated by Alice Buxton Winnicott, this pottery
operated c.1947-50 making Studio-type wares.
This impressed or printed mark was used.

Wade (Ulster) Ltd., Portadown, Co. Armagh,
Northern Ireland, UK
See p.182. Many marks featuring the clover were
used by this firm, including this one that appears
on die-pressed wares c.1955. The letter below is
the potter's mark.

Cook Pottery Company, Trenton, New Jersey, USA
See p.208. "Mellor & Co." was often incorporated into this company's marks, because F. G. Mellor was one of the original founders.

Robert Stewart (Robert Stewart Ceramics Ltd.), Paisley, Strathclyde, Scotland, UK
From 1960 this firm made earthenwares such as covered jars. This mark appears.

J. Glatz, Villingen, Baden, Germany
This firm produced "Majolika" wares from 1870. This mark was used.

Beddgelert Pottery, Beddgelert, Wales, UK
Operated by Mrs A. Davey and Mrs P. Hancock, this pottery was established in 1962, producing Studio-type earthenwares. This mark was used.

Ashtead Potters Ltd., Ashtead, Surrey, UK
Earthenwares were produced by this firm 1926-36 at the Victoria Works in Ashstead, with this printed mark.

Arequipa Potteries, Fairfax, California, USA
A pottery was started in 1911 by tuberculosis patients recuperating in this northern California village, who produced ware under the direction of Frederick Hurten Rhead. A worker made the pots and the tubercular women decorated them. Albert L. Solon replaced Rhead in 1913. The product was almost entirely ornamental, with output consisting primarily of vases, covered jars, jardinières and tiles, in a variety of finishes, some of which were very high quality. The factory closed c.1918.

Orange Tree Pottery, Rainton Gate, Noth Yorkshire, UK
Studio-type wares were made by this company (owned by Mrs. Alethea Short) from 1952, with this impressed or printed mark.

G. L. Ashworth & Bros. (Ltd.), Hanley, Staffordshire, UK
See p.194. This printed mark was used on Mason's Patent Ironstone China from 1957 onwards.

Hewitt & Leadbeater, Longton, Staffordshire, UK
Based at the Willow Pottery, this firm produced porcelain and parian 1907-19. The company became Hewitt Brothers in 1919 and continued until c.1926. This printed mark was used 1907-26.

Campbellfield Pottery Co. (Ltd.), Springburn, Glasgow, Scotland, UK

This firm was established at 60 Rochester St. in the 1870s, and from c.1884 was moved to Flemington St. in Springburn. Earthenwares were made until 1905. A thistle mark was used in various forms; the printed example seen here appears c.1884-1905.

A. W. Buchan & Co. (Ltd.), Portobello, Nr. Edinburgh, Scotland, UK

The Portobello Pottery was established in 1770. They were carried on by Murray & Buchan from 1867 and by A.W. Buchan & Co, from c.1877. Stonewares were produced, with output including bottles, jars, jugs, spirit bottles and other items. From 1949 the printed trade name of the firm was a thistle as seen here.

Robert Heron (& Son), Sinclairstown, Strathclyde, Scotland, UK

This firm was located at the Gallatown Pottery from 1850, with the address changing to the Fife Pottery from 1884. They produced earthenwares, Rockingham ware and "Wemyss" ware. This printed mark appears 1920-29.

J. E. Heath Ltd., Burslem, Staffordshire, UK

Earthenwares such as hotel wares were made by this firm at the Albert Potteries from 1951. This printed mark was one of those used.

Western Stoneware Company, Monmouth, Illinois, USA

The Western Stoneware Company was an extremely large firm created by the merger of many successful stoneware potteries in the Midwest from 1906. The Monmouth Pottery Co., Weir Pottery Co., Macomb Stoneware Co., Macomb Pottery, Whitehall Pottery Co., Fort Dodge Pottery Co., and the Clinton Pottery all combined to produce utilitarian stoneware, both white Bristol and Albany slip-glazed. Their mark is most frequently found on crocks, jugs, and preserve jars. The maple leaf appears in a number of marks used by the firm; this may feature the name of the firm, or "Monmouth, USA".

Fine Arts Porcelain Ltd., Charlton, London, UK

Between 1948 and 1952 this company, based in south-east London, made earthenwares with this printed mark.

Buildings

Tournai, Belgium
See p.221. This early mark was used at the porcelain factory 1751-96 and may appear in blue, gold, crimson or other colours.

La Tour d'Aigues, Vaucluse, France
Baron de Bruni established a faience factory in La Tour d'Aigues in the mid-18thC. Bruni made an application to produce porcelain in 1773. This marks apppears on a faience dish with the words "fait à la Tours Daigues".

Edward Bingham, Castle Hedingham, Essex, UK
Edward W. Bingham established his pottery in 1864, and together with his family produced earthenwares decorated with applied relief motifs and coloured glazes. As well as English wares, the pottery also made copies of German stoneware, Palissy ware, and Greek and Roman pottery. In 1899 the pottery passed to his son who sold the business in 1901. After this date the company became Essex Art Pottery. This applied castle mark above a scroll was used 1864-1901.

John Maddock & Sons (Ltd.), Burslem, Staffordshire, UK
Originally established in c.1830 and known under a number of titles, John Maddock & Sons (Ltd.) produced earthenwares and ironstone from 1855. This mark was used before 1855.

C. T. Maling & Sons (Ltd.), Newcastle-upon-Tyne, Tyne and Wear, UK
See p.165. This printed mark and other variations were used 1890-1963.

New Hall Pottery Co. Ltd., Hanley, Staffordshire, UK
Formerly Plant & Gilmore, this firm based at the New Hall Works made earthenwares 1899-1956. This printed mark was used c.1930-51. Between 1951 and 1956 a similar mark appears, printed in black on a white ground.

Old Hall Earthenware Co. Ltd., Hanley, Staffordshire, UK
Based at the Old Hall Works in Hanley, which was built in 1770. Job Meigh started a business there that was subsequently operated by his son and his grandson (Charles Meigh). In 1861 the company became known as the Old Earthenware

Company Ltd., and after 1886 as the Old Hall
Porcelain Co. Ltd. All types of earthenware, as
well as stoneware, jet ware and parian. Output
comprised services of all kinds, in particular toilet
services, water bottles, tea kettles, spill vases,
figures, busts and other ornaments. This printed
trademark was registered in 1884, and was
continued by the Old Hall Porcelain Co. Ltd. after
1886. The word "England" was added between
c.1891 and c.1902, when the factory closed.

Sibley Pottery (Ltd.), Wareham, Dorset, UK
This pottery produced earthenwares and stonewares 1922-62. This impressed mark was used
1946-53.

Slack & Brownlow, Tonbridge, Kent, UK
Operating between c.1928 and 1934, this company
produced ornamental earthenwares with this
printed or impressed mark.

J. Green & Co. (or & Sons), London, UK
A London-based retailers. Porcelains distributed
by this firm 1834-42 (later at other addresses)
occur with this printed mark featuring St Paul's
Cathedral.

T. G. Green & Co. (Ltd.), Church Gresley,
Derbyshire, UK
See p.214. The mark (top) was first registered in
1888; the marks (centre and bottom) represent
typical printed marks of the 1930s. As well as
marks featuring a church device in a variety of
forms, others feature pattern names.

William De Morgan, London, UK
See p.110. This mark relates to the period 1882-88
when De Morgan's studio was based at Merton
Abbey, situated to the south-west of London.
Other marks from this period include the name.

Clignancourt, Paris, France
Pierre Deruelle founded a porcelain factory
known as Fabrique de Monsieur in 1771, and was
given the protection of the brother of Louis XV.
Continued by his son-in-law, the factory operated
until c.1798. High quality porcelain was produced,
decorated by skilled artists from Vienna and
Sèvres. Before 1784, factories other than Sèvres
were forbidden from using gilding or polychrome
decoration. This is one of the marks used and
appears in gold or red.

Lovatt & Lovatt, Langley Mill, Nottinghamshire, UK
Formerly Calvert & Lovatt, this factory was
founded in 1895 producing stonewares and
earthenwares. The name of the firm changed
to Lovatty's Potteries Ltd. in 1931, and was
bought by J. Bourne & Son in 1959, but continued
under the same name. This trademark was used
c.1931-62, with a revised version appearing after
c.1962.

Miland Pottery, Liphook, Hampshire, UK
Run by Mr and Mrs Hawkins, this pottery made
earthenwares from 1948. This printed or
impressed mark appears.

Levantino Family, Savona, Liguria, Italy
This mark, which is believed to represent one of
the beacon lights in the harbour at Genoa, has
been ascribed to the Levantino family of Albissola
in the late 17th and early 18thC, but has also been
claimed for the town of Genoa itself.

Leonard Acton, Bramber, West Sussex, UK
Hand-made pottery and items such as animals
were made by this potter from 1945. Pieces were
marked with this incised outline of a bridge,
sometimes accompanied by the initials L.A.

Bancroft & Bennett, Burslem, Staffordshire, UK
Earthenwares were made by this firm, based at
Newcastle Street 1946-50. This printed mark was
used.

Paden City Pottery, Nr. Sisterville, West Virginia, USA
This large pottery (active 1914-63) made a variety
of high quality semi-porcelain dinnerware with
decal decoration that effectively mimicked a broad
style of hand painting. They also produced a line
of baking ware.

Morley Fox & Co. Ltd., Fenton, Staffordshire, UK
See p.187. This mark used by Morley Fox & Co.
Ltd. from 1938 was also used by the firm's
successor William Morley & Co. Ltd 1944-57.

Boats

Ann Stannard, Potbridge, Odiham, Hampshire, UK
Studio-type pottery was produced by Ann
Stannard and Marigold Austin from 1959. This
basic painted mark appears.

A. E. Gray & Co. Ltd., Stoke, Staffordshire, UK
Based at the Glebe Works in Hanley c.1913-33
and at Whieldon Road in Stoke 1934-61, this
pottery operated 1912-61 producing earthenwares.
A. E. Gray was formerly a ceramic decorator. The
printed mark (above) was used 1912-30; the mark
(below) was used 1934-61, and may feature the
words "England" or "Made in England". From
1961 this firm was known as Portmeirion
Potteries Ltd.

W. T. Copeland (& Sons Ltd.), Stoke,
Staffordshire, UK
See p.245. This printed mark was used c.1894-
1910. A variety of name marks and devices were
used around this time.

William Alsager Adderley (& Co.), Longton,
Staffordshire, UK
See p.194. This printed trademark was used by
this firm 1876-1905 (and by its predecessor at the
Daisy Bank Works, Hulse & Adderley 1869-75). It
was also used by the firm's successor Adderleys
Ltd. 1906-26.

W. H. Grindley & Co. (Ltd.), Tunstall,
Staffordshire, UK
See p.199. This printed mark appears c.1936-54.
Slight variations do occur.

Karl Nennzoff, Altenkunstadt, Germany
This factory was originally established in 1933 to
produce artistic porcelain. This mark and other
variations occur.

F. & R. Pratt & Co. (Ltd.), Fenton, Staffordshire, UK
The Fenton Potteries were operated by F. & R.
Pratt & Co. from the beginning of the 19thC,
producing earthenware services, and functional
and ornamental items. Specialities were terracotta and a particular type of underglaze
multi-colour printing. Etruscan-style wares
were also made. In the 1920s the firm was taken
over by the Cauldon Potteries Ltd. This early
mark was used: the absence of "& Co." indicates
a date before 1840.

Furnivals (Ltd.), Cobridge, Staffordshire, UK
See p.217. This mark was used c.1905-13. In 1913
the style of the firm changed to Furnivals (1913)
Ltd; A similar mark featuring the new title was
used from 1913.

Greenock Pottery, Greenock, Scotland, UK
Established by James Stevenson in the early
19thC, this firm produced Staffordshire-type
earthenwares c.1820-60. This mark has been
attributed to James Stevenson & Co. of the
Greenock Pottery, but is usually associated with
Andrew Stevenson of Staffordshire.

Viking Pottery Co., Cobridge, Staffordshire, UK
Formerly the Viking Tile Co., this firm operated
1950-64 making general ceramics. This printed
mark was one of those used.

Pots

Geoffrey Maund, Croydon, Surrey, UK
See p.79. This printed or impressed mark was
used from c.1961.

C. P. Sutcliffe & Co. Ltd., Higher Broughton,
Greater Manchester, UK
Between c.1885 and 1901 this firm produced tiles
bearing this printed or impressed mark.

Henry Kennedy & Sons (Ltd.), Glasgow, Scotland,
UK
The Barrowfield Potteries were established by
Henry Kennedy in 1866, and produced glass-lined
stonewares including bottles and jars. The firm
continued until 1929. This trademark was used
from 1866.

William Ault, Swadlincote, Staffordshire, UK
Born in 1841, William Ault established a pottery
at Swadlincote in 1887. He produced glaze effects
and impasto paintings assisted by his two
daughters. Several forms made at the pottery were
designed by Christopher Dresser. After 1923 the
firm became Ault & Tunnicliffe (1923-37) and
then Ault Potteries Ltd. (from 1937).

John Shaw & Sons (Longton) Ltd., Longton,
Staffordshire, UK
Formerly J. Shaw & Sons, this pottery operated
1931-63 producing general ceramics. This mark
was used from c.1949.

Bailey Potteries Ltd., Fenton, Staffordshire, UK
Operating between 1935 and 1940, this firm
produced earthenwares. Several printed marks
were used such as this example.

Blue John Pottery Ltd., Hanley, Staffordshire, UK
See p.104. This printed mark was used 1947-49; a similar mark, also printed, featuring a single pot and the words "Made in England", was used from 1949.

Edwin M. Knowles China Company, East Liverpool, Ohio, USA
This pottery (active 1900-1963) produced high-quality table and toilet wares in semi-porcelain and ironstone with good printed or decal decorations. The first pottery plant was in Chester, West Virginia; in 1913 they moved to Newell, West Virginia. Offices remained in East Liverpool until 1931. Knowles was the son of Isaac M. Knowles of Knowles, Taylor and Knowles (see p.176).

Sterling Pottery Ltd., Fenton, Staffordshire, UK
Formerly Sterling Pottery Co., this firm produced earthenwares 1947-53. This mark was used from c.1947.

Jugtown Pottery, Jugtown, North Carolina, USA
Established by Jacques (d.1947) and Juliana Busbee in 1921 to revive the potter's art in North Carolina, the Jugtown Pottery has specialized in table and decorative ware for quaint interiors. Traditional North Carolina shapes and glazes, were supplemented with simple forms and transmutational glazes adapted from Asian ceramics. Notable glazes are an orange glaze, and a brown glaze called "Tobacco Spit". This impressed mark is used. The pottery has subsequently been operated by other firms.

Holmes & Son, Longton, Staffordshire, UK
Earthenwares were made by this firm 1898-1903 at the Clayton Pottery. This printed mark was used.

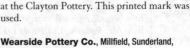

Wearside Pottery Co., Millfield, Sunderland, Tyne and Wear, UK
Previously known as the Sunderland Pottery Co. Ltd., this firm made earthenwares and utility wares 1928-57 with this printed or impressed mark.

Wedgwood & Co. (Ltd.), Tunstall, Staffordshire, UK
See p.206. This printed mark was used from c.1951. The tradename "Wacol" also appears in other marks.

Josiah Wedgwood (& Sons Ltd.), Various locations, Staffordshire, UK

WEDGWOOD

See p.136. The printed mark (above) was used on porcelain (and rarely earthenwares) from c.1878, with the word "England" added after 1891. The mark (centre) was used from c.1900 onwards on Wedgwood porcelain; note the addition of three stars under the vase, which do not appear on the previous mark. The mark (below) is the version that was used by Wedgwood from 1962; the pattern name may also appear below the mark on some examples.

D.& J. Henderson/American Pottery Company, Jersey City, New Jersey, USA

See p.119. This mark was one of those used by this firm.

Wood & Son(s) (Ltd.), Burslem, Staffordshire, UK

See p.206. This mark was used from c.1917. A similar later version, with a description of the type of ware underneath, was used from c.1960.

Arij de Milde, Delft, Holland

See p.244. This mark was also used by this potter c.1680-1708.

Figures

Bates Elliot & Co., Burslem, Staffordshire, UK

Founded 1870, this pottery produced earthenwares, porcelain and other wares at the Dale Hall Works. In 1875 the company became Bates Walker & Co. This staple trademark was used and was continued by the firm's successors, including Gildea & Walker (1881-85) and James Gildea (1885-88).

Pisgah Forest Pottery/Stephen Pottery, Pisgah Forest, North Carolina, USA

Walter Stephen began making pottery in 1901, but his production was very sporadic until he moved to Pisgah Forest and started a new venture in 1926. Vases, tea wares, candlesticks, jugs, bowls and teapots were decorated with sprigged-on scenes of covered wagons, buffalo hunts, etc. or with overall Persian blue or silvery blue crystalline glazes. The company name was Stephen Pottery for a few years in the 1940s. The factory continues today. A few pieces are incised with the names "Pisgah Forest" or "Stephen".

Sèvres, France
See p.72 This mark was used on paste invented by the great ceramicist Théodore Deck who was director of the factory 1887-91. It appears in relief or printed in underglaze brown.

Fulper Pottery, Flemington, New Jersey, USA
See p.114. This mark also appears. The date 1805 seen on this mark, was used by the factory as a starting date although this is not universally agreed.

A. E. Hull Pottery, Crooksville, Ohio, USA
Organized by Addis E. Hull from 1905, the company has made stoneware vessels and much relief-moulded whiteware in kitchen ware, including covered storage jars (called cereal sets), tea and coffee sets, candlesticks, florists' crockery, bowls, jugs, biscuit jars, smoking sets and some ornamental wares such as figures and vases. The firm was reorganized in 1952 after a disastrous fire. This mark appears in many forms, such as impressed marks or paper labels. Several written marks featuring the name "Hull" were also used.

Pearson & Co., Chesterfield, Derbyshire, UK
Established c.1805, this company made stone-wares and earthenwares. This impressed or printed mark was used from 1880. The name of the company changed in c.1925 to Pearson & Co. (Chesterfield Ltd.). This mark has also been used as a trade mark since 1945 with the addition of the words "Pearsons of Chesterfield" and "Made in England".

Britannia Pottery Co. Ltd., Glasgow, Scotland, UK
Operating 1920-35, formerly known as Cochran & Fleming (1896-1920), this firm made earthenwares marked with the figure of Britannia 1920-35. The mark may also feature the initials "B. P. Co. Ltd." and "Made in Scotland".

Dudson, Wilcox & Till Ltd., Hanley, Staffordshire, UK
Earthenwares were made by this firm 1902-26 at the Britannic Works, with a printed or impressed Britannia mark such as this example.

Samuel Johnson Ltd., Burslem, Staffordshire, UK
Based at the Hill Pottery (subsequently known as the Britannia Pottery), this firm operated between 1887 and 1931. This printed mark was used c.1916-31.

Powell, Bishop & Stonier, Hanley, Staffordshire, UK
From 1878, this company (previously Powell &
Bishop), produced a wide range of products at
various locations in Hanley, including earthenware (Stafford Street Works), white granite
(Church Works) and porcelain (Waterloo Works).
A notable product was their "Oriental Ivory" or
cream-coloured ware. This mark was used by
Powell, Bishop & Stonier 1878-91, and was
continued by their successors Bishop & Stonier
1891-1939, sometimes with the word "Bisto"
underneath.

Crown Staffordshire Porcelain Co. Ltd., Fenton,
Staffordshire, UK
See p.197. This printed mark was used from 1930.
Other examples were used for special patterns on
wares, all featuring the words "Crown
Staffordshire".

Biltons (1912) Ltd., Stoke, Staffordshire, UK
See p.104. This printed mark was used from 1912.
Other marks feature the name of the firm without
a device.

Lonhuda Pottery Company, Steubenville, Ohio, USA
See p.87. This mark was also used. This mark of a
Native American head may also appear as a
silhouette.

Globes

Edwin Bennett Pottery, Baltimore, Maryland, USA
See p.103. Most of the marks used by this firm
feature the name "Bennett" or the initials "E. B."
Decorator marks, usually in the form of monograms, may also appear.

George Clews & Co. (Ltd.), Tunstall,
Staffordshire, UK
Operating 1906-61, this pottery produced
earthenwares at the Brownhills Pottery. A globe
mark was used by the firm from 1906, with this
example appearing from 1935.

Globe Pottery Co. Ltd., Cobridge and Shelton,
Staffordshire, UK
Established in 1914, this pottery was based at
Shelton from c.1934. Earthenwares were
produced. This printed mark was used from 1917.
Some marks feature a figure holding the globe.

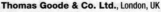

Thomas Goode & Co. Ltd., London, UK
See p.199. The mark seen here was also used by
this firm of retailers.

Grimwades Ltd., Stoke, Staffordshire, UK
See p.205. A number of globe marks were used
from 1906, with this example appearing from
c.1930. Other globe marks may appear beneath a
crown, and may also feature a sash which includes
the pattern name.

W. H. Grindley & Co. (Ltd.), Tunstall,
Staffordshire, UK
See p.199. This printed mark was used from 1925,
but globe marks in various forms were used from
c.1880. These earlier marks may feature a ship
above the globe.

James Kent (Ltd.), Longton, Staffordshire, UK
Porcelain and earthenwares were produced by this
firm at the Old Foley Pottery from 1897. Several
printed marks were used, including some
featuring a globe. These first appeared in c.1910;
this example is from c.1950.

Locke & Co., Worcester, Hereford and Worcester, UK
Porcelain was produced here 1896-1914, before
this company based at the Shrub Hill Works was
taken over by the Worcester Royal Porcelain Co.
Ltd. This printed mark was used c.1898-1902. A
similar mark was used after 1902, with the word
"Ltd." added to the style.

Alfred Meakin (Ltd.), Tunstall, Staffordshire, UK
See p.201. This globe-type mark was used c.1875-
97. After 1897 "Ltd." was added to the style of the
firm.

Minton, Stoke, Staffordshire, UK
See p.164. The standard printed globe trademark
first appeared in c.1863. This example was used
c.1863-72. A revised version with a crown, and the
letter "S" added to the company name was used
from c.1873, with "England" added below from
1891. "Made in England" appears c.1902-11. From
c.1912 the mark featured a wreath.

Moore (Bros.), Longton, Staffordshire, UK
See p.147. This printed mark was used from
c.1880, with "England" added from c.1891. An
earlier mark features the name "Moore" printed
or impressed.

J. Mortlock/Mortlock Ltd., London, UK

This leading firm of 19thC retailers was established in 1746 and stopped trading in c.1930. This printed trademark was first registered in 1877. Marks used by this firm often also include the name of the manufacturer.

Wheeling Pottery Company/Wheeling Potteries Company, Wheeling, West Virginia, USA

This company (active 1879-1910) was organized to produce plain and decorated white granite table and toilet wares. In 1889, several potteries were consolidated under the Wheeling Potteries Company, each making a different type of ware including utilitarian pottery, semi-porcelain, sanitary ware and art ware, including a line of highly-decorated faience ware. A large concern, by 1904 the firm was employing about 1,200 people. The company was reorganized as the Wheeling Sanitary Manufacturing Company in 1910. Many different marks were used, including a number of variations of the globe mark seen here.

Thomas Till & Son(s), Burslem, Staffordshire, UK

See p.249. Many forms of globe mark were used by this firm, including this example which appeared from c.1919. Other feature the name "Thos. Till & Sons" or "Till & Sons".

Arthur Wood & Son (Longport) Ltd, Longport, Staffordshire, UK

Established in 1928, this firm produced earthenwares at the Bradwell Works. Several globe marks appear, including this one from c.1934.

William Brownfield (& Son(s)), Cobridge, Staffordshire, UK

Between 1850 and 1891 this company produced earthenware, with porcelain made after 1871. The firm subsequently became Brownfields Guild Pottery Society Ltd. (1891-c.1898) and Brownfields Pottery Ltd. (c.1898-1900). This printed mark was used 1871-91. A similar double globe mark was used 1891-1900.

Clementson Bros. (Ltd.), Hanley, Staffordshire, UK

See p.196. This printed double globe mark appears 1901-13. The marks used by this firm all feature the name "Clementson Bros.", with the addition of "Ltd." after 1910.

David Chapman & Sons, Longton, Staffordshire, UK
Based at the Atlas Works from 1889, this pottery
produced porcelain. This printed mark was used
with or without the word "Longton" underneath.
A similar mark was used by this firm's successor
the Atlas China Co. Ltd. 1906-10, with the words
"Atlas China".

Hawley Bros. (Ltd.), Rotheram, South Yorkshire, UK
Established in 1868, this firm produced earthenwares. This trademark was registered in 1898 and
occurs printed on wares. The same mark was
continued by the Northfield Pottery Co. until
c.1919.

Bells

J. & M. P. Bell & Co. (Ltd.), Glasgow, Scotland, UK
This firm established the Glasgow Pottery in
1842, where they produced high quality white and
printed earthenware. Later, porcelain, white and
pearl granite ware, and decorated sanitary ware
were also made. A bell mark appeared from 1881,
and may appear within a garter mark. The factory
continued until 1928.

Belle Vue Pottery, Hull, Humberside, UK
This factory was started c.1802 by two potters
named Smith from Hull and Job Ridgway of
Shelton. In 1826 the works were taken by William
Bell who produced cream, white, blue-printed,
and green-glazed wares principally for export
until 1841. This mark was used c.1826-41. The
mark may also appear without the factory name.

Wings

Red Wing Stoneware, Red Wing, Minnesota, USA
See p.129. This mark was one of those used by this
firm.

Powell & Bishop, Hanley, Staffordshire, UK
Previously Livesley Powell & Co., this firm
was known under this title 1867-78, before
becoming Powell, Bishop & Stonier (see p.261).
This Caduceus was registered as a trademark in
1876. A similar mark was also used by the
successors of Powell, Bishop & Stonier, Bishop &
Stonier (Ltd.) (1891-1939), and may feature the
words "Bisto" or "Bishop England".

Winkle & Wood, Hanley, Staffordshire, UK
Operating 1885-90, this pottery used this printed
mark. The firm subsequently became F. Winkle &
Co. (1890-1931).

R. H. & S. L. Plant (Ltd.), Longton, Staffordshire, UK
Formerly R. H. Plant (1881-98), this firm was
based at the Tuscan Works, producing a wide
range of porcelain. The tradename "Tuscan" was
incorporated into many marks from c.1907.

Villeroy & Boch, Septfontaines, Luxembourg
This firm was originally started c.1766 by three
brothers Jean-François, Dominique and Pierre-
Joseph Boch. Jean-François became sole
proprietor in 1795. White and cream-coloured
earthenwares were made usually with blue
painted or printed Chinese-style landscapes.
Plaques were made from 1784. The Boch family
merged with the Villeroy family (which founded
the factories at Frauenberg (1760), Wallerfangen
(1789) and Schramberg (1820), in 1836, and they
went on to establish a works at Mettlach in
Germany in 1842. This mark appears at
Septfontaines and Mettlach.

Miscellaneous

Chantilly, Oise, France
See p.190. This mark usually appears in red enamel and occasionally black for the early period,
underglaze blue and sometimes crimson for the
later period. Other colours occasionally occur.

Hornsea Pottery Co. Ltd., Hornsea, Humberside, UK
Based at the Edenfield Works, this pottery
produced earthenwares from c.1951. This printed
mark was used from 1951.

Joseph Bourne & Son Ltd., Denby, Derbyshire, UK
The works at Denby were started in 1809 by a
Mr Jager. In 1812 Joseph Bourne, son of potter
William Bourne, took over the works and
produced useful stoneware items such as bottles,
for which he won a medal in 1851. As well as
bottles, footwarmers, pestle and mortars, pie
moulds and medical appliances were made. A
variety of items in terracotta were also produced.
Joseph Bourne died in 1860. The tradename
Denby appears in many marks, including this
one from c.1895.

Thomas Lawrence (Longton) Ltd., Longton, Staffordshire, UK

Based at the Falcon Works (1897-1957) and the Sylvan Works (from 1957), this pottery produced earthenwares from 1892. It was originally established at Trent Bridge Pottery in Stoke. Early wares were unmarked. This printed or impressed mark appears from 1947. Other marks feature the tradename Falcon Ware.

J. H. Baum, Wellsville, Ohio, USA

Baum (active 1880-97) made white granite and cream-coloured earthenware table and toilet wares.

Het Bijltje, Delft, Holland

This factory ("The Hatchet") was first recorded as owned by B. van Houten and Jacob Wemmertz Hoppesteyn. Between 1739 and 1775 the proprietor was Justus Brouwer, who registered this mark in 1764.

Cafaggiolo, Nr. Florence, Tuscany, Italy

See p.95. This trident mark has been attributed to Cafaggiolo.

J. B. Owens Pottery Company, Zanesville, Ohio, USA

Owens (active 1896-1907) built and operated several potteries during his life, but this one featured art wares that were designed, made and decorated by leading potters, chemists and decorators during the brief time that the pottery was in production. Overall the work was derivative, with many references to the pottery produced at Rookwood (see p.92), but Owens' ware won gold medals in at least one international fair.

Basing Farm Pottery, Ashington, West Sussex, UK

See p.23. This seal-type mark was used at this pottery from 1962.

The Royal Factory, Copenhagen, Denmark

See p.203. The "wave mark" (above) was adopted by the factory in 1775, and appears in underglaze blue. The vertical wave mark (below) is found on figures.

Leslie G. Davie, Rye, East Sussex, UK

Located at The Needles Studio, this potter made Studio-type ware 1954-62. This Needles mark was used; major pieces were signed and dated.

Josiah Spode, Stoke, Staffordshire, UK
See p.223. This workman's mark appears on some early porcelains c.1790-1805. A similar mark also appears on Coalport porcelains c.1810-20.

Alpha Potteries, Sidcup, Kent, UK
See p.101. This incised mark was used 1954-58. This symbol was also used in an impressed seal-mark 1954-58.

Roger Fry, London, UK
Tin-glazed earthenwares were made at the Omega Workshops c.1913-19. This impressed or incised mark appears.

Chelsea Pottery, London, UK
Earthenwares were produced at this pottery from 1952. This impressed or incised Chelsea Pottery mark appears, sometimes with the words "Chelsea Pottery. Hand Made in England".

Saint-Cloud, Seine-et-Oise, France
See p.60. This "sun-face" mark appears, always in blue.

Girolamo Salomini, Savona, Liguria, Italy
This potter and his family were active in Savona in the 17th and 18thC. This mark has been attributed to Salomini.

Tooth & Co., Woodville, Derbyshire, UK
See p.83. This trademark was registered by Tooth & Co. in 1884. The word "England" was added after 1891. "Made in England" appears on 20thC examples.

A. B. Jones & Sons (Ltd.), Longton, Staffordshire, UK
Based at the Grafton Works and other addresses, this firm made general ceramics 1900-72. Many marks were used, including this one that appears from c.1913. The company became Royal Grafton Bone China Ltd.

Ott and Brewer/Etruria Pottery, Trenton, New Jersey, USA
See p.149. This mark was also used, and features both the company name and the name "Trenton".

Staffordshire-type marks

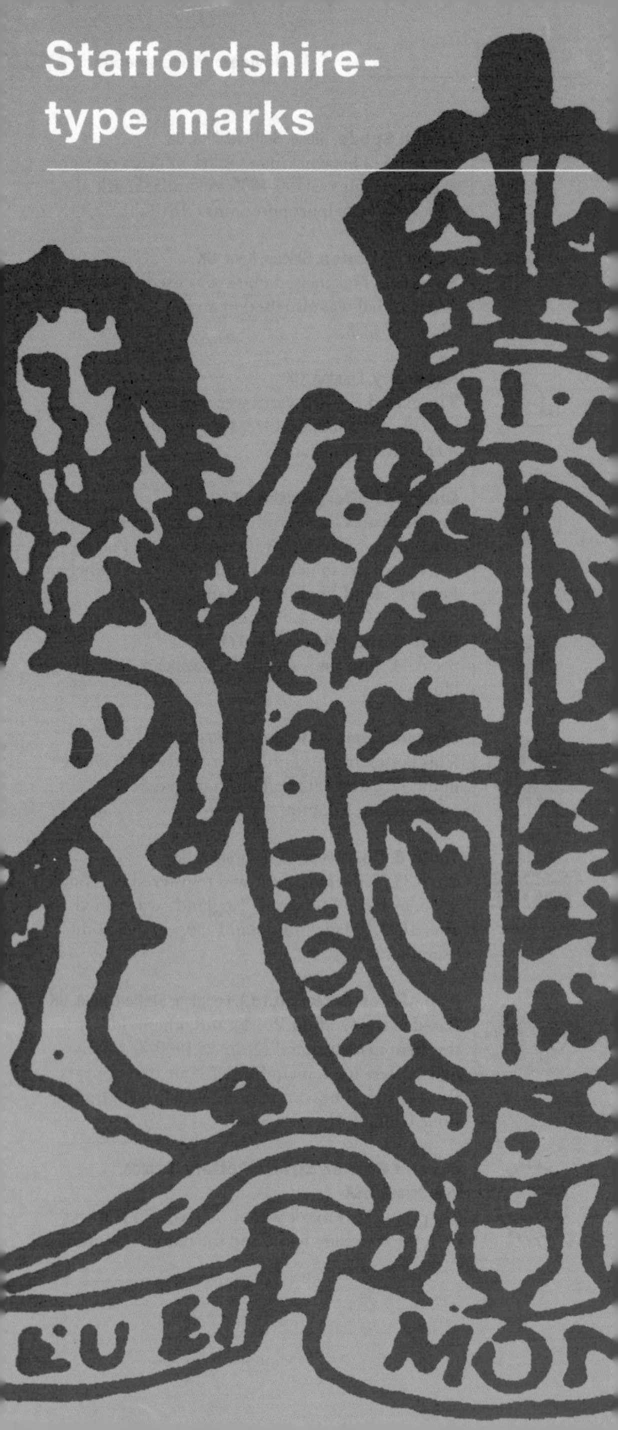

Royal Arms

The British Royal Arms have been the basis for many printed or impressed marks used by several 19th and 20thC British, and some overseas manufacturers.

For British manufacturers the form of this mark can act as a guide to dating: those engraved after 1837 feature the quartered shield (see below right), but pre-1837 arms have an extra shield (inescutcheon) in the centre (see below left). From 1801-14 the inescutcheon is capped; 1814-37 the inescutcheon is crowned.

For the factories and makers below the Royal Arms appear with the following wording:

A.C.CO.
Akron China Company, Akron, Ohio, USA
See p.67. These initials appear on the coat of arms used by this company, together with the words "Extra Quality Ironstone China Warranted".

A.C.CO.
American Crockery Company, Trenton, New Jersey, USA
The pottery (active 1876-99) made white granite table and toilet ware with printed decoration. These initials were used, together with "Iron Stone China".

ADAMS/TUNSTALL/ENGLAND
William Adams & Sons (Potters) Ltd., Tunstall and Stoke, Staffordshire, UK
See p.194. This mark was used 1890-1914. The word "Tunstall" was added after 1896.

W. & T. ADAMS
William & Thomas Adams, Tunstall, Staffordshire, UK
Based at Greenfields in Tunstall, this firm (1866-92) produced earthenwares. This name mark appears with the Royal Arms. Other emblems were used with the name of the firm in full.

SAML. ALCOCK & CO.
Samuel Alcock & Co., Cobridge and Burslem, Staffordshire, UK
Active c.1828-59, this firm was based initially in Cobridge (c.1828-53), and at the Hill Pottery in Burslem (c.1830-59). Wares produced included porcelain, parian and fine earthenwares. Notable was a particularly fine and durable semi-porcelain. The firm sometimes used a version of the Royal Arms with the name of the firm or initials below.

A. & M.

Alpaugh and Magowan, Trenton, New Jersey, USA

The Empire Pottery where this firm was based, was purchased by Alpaugh and Magowan (active 1884-92) from Coxon & Company (see p.238), but the product line was improved. The new owners made thin porcelain dinner, tea and toilet wares and decorated white granite wares. In 1892, this works became part of the Trenton Potteries Company (see p.62), which specialized in sanitary ware.

AP (IN MONOGRAM)

Anchor Pottery, Trenton, New Jersey, USA

See p.218. This firm also used a coat of arms with an "AP" monogram, and the words "Iron Stone China Warranted".

ASHWORTH

G. L. Ashworth & Bros. (Ltd.), Hanley, Staffordshire, UK

See p.194. The Royal Arms were used on Ashworth earthenwares from 1862 usually with the name "Ashworth".

B.B./BURFORD BROS

Burford Brothers, East Liverpool, Ohio, USA

See p.163. These initials and the firm name appears on the mark together with "Iron Stone China" and "Warranted".

BIRKS BROS. & SEDDON

Birks Brothers & Seddon, Cobridge, Staffordshire

This firm produced Ironstone wares 1877-86; the mark features their name.

BROWN-WESTHEAD, MOORE & CO.

Brown-Westhead, Moore & Co., Hanley, Staffordshire, UK

See p.155. This printed mark was used from 1890. Slight variations of the wording occur.

HENRY BURGESS

Henry Burgess, Burslem, Staffordshire, UK

Formerly T. & R. Boote, this firm was active 1864-92, producing earthenwares. The Royal Arms were used, with the name or initials of the firm below.

CLEMENTSON BROS.

Clementson Bros. (Ltd.), Hanley, Staffordshire, UK

See p.196. This mark was used 1867-80.

R. COCHRAN & CO.

R. Cochran & Co., Glasgow, Scotland, UK

Based at the Verreville Pottery (and the Britannia Pottery to 1896), this firm was active 1846-1918. Earthenwares, stonewares (including white graniteware), and porcelain (until 1846) were produced. The Royal Arms was one of the marks used.

COCHRAN & FLEMING

Cochran & Fleming, Glasgow, Scotland, UK

Based at the Britannia Pottery in St Rollox, a works established by Robert Cochran in 1857 and operated by him until 1896, this firm was established by Alexander Cochran (son of Robert) and James Fleming in 1896. All types of earthenware were made for the home and export markets. The firm continued until 1920 when it became the Britannia Pottery Co.

COCKSON & SEDDON

Cockson & Seddon, Cobridge, Staffordshire, UK

Known by this name 1875-77, this firm subsequently became Birk Bros. & Seddon. A printed Royal Arms mark was used.

C.P.CO. (IN MONOGRAM)

Cook Pottery Company, Trenton, New Jersey, USA

See p.208. The Royal Arms were used with a "CPCo" monogram in the centre of the shield, and may also feature the name "Mellor & Co." after F. G. Mellor, one of the original founders.

C.P.CO. (IN MONOGRAM)

Crown Pottery Company, Evansville, Indiana, USA

See p.202. This mark was used with the words "Iron Stone China Warranted".

D.D./DALE AND DAVIS

Dale and Davis, Trenton, New Jersey, USA

This firm based at the Prospect Hill Pottery 1880-94 produced a large line of decorated semi-porcelain and white granite table and toilet wares. Isaac Davis had previously been in business on his own. His souvenirs of the 1876 Centennial Exhibition with views of the buildings are attractive. Mr. Davis had worked for John Moses at the Glasgow Pottery (see p.176).

DRESDEN

Dresden Pottery Works, East Liverpool, Ohio, USA

Organized originally as Brunt, Bloor, Martin and Company, Dresden Pottery Works (active 1875-1927) became part of the Potter's Co-operative Company in 1882 under the direction of H. A. McNicol. The Dresden Pottery Company owned the works in its last two years. The works made award-winning white granite table and toilet wares, cuspidors, toys and hotel ware in 1876. The nature of the body improved over the years and decal decorations were added, but the character of the ware remained much the same.

E.L.P. CO.

East Liverpool Pottery Company, East Liverpool, Ohio, USA

See p.77. These initials appear with "Ironstone China".

ELSMORE & FORSTER
Elsmore & Forster, Tunstall, Staffordshire, UK

Earthenwares, parian and other wares were produced by this firm 1853-71. Variations of the Royal arms mark appear with the name of the firm on a ribbon below. The firm subsequently became Elsmore & Son (1872-87).

F.C. & CO.
Ford, Challinor & Co./Ford and Challinor, Tunstall, Staffordshire, UK

Earthenwares were made by this firm at the Lion Works 1865-80. These initials appear with the Royal Arms, and a number of other marks 1865-80.

T. FURNIVAL & SONS
Thomas Furnival & Sons, Cobridge, Staffordshire, UK

See p.217. Known by this title 1871-90, the firm used a Royal Arms mark with the name of the firm c.1881-90. Variations do occur.

HB
Henry Burgess, Burslem, Staffordshire, UK

See p.270. The firm's initials also appear with the Royal Arms.

H. & D.
Hallam & Day, Longton, Staffordshire, UK

Formerly Hallam & Johnson, this firm produced earthenwares 1880-85 at the Mount Pleasant Works. These initials appear with the Royal Arms and other marks.

C. & W.K. HARVEY
C. & W. K. Harvey, Longton, Staffordshire, UK

Based at various addresses in Longton, this firm produced earthenwares, porcelain and other wares 1835-53. The Royal Arms mark with initials and name was used 1835-53.

JC (IN MONOGRAM)
New York City Pottery, New York, New York, USA

See p.126. This monogram appears within the mark with "Trade Mark" and "Stone China".

J. & T.F.
Jacob & Thomas Furnival, Hanley, Staffordshire, UK

Based at Miles Bank, this firm produced earthenwares c.1843. In c.1844 the firm became Thomas Furnival & Co. These initials occur with the Royal Arms.

JOHNSON BROS
Johnson Bros. (Hanley) Ltd., Hanley, Staffordshire, UK

See p.200. The Royal Arms was one of the marks used that featured the name "Johnson Bros."

J.R. & CO.

John Ridgway (& Co.), Hanley, Staffordshire, UK

Formerly J. & W. Ridgway (1814–c.1830), John Ridgway
continued the Cauldon Place Works with various partners
until 1855, when the title of the firm became J. Ridgway,
Bates & Co. (and then Brown-Westhead, Moore & C.
1858-61). Fine quality porcelains, and earthenwares were
produced, including a "Stone China" body. Many variations
of the Royal Arms occur, either with or without the initials
"J. R." or "J. R. & Co.", or the name of the firm in full.

JAMES KENT

James Kent (Ltd.), Longton, Staffordshire, UK

See p.262. The Royal Arms mark was used by this firm, also
featuring the words "Royal Semi China" above the mark,
1897-1915.

L.B.B. & CO.

L. B. Beerbower, Elizabeth, New Jersey, USA

See p.229. A coat of arms was used with these initials and
"Warranted Stone China".

JOHN MATTHEWS/LATE PHILLIPS

John Matthews, Weston-Super-Mare, Avon, UK

Formerly C. Phillips, this firm made terracotta and other
wares 1870-88. An impressed Royal Arms mark with this
factory name was used. The firm subsequently became
C. G. Warne.

ALFRED MEAKIN LTD.

Alfred Meakin (Ltd.), Tunstall, Staffordshire, UK

See p.201. A Royal Arms mark was used by this firm from
c.1897. Early versions occur without "Ltd."

CHARLES MEAKIN

Charles Meakin, Hanley, Staffordshire, UK

Based at the Eastwood Pottery (previously at Burslem 1870-
82), this firm produced earthenwares 1883-89. A printed
Royal Arms mark was used 1870-89; the word "Hanley"
was added 1883-89.

H. MEAKIN

Henry Meakin, Cobridge, Staffordshire, UK

Earthenwares were made at the Abbey Pottery 1873-76. A
number of printed marks with this name were used including
the Royal Arms. Other "H. Meakins" were operating in
Staffordshire during this period.

J. & G. MEAKIN

J. & G. Meakin, Hanley, Staffordshire, UK

The Royal Arms were used in many of this firm's marks. The
word "England" was added from c.1890.

MEIGH'S CHINA

Charles Meigh & So, Hanley, Staffordshire, UK

Based at the Old Hall Pottery, (formerly C. Meigh, Son & Pankhurst 1850-51) this firm produced earthenwares 1851-61. Many different types were produced, including white and blue-printed wares, stoneware, jetware and parian. Several marks including the Royal Arms occur with the name Meigh, Meigh's or C. Meigh & Son. The firm became Old Hall Earthenware Co. Ltd in 1861 (see p.253).

MELLOR & CO.

Cook Pottery Company, Trenton, New Jersey, USA

See p.208. The designation Mellor & Co. was frequently used by the Cook Pottery Company. F. G. Mellor was one of the founders of the company.

MELLOR TAYLOR & CO.

Mellor, Taylor & Co., Burslem, Staffordshire, UK

See p.201. A printed or impressed Royal Arms mark was one of those used 1880-1904.

MORLEY & ASHWORTH

Morley & Ashworth, Hanley, Staffordshire, UK

Formerly F. Morley & Co. (see p.201). Operating between 1859-62, this firm produced earthenwares, Ironstones and other wares. The firm subsequently became G. L. Ashworth & Bros. (Ltd.) 1862-1968 (see p.194).

P. & CO. LTD.

Pounty & Co. (Ltd.), Bristol, Avon, UK

See p.105. A printed Royal Arms mark was used from c.1889 with these initials and "Bristol Semi Porcelain".

PARAGON

Paragon China (Co.) Ltd., Longton, Staffordshire, UK

Fomerly the Star China Co. (1900-19), this firm made porcelain at the Atlas Works in Longton from 1920. The name "Paragon" appears on a number of Royal Arms marksThe same mark was also used by the Star China Co. The firm was taken over by T. C. Wild & Sons Ltd. in 1960 but continued under the same title.

J.L. PASMANTIER AND SONS

Sterling China Company, East Liverpool, Ohio, USA

See p.137. A coat of arms mark with this name appearing underneath was used.

PINDER BOURNE & CO.

Pinder, Bourne & Co., Burslem, Staffordshire, UK

See p.224. The Royal Arms was one of the marks used by Pinder & Bourne & Co. 1862-82. "Burslem Staffsordshire" appears beneath the Royal Arms.

P.P.COY. L.

> **Plymouth Pottery Co.**, Plymouth, Devon, UK
> Active 1856-63, this firm produced blue-printed earthen-
> wares. These initials appear with the Royal Arms. (It is
> important to note that other firms existed with the same
> initials, and could have used this mark.)

F. PRIMAVESI

> **F. Primavesi (& Son)**, Cardiff and Swansea, Wales, UK
> This firm of retailers operated between c.1850 and 1915. The
> mark includes the words "& Son" after c.1860.

R. & M./RIDGWAY & MORLEY

> **Ridgway & Morley**, Hanley, Staffordshire, UK
> Between 1842 and 1844 this firm produced earthenwares at
> the Broad Street Works in Shelton. Many marks occur
> including the Royal Arms, with this name or initials.

RIDGWAYS, BEDFORD WORKS

> **Ridgways (Bedford Works) Ltd.**, Hanley, Staffordshire, UK
> See p.202. The firm operated under this title 1920-52. One
> of the marks used was the Royal Arms.

ROYAL BAYREUTH/BAVARIA

> **Porzellanfabrik Tettau**, Tettau, Franconia, Germany
> See p.35. This factory used a version of the Royal Arms with
> the initial "T" on a shield in the centre.

ROYAL IRONSTONE CHINA/WARRANTED

> **East End Pottery Company**, East Liverpool, Ohio, USA
> This pottery (active 1894-1908) made and decorated white
> granite and semi-porcelain dinner and toilet ware. From 1900
> to 1903, the firm was part of the East Liverpool Potteries
> Company, a co-operative, but by 1905 it was operating
> independently as East End China Company. The name was
> changed to Trenle China Company in 1909, under new
> management.

ROYAL IRONSTONE CHINA/WARRANTED/STAR
DEVICE

> **Wheeling Pottery Company/Wheeling Potteries
> Company**, Wheeling, West Virginia, USA
> See p.263. This mark was one of those used.

R. & T.

> **Jersey City Pottery**, Jersey City, New Jersey, USA
> See p.119. This mark appears; the initials are those of the
> proprietors.

S.A. & CO.

> **Samuel Alcock & Co.**, Cobridge and Burslem, Staffordshire, UK
> See p.269. These initials were used.

S.P. CO.
Steubenville Pottery Company, Steubenville, Ohio, USA
See p.184. These initials appear within a coat of arms used
by this firm. Another arms mark was used with "Royal
Ironstone China Warranted".

STONE CHINA
Hicks, Meigh & Johnson, Shelton, Staffordshire, UK
See p.193. Both this firm and its predecessor Hicks & Meigh,
used as one of its marks a Royal Arms mark with the words
"Stone China" only, and a number printed below. The name
of the pattern may also appear. The example used by Hicks &
Meigh (c.1806-22) was more detailed then the version used by
Hicks, Meigh & Johnson (1822-35). On wares made by Hicks
& Meigh, the mark varies in size, and on large pieces may
measure over 3in (7.6cm).

SWINNERTONS
Swinnerton's Ltd., Hanley, Staffordshire, UK
Earthenwares were produced here 1906-70. Many marks
were used including the Royal Arms.

T.P.C. CO.
Dresden Pottery Works, East Liverpool, Ohio, USA
See p.271. These initials are among those that appear in the
mark.

TURNER'S
G. W. Turner & Sons, Tunstall, Staffordshire, UK
Formerly Turner & Tomkinson (see p.63), earthenwares were
made by this firm 1873-95. A Royal Arms printed mark was
used 1891-95.

U.P.CO. IN MONOGRAM
**Union Co-operative Pottery Company/Union Potteries
Company**, East Liverpool, Ohio, USA
See p.97. This mark was one of those used.

A.J. WILKINSON LTD.
Arthur J. Wilkinson (Ltd.), Burslem, Staffordshire, UK
See p.206. The Royal Arms were used by this firm. On pieces
made earlier than c.1896, the word "Ltd." does not appear.
The words "Royal Ironstone China" were also used.

W.M.CO.
Willets Manufacturing Company, Trenton, New Jersey, USA
See p.98. This mark appears.

WOOD & SONS LTD.
Wood & Son(s) (Ltd.), Burslem, Staffordshire, UK
See p.206. The Royal Arms was one of the marks used by this
firm, and appears from c.1910.

WOOD, SON & CO.

Wood, Son & Co., Cobridge, Staffordshire, UK

Earthenwares and Ironstones were produced by this firm 1869-79, when it became known as W. E. Cartlidge. This name mark appears below the Royal Arms.

W Y S

William Young & Sons/William Young's Sons, Trenton, New Jersey, USA

Based at the Excelsior Pottery Works, this firm (1857-79) made white ware household crockery as well as porcelain hardware trimmings. A few porcelain pitchers were made with ivy in relief overall. When William Young retired in 1870, his sons continued the pottery, eventually selling the works to the Willets Manufacturing Company.

Garter marks

Garter marks appear with or without a crown, many variations occur in the 19thC on pieces made in Britain, France and Europe. The firm's initials or name may occur in the centre or in the border of the mark.

GEBRUDER BENEDIKT/MAYERHÖFEN

Benedikt Brothers, Meierhöfen, Bohemia, Czech Republic

See p.228. This mark was used.

C. & H.

Cockson & Harding, Shelton, Staffordshire, UK

Based at the New Hall Works in Shelton, this company produced earthenwares 1856-62, before becoming known under the title W. & J. Harding. A garter featuring the pattern name and the firm's initials is a typical example of one of their marks.

A.B. DANIELL & SON

A. B. & R. P. Daniel, London, UK

Known under a variety of different titles such as the one detailed above, this firm of retailers operated c.1825-1917. Wares were made for the firm by Coalport and other manufacturers. A garter mark was one of those used, and features the name and the address of the firm.

DERBY

Derby Porcelain Works, Derbyshire, UK

See p.151. Garter marks were used by workmen and artists at the King Street Works, c.1849-61. These are distinguished by the words "Derby" and "Late Bloor".

F. & C.

Ford, Challinor & Co./Ford and Challinor, Tunstall, Staffordshire, UK

See p.272. A garter mark featuring the initials F. & C. or F. C. was one of those used 1865-80.

F. & R.

Ford & Riley, Burslem, Staffordshire, UK

See p.180. The garter mark was one of those used 1882-93.

H. & B.

Heath & Blackhurst/Heath, Blackhurst & Co., Burslem, Staffordshire, UK

Earthenwares produced 1859-77 with many different marks with these distinguishing initials. A garter-shaped mark was favoured.

CHARLES HOBSON

Charles Hobson (& Son), Burslem, Staffordshire, UK

This firm produced earthenwares 1865-80. The name of the firm appears in full on a garter-shaped mark on a design registered in 1883.

K. & B.

Knapper & Blackhurst, Tunstall and Burslem, Staffordshire, UK

Based at the Boston Works 1867-71, and at Dale Hall 1883-88, this firm produced earthenwares during these periods. These initials may have been used by other manufacturers.

W. & R. MEIGH

W. & R. Meigh, Stoke, Staffordshire, UK

This firm operated at the Bridge Bank Works 1894-99 producing earthenwares. The title then changed to F. Hancock & Co. A printed garter-shaped mark was used 1894-99.

M. & CO. (IN MONOGRAM)

Minton, Stoke, Staffordshire, UK

See p.164. A garter-shaped mark was used by Minton c.1841-73 while, known by the title Minton & Co. Many other marks were used.

P. B. & CO.

Pinder, Bourne & Co., Burslem, Staffordshire, UK

See p.224. A garter-shaped mark was one of those used by this firm.

S.B. & S.

Samuel Barker & Son, Swinton, Yorkshire, UK

Earthenwares were produced by this firm at the Don Pottery
1834-93. A garter mark surrounding a lion occurs c.1851-93,
and may also include the name "Don Pottery"; "& Son" or "&
S" appears on all marks from 1851.

T.I. & J.E.

Thomas, Isaac & James Emberton, Tunstall, Staffordshire, UK

Based at the Highgate Pottery, this firm produced earthenwares 1869-82. A printed garter-shaped mark was used with
the initials shown above.

T.M. & S.

Thomas Maddock & Sons, Trenton, New Jersey, USA

Thomas Maddock had an interest in Astbury and Maddock
which preceded this company in the same pottery works,
although only sanitary ware was made by the earlier concern.
Maddock and Sons, which operated 1882-1929, added white
earthenware tableware to the sanitary products. A third
Maddock pottery – John Maddock and Sons – made only
sanitary ware.

T.N. & CO.

Thomas Nicholson & Co., Castleford, Yorkshire, UK

Earthenwares were produced by this firm c.1854-71. A
garter-shaped mark was one of those used, featuring these
initials.

T.R. & CO

T. Rathbone & Co., Tunstall, Staffordshire, UK

See p.178. A crowned garter-shaped mark was used from
c.1898. These initials were also used in an earlier period by
Thomas Rathbone & Co. of Portobello, Scotland.

T.T.CO. (IN MONOGRAM)

Taylor, Tunnicliffe & Co., Hanley, Staffordshire, UK

See p.152. Garter-type marks and other marks featuring this
monograms were used c.1875-98.

T.W. & S.

Thomas Wood & Sons, Burslem, Staffordshire, UK

Earthenwares were made by this firm at the Queen Street
Pottery 1896-97. These initials were found on many marks,
including garter-type examples.

VICTORIA

Blakeney Art Pottery, Stoke, Staffordshire, UK

This pottery (run by M. J. Bailey and S. K. Bailey) produced
earthenwares from 1968. Output included "Flow Blue
Victoria" printed ware, Staffordshire figures and floral art
containers. A printed backstamp with this name was used.

Staffordshire knot marks

Many 19thC British printed marks are based on the Staffordshire knot. The mark appears often with the manufacturer's initials or names inside the segments of the knot.

The firms detailed below used the knot mark as one of their principal devices, although their names and initials may also appear within other marks. The title of the firm is preceded by the wording that appears on the mark.

AJM

Arthur J. Mountford, Burslem, Staffordshire, UK
From 1897-1901 earthenwares were made by this potter at the Salisbury Works bearing this printed mark.

B & CO.

Bodley & Co., Burslem, Staffordshire, UK
Based at the Scotia Pottery in 1865, this company produced earthenwares with these initials.

B & H

Bodley & Harrold, Burslem, Staffordshire, UK
Also based at the Scotia Pottery (see above) 1863-65, this firm made earthenwares.

BSA

Burslem School of Art, Burslem, Staffordshire, UK
Between 1935 and 1941 pottery figure, groups and other similar wares were made by this firm, marked with these initials. Pieces may also include the name of the instructor (William Ruscoe), or of the pupils, and the date.

E.B. & CO.

E. Brain & Co. Ltd., Fenton, Staffordshire, UK
See p.237. A printed Staffordshire knot mark with the date 1850 and "Foley China" was used from 1903.

G & B

Goodwin & Bullock, Longton, Staffordshire, UK
Based at the Dresden Works 1852-58 (and 1858 at High Street, Longton), this firm produced porcelain.

GFB

George Frederick Bowers (& Co.), Tunstall, Staffordshire, UK
Porcelain and earthenware was made 1842-68 at the Brownhills Works. These initials appear inside the knot.

H.A. & CO.

H. Aynsley & Co. (Ltd.), Longton, Staffordshire, UK
This firm, active from 1873 at the Commerce Works, produced lustre, Eqyptian Black, turquoise and painted ware, and stoneware mortars. The name and initials of the firm appear in many marks, including the Staffordshire knot mark. "Ltd." was added in 1932. Late marks include the name in full.

HC CO.

Hanley China Co., Hanley, Staffordshire, UK
Formerly Hanley Porcelain Co. (see below), this firm made porcelain at Burton Place 1899-1901. A crowned knot mark was used.

HJW

H. J. Wood (Ltd.), Burslem, Staffordshire, UK
Established in 1884, in its early years this firm produced jet and Rockingham-glazed earthenware, and later produced general earthenwares. The rope mark was used from c.1884 with these initials.

HPCO.

Hanley Porcelain Co., Hanley, Staffordshire, UK
Formerly Thomas Bevington, this company produced porcelain 1892-99. A Staffordshire knot was used with these initials.

KENT

William Kent Porcelain (Ltd.), Burslem, Staffordshire, UK
Earthenwares were made by this firm 1944-62 (electrical porcelain continued to be made after this date). The name 'Kent' appears together with "Staffordshire Ware" on the mark.

KPH

Kensington Pottery Ltd., Hanley and Burslem, Staffordshire, UK
Based at the Kensington Works in Hanley (c.1922-37), and Trubsham Cross, Burslem (from c.1937), this company produced earthenwares. These initials appear with "Kensington Ware" and "England" from c.1922.

NEW BRIDGE POTTERY

Edward F. Bodley & Son, Longport, Staffordshire, UK
Formerly E. F. Bodley & Co. (see p.282), this firm moved to the New Bridge Pottery in Longport 1881-98. A printed mark with this name was used 1883-98.

NEW WHARF POTTERY

New Wharf Pottery Co., Burslem, Staffordshire, UK
Active 1878-94, this firm produced earthenwares. A crowned knot mark was used c.1890-94.

PHILLIPS
George Phillips, Longport, Staffordshire, UK
A producer of earthenwares 1834-48, this firm used a number of marks featuring the name Phillips or G. Phillips. The Staffordshire knot appears with the name and "Longport".

RHP
R. H. Plant & Co., Longton, Staffordshire, UK
All types of porcelain and stone china ware were produced by this firm at the Carlisle Works 1881-98, including tea and breakfast services, trinket sets, and fancy goods. A crowned and winged printed knot mark was used.

R.H. & S.L.P.
R. H. & S. L. Plant (Ltd.), Longton, Staffordshire, UK
Formerly R. H. Plant & Co. (see above and p.265), a crowned and winged printed knot mark was used from c.1898.

R & S
Robinson & Son, Longton, Staffordshire, UK
Porcelain was produced by this firm at the Foley China Works 1881-1903. A printed trade mark incorporated the Staffordshire knot mark with "Established 1850". This firm subsequently became E. Brain & Co. (see p.237).

RSR
Ridgway, Sparks & Ridgway, Hanley, Staffordshire, UK
Based at the Bedford Works in Shelton, this firm produced earthenwares 1873-79. These initials appear in many marks including the Staffordshire knot.

S & B
Smith & Binnall, Tunstall, Staffordshire, UK
Formerly Rathbone, Smith & Co. (1883-97), this firm based at the Soho Pottery produced earthenwares 1897-1900. The firm subsequently became the Soho Pottery. The firm used a printed knot mark.

SCOTIA POTTERY
Edward F. Bodley & Co., Burslem, Staffordshire, UK
Established at the Scotia Pottery 1862, this firm produced earthenwares together with Bodley & Co. (see p.280). It continued until 1881. This printed mark was one of those used. The mark was also used by Bodley & Harrold, based at the Scotia Pottery 1863-65.

T.A. & S.G.
T. A. & S. Green, Fenton, Staffordshire, UK
Formerly M. Green & Co., from 1876-89 the style of this firm was T. A. & S. Green. From 1889 it continued as the Crown Staffordshire Porcelain Co. These initials appear within a crowned knot mark.

T.G.

Thomas Green, Fenton, Staffordshire, UK

Formerly Green & Richards (1833-47), Thomas Green ran this firm, based at the Minerva Works until his death in 1859 when the firm became M. Green & Co. (1859-76). Good quality porcelain sevices of all types, toy sets, jugs, mugs, feeders and other items were produced in both porcelain and earthenware. A printed crowned knot mark with these initials was used 1847-59.

TT

Thomas Twyford, Hanley, Staffordshire, UK

Based at the Bath Street Works and Cliffe Vale Potteries (from c.1888), this firm made sanitary earthenwares 1860-98. These initials appear on the mark 1860-98. The firm was known as Twyfords Ltd. from 1898.

JOHN WARDLE & CO.

John Wardle & Co., Mexborough, Yorkshire, UK

Based at the Denaby Pottery, this firm operated 1866-70, making earthenwares, printed creamwares and other items. The knot mark appears with this name mark, and "Near Rotheram Denaby Pottery".

WB

William Brownfield (& Son(s)), Cobridge, Staffordshire, UK

See p.263. These initials appear with a knot mark.

WPCO

Wellington Pottery Co., Hanley, Staffordshire, UK

Formerly Bednall & Heath (1879-99), this firm produced earthenwares at the Wellington Pottery 1899-1901. The firm subsequently became W. H. Lockitt (1901-19) (see p.171).

WW/DENABY POTTERY

Wilkinson & Wardle, Mexborough, Yorkshire, UK

This firm made earthenwares at the Denaby Pottery 1864-66. Printed or impressed marks feature these initials, or the full title of the firm. From 1866 the firm became John Wardle & Co. (see above).

WW & CO.

W. Wood & Co., Burslem, Staffordshire, UK

Based at the Albert Street Works 1873-1932, this firm made earthenwares, door furniture and other wares. A printed knot mark was used 1880-1915 with these initials; a crowned mark was used 1915-32.

Name & initial marks

Some pottery and porcelain
producers use marks that feature
just their name or initials, and do
not have a particular illustrated
form. Others use a wide range of
marks, which are characterized
either by distinguishing names
and initials, or trademarks.
These may be stencilled, incised,
impressed, printed or painted.
In this section the name or initial
marks used are featured written
in the way that they would appear
on the mark (together with
possible variations).

In this section, name and initial marks appear alphabetically according to the form in which they appear in the mark. Variations of the names used by the same potter or factory may appear in brackets, or on a new line.

ALABAMA POTTERY CO./FT. PAYNE, ALA.
Alabama Pottery Company, Fort Payne, Alabama, USA
One of the most productive of the Alabama potteries was the Alabama Pottery Company (active 1890-1910) recorded at Fort Payne in 1890. Earlier, traditional alkaline-glazed stoneware had been made there by Elizer McPherson from 1875-1900, but the Pottery Company focused on Albany-slip and Bristol-white glazed wares. This stencilled mark appears.

ALDRIDGE
Aldridge & Co., Longton, Staffordshire, UK
Based at the Normacot Works, this pottery produced earthenwares 1919-49. It was later known as Aldridge Pottery Co. (Longton) Ltd. Name marks are impressed.

AMERICAN LIMOGES
Limoges China Company, Sebring, Ohio, USA
This pottery produced a large quantity of semi-porcelain dinnerware with decal patterns on traditional and stylish forms from 1900. In 1920, for example, the daily output was 45,000 pieces. Viktor Schreckengost designed a number of shapes and decorations for the firm. It closed in 1955. A variety of devices are used with the pattern names, but the company name "Limoges" is usually present, sometimes as "American Limoges" due to conflicts with Haviland and other French companies. Also for this reason "Lincoln China Co." appears in some marks along with "American Limoges".

ARABIA
O/Y Arabia A/B, Helsinki, Finland
Founded in 1874, this company produced domestic earthenware and porcelain. Style was influenced by a Belgian teacher of ceramics, A.W. Finch, who taught in Finland 1897-1902. In 1948 the firm was taken over and renamed Wärtsilä-koncernen A/B Arabia.

ARCADIAN (CHINA)
Arkinstall & Sons (Ltd.), Stoke, Staffordshire, UK
Based at the Trent Bridge Pottery, and subsequently at the Arcadian Works 1904-24, this company produced porcelain before it was taken over by Robinson & Leadbeater in 1908.

D.L. (H.R.) ATCHESON/ ANNAPOLIS, IA/IND.
Atcheson Pottery, Annapolis, Indiana, USA
Three potters from Ohio, David L. Atcheson, David Huggins, and Jacob Bennage, established a stoneware

manufactory at Annapolis, Parke County, Indiana, in 1841.
The Atcheson family remained involved through various
partnerships until at least 1904, when white Bristol-glazed
wares were being made. During the early years ovoid storage
jars and jugs were produced in salt-glazed stoneware.

AVON
Avon Pottery, Cincinnati, Ohio, USA

Founded by Karl Langenbeck, this pottery (active 1886-88)
used yellow Ohio clay or a white body to make a variety of art
wares with glossy coloured glazes, some taking advantage of
the clarity of the glaze to show white decorations beneath the
glaze or to be subtly shaded from bottom to top. This incised
mark appears. This pottery and mark should not be confused
with another called Avon Faience Company that was located
in Wheeling, West Virginia, and made slip-decorated art
wares in 1902 and 1903.

R & J BADDELEY
Ralph & John Baddeley, Shelton, Staffordshire, UK

These potters produced earthenwares 1750-95 using this
impressed mark.

T. (THOS) BADDELEY/HANLEY
Thomas Baddeley, Hanley, Staffordshire, UK

An engraver active 1800-34 at various addresses in Hanley.
He used these signature marks on pieces that featured his
engravings. Pieces may also be dated.

W. BADDELEY
William Baddeley, Longton, Staffordshire, UK

A potter named William Baddeley worked at the Drury
Court Works in Longton c.1864-75, producing terracotta
and similar wares. Pieces feature this impressed mark.

(C. J. C.) BAILEY/FULHAM (POTTERY LONDON)
C. J. C. Bailey (or Bailey & Co.), Fulham Pottery, London, UK

See p.69. Several incised or impressed marks were used by
this firm, many of which incorporated the above names.

BAKER BEVANS & IRWIN
Baker, Bevans & Irwin, Swansea, Wales, UK

Based at the Glamorgan Pottery, this firm produced
earthenwares c.1813-38. This name mark appears.

BAKEWELL BROS. LTD.
Bakewell Bros. Ltd., Hanley, Staffordshire, UK

Based at the Britannic Works, this pottery made earthenwares and stonewares 1927-43. Many marks feature the
factory name. The name of the body "Royal Vitreous" may
also be added. The addition of "Stoke-on-Trent" indicates a
date after 1931.

COPYRIGHT BALL BROS./SUNDERLAND
Ball Brothers, Sunderland, Tyne and Wear, UK

The Deptford Pottery in Sunderland was founded in 1857 by William Ball for the manufacture of flower pots. In 1863 he began to produce "Sunderland ware" for the domestic market. Output also included flower vases and seed boxes. From 1884-1918 the firm was known as Ball Brothers. Most pieces are unmarked, but this mark does appear.

O.L. & A.K. (A.K.) BALLARD/BURLINGTON, VT.
Ballard Brothers, Burlington, Vermont, USA

Three brothers, Alfred K., Orrin L., and Hiram N. Ballard bought out an existing stoneware manufactory in Burlington, Vermont, in 1856. The city, on Lake Champlain, was an important ceramics centre at least as early as 1806. After 1867, Alfred was a sole proprietor until 1875 when the pottery was sold to F. Woodworth. Wares made by the Ballard Brothers include Rockingham hound-handled pitchers, flasks, and washbowl and pitcher sets in addition to the usual blue-decorated, salt-glazed stoneware.

BARKER
John, Richard and William Barker, Longton, Staffordshire, UK

These three brothers based at Lane End, produced earthenwares, basaltes and similar wares in the late 18th and early 19thC. This name mark has been found.

BARRATTS OF STAFFORDSHIRE
Barratt's of Staffordshire Ltd., Burslem, Staffordshire, UK

See p.197. This name mark was incorporated into many of the marks used by this firm from 1945.

BATCHELDER/LOS ANGELES
Batchelder Tile Company, Pasadena and Los Angeles, California, USA

Tiles were first made in Batchelder's backyard workshop in Pasadena from 1909. The business was enlarged and production was moved into a small factory in 1912, and in 1920 to a larger facility in Los Angeles. Relief-moulded tiles for walls and floors, fountains, door frames and mantels as well as special-order architectural pieces were made. Although these tiles were not glazed, they were coloured with slips rubbed onto the surface. The company failed in 1932 during the Great Depression. The mark appears in a mould on the back of the tiles after 1916.

BATES WALKER & CO.
Bates Walker & Co., Burslem, Staffordshire, UK

Based at the Dale Hall Works, this firm operated 1875-78 producing earthenwares, jasper-type wares and porcelain. Formerly Bates, Elliot & Co. (see p.259), the firm became Bates, Gildea & Walker. 1878-81.

B. B. & I.
Baker, Bevans & Irwin, Swansea, Wales, UK
See p.287. A number of marks were used by this firm incorporating these initials.

BEAVER FALLS, ART TILE CO. LTD./BEAVER FALLS PA.
Beaver Falls Art Tile Company, Beaver Falls, Pennsylvania, USA
Chemist Francis W. Walker organized the company (active 1886-1927) to make plain and relief-moulded tiles covered with glazes of brilliant colouring that showed little or no crazing over time. This characteristic made them desirable for mounting in parlour stoves. Although popular designs were made, heads and full figures were a speciality of this pottery in the late 19th century. Sculptor Isaac Broome worked for the company in the 1890s. Marks are frequently moulded into the backs of the tiles.

BEECH & HANCOCK
Beech & Hancock, Tunstall, Staffordshire, UK
Based at the Church Bank Works (c.1857-61) and the Swan Bank Pottery (c.1862-76) in Tunstall, this firm made ceramic wares for the domestic market in "sponged", painted, gilded, enamelled and lustred styles. High quality stonewares and blackwares were also produced. This name mark appears in many printed marks. The initials "B. & H." may also appear.

S. BELL
Samuel and Solomon Bell, Strasburg, Virginia, USA
Peter Bell came from Maryland to Winchester, Virginia, in 1824, where he manufactured redware and, later, stoneware. Samuel and Solomon were his sons, and they founded their own pottery in Strasburg (1833-82). Decorated earthenwares and decorated salt-glazed stoneware were made, which may still be readily found. This impressed mark was used.

BELLEEK/CO. FERMANAGH
Belleek Pottery, Co. Fermanagh, Northern Ireland, UK
See p.244. This impressed or relief mark was used 1863-90.

BELPER (& DENBY)/BOURNES POTTERIES, DERBYSHIRE
Belper Pottery, Nr. Derby, Derbyshire, UK
Brownwares were produced here towards the end of the 18thC. From 1800, the pottery was taken over by William Bourne who continued the production of salt-glazed blacking, ink, ginger-beer and spirit bottles. High quality brownwares were also made and included bowls, pans, dishes, jugs and other domestic wares. In 1812 William Bourne's son Joseph moved to the Denby Pottery and the two works were carried on simultaneously until 1834 when the Belper Pottery closed, and the concern was entirely transferred to Denby.

BEVINGTON & CO./SWANSEA

Bevington & Co., Swansea, Wales, UK

Operating 1817-21, this firm produced creamwares and
porcelain. Pieces occasionally feature this impressed name
mark. The firm subsequently became known as T. & J.
Bevington.

B. G. & W.

Bates, Gildea & Walker, Burslem, Staffordshire, UK

See p.288. This firm produced earthenwares and china 1878-
81, with these distinguishing initials. The firm subsequently
became Gildea & Walker (see p.259).

B. H. & CO.

Beech, Hancock & Co., Burslem, Staffordshire, UK

This firm produced earthenwares at the Swan Bank Pottery
in Burslem 1851-55. After 1857 the firm relocated to Tunstall,
and was known as Beech & Hancock (see p.289). These
distinguishing initials appear.

B. M. & CO./SARACEN POTTERY

Bailey Murray & Co., Glasgow, Scotland, UK

The Saracen Pottery was established in 1875 by Bailey,
Murray & Brammer at Possil Park. The firm produced
Rockingham ware, cane-coloured, Egyptian black, jet and
mazarine blue ware on a large scale. Output mainly
comprised teapots, jugs and other domestic items. From
c.1884 the style of the firm changed to the Saracen Pottery
Co. The works closed c.1900.

BOSTON

Jonathan Fenton & Charles Carpenter, Boston and
Charlestown, Massachusetts, USA

An early Boston, Massachusetts, stoneware manufactory was
established in 1793 by Jonathan Fenton (of New Haven,
Connecticut) and Charles Carpenter (of Lebanon, Connecticut). Exceptional work was produced by the partners in two
different styles: salt-glazed with stamped and blue decorated
birds, fish, etc. and wares dipped top and bottom in an iron-
brown glaze. They marked their wares "BOSTON" with
letters of same size. After dissolving the partnership in 1796,
Carpenter returned to Massachusetts in 1801 to start a
stoneware pottery in Charlestown. Dipped wares similar to
those made earlier were produced, marked "Boston" (two
sizes of letters) and, later, "Charlestown," until Carpenter
died in 1827.

BRAMELD

Rockingham Works, Swinton, Yorkshire, UK

See p.243. This name appears in several of the marks used by
the Bramelds at the Rockingham Works 1806-42. Various
crosses or stars may appears after the name "Brameld".

C.W. BRAUN/BUFFALO N.Y.

Charles W. Braun, Buffalo, New York, USA
Charles W. Braun, a Prussian potter, bought the old Heiser family pottery in Buffalo in 1857 and directed various kilns, producing blue-decorated stoneware, until his retirement in 1896. Bird designs, frequently matching in quality those found on Rochester and Utica wares, were popular with customers in Buffalo's German-American community.

BRENTLEIGH WARE

Howard Pottery Co. (Ltd.), Shelton, Staffordshire, UK
This firm produced earthenwares from 1925. This trade name was incorporated in marks from 1925.

(JAS.) BROADHURST

James Broadhurst & Sons Ltd., Fenton and Longton, Staffordshire, UK
Established in c.1862, this firm was based at the Crown Pottery, Longton, until 1870. Here James Broadhurst made a range of gold and silver lustrewares. In 1870 the firm moved to the Portland Pottery at Fenton, and continued to produce good quality earthenware. In 1897 "& Sons" was added to the company name, and "Ltd." from c.1922. The full name seen above appears on marks from 1957.

JOHN BURGER (J. BURGER JR., BURGER & LANG)/ROCHESTER, N.Y.

John Burger, Rochester, New York, USA
See p.105. These impressed name marks were used.

B. W. & B.

Batkin, Walker & Broadhurst, Lane End, Staffordshire, UK
This firm produced earthenwares, stone china and other wares 1840-45. These initials appear in printed marks of differing design; the pattern name may also appear.

A. CADMUS/CONGRESS POTTERY/SOUTH AMBOY N.J.

Abraham Cadmus/Congress Pottery, South Amboy, New Jersey, USA
Cadmus's pottery (active 1849-54) made Rockingham and yellow ware in table and kitchen forms and is especially known for his pitchers, one of which has a fire brigade marching around the sides. The mark was impressed.

CANONSBURG POTTERY CO./CANONSBURG, PA./USA

Canonsburg Pottery/Canonsburg China Company, Canonsburg, Pennsylvania, USA
This pottery (active 1901-78) made large quantities of semi-porcelain dinner and toilet sets and sets of odd dishes decorated with decals. In later years, it was making ceramic

inserts for electric slow-cooking devices (crock pots). This printed name mark appears with many pattern and shape names.

CAMBRIA (CAMBRIAN POTTERY)

Swansea Pottery, Swansea, Wales, UK
See p.323. These impressed or printed marks appear in many forms c.1783–c.1810.

CATALINA POTTERY

Gladding, McBean and Company, California, USA
Although known for its ceramic architectural products, this company also owned several important potteries for domestic products, including Tropico Pottery from 1923, which made tiles, garden ware and vases; Catalina Pottery from 1937, which made tableware; and Franciscan Ware, an earthenware line that the company developed beginning in 1934 to make dinner and ornamental wares. The company was acquired by Wedgwood from Interpace Corporation in 1979 and in 1985 the factory was closed and production of Franciscan moved to England. This mark appears printed and on sticker labels.

B. G. & C. (L. & B. G.) CHACE/SOMERSET

Somerset Potters' Works, Somerset, Massachusetts, USA
The potter Asa Chace made redware in Somerset, Massachusetts, by 1768, and, later, in 1847 his grandsons, Leonard, Benjamin G., and Clark opened a stoneware factory which continued until 1882. It was called the Somerset Potters' Works and remained in the family, although different individuals were involved through the years. Most common forms were produced and some salt-glazed, cobalt-blue brush-decorated examples may be found.

CHAMBERS, LLANLLEY

Chambers & Co., Llanelly, Wales, UK
This firm was owned by William Chambers, the founder of the South Wales Pottery (see p.332), and operated c.1839-54.

CHARLESTOWN

Jonathan Fenton & Charles Carpenter, Boston and Charlestown, Massachusetts, USA
See p.290. This impressed mark appears on later wares.

C. J. M. & CO.

Charles James Mason & Co., Lane Delph, Staffordshire, UK
See p.200. This firm operated under his style 1829-45. These initials are found incorporated into a number of marks.

N. CLARK (JR.)/ATHENS (N.Y.) (N. CLARK & CO., LYONS, N.Y.)

Nathan Clark Pottery, Athens, New York, USA
See p.106. These impressed marks were used.

G. COCKER

George Cocker, Various addresses, UK

A figure modeller trained at the Derby Works, George Cocker (d.1868) later modelled for various firms and also independently. Figures and groups in unglazed porcelain or parian occur with his incised signature. The periods of his work are: Derby 1808-c.1817 and 1821-40; Coalport 1817-19; Worcester 1819-21; London c.1840-50; Mintons c.1850-60.

COPELAND & GARRETT

Copeland & Garrett, Stoke, Staffordshire, UK

Formerly Spode (see p.223), this firm operated between 1833 and 1847. Porcelain, earthenwares, parian and other wares were produced with several marks that included the factory name. The firm subsequently became W. T. Copeland (see p.245).

W. & E. CORN

W. & E. Corn, Burslem and Longport, Staffordshire, UK

Producers of earthenwares 1864-1904. Pieces are rarely marked before 1900; this name mark appears in different printed marks 1900-04.

COWDEN & WILCOX (F.H. COWDEN)/HARRISBURG, PA.

Cowden & Wilcox, Harrisburg, Pennsylvania, USA

Among the most important of the eastern Pennsylvania stoneware potteries was the firm started in 1860 at Harrisburg by John Wallace Cowden and Isaac J. Wilcox. After 1867, John's son Frederick took part in the business and remained after his father's death in 1872 and Wilcox's retirement in 1885. In 1896, J. W. Cowden joined his father Frederick, and the company remained in business until 1915. Excellent decorated stoneware was made there, and designs included the man-in-the-moon, ducks, eagles, and boats.

C.P.CO.

Crown Pottery Company, Evansville, Indiana, USA

This pottery (active 1891-c.1955) made decorated ironstone and semi-porcelain dinner and toilet ware. In later years their ware was sold in the white, and their business declined when they could not expand from their original building. These initials appear with the pattern name.

CROWN DUCAL

A. G. Richardson & Co. Ltd., Cobridge, Staffordshire, UK

See p.197. This tradename was used in several different marks used by this firm.

CROWNFORD

Ford & Sons (Ltd.), Burslem, Staffordshire, UK

See p.296. This tradename was used from the 1930s.

PAUL CUSHMAN
Paul Cushman, Albany, New York, USA
About 1807, Paul Cushman established Albany's best-known stoneware manufactory on Lion (Lyon) Street (later Washington Street) "half a mile west of Albany gaol" (an address that is incorporated into some marks). A variety of utilitarian forms, often decorated with incised designs and cobalt blue were produced until Cushman's death in 1833. They are popular with today's collectors and highly valued.

AUGUSTE DELAHERCHE
Auguste Delaherche, Various locations, France
Born in 1857, this potter worked at the Ecole des Arts Décoratifs, Paris (1877 and 1879-83), and was director of the L. Pilleux factory in Goincourt (1883-86) producing ceramic architectural decoration. From 1894-1904 he operated his own pottery at Armentières. He was awarded a gold medal at the Paris World Exhibition of 1889. His name mark appeared in a circle; his initials were also used with a number of devices.

DILLWYN (& CO.)/SWANSEA
DILLWYN'S ETRUSCAN WARE
Dillwyn & Co., Swansea, Wales, UK
See p.323. This firm operated the Cambrian Works at Swansea c.1811-17 and c.1824-50. "Dillwyn & Co" appeared in impressed or printed marks of various forms c.1811-17. "Dillwyn" or "Dillwyn, Swansea" was used c.1824-50. The printed mark "Dillwyn's Ertruscan Ware" appears c.1847-50.

DIXON (AUSTIN, PHILLIPS) & CO.
Sunderland or "Garrison" Pottery, Sunderland, Tyne and Wear, UK
See p.312. The style "Dixon & Co." appears on marks c.1813-19; "Dixon, Austin & Co." was used c.1812-40; "Dixon, Austin, Phillips & Co." appears c.1827-40; "Dixon, Phillips & Co." c.1840-65.

DUCHESS
A. T. Finney & Sons (Ltd.), Longton, Staffordshire, UK
See p.198. Many marks feature the tradename "Duchess".

(J.) DUDSON
James Dudson, Hanley, Staffordshire, UK
Based at the Hope Street Works (originally established in 1800) from 1838, James Dudson operated a pottery until his death in 1882, when it was carried on by his son. At various times, ornamental porcelain, white and coloured stonewares, Wedgwood-type jasper wares, mosaic wares, metal-mounted items, flower pots and candlesticks were produced. Many designs were registered. The mark "Dudson" appears on wares 1838-88; "J. Dudson" was used 1888-98. From 1898 the firm became Dudson Bros. Ltd.

DUNN, DUNLAP & CO.

Van Schoik & Dunn/Dunn, Dunlap & Co, Matawan, New
Jersey, USA
Founded by Josiah Van Schoik in 1802, the pottery made a
large quantity of salt-glazed stoneware utilitarian vessels for
many years, many with small flowers drawn in blue. They
also continued to make drape-moulded redware pie plates.
Although these latter are not marked, a number of jigger
moulds for plates of this shape survive from the 1860s and
1870s that were incised "DD&Co" (Dunn Dunlap & Co) by
their potter William Lowe. The factory continued until
c.1875.

J. DUNTZE/MANUFACT/R/N. HAVEN, CT.

John Duntze, New Haven, Connecticut, USA
A stoneware manufactory owned and operated by Absalom
Stedman from 1825-33 in New Haven, Connecticut, was
taken over in 1833 by the potter John Duntze. He maintained
this East Water Street Works until 1852. Fine, early, ovoid
salt-glazed stoneware forms were produced, occasionally
decorated in manganese brown.

EAST LAKE POTTERY/BRIDGETON, N.J.

East Lake Pottery, Bridgeton, New Jersey, USA
George F. Hamlyn (active c.1885-c.1910) advertised in 1889
as a manufacturer and dealer in stoneware, earthenware,
rockingham and terracotta at the East Lake Pottery. However, only redware has been found with his mark. It is
possible that he was a dealer in the other wares. The mark
appears impressed.

EASTWOOD

William Baddeley, Hanley, Staffordshire, UK
William Baddeley produced Wedgwood-type earthenwares
and basaltes at Eastwood, Hanley c.1802-22. His mark was
the word "Eastwood". The word "East" may sometimes be
indistinct and can be mistaken for "Wedgwood": collectors
must be wary of this.
   Another potter named William Baddeley worked at
Longton c.1864-75, producing terracotta and similar wares
(see p.287).

B(ARNABAS) EDMANDS (EDMANDS & CO.)/CHARLESTOWN

Edmands & Co., Charlestown, Massachusetts, USA
See p.111. These impressed marks were used.

D.J. (I.) EVANS & CO.

D.J. Evans & Co., Swansea, Wales, UK
Formerly known as Evans & Glasson (see p.296), this firm
operated the Cambrian Works from 1862 until its closure in
c.1870. The name marks above were used c.1862-70.

EVANS & GLASSON/SWANSEA

Evans & Glasson, Swansea, Wales, UK

David Evans operated the Cambrian Works at Swansea (see
p.323), in this style c.1850-62. He produced blue and white,
and agate earthenwares, which were sold mainly in Wales,
Ireland, the south-west of England and Chile. Production
was discontinued after 1870.

F. & SONS (LTD.)

Ford & Sons (Ltd.), Burslem, Staffordshire, UK

Based in Newcastle Street, Burslem, this company operated as
Ford & Sons c.1893-1938, then became Ford & Sons (Crown-
ford) Ltd. "F. & Sons" was used in many marks 1893-1938.
"Ltd." may occur after 1908.

FERRYBRIDGE

Tomlinson & Co., Ferrybridge Pottery, Yorkshire

See p.325. This mark (the "D" is sometimes reversed) was
used from 1804.

FRANCISCAN WARE/MADE IN CALIFORNIA U.S.A.

Gladding, McBean and Company, California, USA

See p.292. This printed mark was used. A number of
variations were used.

FRANKOMA

Frankoma Pottery, Sapulpa, Oklahoma, USA

Founded and operated by the Frank family from 1936, this
pottery has made earthenware dinnerware in a variety of
patterns (such as Mayan-Aztec, a line introduced in the
1940s), as well as Christmas plates, sculptured wares, souvenir
items, florists' crockery and miscellaneous novelties as commissioned. State plates in a variety of colours were also
produced. Marks are usually printed. The name "Frankoma"
appears in the mark, sometimes with pattern name; stickers
are also used; descriptions and marks are sometimes moulded
into the backs or bottoms of souvenir items.

FRAUENFELTER CHINA (USA)

Frauenfelter China Company, Zanesville, Ohio, USA

Charles Frauenfelter, who was director of the Ohio Pottery
from 1915, purchased the works in 1923 and gave it his name.
In 1918 he started making restaurant and kitchenware in the
pottery that had been producing chemical china. In 1920 he
further refined the product and began making stylish shapes
on a cream-coloured vitreous body. The firm continued until
1939. The marks are printed.

G. & C. J. M.

G. M. & C. J. Mason, Lane Delph, Staffordshire, UK

See p.200. Marks incorporating the initials of George Miles
and Charles James Mason occur before 1829.

JOHN GEDDES/VERREVILLE POTTERY
John Geddes (& Son), Glasgow, Scotland, UK

This firm was based at the Verreville Pottery, which was originally built for a glass-house in 1777. They were sold in 1806 to John Geddes subject to the understanding that he was not to produce crown or bottle glass. He produced flint glass, and after 1820 began to produce earthenwares. Geddes worked with various partners, including Robert Alexander Kidston after 1827. In 1838 the works passed into the hands of Kidston, who began to make porcelain as well as glass and earthenware. Figures, porcelain basket work and flowers were produced by skilled craftsmen who had previously worked at Derby and Coalport. Kidston and his partners carried on the concern until 1846, when the company became Robert Cochran & Co. This concern produced only earthenwares and white granite wares. Robert Cochran died in 1869 and the business was taken over by his son. The firm continued until 1918. The mark above was used c.1806-24; "& Son" was added 1824-27.

W.S. GEORGE
W. S. George Pottery Company, East Palestine, Ohio, USA

Although this was called the Continental China Company from 1904-09, W. S. George had controlling interest in the operation which was set up in the old factory of the East Palestine Pottery Company (1884-1904). Like its predecessors, the W. S. George Pottery Company made white and decorated ware, including semi-porcelain dinner and toilet ware. The firm continued until 1960. Many marks appear with pattern names arranged in circles, lines, wreaths or other devices, but all include "W. S. George".

GIBSON & SONS (LTD.)
GIBSONS
Gibson & Sons (Ltd.), Burslem, Staffordshire, UK

See p.187. Many marks were used by this firm incorporating these name marks. "Gibsons" mainly appears in marks used after c.1940.

GLASGOW POTTERY CO./TRENTON N.J.
Glasgow Pottery, Trenton, New Jersey, USA

See p.176. This printed mark was used.

GLOBE POTTERY CO. LTD.
Globe Pottery Co. Ltd., Cobridge and Shelton, Staffordshire, UK

See p.261. This name mark was incorporated into a large number of marks used by this firm.

GOODWIN'S HOTEL CHINA
Goodwin Pottery/Goodwin Brothers, East Liverpool, Ohio, USA

See p.239. This printed mark was used.

GORHAM/EST. 1831/ FINE CHINA/FLINTRIDGE/USA

Gorham Company, Providence, Rhode Island, USA

This company, known for many generations for its high-quality silver products (produced from 1831), expanded into the general tabletop business during the late 1960s and early 1970s by buying selected manufacturers, including the Flintridge China Company, Pasadena, California, making dinnerware since 1945. Gorham/Flintridge produced fine porcelain tableware in shapes and patterns to compete with Lenox China. Indeed, Lenox bought the Gorham Company in 1991. This printed mark appears.

GRAFTON CHINA

A. B. Jones & Sons (Ltd.), Longton, Staffordshire, UK

See p.155. This tradename was used in marks.

G. (GEO) GRAINGER/WORCESTER

George Grainger (& Co.), Worcester, Hereford and Worcester, UK

See below and p.156. Many painted or printed marks include this name mark. After c.1850 "& Co." was added to most marks.

GRAINGER LEE & CO./WORCESTER

Grainger, Lee & Co., Worcester, Hereford and Worcester, UK

A porcelain works was established by Thomas Grainger in 1801. He went into partnership with a skilled painter, and the company was known as Grainger, Wood & Co. In 1812 Grainger went into partnership with his brother-in-law, and the style changed to Grainger & Lee. After Mr. Lee retired from the business, it was carried on by Thomas Grainger until 1839, when he was succeeded by his son George, and the firm became G. Grainger & Co. Early wares feature this written mark; printed marks also occur in many forms.

GRAINGER WOOD & CO./WORCESTER/WARRANTED

Grainger, Wood & Co., Worcester, Hereford and Worcester, UK

See above. This company produced porcelains c.1801-12. Most examples are unmarked, but some written marks similar to the one above were used.

GREATBATCH

William Greatbatch, Fenton, Staffordshire, UK

Potter and modeller, William Greatbatch was apprentice to Thomas Whieldon. He was later associated with Josiah Wedgwood from c.1760, and among other things, modelled relief designs on wares including landscapes that were used on salt-glazed and green-glazed ware. His name appears on some wares with transfer prints coloured by hand in the 1770-80 period. Later printed creamwares may bear the name on the print.

B. GREEN/PHILAD:

Branch Green, Philadelphia, Pennsylvania, USA

Branch Green had been a stoneware potter in Troy, New York, as early as 1799 and moved to New Jersey by 1805. In 1809 he located his stoneware factory in Philadelphia at "2nd above Germantown Road." His production consisted of jugs, pitchers, jars, butter tubs, and milk pots. Many of the jugs were evidently intended for liquor distillers or retail spirits merchants since they are stamped "Wine", "Rum", etc. He operated until 1827.

GREENWOOD CHINA/TRENTON, N.J.

Greenwood Pottery Company, Trenton, New Jersey, USA

See p.210. This impressed name mark was used.

GRINDLEY HOTEL WARE

Grindley Hotel Ware Co. Ltd., Tunstall, Staffordshire, UK

Established in 1908, this company produced earthenwares with this name mark.

W.H. GRINDLEY & CO.

W. H. Grindley & Co. (Ltd.), Tunstall, Staffordshire, UK

See p.199. This name was incorporated into many marks.

GROSVENOR CHINA

Jackson & Gosling, Longton, Staffordshire, UK

Initially founded in c.1866 at King Street, Fenton, this firm was later based at the Grosvenor Works in Longton (from c.1909). It operated under various owners 1866-1961. Porcelain services were produced, and the firm produced for the home and export markets.

(W. H.) HACKWOOD

William Hackwood, Hanley, Staffordshire, UK

This potter produced earthenwares at the Eastwood Pottery 1827-43. The impressed name "Hackwood" is found. The firm subsequently became William Hackwood & Son.

HAIDINGER

Gebrüder Haidinger, Elbogen (Locket n.0), Czech Republic

The Haidinger Brothers founded a porcelain factory in 1815, with the support of Niedermayer, director of the Vienna Porcelain Works 1805-27. Initially white porcelain was made, which was greyish in colour. Output later improved, and pieces were taken to Sèvres in 1836. The last of the Haidinger Brothers died in 1870 and in 1873 the factory was sold to Springer & Oppenheimer.

HALL

Samuel Hall, Hanley, Staffordshire, UK

This potter produced earthenwares c.1841-56. The name "Hall" appears on some rare earthenware figures which were attributed to John and Ralph Hall (see below). However, directories do not list John and Ralph Hall as producers of figures, while Samuel Hall is listed as such a manufacturer.

I. HALL (& SONS)

John Hall (& Son), Burslem, Staffordshire, UK

Active as a potter 1814-32, John Hall was in partnership with Ralph Hall between 1802 and 1822. In 1822 he took over the Stych Pottery in Burslem and continued until 1832. The mark "I. Hall" appears in many marks 1814-22; "I. Hall & Sons" was used c.1822-32, and may be impressed or printed.

R. HALL (& SON, & CO.)

Ralph Hall & Co. (& Son), Tunstall, Staffordshire, UK

Ralph Hall owned the Swan Bank Works c.1822-48 and produced earthenwares. He was formerly in partnership with John Hall at the Stych Pottery in Burslem 1802-22, and in Tunstall 1811-22 (see above). His name was found in several printed marks: "R. Hall" appears 1822-41; "R. Hall & Son" was used on American subject prints c.1836; "R. Hall & Co." was incorporated into several printed marks 1841-49.

HAMMERSLEY & CO.

Hammersley & Co., Longton, Staffordshire, UK

Based at the Alsager Pottery, this firm produced porcelain 1887-1932 before becoming Hammersley & Co. (Longton) Ltd. The factory name appears in many marks.

HAMPSHIRE POTTERY

Hampshire Pottery Company/James S. Taft & Company, Keene, New Hampshire, USA

See p.52. This printed mark appears in a double circle.

GEO. F. HAMLYN/EAST LAKE POTTERY/BRIDGETON, N.J.

East Lake Pottery, Bridgeton, New Jersey, USA

See p.295. The mark is impressed.

(T.) HARLEY

Thomas Harley, Lane End, Staffordshire, UK

Thomas Harley produced some good earthenware services, jugs and other items c.1802-08. His name mark appears impressed on fine lustre decorated jugs, and printed or written in writing letters.

(T.) HARRINGTON/LYONS (N.Y.)

Thompson Harrington, Lyons, New York, USA

In 1852, Thompson Harrington, a potter who had worked in Hartford, Connecticut, took over the Lyons, New York, pottery that George G. Williams had run for Nathan Clark & Co. Harrington, too, specialized in utilitarian salt-glazed stoneware. However, his marked wares are especially prized by collectors for their cobalt-blue trailed lions, horses, and sunbursts with human faces at the centres. This successful manufacturer also produced brown Albany-slip glazed stoneware. The firm was active until 1872. These impressed marks appear.

HARTLEY, GREENS & CO./LEEDS POTTERY
Hartley, Greens & Co., Leeds, West Yorkshire, UK

This firm was based at the Leeds Pottery from c.1781, producing creamwares for export until the firm became bankrupt in 1820. This name mark appears in many impressed marks of differing form.

HAVILAND (& CO.)
David Haviland, Limoges, France

An important porcelain factory was founded here in 1842, producing porcelain wares, and also decorating pieces from other factories. David Haviland's sons Charles and Théodore became owners in 1879. A subsidiary firm at Auteil (1873-85) produced wares decorated in the Impressionist style. Haviland also used Tang shell motifs from c.1870. A number of marks feature the name above.

HAWLEY BROS. (LTD.)
Hawley Bros. (Ltd.), Rotheram, South Yorkshire, UK

In 1855 the Northfield Pottery in Rotheram was bought by George Hawley who produced the common types of earthenware. After George Hawley's death the business was continued by his son William, and his two brothers. The style was for a time W. & G. Hawley, and then Hawley Bros. until 1903 when the form became Northfield Hawley Pottery Co. Ltd. This name mark was used; "Ltd." appears on some marks from 1897.

THÉODORE HAVILAND
Théodore Haviland, Limoges, France

See above. Théodore Haviland founded his own porcelain factory in 1893, producing table services and luxury ware. Renowned artists were employed by him as decorators. His name appears in many marks.

H. B.
Hawley Bros. (Ltd.), Rotheram, South Yorkshire, UK

See above. A printed mark featuring these intertwined initials was used 1868-c.1898.

H. & C.
Hope & Carter, Burslem, Staffordshire, UK

Based at Fountain Place, this company produced earthenwares 1862-80. The works were taken over by G. L. Ashworth & Bros. c.1880. These initials were found in several printed marks, often with the pattern name.

H. D./DUBLIN

Henri Delamain, Dublin, Eire

The Belgian Henri Delamain (d.1757), made pottery in
Dublin from 1752, although a delftware pottery had been in
existence from 1735. Wares are characterized by bright blue
or manganese purple decoration, usually comprising elaborate
scroll borders around landscape paintings. Most wares are
unmarked, but the monogram "HD" is known with the name
"Dublin" added.

HEREND

Moritz Farkashazy-Fischer, Herend, Hungary

A porcelain factory was founded here in 1839 by Moritz
Farkashazy-Fischer with the help of Prince Esterhazy. Many
of the pieces made were replacements for pieces from famous
collections; these were made to such a high standard that only
the marks gave them away. Polychrome decoration was used
that required items to be fired up to three times. Quality of
later pieces was variable. The place name "Herend" is
incorporated into numerous marks used by the company.

HOLLAND & GREEN

Holland & Green, Longton, Staffordshire, UK

This firm produced earthenwares, ironstones and other wares
at the Stafford Street Works 1853-82. Toilet services of high
quality were made in rich colours with elaborate gilding.

S. HOLLINS

Samuel Hollins, Shelton, Staffordshire, UK

Samuel Hollins made fine redware teapots and other items,
basaltes and other Wedgwood-type wares at Vale Pleasant
c.1774-1813. He was also a partner in the New Hall China
Works, and remained so until his death in 1820. His name
mark appears impressed.

HONITON (LACE ART) POTTERY (CO.)

Honiton Art Potteries Ltd., Honiton, Devon, UK

Established in 1881, this company which operated under
various titles and owners, produced earthenwares. Early
wares were usually unmarked. "The Honiton Lace Art
Pottery Co." appears as a printed or impressed mark and
was registered in 1915. "Honiton Pottery Devon" appears as
a printed, moulded or impressed mark from 1947.

F. M. (F. D.) HONORÉ

F. M. Honoré, Boulevard St. Antoine, Paris, France

A porcelain factory was established by F.M. Honoré in 1785.
In 1812 he took his sons Edward and Théodore into partnership. They then collaborated with Dagoty and opened a
new factory, and the style of the firm changed to "Dagoty et
Honoré". The partnership ended in 1820 and the factories
were divided between them.

HOWE & CLARK/ATHENS
Nathan Clark Pottery, Athens, New York, USA
See p.106. This impressed mark was used.

HÜTTL
Theodor Hüttl, Budapest, Hungary
A factory was founded by Theodor Hüttl in 1852, initially for porcelain painting, but later full production began. Work was mainly commission-based. Hüttl himself died in 1910, and the concern was continued by his sons. Wares include table settings, tea and coffee services and restaurant ware.

I. I.
John Ifield, Wrotham, Kent, UK
The above initials occur on examples of Wrotham earthenware, with dated examples from 1674 and 1676. The initial "I" was often used instead of "J" during this period.

IMPERIAL (PORCELAIN)
Wedgwood & Co. (Ltd.), Tunstall, Staffordshire, UK
See p.206. This tradename appears from c.1906.

I. M. & S.
John Meir & Son, Tunstall, Staffordshire, UK
See p.304. These initials also refer to this firm.

INTERNATIONAL CHINA/TRENTON, N.J.
International Pottery/Burgess & Campbell, Trenton, New Jersey, USA
See p.213. This printed mark was used.

IROQUOIS CASUAL CHINA BY RUSSEL WRIGHT
Iroquois China Company, Syracuse, New York, USA
Semi-porcelain tableware for domestic and institutional consumption was made early in the history of this pottery. Beginning in 1939, the new owner made only hotel ware. In 1946, the company started three new dinnerware lines, including "Casual China" by designer Russel Wright, and "Impromptu" and "Informal" designed by Bob Seibel. By about 1960, hotel ware was abandoned so that the company could concentrate on the three dinnerware lines. The factory continued until 1969. This printed mark appears.

JACKSON & GOSLING
Jackson & Gosling, Longton, Staffordshire, UK
See p.299. This name mark was used in many marks.

J. B.
James Beech, Tunstall and Burslem, Staffordshire, UK
This firm operated at the Swan Bank Potteries in Burslem and Tunstall 1877-89. These initials appear with the printed mark of a swan, often with the pattern name.

These initials were also used by James Broadhurst & Sons Ltd. (see p.291), 1862-70.

J. B. & S. (SON)

James Beech & Son, Longton, Staffordshire, UK
Producers of porcelain 1860-98, this firm should not be confused with James Beech (above). Several printed marks include the initials above, including a crowned Staffordshire knot mark (with the word "England" 1891-98).

The initials "J. B. & S." were also used by James Broadhurst & Sons Ltd. (see p.291), 1870-1922. "Ltd." was added from 1922.

J. (F.) & C. W.

James & Charles Wileman, Longton, Staffordshire, UK
Based at the Foley China Works, this firm (formerly Henry Wileman) produced earthenwares 1864-69. These distinguishing initials were found in several printed marks.

J. F. W.

James F. Wileman, Longton, Staffordshire, UK
The firm James & Charles Wileman (see above) was continued by James F. Wileman 1869-92. His name or initial mark appears on printed marks of differing design.

J. M. & S.

Job Meigh (& Son), Hanley, Staffordshire, UK
See p.308. These initials appear c.1812-34, but usually relate to J. Meir & Son, an earthenware-producing firm based at the Greengates Pottery in Tunstall 1837-97. Originally John Meir (c.1812-36) this firm made services from the ordinary classes of earthenwares, and the initials appear in many different marks.

J. T. (& S.)

John Tams (& Son) (Ltd.), Longton, Staffordshire, UK
Based at the Crown Pottery from c.1875, this firm specialized in the production of Government measures, jugs and mugs. The initials "J. T." appear 1875-90, and may also appear as a monogram within a garter, crown and wreath mark. "J. T. & S." appears c.1903-12 when the company was known as John Tams & Son. After 1912, the firm became John Tams Ltd.

J. & W. R.

John & William Ridgway, Shelton, Staffordshire, UK
Originally Job Ridgway & Sons (see p.314), this firm used a variety of marks that featured the distinguishing initials seen here.

K. E. & K.

Knight Elkin & Knight, Fenton, Staffordshire, UK
Also listed as Knight, Elkin & Co., this firm succeeded Elkin,

Knight & Bridgwood after 1840. These initials appear in many printed marks, which may also feature the pattern name. After the retirement of Mr. Elkin in 1846, the style was changed to J. K. Knight.

KELSBORO' WARE
Longton New Art Pottery Co. Ltd., Longton, Staffordshire, UK
Based at the Gordon Pottery, this company produced earthenwares 1932-65. Variations of the mark occur, but all include the tradename "Kelsboro".

KISHERE (POTTERY)/MORTLAKE (SURREY)
Joseph Kishere, Mortlake, London, UK
Stonewares were made by Joseph Kishere at the Mortlake Pottery during the first quarter of the 19thC, c.1800-43. Impressed marks appear in a number of forms, including those above. William Kishere succeeded his father.

KIRKHAM (S)
Kirkham's Ltd., Stoke, Staffordshire, UK
Operating between 1946 and 1961, this company produced earthenwares, with a variety of marks that feature this name.

J. K. KNIGHT
John, King, Knight, Fenton, Staffordshire, UK
See p.304. This name mark was used 1846-53, before the firm became Knight & Wileman. The name "Foley" sometimes appears with these marks.

KNOWLES
Matthew Knowles & Son, Brampton, Derbyshire, UK
The Welshpool and Payne Potteries came into the hand of Matthew Knowles in 1835. He was later joined in business by his son, and the style of the firm changed to Matthew Knowles & Sons. All types of brown and stonewares were made for export to Australia, Russia, Africa and Jamaica, as well as for the domestic market. The output included good quality stoneware spirit bottles, kegs and barrels, ginger beer bottles made in both stoneware and brownware, jam jars, stew and sauce pots, bowls, colanders, tobacco jars, jugs and a wide variety of other items. Notable were high quality water filters, and finely-coloured Chesterfield ware. The firm continued until 1911.

KORZEC
Prince Iwan Czartorsky, Korzec, Poland
A porcelain factory was founded here by Prince Iwan Czartorsky, and was active 1790-97. The factory was burned down in 1798 and production transferred to Gorodnitza. In 1803 Mérault from Sèvres managed the factory, and some very beautiful pieces were produced. The name "Korzec" appears in many marks used by the factory.

K.T. & K./CHINA
Knowles, Taylor and Knowles, East Liverpool, Ohio, USA
See p.176. This is one of the marks used.

KUZNECOVS (/LATVIJA)
T. J. Kusnetzoff, Various locations, Europe
T. J. Kusnetzoff was one of a family of porcelain factory
owners that ran large, successful factories throughout the
19thC and into the 20thC, producing utility wares. A large
number of marks are used; some feature the name as it
appears above, on others the name appears in Cyrillic script.

LAMSON & SWASEY/PORTLAND, ME.
Lamson & Swasey, Portland, Maine, USA
In 1875, an earthenware pottery was opened by Rufus
Lamson and Eben Swasey at Portland, Maine, but, within
three years, the Portland Pottery Works began to make salt-
glazed utilitarian stoneware, sometimes decorated in blue.
After Lamson left in 1883, Swasey took on a new partner,
L. Frank Jones, until Lamson's return in 1886. The firm
continued until c.1905. Many of their examples are half
dipped in Albany slip producing a distinctive glaze contrast.
This impressed mark was used.

LANCASTER SADLAND LTD.
Lancaster & Sadland Ltd., Hanley, Staffordshire, UK
Formerly Lancaster & Sons (Ltd.) (see p.157), this name mark
appears in several marks of differing design from 1944.

J. LOCKETT & CO.
J. Lockett & Co., Lane End, Staffordshire, UK
This firm produced earthenwares c.1812-89 at King Street,
Lane End, 1882-1960 at Longton, and from 1960 at Burslem.
Impressed or printed marks appear with the name in full as
seen above.

J. LOCKETT & SONS
J. Lockett & Sons, Longton, Staffordshire, UK
A firm with this name produced earthenwares 1828-35 with
this impressed mark. The firm subsequently became John &
Thomas Lockett.

L. S.
Lancaster & Sons (Ltd.), Hanley, Staffordshire, UK
See p.157. These initials were used in many marks 1900-06;
"& Sons" or "& S" was added from 1906.

MCCOY (USA)
Nelson McCoy Pottery, Roseville, Ohio, USA
This pottery (active 1910-present) made stoneware churns,
butter jars, crocks and drainage tiles when it was first
organized, but for many years has manufactured a variety

of novelty consumer items, including biscuit jars, planters, ash trays, mugs and florists' crockery. Today it is owned by the Mount Clemens Pottery Company, Michigan, but continues to operate under its original name. (Note that this company should not be confused with J. W. McCoy Pottery, Roseville OH, which made florists' crockery in the style of Rookwood, 1899-1911.) "McCoy" and "McCoy USA" are the most common name marks; sometimes the "M" and "c" overlap at the beginning of the name.

J. MCCULLY/TRENTON
Joseph McCully Pottery, Trenton, New Jersey, USA
Joseph McCully and his nephew, Joseph McCully, made and marked slip-decorated redware plates, platters and jars c.1800-52. They may have made other forms also, but these were not marked. This name mark is impressed in an oval.

MALING
Maling (various christian names), Sunderland, Tyne and Wear, UK
William Maling established the North Hylton or Hylton Pottery in 1762 for his sons Christopher and John. John's son Robert joined the business in 1797, and the concern continued until 1815 when a new factory was built at Ouseburn, Newcastle. Early wares are unmarked, but an impressed name mark was occasionally used on early 19thC pieces, c.1800-15.

This mark was also used at the Ouseburn Pottery by Robert Maling on general earthenwares c.1817-59.

In 1859, Robert's son Christopher became the owner of the firm. The style changed to C. T. Maling, and he built the Ford Potteries in Newcastle and the firm continued there until 1963 (see p.165). He used the "Maling" name mark c.1859-90.

J. MANTELL/PENN YAN
James Mantell, Penn Yan, New York, USA
This pottery was operated near the village of Penn Yan before 1830 by the Campbell family, but by 1855 James Mantell, who had been born in England and worked as a potter at Lyons, New York, owned the factory, first with Shem Thomas, and later alone. The business was a successful one, and well-decorated examples survive in substantial number. Mantell's partner, Shem Thomas, went on to operate his own stoneware kiln at Harrisburg, Pennsylvania, in 1856 and also worked at the Cowden & Wilcox Pottery until his death in 1871. This impressed mark appears.

MAW (& CO.)
Maw & Co. (Ltd.), Broseley, Shropshire, UK
Originally established at Worcester in 1850, this firm produced plain, geometric, mosaic and ordinary encaustic

tiles. The concern was moved to the Benthall Works at Broseley in 1852. A great deal of experimentation was carried out, and many different decorative techniques were used. Notable were *tesserae* (small pieces of pottery) for mosaic work decorated with rich enamels, embossed tiles, *sgraffiato* decorated tiles, "slip painting", and *pâte-sur-pâte*. Art pottery was produced from c.1875, which comprised a variety of majolica wares. The firm continued until c.1970.

T. J. & J. MAYER

Thomas, John & Joseph Mayer, Burslem, Staffordshire, UK
This firm was based at the Dale Hall Works 1843-55 before becoming Mayer Bros. & Elliot and then Mayer & Elliot (see p.55). The firm's wares were shown at the 1851, 1853 and 1855 Exhibitions, and their range of general ceramics including parian, were highly regarded, particularly their moulded parian ware. The title "Mayer Bros." was also used.

MAYER CHINA/BEAVER FALLS, PA.

Mayer China Company/Mayer Potteries Company,,
Syracuse, New York, USA
See p.226. This printed mark was used in the 20thC.

C J MEADERS/CLEVELAND, GA.

Cheever and Q. Lanier Meaders, White County, Georgia, USA
Cheever Meaders (1887-1967) took over the management and production of the original Meaders family pottery in 1920 and continued to make traditional alkaline-glazed stoneware for local use. His wife, Arie, developed a line of decorated tablewares and inspired her husband to produce some original forms of his own. Their son, Q. Lanier Meaders (b.1917), eventually joined in the family business in 1967, and he is best known for the humorous face-jugs he fashions in stoneware. The business continued until 1989. The name "Lanier Meaders" also appears incised in script.

MEIGH

Job Meigh (& Son), Hanley, Staffordshire, UK
Based at the Old Hall Pottery, this firm produced earthenwares c.1805-34 (& Son from c.1812). This impressed name mark was used 1805-34.
   The firm subsequently became Charles Meigh, and this name appears on wares made 1835-49, sometimes with the date of the introduction of the design or other information. The firm became C. Meigh, Son & Pankhurst in 1849, and the Charles Meigh & Son in 1850 (see p.274).

MELBAR WARE

Barlows (Longton) Ltd., Longton, Staffordshire, UK
Based at the Melbourne Works, this company produced earthenwares 1920-52. This trade name appears in their marks.

MERCER POTTERY/TRENTON N.J.

Mercer Pottery Company, Trenton, New Jersey, USA

Established by James Moses in 1868, this large pottery specialized in decorated semi-porcelain table, toilet wares, druggist's wares (such as pestles and mortars). Mercer shared business partners and products with the International Pottery Company (see p.213), organized in 1879, and the New York City Pottery (see p.176); thus the three potteries also shared for a time a mark with two shields differentiated only by the name that appears below the shields. The tradename "Mercer China" also appears in a number of marks. The Mercer Pottery Company continued until 1900.

MIDDLESBORO POTTERY (CO.)

Middlesbrough Pottery Co., North Yorkshire, UK

See p.161. The name "Middlesboro Pottery" or "Middlesboro Pottery Co." appeared in impressed or printed marks c.1834-44, and may feature an anchor device. "Middlesboro Pottery" was also used by this firm's successor, the Middlesbrough Earthenware Co. 1844-52, again with an anchor device.

MIDWINTER

W. R. Midwinter (Ltd.), Burslem, Staffordshire, UK

See p.201. This distinguishing name mark appears in many different marks.

C. J. (W. F.) MILLER/VICKSBURG, MISS.

C. J. and W. F. Miller, Vicksburg, Mississippi, USA

C. J. Miller established his stoneware pottery along the Mississippi River at Vicksburg in 1890 and produced white Bristol-glazed wares until his son, W. F. Miller, took over the pottery in 1910. Manufactured jugs, crocks and jars continued in production until at least 1930. These stencilled marks appear.

MONMOUTH/POTTERY CO./MONMOUTH, ILL.

Monmouth Pottery Company, Monmouth, Illinois, USA

A major commercial stoneware factory was erected at Monmouth, Illinois, in 1893 by William Hanna, a banker, and associates, to take advantage of rich and extensive local deposits of stoneware clays. The factory had an annual production of over 6 million gallons of pottery when, in 1906, it merged with the Western Stoneware Company. Bristol and Albany slip glazed wares are frequently found, and blue sponge-decorated pitchers, crocks, etc. are avidly collected. This mark in raised letters appears.

MOORE (BROS.)

Moore (Bros.), Longton, Staffordshire, UK

See p.147. "Moore" printed or impressed, was used c.1868-75; "Moore Bros." appears 1872-1905. "Moore Bothers England" was used 1891-1905.

MORLEY WARE
William Morley & Co. Ltd., Fenton, Staffordshire, UK
See p.187. This tradename appears in marks used by both
Morley Fox & Co. Ltd. and William Morley & Co.

MORRISON & CARR
New York City Pottery , New York, New York, USA
See p.176. This mark appears impressed in an oval.

NANTGARW
Nantgarw China Works, Glamorgan, Wales, UK
This works was opened by William Billingsley of Derby
in 1813. Following an inspection of the premises and the
production by Mr Dillwyn of the Cambrian Pottery,
Billingsley and his partner Samuel Walker were persuaded to
move to Swansea. This arrangement ended after two years
and Billingsley and Walker returned to Nantgarw where they
produced high quality porcelain for about four years before
production ended. Notable is a service presented to the Prince
of Wales (later George IV). This impressed, painted or
stencilled name mark was used; sometimes the initials "C.
W." for "China Works" are also included.

NASHVILLE POTTERY
Nashville Pottery Co., Nashville, Tennessee, USA
In 1888, William McLee and C. C. Laitenberger started a
stoneware pottery at Nashville, which produced a fine Albany
slip-glazed ware. Many common utilitarian forms were
manufactured, including jugs, crocks, pans, preserve jars, and
churns. The pottery remained in operation until 1900; in the
1901 Nashville City Directory, the factory is listed as "vacant."
This impressed mark was used.

NEALE (& CO.)
(James) Neale & Co., Hanley, Staffordshire, UK
See p.144. This name mark was used in a number of forms;
"& Co." was added c.1778-86.
    This firm's predecessor Neale & Palmer marked their
wares with their name c.1769-78.

N(ORTH) STAFFORDSHIRE POTTERY CO. LTD.
North Staffordshire Pottery Co. Ltd., Cobridge & Hanley,
Staffordshire, UK
This firm produced earthenwares 1940-52 before being taken
over by Ridgway Potteries Ltd. The firm's registered
trademark was a rock emerging from water, and the slogan
"Strong As The Rock". This trademark was continued by
Ridgways.

E. & L. P. (J. & E.) NORTON/BENNINGTON, VT.
Edward & Luman P. Norton, Bennington, Vermont, USA
The most prolific of the stoneware potteries of Bennington,

Vermont, was run by Edward and Luman Preston Norton, after the death of Julius Norton, who, with his cousin Edward, had managed the factory since 1850. Wares dating from their partnership include some of the finest and most elaborate cobalt-blue trailed lions, deer, eagles, etc. found on American stoneware. While under Edward and Luman's partnership, decorated wares continued to be made, though they were not as consistently imaginative. They did, however, manufacture fancy Rockingham pottery forms, including hound-handled pitchers, teapots, and spittoons. This firm continued until 1881. These impressed marks appear.

F. B. NORTON (& CO., SONS, & SONS)/ WORCESTER, MASS.

Frank B. Norton, Worcester, Massachusetts, USA

In 1858 Frank B. Norton of the Bennington, Vermont, family of potters and Frederick Hancock opened a successful stoneware manufactory at Worcester, Massachusetts. Norton's sons entered the pottery business in 1868, and Hancock left the business in 1877. A highly popular, blue-decorated and saltglazed stoneware was produced using some of the slip-trailed designs introduced at Bennington. He continued until 1894.

O. P. CO/CHINA (IMPERIAL)

Onondaga Pottery, Syracuse, New York, USA

See p.158. This printed mark was used.

O.P. CO./SYRACUSE/CHINA

Syracuse China Company, Syracuse, New York, USA

Although this company was not officially created until 1966, the trade name "Syracuse China" had been used since 1897 on an individual product line made by the Onondaga Pottery Company (see p.158). When the line was created in the 19thC it was a vitreous china dinnerware apart from the pottery's graniteware line. Today Syracuse specializes in high-quality hotel and institutional ware. This mark was printed on wares pre-1966.

PALISSY

Albert E. Jones (Longton) Ltd., Longton, Staffordshire, UK

Formerly A. B. Jones & Sons (Ltd.) (see p.155), this name mark was used both by this firm 1905-46, and its successor Palissy Pottery Ltd. 1946-89.

PATTERSON & CO.

Patterson & Co., Newcastle-upon-Tyne, Tyne and Wear, UK

This firm was based at the Sheriff Hill Pottery from c.1830. He produced mainly white wares, much of which was exported to Scandinavia. The firm operated until 1904 when the Sheriff's Hill Pottery Co. was formed. Many printed or impressed marks include this name.

APSLEY PELLATT & CO.
Apsley Pellatt (& Co. Ltd.), London, UK
The name of this firm of ceramics and glass retailers (established in c.1789) appears on some marks, mainly during the second half of the 19thC or the 20thC.

PENN YAN
James Mantell, Penn Yan, New York, USA
See p.307. This impressed mark was used.

J. PHILLIPS/SUNDERLAND POTTERY
PHILLIPS & CO.
Sunderland or "Garrison" Pottery, Sunderland,
Tyne and Wear, UK
Established by John Phillips c.1807, this works was carried on by Dixon, Austin, Phillips & Co., who produced white and Queen's ware with all types of decoration. The works was discontinued in c.1865. The mark above was used c.1807-12. Phillips & Co. appears c.1813-19.

PHOENIX/FACTORY/ED SC
Phoenix Factory, Shaw's Creek, South Carolina, USA
In 1840 Collin Rhodes and Robert Mathis established the Phoenix Factory pottery, which made probably the most elaborate and decorative southern stonewares. Thomas Chandler is credited with the development of the brown and white slip-decorated alkaline-glazed pieces produced at the Phoenix Factory, though Collin Rhodes maintained this style of decoration after Chandler left in 1845 and Rhodes' partner, Mathis, withdrew in 1846. The factory continued until 1853. This impressed mark was used.

PORT DUNDAS/GLASGOW POTTERY
Port Dundas Pottery Co. Ltd., Glasgow, Scotland, UK
These works were established for the production of stoneware c.1816, and operated under many owners until 1845 when they were taken over by James Miller who traded as James Miller & Co. and then the Port Dundas Pottery Co. Output included chemical vessels, apparatus of various types and later water pipes. Stoneware beer, ink and spirit bottles and other items with a cream-coloured glaze were also produced. This firm was one of those that pioneered the development of the steam-driven potter's wheel. The firm continued until 1932.

PRAG
K.L. Kriegel and others, Prag, Bohemia, Czech Republic
Originally a stoneware factory founded by the Kunerle brothers in 1793, the factory began to produce porcelain in 1837 when K.L. Kriegel became the director. Kriegel, together with K. Wolf, became the leaseholder 1837-41. Kriegel and E. Hoffman Von Hoffmansthal became the

owners in 1882. Attractive porcelain figures dominated the
production. The name "Prag" is incorporated into many
marks, including "Prag-Smichow", the mark used 1854-94.

PRATT
William Pratt, Lane Delph, Staffordshire, UK

In c.1780 William Pratt (d.1799) founded a factory which
produced lead-glazed earthenware, coloured and moulded
figures, jugs and other wares. The works were taken over by
his eldest son Felix in 1810. Later the ware was copied by
local potters. In the mid-19thC the Pratt family also produced
ware decorated with polychrome transfer prints, such as the
well-known "pot-lids" (pottery covers for shallow circular
containers, which often contained bear's grease which was
used as a dressing for men's hair). The impressed name
"Pratt" occasionally appears, but it is difficult to state with
certainty which member of the family employed this mark.

PRICE (BROS.)
Price Brothers, Burslem, Staffordshire, UK

Established in 1896, this earthenware-producing firm was
initially based at the Crown Works. This name mark was
used by this firm 1896-1903, and by its successors, Price Bros.
(Burslem) Ltd. (1903-61), and Price & Kensington Potteries
Ltd. at Longport (from 1962).

S. (H.) PURDY/OHIO
Solomon and Henry Purdy, Mogadore, Ohio, USA

Solomon Purdy arrived from Connecticut to Zanesville,
Ohio, in 1812 and quickly established a stoneware pottery. He
moved to Akron in 1828 and, later, to Mogadore, five miles
south-east of Akron. His early ovoid shapes in cobalt-blue,
brush-decorated salt-glazed stoneware are among the more
highly sought-after examples of Ohio pottery. In 1840,
Solomon's son, Henry Purdy, took over management of the
shop and continued in business until 1850. These impressed
marks were used.

QUEEN ANNE
Shore & Coggins, Longton, Staffordshire, UK

See p.319. This tradename was one of those used from c.1949.

ERIC RAVILIOUS
Eric Ravilious, Staffordshire, UK

Utility wares were designed by Eric Ravilious for Wedgwood
during the late 1930s. *Alphabet* nurseryware was designed in
1937; another well-known design is the zodiac series. Most
designs were not executed until the 1950s. Some were
reissued in the late 180s due to popular demand, but these
lack the characteristic signs of wear of the originals. Wares
are signed in a small rectangular panel "designed by Eric
Ravilious", and carry an imprinted Wedgwood mark.

HENRY REMMEY/MANUFACTORY/ PHILADELPHIA

Remmey Manufactory, Philadelphia, Pennsylvania, USA

Henry H. Remmey, the son of potter John Remmey of Manhattan, New York, purchased c.1827 an existing stoneware factory in Philadelphia, Pennsylvania. After 1859 his son, Richard C. Remmey, assumed control of the company and it flourished for many years. Some fine decorated "after-hours" and gift pieces are known, but the main production was simply decorated with leaves in cobalt blue.

J. REMMEY/MANHATTAN WELLS/NEW YORK

John Remmey, Sr., Jr., and III, Manhattan, New York, USA

The first John Remmey operated a stoneware factory on Pottbaker's Hill in southern Manhattan from c.1735. After his father's death in 1762, John Remmey, Jr. continued to operate the pottery until he died in 1792. By then, he had been joined by his two sons, John III and Henry, who were also potters. The pottery adjoined the water works, and this explains the use of "Manhattan Wells, New York" to identify their location on their marked pots. Infrequently, blue incised floral decoration was added to the utilitarian wares. The concern continued until 1820.

C. RHODES MAKER

Phoenix Factory, Shaw's Creek, South Carolina, USA

See p.313. This slip-trailed mark was used by Collin Rhodes.

G. RICHARD & C.

Giulio Richard, Milan, Italy

A factory was founded here in 1833 by Luigi Tinelli and produced porcelain and faience. Copies of Wedgwood wares were made but feature the mark of this factory. Luigi's brother Carlo took over the business and went into partnership with Giulio Richard from Turin in 1841. Richard became the sole owner in 1870, and in 1896 his company amalgamated with Ginori of Doccia.

RIDGWAY (& SONS)

Job Ridgway & Sons, Shelton, Staffordshire, UK

Job Ridgway originally established a firm at Cauldon Place c.1802, having formerly been in partnership with his brother George at the Bell Works (c.1782-1802). Job took his sons into partnership in c.1808. Job died in 1814, and the firm became John & William Ridgway until c.1830 when John Ridgway took over the firm (see p.273).

RIDGWAYS

Ridgways, Shelton, Hanley, Staffordshire, UK

See p.202. This name mark appears in the wide ranged of marks used by this firm 1879-1920, and its successor Ridgways (Bedford Works) Ltd. 1920-52.

S. RISLEY/NORWICH

Sidney Risley, Norwich, Connecticut, USA

Around 1836 a stoneware pottery was established in Norwich, Connecticut, on Yantic Cove by Sidney Risley. He had been a potter in East Hartford, Connecticut, but opened the shop in Norwich after the old Armstrong and Wentworth pottery closed. Risley died in 1875, though his son, George S. Risley, kept the pottery in business until he was killed in an explosion in 1881. Some Rockingham ware was produced in addition to utilitarian stoneware. This impressed mark appears.

R. M. (& S)

Ralph Malkin (& Sons), Fenton, Staffordshire, UK

Based at the Park Works in Fenton, this firm made the ordinary classes of earthenwares 1863-92. The name of the firm changed to Ralph Malkin & Sons in 1882. These initials are found in many printed marks, often including the pattern name.

W. ROBERTS/BINGHAMTON, N.Y.

William Roberts, Binghamton, New York, USA

William Roberts was born in Llanfachreth, Merionethshire, North Wales, in 1818 and arrived with his family in the USA in 1827. By 1848 he was operating a Binghamton pottery in partnership with his father-in-law, Noah White of Utica, New York. Cobalt blue slip-trailed decorated wares may be found, dating from the later years of the pottery's production. The concern continued until 1888.

ROGERS

John & George Rogers, Longport, Staffordshire, UK

These brothers owned the Dale Hall Pottery from c.1784, and produced good quality tableware. Notable are their light blue "Willow" pattern services. Their early mark was simply the name "Rogers" impressed or printed. After the death of George Rogers, the firm continued as John Rogers & Son until c.1836; the name "Rogers" was also used up to this time.

(J.) ROSE

Coalport Porcelain Works, Coalport, Shropshire, UK

See p.72. The founder of the Coalport Works, John Rose's name mark appears in various forms on many pieces.

ROSLYN CHINA

Reid & Co., Longton, Staffordshire, UK

See p.201. This tradename was continued by this firm's successor Roslyn China 1946-63.

ROYAL ART POTTERY/ENGLAND

Clough's Royal Art Pottery, Longton, Staffordshire, UK

Formerly Alfred Clough Ltd. (Royal Art Pottery), this company produced earthenwares from 1961. This name mark appears above a crown device, with the word "England" appearing underneath. The same mark was used by the firm's predecessor 1951-61.

ROYAL BARUM WARE
C. H. Brannam Ltd., Barnstaple, Devon, UK
See p.210. This tradename appears on 20thC marks.

ROYAL BOURBON WARE
New Pearl Pottery Co. Ltd., Hanley, Staffordshire, UK
Based at the Brook Street Potteries, this firm (formerly Pearl Pottery Co. Ltd.) operated 1936-41. The firm was closed during the World War II, and the factory was sold in 1947. This tradename was used.

ROYAL BRADWELL
Arthur Wood & Son (Longport) Ltd., Longport, Staffordshire, UK
Formerly Arthur Wood (1904-28), this firm was based at the Bradwell Works from 1928. Earthenwares were produced.

ROYAL CHELSEA
New Chelsea Porcelain Co. (Ltd.), Longton, Staffordshire, UK
See p.218. This tradename was used c.1919-61.

ROYAL CHINA
E. Hughes & Co., Fenton, Staffordshire, UK
See p.168. This tradename appeares in a number of marks.

ROYAL (CHINA)/SEBRING, OHIO
Royal China Company, Sebring, Ohio, USA
This pottery made semi-porcelain tableware and vitreous hotel ware with printed or decal decoration in traditional and contemporary styles 1934-c.1985. In 1969, the company was purchased by the Jeannette Corporation and continued making vitreous dinnerware. The mark above usually appears with the pattern name.

ROYAL CROWN POTTERY
Trentham Bone China Ltd., Longton, Staffordshire, UK
Based at the Royal Crown Pottery, this firm produced porcelain 1952-57. This name appears in the marks used by this firm.

ROYAL GRAFTON
A. B. Jones & Sons (Ltd.), Longton, Staffordshire, UK
See p.155. The tradename "Royal Grafton" was used from c.1949; the company subsequently became Royal Grafton Bone China Ltd.

ROYAL HARVEY
Gibson & Sons (Ltd.), Burslem, Staffordshire, UK
See p.187. This tradename was used c.1950-55.

ROYAL LANCASTRIAN
Pilkington's Tile & Pottery Co. Ltd., Manchester, UK
See p.183. The impressed "P" mark of the Pilkington Factory
sometimes includes the words "Royal Lancastrian". Some
wares bear only these words, c.1914-38. "England" was added
c.1920; "Made in England" appears c.1920-38.

ROYAL LEIGHTON WARE
Leighton Pottery, Burslem, Staffordshire, UK
See p.214. This tradename was used c.1946-54.

ROYAL MAYFAIR
Chapmans Longton, Ltd., Longton, Staffordshire, UK
See p.204. This tradename appears in some marks during the
period 1938-41.

ROYAL NORFOLK
Norfolk Pottery Co. Ltd., Shelton, Staffordshire, UK
See p.203. This tradename appears in marks used by this firm
from 1958.

ROYAL PRINCE
Hall Bros. (Longton) Ltd., Longton, Staffordshire, UK
From 1947 this firm produced porcelain figures, vases and
other wares at the Radnor Works. This tradename appears in
marks 1947-51.

ROYAL STAFFORD CHINA
Thomas Poole, Longton, Staffordshire, UK
See p.193. This tradename was used in many of the marks
used by this firm from 1912-52. The firm became Thomas
Poole (Longton) Ltd. in c.1925. In 1948 it merged with
Gladstone China Ltd., and after 1952 continued as Royal
Stafford China.

ROYAL STANDARD
Chapmans Longton, Ltd., Longton, Staffordshire, UK
See p.204. Several marks featuring this tradename were used
from c.1930.

ROYAL STUART
Stevenson, Spencer & Co. Ltd., Longton, Staffordshire, UK
Porcelain was produced by this firm 1948-60 (after 1960 the
firm became a distributor only). This was one of the
tradenames used, and appears from c.1951.

ROYAL TORQUAY POTTERY
Royal Aller Vale & Watcombe Pottery Co., Torquay, Devon, UK
Formerly Aller Vale Art Potteries (1887-1901), this company
produced earthenwares c.1901-62. This impressed or printed
name mark was one of those used by this firm from c.1901
onwards.

ROYAL TUDOR WARE
Barker Bros., Lane End, Staffordshire, UK
See p.195. This tradename was incorporated into a number of marks from c.1937.

ROYAL TUNSTALL
Wedgwood & Co. (Ltd.), Tunstall, Staffordshire, UK
See p.206. This tradename was used from c.1957.

ROYAL VALE
ROYAL VITRIFIED
Ridgway Potteries Ltd., Hanley, Staffordshire, UK
See p.202. "Royal Vale" was one of several different tradenames used. The tradename "Royal Vitrified" was used c.1905-20 while this firm was operating under the name Ridgways.

ROYAL WATCOMBE
Royal Aller Vale & Watcombe Pottery Co., Torquay, Devon, UK
See p.317. This name mark was used in a printed or impressed mark c.1958-62.

ROYAL WINTON
Grimwades Ltd., Stoke, Staffordshire, UK
See p.205. This tradename appears in many marks used by this firm from c.1910.

ROYAL WORCESTER
Worcester Porcelains, Hereford and Worcester, UK
See p.23. This company became the Worcester Royal Porcelain Co. Ltd. in 1862. Several marks feature this name.

R.R.P.CO./ROSEVILLE, O./USA
Ransbottom Brothers Pottery Company/Robinson-Ransbottom, Roseville, Ohio, USA
This is one of the few US companies to make stoneware products profitably throughout the 20thC. Since its founding in 1900, the pottery has produced poultry feeders, flower pots, and garden crockery such as bird baths, jardinières, vases, urns and strawberry jars. Jars, jugs, bowls, milkpans and cuspidors (a globular-shaped spittoon with a wide, flaring rim or a high, funnel-shaped mouth) were also made early, and kitchenware was added in the later part of the century. The Robinson Clay Products Company bought the Ransbottom brothers' pottery in 1920 and renamed the operation Robinson-Ransbottom. This mark appears in a number of variations

RYE
Rye Pottery, Rye, East Sussex, UK
See p.173. The name "Rye" appears in many of the marks used by this firm, c.1869-1939, and from 1947.

SALEM
Salem China Company, Salem, Ohio, USA
This pottery made conventional ironstone and earthenware from 1898, before developing a line of better dinnerware which has been heavily decorated with brilliant decals in a wide variety of patterns. Since 1967, the firm has been a distributor of Japanese and English wares made with the Salem China backstamp. The name "Salem" appears within a variety of marks.

SALON CHINA
Salt & Nixon (Ltd.), Longton, Staffordshire, UK
Based at the Gordon Pottery and the Jubilee Works from 1910, this firm produced porcelain 1901-34. This tradename appears on many of their marks.

SATTERLEE & MORY/FORT EDWARD
New York Stoneware Company, Fort Edward, New York, USA
See p.125. This impressed mark was used.

S. B. & CO.
Thomas Sharpe (Sharpe Brothers & Co.), Burton-on-Trent, Staffordshire, UK
See p.320. These initial marks appear in many forms c.1838-95. "Ltd." was added from 1895.

S. & C.
Shore & Coggins, Longton, Staffordshire, UK
See p.151. This firm operated under this style 1911-66 producing porcelain. These initials appear on a number of marks.

SCHERZER
Zeh Scherzer & Co., Rehau, Bavaria, Germany
Founded in 1880, this company produced porcelain coffee and tea services and gift items. Between 1924 and 1926 the company owned the Elsterwerke, Mühlhausen. This name was incorporated into some of the factory marks used by the firm.

A.(NTHONY) SCOTT (& SONS)
Southwick Pottery, Sunderland, Tyne and Wear, UK
The Southwick Pottery was built in 1788 by Anthony Scott, and was carried on by various members of the Scott family until c.1897. The factory produced white, coloured and brown earthenwares. The style of the firm changed many times, and the marks used were as follows: "A. Scott & Co." (c.1800-29); "Anthony Scott & Sons" (c.1829-38); "Scott Brothers & Co." (c.1838-54); A. Scott (c.1854-72 and c.1882-97); "A. Scott & Son" (c.1872-82).

These marks should not be confused with Scott Bros. of Portobello (see p.320).

SCOTT BROS. (P.B.)

Scott Brothers, Portobello, Nr. Edinburgh, Scotland, UK

This firm operated c.1786-96 producing earthenwares. Marks are impressed.

SEBRING/SEBRING POTTERY COMPANY

Sebring Pottery Company, East Liverpool and Sebring, Ohio, USA

Although the company began production in East Liverpool in 1887, the pottery was moved to Sebring in 1898 when the town was founded to support the several potteries being created by the Sebring brothers. The pottery first made white granite dinner and tea sets and later changed to semi-porcelain dinnerware and hotel ware with decal decorations. "Ivory Porcelain" was introduced in 1923. The company continued until 1934. The names above appear in many marks that incorporate pattern names.

SEWELL (& DONKIN, & CO.)

St Anthony's Pottery, Newcastle-upon-Tyne, Tyne and Wear, UK

See p.323. The impressed or printed name "Sewell" appears 1804-c.1828; "Sewell & Donkin" was used 1828-52; "Sewell & Co." appears 1852-78.

(T.) SHARPE

Thomas Sharpe (Sharpe Brothers & Co.), Burton-on-Trent, Staffordshire, UK

The Swadlincote Works were established by Thomas Sharpe in 1821, and operated by him until his death in 1838. The firm was then continued by his brothers, and was known by the name Sharpe Bros. & Co. Production included Derbyshire ironstone, cane (yellow) ware, drab ware, Rockingham ware, mottled ware and black lustreware. All types of domestic wares were produced, including some speciality wares such as Toby jugs. After 1895 output mainly comprised sanitary wares. Various combinations of Sharpe's name appear.

A.(NTHONY) SHAW

Anthony Shaw (& Co.) (& Son), Tunstall and Burslem, Staffordshire, UK

Founded c.1851, this firm made wares principally for the American export markets, including white graniteware and cream-coloured ware for the United States, and printed, lustred and painted wares for the South American markets. This name appears in many printed or impressed marks of differing design; the Royal Arms is often used. "& Son" was added to the style and marks c.1882-98; "& Co." was substituted for "& Son" from c.1898. The firm was taken over by A. J. Wilkinson Ltd. in c.1900.

SHAWNEE/USA

Shawnee Pottery Company, Zanesville, Ohio, USA

Named because of an Indian arrowhead found on the

property during construction, the pottery (active 1937-61) specialized in inexpensive colourful florists' crockery and novelty table and kitchen ware. As an example, for the Corn King pattern all forms were based on the shape and texture of an ear of corn including the husks. Marks and paper labels include the name "Shawnee, USA" along with pattern names.

SHELLEY
Wileman & Co., Longton, Staffordshire, UK
See p.304. This pottery operated 1892-1925 producing porcelain. This tradename was used from c.1911. The firm became Shelley Potteries Ltd. in c.1925 (Royal Albert Ltd. from 1967), and marks in various forms incorporating this tradename continued to be used.

SHENANGO CHINA
Shenango Pottery Company, New Castle, Pennsylvania, USA
Formed in 1901, after some initial problems, this pottery has prospered under its own and other names. In its early years the company made semi-porcelain dinner and toilet sets. Between 1936 and 1958, the pottery made porcelain for the Theodore Haviland Company of Limoges, France, under the style "Haviland, New York," in addition to its regular production of vitreous dinner and hotel ware. By 1951, Shenango fully owned the fine porcelain company Castleton China, which was known for its "Museum" shape designed by Eva Zeisel and for the service made for the White House during Lyndon Johnson's administration (1963-69). Today, Castleton and Haviland have passed as trade names, but Shenango continues to make high-grade hotel and institutional ware.

SHORTHOSE (& HEATH)
Shorthose & Heath (John Shorthose), Hanley, Staffordshire, UK
Shorthose & Heath (or Shorthose & Co.) were based in Hanley c.1795-1815 and produced cream-coloured services, white and printed goods, black basaltes and other wares. John Shorthose worked in Hanley from c.1807-23, and made good quality lustrewares, often with white relief patterns. His pieces are occasionally marked.

JOHN SIMPSON
John Simpson, Burslem, Staffordshire, UK
This potter made slip-decorated earthenwares in the early 18thC. This name occurs. Three potters of this name were included on Wedgwood's list of Burslem potters c.1710-15.

RALPH SIMPSON
Ralph Simpson, Staffordshire, UK
Active in the late 17th to early 18thC, Ralph Simpson (b.1651, d. c.1724), made slip-decorated earthenwares similar to those made by the Tofts (see p.325).

WILLIAM SIMPSON
William Simpson, Staffordshire, UK
This name appears on a slip-decorated posset-pot dated 1685, and also appears in contemporary records in various Staffordshire centres during this period.

SIMPSONS (POTTERS) LTD.
Simpsons (Potters) Ltd., Cobridge, Staffordshire, UK
Formerly the Soho Pottery Ltd. (see p.204), this firm produced earthenwares at the Elder Works from 1944. This name mark appears in their marks which also feature a number of different tradenames.

S. M.
Samuel Malkin, Burslem, Staffordshire, UK
This potter produced slip-decorated earthenwares during the early 18thC. Some pieces include these initials within the designs; one example is signed in full. Dated examples range between 1712 and 1734.

W.J. SMITH/BRIDGETON, N.J.
Cohansey Street Pottery, Bridgeton, New Jersey, USA
William J. Smith (active 1865-95) made brown glazed redware in kitchen forms, such as pie plates and handled jars, as well as whimsies or what were called image toys, especially of birds. This mark was incised in script.

SOHO POTTERY (LTD.)
Soho Pottery (Ltd.), Tunstall and Cobridge, Staffordshire, UK
See p.204. This name appears in the wide variety of marks used by this firm.

SOMERSET POTTERS WORKS
Somerset Potters' Works, Somerset, Massachusetts, USA
See p.292. This impressed mark was used.

SOUTH WALES POTTERY
South Wales Pottery, Llanelly, Wales, UK
This pottery was established by William Chambers in 1839, and was operated by him until 1854. He produced white and cream-coloured, edged, painted and printed ware. Other types of wares produced at one time or another, include parian, figures and enamelled wares. From 1850 white granite and underglaze printed wares were produced for sale in the United States. Coombs and Holland took over the pottery in 1854, but the partnership ended in 1858, and Mr. Holland continued alone until 1869, when he was joined by D. Guest. In 1877 the firm changed to Guest & Duesbury. The firm purchased the copper-engraved plates from many other Welsh potteries, including the Cambrian Works at Swansea. The firm continued until c.1927. This name mark is one of those used c.1839-58.

SPODE

Josiah Spode, Stoke, Staffordshire, UK

See p.223. This impressed, painted or printed name mark was used in many of Josiah Spode's marks. The name has also been incorporated into the marks of his successor, W. T. Copeland (& Sons Ltd.) (see p.245).

ST. ANTHONY'S

St. Anthony's Pottery, Newcastle-upon-Tyne, Tyne and Wear, UK

One of the oldest potteries in the area, St. Anthony's Pottery was established c.1780. It became the property of Mr. Sewell in 1803 or 1804, and was continued by his family until c.1828, when the firm became Sewell & Donkin (1828-52) and Sewell & Co. (1852-78). Production mainly comprised cream-coloured, printed and blue-painted wares. Several forms of mark were used, including this one 1780-1820.

STANGL

Stangl Pottery Company, Trenton, New Jersey, USA

After the Fulper Pottery of Flemington, New Jersey (see p.114), suffered a devastating fire in 1929, the pottery's manager J. M. Stangl took over the company and concentrated production in their Trenton factory, where they made novelty finishes on casual dinnerware. *Sgraffiato* decorations through white slip on red earthenware were produced in many popular patterns. The company also produced a large line of colourful bird figurines in earthenware that is extremely popular with collectors today. The Stangl trade name was sold to Pfaltzgraff (see p.185) in 1978. Marks appear printed and on paper labels; the name appears often with the pattern name.

STEUBENVILLE (CHINA)

Steubenville Pottery Company, Steubenville, Ohio, USA

See p.184. Later marks usually feature the mark above, along with the pattern names.

SWANSEA

Swansea Pottery, Swansea, Wales, UK

A works had existed here since at least the middle of the 18thC, originally built to produce copper, but it was later converted into a pottery. Bought by Messrs. Coles & Haynes in 1783, the works were enlarged by George Haynes after the death of Mr. Coles in 1800, and named the Cambrian Pottery. Earthenwares were made at first, but under George Haynes a refined cream-coloured ware was produced, together with an opaque porcelain and other types of wares. Lewis Dillwyn took over the works in 1802, and under him the decoration became more artistic as he employed talented painters, including William Young. High quality porcelain was produced for Dillwyn after 1814 by William Billingsley and Samuel Walker, but these men were dismissed after it

transpired that they had illegally left their positions at the
Worcester Porcelain Works. T. & J. Bevington took over the
works in 1817, but they returned to Lewis Dillwyn in 1824,
and were subsequently operated by his son from 1840.
Notable are imitations of Wedgwood's Etruscan wares,
known as "Dillwyn's Etruscan Ware", made from c.1847. In
c.1851 the works were taken over by David Evans. The works
closed c.1870, and the engraved copper plates were sold to the
South Wales Pottery, Llanelly.

E. SWASEY & CO./PORTLAND, ME.
Lamson & Swasey, Portland, Maine, USA
See p.306. This impressed mark was used.

SYRACUSE/CHINA/U.S.A.
Syracuse China Company, Syracuse, New York, USA
See p.311. This modern mark appears printed in several
different ways.

J. S. TAFT (& CO.)/KEENE, N.H.
J. S. Taft & Co., Keene, New Hampshire, USA
James Scholly Taft and his uncle, James Burnap, purchased a
woodenware factory in Keene, New Hampshire, in 1871 and
converted it to the production of earthenware. Stoneware was
quickly added to their output, and in 1874 the company
bought out a local competitor, whose factory they used for
subsequent redware production. Simple utilitarian wares
were only infrequently decorated with cobalt blue. The
company continued until 1898.

WILLIAM TALOR (TALLOR)
William Talor (or Tallor), Burslem, Staffordshire, UK
This name appears on rare slip-decorated earthenwares; one
features the date 1700. Another is known, marked with the
name "William Tallor".

TAMS
John Tams (& Son) (Ltd.), Longton, Staffordshire, UK
See p.304. The name "Tams" or "Tams Ware" appears in a
number of different marks from c.1930; others include the
words "Tams England".

D. G. THOMPSON/MORGANTOWN
David Greenland Thompson, Morgantown, West Virginia, USA
John Wood Thompson purchased a redware pottery at
Morgantown, West Virginia, in 1827 and produced both
redware and, later, stoneware until his retirement in 1853.
Then the firm passed to three sons, including David Greenland Thompson who was manager of the pottery until he
died in 1890. Blue-decorated brushed and stencilled designs
may be found along with impressed designs. This impressed
mark appears.

J. THOMPSON

Joseph Thompson, Ashby de la Zouch, Leicestershire, UK

Based at the Hartshorne or Wooden Box Pottery, this firm
was first operated by Joseph Thompson who founded the
works in 1818. He was succeeded by his sons Richard and
Willoughby, and the title of the firm changed to Thompson
Brothers from 1856. Derby ironstone, brown, cane, buff, and
yellow ironstone ware, blackware, Rockingham ware, terracotta and sanitary goods were produced. White wears,
porcelain and other decorated items were also made by
Thompson Brothers. Holland & Thompson continued the
firm until it closed in 1882.

J. T. (& SONS)/ANNFIELD (GLASGOW)

John Thomson (& Sons), Glasgow, Scotland, UK

This firm was based at the Annfield Pottery c.1816-84, and
produced general ceramics for the home and export markets.
The works closed c.1884. Many different marks were used:
"J. T." with or without "Annfield" was used c.1816-65.
"& Sons" was added from c.1866, and "Glasgow" may
also appear.

JAMES (RALPH, THOMAS) TOFT

James, Ralph, Thomas Toft, Hanley, Staffordshire, UK

Three brothers, James (b.1673), Ralph (b.1638) and Thomas
(b.1689), produced slip-decorated earthenwares, some of
which bear the names of the potters as part of the decoration.
Thomas Toft's work is most frequently marked, over 30
signed examples are recorded.

TOMLINSON & CO.

Tomlinson & Co., Ferrybridge Pottery, Yorkshire, UK

Ferrybridge Pottery was established by William Tomlinson
and partners in 1792, and the firm was known as William
Tomlinson & Co. until 1796, when Ralph Wedgwood joined
the business and the name changed to Tomlinson, Foster,
Wedgwood & Co. Ralph Wedgwood was the eldest son of
Thomas Wedgwood of Etruria (cousin and partner of Josiah
Wedgwood). This partnership was dissolved c.1800, and the
company once again became known as Tomlinson & Co. until
1834, when it changed to Tomlinson, Plowes & Co. In 1804
the name of the works was changed from the Knottingley
Pottery to the Ferrybridge Pottery. William Tomlinson's son
Edward continued the works until 1826. Wares were
principally cream, cane and greenwares; blackwares and fine
white earthenwares were also produced. Shortly afterwards,
the works were taken over by James Reed and Benjamin
Taylor who made great improvements in the output and
began production of porcelain. After 1856 the works were
owned by Lewis Wolf, and later by his sons. Subsequent
owners include Poulson Bros. (1897-1919) and T. Brown &
Sons (Ltd.)

TRENT
Trent Tile Company, Trenton, New Jersey, USA

Isaac Broome was the first modeller for the company, active 1882-1938, specializing in heads and figures. English modeller William W. Gallimore followed Broome. The firm made floor, wall and fireplace tiles mostly covered in glossy coloured glazes. In 1938, the company went into receivership and was purchased by Wenczel Tile Company, which continued to make tiles until 1994. The name "Trent" appears impressed or raised on the back of tiles.

TROPICO
Gladding, McBean and Company, Various locations, California, USA

See p.292. This mark appears raised on tiles.

TUSCAN CHINA
R. H. & S. L. Plant (Ltd.), Longton, Staffordshire, UK

See p.265. This tradename appears on many marks.

UHL POTTERY WORKS/EVANSVILLE, IND.
Uhl Pottery Works, Evansville and Huntingburg, Indiana, USA

One of the best-known of the many Indiana pottery manufactories is the Uhl Pottery Works of Evansville, Indiana, founded in 1854 by German potters, August and Louis Uhl. In 1891 the pottery moved to the site of major clay deposits, Huntingburg, Indiana, and continued in production into the 20th century. Utilitarian forms comprised the bulk of their production, though in the later years decorative vases, piggy banks, and planters were made in bright enamel glazes. Production continued until 1944.

UNWIN
Joseph Unwin (&Co.), Longton, Staffordshire, UK

Formerly Poole & Unwin (1871-76), based at the Cornhill Works in Longton, this firm produced earthenwares, figures and other wares 1877-1926. This moulded name mark appears within a diamond-shaped outline. "& Co." was added to the firm's title in 1891.

U. H. P. CO. (LTD.)/ENGLAND
Upper Hanley Pottery Co. (Ltd.), Hanley and Cobridge, Staffordshire, UK

Based in Hanley (c.1895-1902) and Brownfield's Works in Cobridge (c.1902-10), this pottery produced earthenwares 1895-1910. The initial mark "U. H. P. & Co." appears in various forms 1895-1900; "Ltd." was added from c.1900.

VAN SHOIK & DUNN
Van Schoik & Dunn/Dunn, Dunlap & Co, Matawan, New Jersey, USA

See p.295. This impressed mark was used.

VERNON/CALIFORNIA
VERNONWARE/MADE IN U.S.A.

Vernon Kilns/Vernon Potteries, Vernon, California, USA

This pottery (active 1928-58) produced a wide variety of
casual earthenware dinnerware, including many designs by
the well-known illustrator Rockwell Kent. Metlox Potteries,
which owned the pottery between 1958 and 1960, its last year
of production, continued to make some Vernon Kilns
patterns. Marks sometimes include the pattern name.

VODREY DUBLIN POTTERY

Vodrey's Pottery, Dublin, Eire

General pottery was produced here c.1873-c.1885. This
impressed mark is known.

VOLKMAR (& CORY)

Volkmar Pottery, Various locations, New York and New Jersey, USA

Charles Volkmar was trained as an artist in Paris and studied
pottery decoration as an apprentice at the Haviland factory.
He worked as a potter first for a few years in Greenpoint,
New York, then moved to Tremont, New York. By 1888, he
was working in Menlo Park, New Jersey, making tiles. He
returned to Brooklyn in 1893 and made cups, mugs and plates
with blue decoration. For a few months in 1896, he made
blue-decorated plaques with Kate Cory, and later produced a
line of vases with matt glazes or painted landscapes. In 1903,
he founded Volkmar Kilns, Charles Volkmar & Son with
Leon in Metuchen, New Jersey, and they worked together,
making a variety of effects until 1911. Many marks appear,
incised or in relief.

WARWICK CHINA

Warwick China Company, Wheeling, West Virginia, USA

See p.221. This printed mark was used.

W. & C.

Walker & Carter, Longton, Staffordshire, UK

Based at Longton 1866-72, and at Stoke 1872-89, this firm
(formerly Walker, Bateman & Co.) produced earthenwares.
These initials appear in many marks, many of which include
an anchor (1866-89).

WEDGWOOD & CO.

Tomlinson, Foster, Wedgwood & Co., Ferrybridge Pottery,
Yorkshire, UK

See p.325. This impressed mark was used c.1796-1801.

WEIR POTTERY CO.
THE WEIR PAT' MAR 1ST 1892

Weir Pottery Company, Monmouth, Illinois, USA

Though it was operated as an independent stoneware pottery
for only a short time (1899-1905), the Weir Pottery Company

of Monmouth, Illinois, left an enormous legacy of signed and marked wares. Founded in 1899 by local banker William S. Weir, the pottery produced 500,000 moulded stoneware pitchers, mugs, steins, vases, etc. as premiums for the Sleepy Eye Milling Co. of Minnesota; these featured a bust portrait of the Sioux Indian Chief, "Old Sleepy Eye." The Weir Pottery also manufactured the patented Weir Stone Fruit Jars, and numerous examples of this form may be found. Marks are impressed.

WELLER (POTTERY)
Weller Pottery/S.A. Weller Company, Fultonham and Zanesville, Ohio, USA
See p.226. This impressed or incised mark was used.

WELLSVILLE CHINA
Wellsville China Company, Wellsville, Ohio, USA
The company purchased the abandoned Pioneer Pottery Company works and by 1912 was producing plain and decorated semi-porcelain dinner and toilet wares, tea sets, cuspidors, and other accessories and speciality items. Vitreous hotel ware was added in 1933. Controlling interest passed to Sterling China (see p.137) in 1959, and the factory was closed in 1969. Many marks appear, featuring the pattern name and "Wellsville China", sometimes appearing as "W. C. Co."

W. H. & S.
William Hackwood & Son, Shelton, Staffordshire, UK
Formerly William Hackwood (see p.299). This firm took over the New Hall Works in 1842. William Hackwood died in 1849 and the firm was continued by his son Thomas. They made various types of earthenware, mainly for the Continental markets. These initials are incorporated into many marks, often with the name of the pattern.

THE WHEELING (STONE CHINA) POTTERY CO.
Wheeling Pottery Company/Wheeling Potteries Company, Wheeling, West Virginia, USA
See p.263. This printed mark was used.

A. O. WHITTEMORE/HAVANA, N.Y.
Albert O. Whittemore, Havana, New York, USA
The businessman, Albert O. Whittemore, rebuilt a modest stoneware pottery in Havana, New York, in 1863, and operated it as the Schuyler Stoneware Works until 1893. Some of the elaborate blue-decorated wares produced there rank among New York's finest and most imaginative; subjects included animals and human figures. Whittemore had originally been a maker of beaver hats in New York City, but established a farm and iron foundry in Havana in addition to his stoneware potteries there and in Elmira, New York. This impressed mark appears.

WILSON
David Wilson (& Sons), Hanley, Staffordshire, UK

This potter and later his sons (from 1815), produced earthen-wares and china, particularly lustred wares c.1802-18. David Wilson made some fine lustrewares, with patterns in gold over a lustre or coloured ground.

This mark was also used by David Wilson's father, Robert Wilson 1795-1801 (see p.140).

ARTHUR WOOD (& SON)
Arthur Wood & Son (Longport) Ltd., Longport, Staffordshire, UK

See p.316. This name mark features in many of the marks used. On some moulded wares the name "Wood" only appears.

R(A). WOOD
Ralph Wood, Burslem, Staffordshire, UK

Ralph Wood (b.1715, d.1772) and his son (b.1748, d.1795) were potters at the Hill factory in Burslem, and produced finely-modelled earthenware figures, Toby jugs and other wares. Marked wares mainly comprise figures, reliefs and Toby jugs.

M. WOODRUFF/CORTLAND, N.Y.
Madison Woodruff, Cortland, New York, USA

This potter, Madison Woodruff, had been associated with several earlier potteries in Homer and Cortland, New York, in the Finger Lakes region, before purchasing the Thomas Chollar Pottery in 1849. Floral decorated utilitarian stoneware was produced at various kiln sites in Cortland until his death in 1885.

W. S. & CO. (STAFFORD POTTERY)
William Smith (& Co.), Stockton-on-Tees, UK

The Stafford Pottery was established by William Smith for the manufacture of brownware in 1825. Earthenware was added to the production soon afterwards. The style changed to William Smith & Co. in 1926, and then to G. Skinner & Co. (c.1855-70), and subsequently Skinner & Walker (1870-c.1880). Production principally comprised "Queen's Ware", a fine, white earthenware, and a fine brown ware, much of which was exported to Europe. In 1848, an injunction was granted preventing this firm using the name "Wedgewood & Co." or Wedgewood" in their marks, which they had been doing illegally before this date.

ZSOLNAY/PECS
Zsolnay, Pécs, Hungary

Established in 1862, this firm produced Islamic-inspired pierced wares until the 1890s, and subsequently vases with organic forms and iridescent glazes. All pieces are marked, and feature a mark showing the five towers of Pécs.

Chinese marks

The first marks on Chinese ceramics probably date from the Warring States period (480-221 BC), but these potter's marks, in the form of inscriptions, are rarely found. Only the porcelains made at Jingdezhen (Ching-tê-chen), have been marked consistently (although not every piece), from the Ming dynasty onwards. The reign marks of the emperors of the Ming (1368-1643) and Qing (1644-1916) dynasties are featured in this section.

Ming dynasty 1368-1643

Apart from Jingdezhen (Ching-tê-chen) porcelain, few Chinese ceramics are marked. The earliest marks probably date from the Warring States Period (480-221 BC), but these are of the greatest rarity, and are not generally encountered by collectors outside museums. Cizhou and Ding wares are occasionally inscribed, but again these are exceptional. The systematic marking of porcelain only began in the early 15thC using six character marks, although four character marks were also employed. Most marked pieces from Jingdezhen are retrospective using reign marks from earlier and respected reigns. The marks of emperors Xuande (1426-35), Chenghua (1465-87), Kangxi (1662-1722), Yongzheng (1723-35) and Qianlong (1736-95) are commonly used on much later wares and therefore should be treated with the greatest caution: always seek expert advice.

Other marks used include commendations or are well-wishing symbols, although these generally are only used from the late Ming onwards. Until the early 18thC marks were written under the glaze in cobalt blue, or much more rarely were incised beneath the glaze. Late in the reign of Kangxi, some Imperial pieces were enamelled on top of the glaze, although the vast majority continued to be written in underglaze cobalt blue. At the turn of the 18thC overglaze iron-red was used increasingly on non-export-type porcelain.

Other marks on Chinese porcelain from the late Ming period onwards include animals, flowers and objects. The hare or the rabbit appears late in the 16thC, followed by the crane or heron. During the Kangxi period (1662-1722), the *lingzhi* or sacred fungus was introduced together with a lotus head, the artemisia leaf, and the *ding* (a bronze vessel form). These marks were sometimes used on 19thC copies of Kangxi porcelain.

Ming reign marks

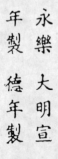

Yongle (Yung-lo) and Xuande (Hsüan-tê),
(1403-24), (1426-35)
The earliest underglaze blue marks of Yongle and Xuande appear on Imperial-quality monochrome and blue and white wares. The porcelain from this early 15thC period are quite varied in form, but almost all have characteristically thick glazes saturated with bubbles which give a blurred appearance to the underlying blue designs and marks. The mainly floral patterns of this period are confidently but carefully painted.

Chenghua (Ch'êng-hua), (1465-87)

Chenghua porcelain is delicately painted with perceptibly less vigour and a more open look to the scrolling foliage. This reign is noted for the so-called "Palace bowls" and the ultra-refined *doucai* or polychrome enamelled porcelains, which feature red, yellow, brown and green overglaze enamels, within an underglaze blue outline.

Hongzhi (Hung-chih), (1488-1505)

Porcelain made during the Hongzhi dynasty, while maintaining the colourful styles developed in the latter part of the 15thC (see Chenghua porcelain above), tended to become increasingly stylized and weaker towards the end of the reign.

Zhengde (Chêng-tê), (1506-21)

Zhengde is arguably the last classic Ming reign, with some pieces recalling the high standards of the previous century, but generally becoming either too crowded or too stylized. The reign is notable for pieces inscribed in Arabic or Persian, and intended for the Imperial household. Wares include brush rests, censers and dishes. It was during this reign that the first Western European traders, the Portuguese, made a landfall in China.

Jiajing (Chia-ching), (1522-66)

The reign of Jiajing is noteworthy for the introduction of a brilliant purplish-blue – in contrast to the steely, greyish-blue which characterizes the late 15th and early 16thC. Other features of this reign include a greater use of figure subjects. This emperor followed the religion of Daoism, and Daoist symbols such as the pine tree (representing longevity), the *lingzhi*, and the crane. These motifs were used through the 16th and 17thC, and are occasionally found on 18thC pieces. Also from this period, Chinese porcelains appear with Western symbols, letters and armorials.

Longqing (Lung-ch'ing), (1567-72)

The wares made during the short reign of Longqing cannot, without reign marks, be distinguished from porcelain made in the dynasties that preceded or followed. Being of such rarity it has attracted the attention of copyists in the 19th and 20thC.

Wanli (Wan-li), (1573-1619)

During the reign of Wanli the export trade in porcelain grew enormously to the detriment of quality. Mass production is evident on most pieces, the poor quality of the clay, improper refinement of the materials leaving pinholes and large dark blemishes on the surface, and the use of simple, repetitive decoration. This latter type was known as "kraakporselein", and formed the backbone of the export market until 1657. There are no reign marks on this type of ware, but animal marks do occasionally appear.

Tianqi (T'ien-ch'i), (1621-27)

Also a relatively short reign, the Tianqi period produced an interesting group of wares made for the Japanese market. Mainly in blue and white, but sometimes in *wucai* colours, this type of porcelain falls into two different categories. The first is an informal type, painted with figures, landscapes or vegetation, and is rarely marked. These simple wares were often used in the Japanese Tea Ceremony. The second type of wares, known as *Shonzui* are more meticulously made, and often feature tight, geometric patterns. Wares from this period may also have rims dressed in an iron-brown glaze to prevent chipping.

Chongzhen (Ch'ung-chêng), (1628-43)

This reign is noted for the so-called "Transitional" wares (porcelain made during the overlapping Ming and Qing dynasties). These heavily-potted wares are often quite brilliantly painted in a lustrous cobalt blue and show a break from the repetitious *kraakporselein*-type. A few pieces are inscribed with cyclical reign marks, but as in the previous reign there are few conventionally-marked specimens from this turbulent period of Chinese history.

Qing dynasty 1644-1916

The early years of the Qing dynasty were marked by internal strife which had a devastating effect on production at Jingdezhen. It was not until well into the reign of Kangxi (1662-1722) that normal production was resumed. In 1683 with the appointment of Ts'ang Ying-Hsuan as director of the imperial kilns, Chinese porcelain enters a long period in which some of the most refined and beautiful objects were made. This brilliant era ends with the retirement of the last great director T'ang Yin (Tang Ying) c.1752.

During the Kangxi period there were a considerable number of innovations and revivals. For example the Ming *wucai* palette in which underglaze blue is combined with overglaze enamels, including red, green, manganese brown and yellow, was abandoned in favour of the *famille verte* colour scheme in which a bright overglaze blue replaces the darker underglaze cobalt. Towards the end of the reign *famille verte* too was superseded by another palette, namely *famille rose* which uses colours saturated in white, creating an opaque and pastel effect, and which also introduces rose-pink for the first time. As well as these developments, a number of new monochromes appeared, such as a luminous green, a fine turquoise and the copper-derived, peach-bloom glaze.

In addition there was the revival of underglaze copper-red painting which had fallen into disuse during the Ming dynasty. Export porcelain from this period was carried out by private kilns and while the designs are somewhat stiff by comparison with the earlier "Transitional" wares, they are invariably well made and thinly-potted using a clean white porcelain and economically-applied glaze. It was in this reign that the practise of putting reign marks on export ware became common. The marks most often encountered were those of the much-admired Chenghua period (1465-87). In fact, contemporary Kangxi reign marks are ironically quite rare on export porcelain. Other marks include the lotus flower, the Ding and the artemsia leaf.

Yongzheng (1723-35) was a period synonymous with the greatest refinement in all Chinese porcelain, and it is important for collectors to be aware that there are a great number of later copies of its wares.

Qing reign marks

Shunzhi, (1644-61)

The first emperor of the Qing or Manchu dynasty. The wares of this period are quite varied, whether in blue and white or in the polychrome *wucai* palette, and are essentially a continuation of the Transitional tradition. Generally, there is a subtle move away from the more academic treatment of figurative and floral subjects of the High Transitional into the casually-drawn and somewhat stiffer style of Kangxi. There are very few marked specimens of this period, and these are marked in conventional script.

Kangxi, (1662-1722)

This is the first of the three most important reigns of the Qing dynasty. In terms of export material the majority of wares are blue and white, the minority *famille verte* (see above). Monochromes both for export or for the domestic market include new and revived colours. In the latter category are a copper-derived glaze termed *sang-de-boeuf* and another called "peach-bloom". Other colours include lavender blue and a flecked darkish cobalt – *bleu soufflé*. Towards the end of this long reign, enamels saturated in white first appear. This pastel palette is known as *famille rose* and while a rose-pink is part of the scheme it often by no means dominates the other colours. For a time *famille verte* and *famille rose* overlap but by about 1730 the earlier green family has virtually disappeared.

The reign mark of Kangxi is relatively rare on non-Imperial pieces; the most frequently-used mark in this period is an "ancestral" Chenghua. Official seal-script marks are of the utmost rarity and should be treated with great suspicion.

Yongzheng, (1723-35)

This relatively short reign is generally regarded as probably the best in terms of ceramic refinement although there is no clear change technically or stylistically between this reign and the early years of the following Qianlong (1736-95). By comparison between this and the preceding Kangxi there is a tendency towards a more intimate scale in graphic subjects. In addition this period is noted for a strong classicising movement with a considerable number of pieces recalling the great mono-chrome stonewares of the Song and the early Ming blue and white and sacrificial red porcelains. It is during this reign that we see reign marks executed both in official and seal script.

Qianlong, (1736-95)

Considered to be the last classic reign of the Qing dynasty, this period saw enormous changes, initially under the directorship of T'ang Ying (active 1736-c.1750), one of the most celebrated figures in Chinese ceramics. While continuing the classical tradition of Yongzheng there is generally a sense of over-elaboration and decadence in the second half of the 18thC. Robin's egg and Tea dust are just two of the more popular colours of this period, but as well as blue and white, *famille rose* porcelains are predominant.

Jiaqing, (1796-1821)

From the early 19thC onwards forms and decoration found in Chinese porcelain are usually based on styles from previous dynasties. Some very fine pieces were produced as well as the usual types of export wares.

Later Qing dynasties

As noted above, the later Qing dynasties did not produce wares in new or inidividual styles. The marks of these dynasties and their corresponding dates are shown below.

Tao-kuang,
(1821-50)

Hsien-Feng,
(1851-61)

T'ung-chih,
(1862-73)

Kuang-hsü,
(1874-1908)

Hsüan-t'ung,
(1909-12)

Hung-hsien,
(1916)

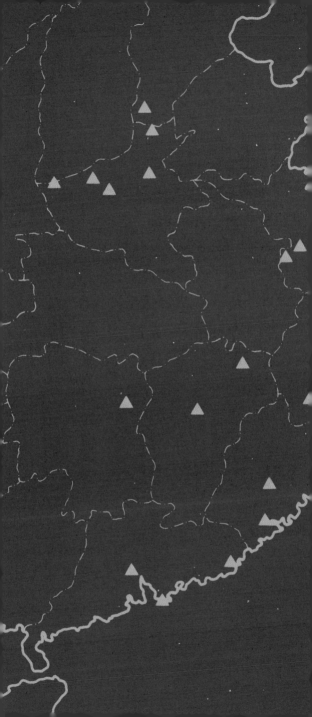

Additional information

This section contains: details of fakes and copies; maps showing the locations of some of the major pottery and porcelain-producing centres in China, Europe and the USA; appendices providing further information on Patent Office Registration marks, year marks and cyphers found on wares made at Derby, Minton, Sèvres, Worcester and Wedgwood; and a list of the decorator marks used by painters, gilders and potters at Sèvres. There is also a detailed glossary, and a list of further reading.

Fakes & copies

China

Chinese reign marks have always been a problematical issue. Until the turn of the 15thC, the six, or more rarely, four-character reign marks appeared almost exclusively on Imperial porcelains. However, in the 16thC Chinese potters began to copy earlier reign marks.

In the 16thC, the most frequently copied marks were those of Xuande (1426-35) and Chenghua (1465-87). A famous example is a bowl dated 1541, made for Pedro de Faria, the Portuguese governor of Goa. The base carries the six-character mark of Xuande who died over 100 years before the bowl was made. The calligraphy of the genuine marks is distinctive when compared to the more casually-drawn versions that appear on faked examples.

17thC copyists used the Xuande mark, and also the mark of Jiajing (1522-66). Chenghua was also used, and became increasingly popular during the reign of Kangxi (1662-1722). Jang Qi Jing, the superintendent of the Imperial kilns, banned the use of the reign mark from 1677-80, perhaps because of the implied disrespect if the mark appeared on lower quality porcelains. We do not know how strictly this ban was enforced but it is clear that as well as using old reign marks, the potters of Jingdezhen used symbols such as the artemisia leaf, the lotus or the *ding* (a bronze tripod vessel). The practise of marking with symbols was probably abandoned later in the reign of Kangxi but was probably revived in the latter half of the 19thC.

It was during the reign of Kangxi that the reproduction of classic wares of the Song and Ming dynasties became popular, a trend which continued to the end of the dynasty, early in the 20thC. Many of these pieces bear deceptively good copies of the reign marks of their original period. A thorough knowledge of the material and, where applicable, an understanding of the brushwork, is important.

This trend continued through the 18thC, and while some of the copies are marked with early marks, the majority carry contemporary reign marks. Unfortunately even these pieces were themselves copied in the 19thC and 20thC, and particularly today.

During the reigns of Yongzheng (1723-35) and Qianlong (1736-95) a number of marks were written in seal script as opposed to the conventional script used on early Qing and Ming porcelains. The characters in this formalized script appear within a square seal. Most marks were painted in underglaze blue, but from the reign of Kangxi onwards a few pieces are marked in overglaze enamels. Towards the end of the 18thC, many pieces are marked in iron-red, a tradition which was carried through into the 20thC.

In the 19thC large numbers of Imperial or Chinese porcelains in 18thC style were made at Jingdezhen. Some of these
pieces bore contemporary reign marks, but many more were
made with the marks of Kangxi, Yongzheng and Qianlong.
These copies are very deceptive, and some have even fooled
experts. Before setting out to acquire pieces of Chinese
porcelain, it is absolutely essential to spend as much time as
possible studying the material and the reign marks, and it
would also be helpful to seek the advice of a specialist.

Italy

From the middle of the 19thC, a number of factories
and individuals began to make their own versions of
Rennaisance-style maiolica, and also some extremely deceptive forgeries. The factory of Ginori at Doccia near Florence,
produced convincing pastiches of 16thC maiolica of which
there is an interesting example in the Wallace Collection
(illustrated in the catalogue, p.312, no.C160). Other centres
included Pesaro, Gubbio, Gualdo Tadino and Florence. In
Pesaro Ferruccio Mengaroni (1875-1925) produced some
outstanding forgeries of early maiolica including Faenza,
Cafaggiolo and Urbino. Mengaroni's work fooled some of
the greatest experts of their day; two of his pieces were
acquired by Henry Oppenheim, one of them later purchased
by the Victoria & Albert Museum and the other going to the
British Museum. Ulisse and Guiseppe Cantagalli, who established a factory in Florence in 1878, produced large numbers
of reproductions of Hispano-moresque, Turkish (Isnik) pottery as well as Renaissance maiolica. The factory mark is a
singing cockerel; in some cases this has been ground away,
presumably so that it could be passed off as the real thing.

For the most part these 19thC copies can be detected by
analysing the material, the design and the brushwork.
Usually the potting is very neat, with smooth, well rounded
rims, and carefully finished footrims. Early maiolica is often
slightly irregular with rims of variable thickness and profile.
The glaze on the original can be patchy or uneven, with a
bubbled surface and zones of stronger colour. 19thC copies
are covered in even, creamy or greyish glazes giving a
mechanical look. In old maiolica studios, flatware was fired
in stacks, each piece supported on a triangular arrangement
of ceramic stilts which left blemishes on the upper surface.
Therefore all but the uppermost dish in a stack would show
these weals. Late pieces do not have such stilt marks. The
types of colours used can also help to distinguish between
the genuine article and a copy, and later examples exhibit a
tendency towards over-elaboration.

France

Earthenwares

Among the earliest wares in France to be copied or faked
are the elaborate, lead-glazed wares produced by Bernard
Palissy and his followers towards the end of the 16thC.
There are two distinct types: first, large dishes, with lizards,
serpents, frogs and other reptiles modelled in high-relief
among ferns and foliage; second, shallow, circular or oval
dishes moulded in low-relief with figure subjects, mainly of
classical inspiration. These types of wares were copied extensively in the 19thC in response to a demand for "historical"
wares. For example, the Portuguese Mafra factory at Caldas
da Rainha made considerable quantities of "Palissy" type
pottery. These crude versions usually feature a factory mark.
French copies by Charles Avisseau or George Pull are more
difficult to distinguish, but the later copies are painted in
slightly harsher, acid colours, whereas Palissy used warmer
earthy tones. In addition, the modelling on later versions is
more cluttered and less spontaneous than the originals.

Faience

The great days of French faience ended with the development of porcelain and more importantly creamware (*faience
fine*) in the latter half of the 18thC. One type of faience
that is still found is low quality ware made for tourists. In
Normandy, Brittany and other parts of northern France,
these items are to be found in almost every town and resort.
Modern pieces are invariably marked with the initials or
name of the pottery, and its location. With the notable
exception of the leading faience factories such as Strasburg,
Niderviller or Marseilles, few 18thC factories marked their
wares as extensively marks were usually confined to initials
or a simple device. Place names such as Rouen or Lille (with
the date 1767) are found on modern copies and forgeries.

Deliberate copies have been made of faience from
Strasburg, Sceaux, Nevers and Marseilles. In particular,
pieces from Marseilles were copied extensively in the late
19th and early 20thC. Perhaps the most commonly faked
mark is the "VP" monogram of the Veuve Perrin factory.

Porcelain

French porcelains have been extensively faked, especially
pieces from the Vincennes-Sèvres factory. It is safe to say that
over 95 per cent of pieces bearing the interlaced "L"s of
Sèvres are later hard-paste copies of high-rococo originals.
It is essential to study the way in which Sèvres enamellers
inscribed their wares in the 18thC. Familiarity with the
Sèvres porcelain in the greatest public collections in France,

the USA and the UK is also a requirement. In addition, a knowledge of the date letters on Sèvres is useful (for further details of date letters, see p.363). For example, the date letter "B" (for 1754) found on a piece of porcelain with a rose-pink ground must be a fake, as the colour was only introduced in 1757. Most fakes tend to carry fairly early (and therefore more desirable) date letters.

At the time of the French Revolution there was a considerable body of undecorated Sèvres porcelain stockpiled at the factory. After the Revolution this was sold off and much of it enamelled in the old style. This group presents some problems as it is perfectly genuine 18thC porcelain, with the decoration added later. The combined result is a forgery, and can be difficult to identify. There were also concerns in England which specialized in reproducing soft-paste Sèvres porcelain, such as John Randall whose work was exceptional. Soft-paste copies are much rarer than French hard-paste copies. Hard-paste porcelain was only made from 1768 onwards; pieces in this material with earlier date letters are fakes.

Other French factories were also copied or faked but these are relatively uncommon. The Samson factory produced hard-paste copies of St Cloud, Mennecy and Chantilly soft-paste porcelains. Most have the Samson entwined "S" mark as well as the original factory mark.

Germany

Stoneware

The classic stonewares of Cologne, Frechen, Raeren, Westerwald, Siegburg and Kreussen have all been copied, particularly in the latter half of the19thC. The copies of Frechen or Cologne stonewares are generally fairly mechanical-looking, compared to the uneven, irregularly glazed originals.

Copies of Raeren wares by Hubert Schiffer, active in the late 19thC, although made in the traditional manner, are too neatly finished to deceive, and most are impressed with the manufacturer's "HS" monogram.

Westerwald blue and white stonewares are still made today, but modern pieces are invariably marked. Many of the *Historismus* pieces from the 19thC are often large and over-elaborate compared to the humbler wares of the 17th and 18thC. Whatever the size or shape, all the copies are tightly and stiffly decorated, with perfectly flat bases; early Westerwald bases tend to be slightly concave. In many cases the dense, blackish cobalt blue of the originals, is replaced by a bright-blue with a sticky appearance. In the late 19thC the

Merkelbach factory made some good quality pieces, However, most have the impressed name or initials on the base.

Copies of Siegburg wares made by Peter Lowenich and
others in the last quarter of the 19thC can be exceptionally
difficult to attribute because they are made in the same
manner and with the same moulded designs as the 16thC
originals. In general the copies appear too well-made.

Finally, the enamelled stonewares of Kreussen made
in the 17th and early 18thC were also faked. These include
the *waltzenkrug* (a short, cylindrical tankard) and the
schraubflasche (a flask with rounded sides). There are many
copies of this group, and these are usually neatly potted, but
decorated in a stiff and over-zealous manner using 19thC
enamels which tend to be slightly duller in colour than those
used earlier.

Porcelain

This category has always been attractive to the copyist and
forger. Meissen, the foremost factory in Europe before the
Seven Years War (1756-63), was the target of almost every
other factory at least in terms of imitation of its style in the
middle of the 18thC. However the distinctive palette of
Meissen eluded them all as did its superlative modelling.
While it is easy to distinguish Meissen from other German
hard-paste factories in the 18thC, it is not so easy to separate
early from late Meissen, particularly on small objects such as
snuff-boxes where there is little undecorated surface to help.
In these cases one has to rely on the quality of the decoration
alone, the appraisal of which is beyond most except the experienced expert. The best copies of Meissen were made by the
Samson factory (established in 1854) but while the modelling
and the colouring are of high standard the pure white paste
of this French factory is totally different from the flecky
greyish paste of Meissen.

The Meissen crossed-swords mark is, together with
the interlaced "L"s of Sèvres, the most copied symbol in all
of western porcelain. Few copies have the sureness of the
original. The mark was copied not only in Germany but in
France and England.

Other German factories such as Fulda, Furstenberg and
Ludwigsburg, as well as many others have been copied in
the 19thC and a thorough knowledge of the different pastes
and enamels is a prerequisite for venturing into this particular area of collecting.

Faience

Most fakes in this category appear to be of the more
expensive enamelled wares although relatively few are
encountered.

Holland

Delftware

Delft became the most important tin-glazed earthenware centre in the middle of the 17thC. At first the emphasis was on Chinese-style blue and white wares although by the early 18thC, polychrome decorated pieces became popular. While many factories closed towards the end of the 18thC (the competition from English creamware and less expensive porcelain administering the death-blow) a few continued in the 19thC making tourist-type wares in the manner of earlier Delftware. These late copies and pastiches are not difficult to spot, but a few with well-known factory marks, such the "PAK" monogram of the *De Griesche A* (The Greek A) factory, are deceptive. This category includes frequently collected Delftware animals and figures.

Britain

Almost every category of British ceramics – Staffordshire slipware, English delftware, Astbury, Wheildon, Wedgwood, Worcester, Chelsea and Lowestoft, and even the humble Staffordshire "flatback" – has been forged or copied.

The 19thC in Britain was a period of deliberate recreation of past styles in all areas of the decorative arts, including ceramics. Spode, Coalport, Minton, Wedgwood and other major manufacturers produced wares in the current styles: neo-rococo, neo-gothic and the Aesthetic Movement. At the same time however, there was interest in genuine old pottery and porcelain from a growing group of collectors. The period from about 1880 until c.1930 probably marks the most prolific activitity of fakers in Britain, not only in the field of ceramics, but also in furniture, arms and armour, bronzes, glass and in the printed book.

Pottery
Slipware

Slipware enjoyed a continuing tradition from the 17thC until well into the 19thC. Pieces made by the great Staffordshire potters, Thomas Toft, William Tallor (or Talor) and Ralph Simpson were eagerly sought by collectors. A number of signed and dated pieces by this group of potters are well known, and the high prices paid for their dishes and vessels encouraged potters to make some very deceptive copies, which they then inscribed with the names of these celebrated figures. Many pieces subsequently passed into some of the most notable collections, some no doubt remaining undetected to this day.

Delftware

Delftware fakes are another intriguing group. Whereas there are a great number of forgeries of French faience there are relatively few of English delftware. This may be explained by the continuous production of French tin-glazed pottery into the 20thC: the basic skills are therefore still available, making it possible to achieve a passable copy. In Britain the manufacture of tin-glazed earthenware virtually ceased in the early 19thC, and the necessary skills were lost.

In the late 19th and early 20thC a number of fakes began to appear on the market in London. They were genuine 17thC wine bottles which had originally been covered in an undecorated, plain white glaze, a fairly common practice in the latter half of the 17thC. Just as with Staffordshire slip-ware there was great demand at the turn of the 19thC for 17thC ceramics, especially pieces bearing a date and/or a name. In order to gain from this apparent shortfall, a group of forgers inscribed these "white" pieces with 17thC dates. This meant that the piece then had to be refired, a difficult task, particularly with a delicate and friable material such as delftware. A number were irretrievably damaged: the globules of moisture trapped within the absorbent clay under the glaze, exploded through the surface of the glaze during firing. Several of these pieces still exist. The more successfully fired wares can still be identified by the unconvincing hand in which the dates and inscriptions are written.

Astbury, Wheildon and Wedgwood

Astbury, Wheildon and Wedgwood wares have also been forged, and of special interest are the celebrated "Pew groups" which can fetch large sums of money. In the 1920s and 1930s a few of these pew groups (so-called because the figures are seated on pews) appeared on the market featuring the names of Staffordshire's most famous potters. As the models were clearly all made by the same person they did not fool experts for long. However, while pew groups with names like Astbury, Wheildon or Wedgwood should arouse the gravest suspicion, unnamed pew groups cannot neccessarily be dismissed as fakes, even if the modelling lacks the sharpness of detail and the finesse of the original.

Other Staffordshire wares

Fakes of other Staffordshire pottery include agate ware and early Wedgwood-Wheildon cauliflower ware, but perhaps most surprising are Victorian flat-back figures and cottages. Within the past 30 years there has been a spate of fakes of this type, not only confined to the more collectable figures such as the boxing group of Heenan and Sayers, Dick Turpin and Tom King, but also cottages and money boxes.

Porcelain

In terms of porcelain, the British factories which have received the most attention from the faker are Chelsea and Worcester, although forgeries of Lowestoft, Longton Hall, Bow and Derby are also known. The majority of copies of Chelsea and Worcester soft-paste that are encountered are made from French hard-paste porcelain, mainly produced by the Samson factory, and are slightly greenish or bluish in tone. Copies of Chelsea almost invariably feature the gold anchor mark, which tends to be a fraction larger than the original. Many other European factories employed the gold anchor, and it is the most commonly faked English mark. These late 19thC copies are decorated in harsh blues and reds, unlike the softer, more irregular colours of the 18thC.

The Samson factory also made copies of Worcester, with panels of exotic birds or flowers: most of these have either the crescent or the seal mark of Worcester. The greenish, glassy glaze of Samson, is quite distinct from the duller, more greyish surface of genuine Worcester porcelain.

Another group of fakes were made in Torquay, c.1945. Produced by a husband and wife team, they are made from a convincingly primitive and fissured material. However their figures and wares of Chelsea, Derby and Longton Hall are poorly cast, modelled and decorated compared to the originals. In their day they duped many experts until A. J. B. Kiddell of Sotheby's, London, proved them to be forgeries. Fortunately this latter type of fake is extremely rare.

USA

Although the domestic ceramics industry developed slowly in the USA, by the 18thC a cottage industry had developed, and a distinctive style of slip-decorated redware was being made in several parts of New England. This type of ware was made commercially until the early 20thC, and is now widely reproduced.

The town of Bennington in Vermont became a potting centre at the end of the 18thC. The forms and standards of the stonewares that were produced, set standards that were widely copied, particularly throughout New England, until the beginning of the 20thC. American stonewares are distinguishable from European by their larger size and relatively thick potting. Other Bennington Potteries, including the United States Pottery, produced lustrous brown "Rockingham" wares and also American porcelain, particularly figures. Very little Bennington pottery is marked, but impressed tradenames or monograms may appear. It should also be noted that the ware is widely reproduced.

Britain & Ireland

It is not certain where the first characteristic British pottery was produced, but it is likely that many of the finer examples from the 14thC were made at monasteries. In the 16th and 17thC glazed, relief-moulded slipwares were produced in Staffordshire (especially in the areas around Burslem), and at Wrotham in Kent.

Tin-glazed earthenware first appeared in Britain in the mid-16thC, in London and Norwich. Potters in London were responsible for the spread of English delftware to many other parts of the country, including Bristol, Wincanton, Liverpool, Glasgow and Dublin.

The production of refined pottery and porcelain was a relatively late development in the British Isles, largely advanced by European immigrants in the 17thC. Until the 18thC no British pottery bore factory marks, and even marking was confined to some porcelains and more sophisticated pottery. Tin-glazed earthenware was made at about half-a-dozen centres scattered about the British Isles; none feature factory marks in the way that pieces made at Dutch Delftware factories do. Attributions are made by excavation or by documentary inscriptions on pieces made for individuals or institutes such as the Livery Companies of London. Other types of pottery – redware, basaltes, jasper-type wares, creamware or Prattware – made in Staffordshire, Lancashire, Yorkshire or elsewhere, were rarely, if ever, marked before about 1770, when Josiah Wedgwood and his contemporaries began to impress their products with their initials or full names, and later a number of different symbols or devices.

The early English porcelain factories were, with the odd exception, based in the great seaports of their day: London (Chelsea, Bow, Limehouse and Vauxhall), Bristol, Plymouth and Liverpool. Oddly enough, the manufacture of porcelain was an unusual activity in Staffordshire, traditionally the home of British ceramics, until the 19thC. By the middle of the 19thC Staffordshire potters were producing millions of pieces of transfer-printed earthenware and other hybrid wares (often referred to under the general term "china") for the domestic and colonial markets. Many of these pieces were marked not only with factory marks, but also with the title of the pattern.

Belfas

Dublin ▲

St Iv

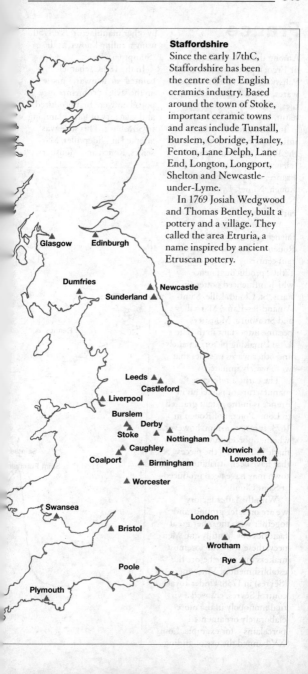

Staffordshire

Since the early 17thC, Staffordshire has been the centre of the English ceramics industry. Based around the town of Stoke, important ceramic towns and areas include Tunstall, Burslem, Cobridge, Hanley, Fenton, Lane Delph, Lane End, Longton, Longport, Shelton and Newcastle-under-Lyme.

In 1769 Josiah Wedgwood and Thomas Bentley, built a pottery and a village. They called the area Etruria, a name inspired by ancient Etruscan pottery.

Glasgow
Edinburgh
Dumfries
Newcastle
Sunderland
Leeds
Castleford
Liverpool
Burslem
Derby
Stoke
Nottingham
Caughley
Coalport
Birmingham
Norwich
Lowestoft
Worcester
Swansea
London
Bristol
Wrotham
Rye
Poole
Plymouth

France

Among the earliest characteristic French pottery is Bernard Palissy's 16thC relief-moulded wares, which feature fish, reptiles, insects, snakes and other naturalistic objects.

Italian maiolica had a great influence on French pottery in the 16thC, and maiolica, or faïence as it was to be called in France, was produced in Brou, Rouen, Nîmes, Lyon and Nevers, the most important early factory.

A native French style of faïence began to develop. Rouen became the most important centre by the end of the 17thC, producing faïence which influenced potters in Paris, St, Cloud, Lille, Saint-Amand-les-Eaux, Marseilles and Strasburg. Moustiers became important in the late 17thC, making pictorial panels and other wares in styles that were widely imitated.

The earliest reference to manufacture of porcelain in France is in the patent granted to Louis Poterat of Rouen in 1673. It is not certain, however, whether porcelain was actually made in Rouen – the pieces that have been attributed to the town may have been produced at Saint Cloud.

With the latter factory we are on safer ground, and together with the other great factories of Chantilly and Mennecy, these were the foremost makers in France before the establishment of Vincennes (Sèvres) in 1738. Under royal control Sèvres enjoyed a virtual monopoly in the more elaborately ornamented porcelains – for example, Louis XV banned the use of gilding by other manufacturers c.1750 using a ruling known as the "Sumptuary Laws".

In the 18thC, enamel-painted earthenwares made in the style of contemporary porcelain were first produced at the factory of Paul Hannong in Strasburg. This style was adopted at Niderviller, Marseilles, Rouen and Moustiers.

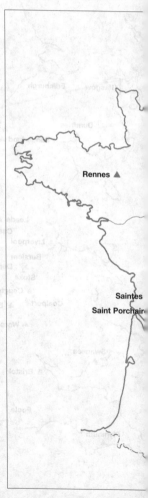

In the years following the Revolution in 1789-93, a large number of factories were set up in Paris producing the characteristic glassy, hard-paste porcelain of the early 19thC. In the second half of the 19thC, the large deposits of fine porcelain clay near Limoges, as well as other economic factors persuaded manufacturers to establish potteries there. Today it is still one of the most important ceramic centres in Europe.

In the late 18th and early 19thC, potteries began to imitate the cream-coloured earthenware made at Staffordshire in England called *faience fine* in France. This was made at Lunéville, Bellevue, Saint Clément, Paris and Orléans.

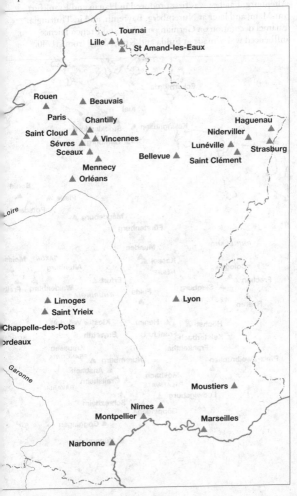

Northern Europe

The main ceramic-producing centres in northern Europe are based in an area now occupied by present-day Holland and Germany. There is a large, complex network of centres situated in Germany, and as a result they are illustrated here.

Some of the earliest German pottery was produced around Cologne in the Rhineland. Salt-glazed stonewares were produced at least from the 14thC in the Rhineland, and during the 16thC in Cologne, Siegburg, Raeren and Westerwald. A number of places in Saxony were important in the 17thC, including Freiburg and Altenburg. Faience was first produced in Hanau and Frankfurt-am-Main, and later at Nuremberg, Bayreuth, and in Thuringia. Enamel decoration on German porcelain and French faience influenced wares made at Fulda and Künersberg from c.1740.

The Royal porcelain factory at Meissen was established in 1710, and was the only factory in Germany producing true porcelain until the mid-18thC, if we exclude Vienna in Austria. After this date, however, other factories were set up in Höchst, Frankenthal, Nymphenburg, Ludwigsburg, Fürstenburg and Berlin. The work of the independent decorator or *Hausmaler*, who worked on both pottery and porcelain is also important c.1720-50.

The main centres in Holland are fewer and better known than those located in Germany. They include Antwerp, Rotterdam, Amsterdam, Middleburg, Makkum, Weesp, and Delft. Blue and white tin-glazed earthenwares were produced at Delft in the 17th and 18thC.

Other important centres in northern Europe include the Royal factory at Copenhagen in Denmark, the Imperial factory at St. Petersburg, and Rörstrand near Stockholm in Sweden.

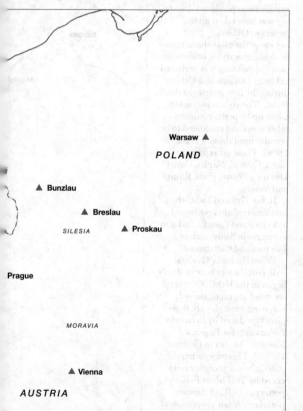

Italy

The first important maiolica-producing centres in Italy in the 15thC were Orvieto (possibly the oldest), Viterbo, Florence and Siena, and Faenza.

The production of maiolica was well-established by the beginning of the 15thC, and output included large dishes and sets of drug jars. An important centre was Deruta where polychrome and lustre maiolica was produced. Lustre-ing was later taken up by potters in Gubbio.

One of the most characteris-tic decorative styles, *istoriato* or pictorial painting was perfected in Castel Durante and Urbino during the first quarter of the 16thC. The style was quickly taken up by pottery painters in other areas and continued to be popular until the end of the 18thC. These areas include Siena, Castelli, Naples, Castel Durante, Pesaro, Forli, Rimini and Verona.

In the 17th and 18thC the maiolica tradition continued at Venice and Castelli, and also at centres in Sicily, such as Palermo and Caltagirone.

Efforts to make Oriental style porcelain in Italy probably began in the 16thC. Of several recorded attempts, the only surviving examples are those pieces produced by Bernardo Buontalenti for Francesco Maria de' Medici in Florence 1575-87. This curious hybrid porcelain was probably influ-enced by Turkish or Persian pottery as well as Chinese porcelain. A fair proportion of them bear one of the most exciting marks in all ceramics - the dome of Florence cathedral – the earliest factory mark on non-Oriental porcelain.

For the further production of porcelain in Italy we have to wait until c.1720, when the Vezzi brothers of Venice

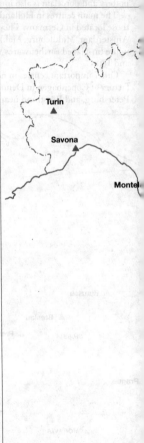

acquired the arcanum, or secret recipe, for hard-paste porcelain, probably from Christoph Conrad Hunger formerly of Dresden and Vienna.

In the 18thC there were two other factories in Venice (Hewelcke and Cozzi) as well as the important porcelain concerns at Capodimonte in Naples, and Doccia, near Florence.

The United States

Aside from Native American pottery, the first pottery was produced in the United States in the 17thC. One of the first makers was Philip Drinker of Charlestown, Massachusetts, active from 1635. Early ware comprised simply-decorated redwares in traditional northern European forms. By the second half of the 18thC, a distinctive style of slip-decorated redware was being made in New England, particularly Connecticut. American-style stonewares also developed during the 18thC. Production was particularly successful in the southern states such as Georgia and Virginia. Porcelain experiments first began in Georgia in the

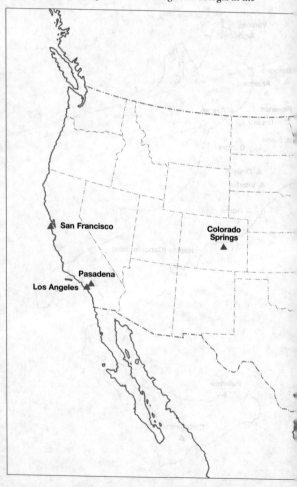

mid-18thC, but the production of porcelain started in earnest in Philadelphia c.1770.

Commercial potting began in the 19thC, with important centres located in Ohio, Pennsylvania, Maryland (in Baltimore), and New Jersey (in Trenton, the "Staffordshire of America") by the 1880s. Most of these manufacturers produced a kind of iron-stone ware evolved from early American stoneware.

The late 19thC saw the establishment of an art pottery industry in North America. Works were founded as far afield as New Orleans, California and New Hampshire. The best-known, largest and most influential art pottery manufacturer was the Rookwood factory, founded in Cincinnati, Ohio in 1880.

China

Almost all types of ceramics made after the Tang Dynasty have borne some kind of mark. Marks on early pottery however, are relatively unusual, and it is only the porcelain wares made at Jingdezhen (Ching-tê-chen) which were marked on a regular basis, from the 15thC onwards.

While celadons, blackwares and Cizhou-type wares continued to be made throughout the Ming Dynasty, it was the blue and white porcelain of Jingdezhen in the southern province of Jiangxi which proved to be the most popular of all Chinese ceramics. At least until the late 17thC well over 90 per cent of production was blue and white. Competition from Japanese Imari and Kakiemon porcelain in the second half of the 17thC forced the Chinese to respond with copies of Japanese porcelain but also develop polychrome decorated porcelains. *Famille verte* and *famille rose* were made in increasing quantities in the 18thC culminating with highly decorated Canton wares. Jingdezhen porcelain made for the Imperial court is very refined, but exportware is generally coarser. In the 15thC it appears that only wares destined for the court or for the Chinese market were inscribed with reign marks. During the 16thC when production at Jingdezhen increased dramatically in response to the export trade, reign marks were less rigorously controlled, this encouraged potters to copy earlier marks (for further information on Chinese fakes and copies see pp.340-41).

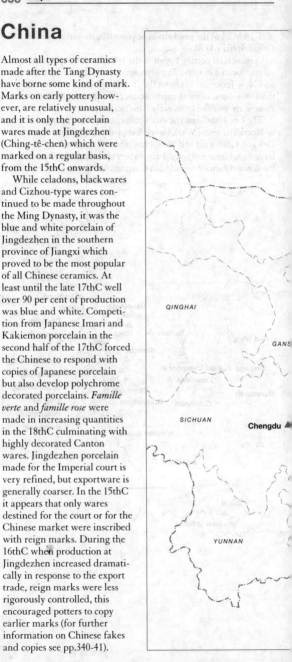

QINGHAI

GANS

SICHUAN

Chengdu

YUNNAN

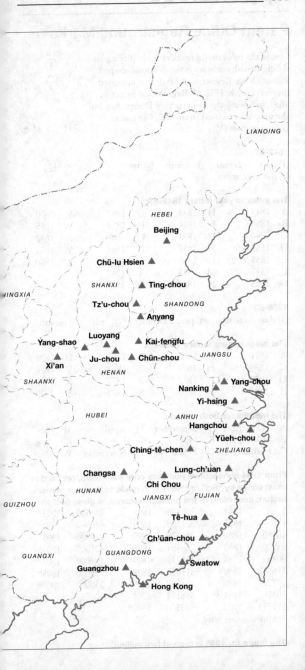

Appendices

Patent Office Registration Marks

One of the most useful marks for identifying and dating British ceramics is the diamond-shaped Patent Office Registration Mark that appeared on pieces made 1842-83. Registration began in 1839, following the Copyright of Design Act, but the insignia was used from 1842. Ceramics belong to class IV.

1842-67

① class ② year ③ month ④ day
⑤ parcel number

The index to year letters 1842-67:

A	1845	H	1843	O	1862	V	1850
B	1858	I	1846	P	1851	W	1865
C	1844	J	1854	Q	1866	X	1842
D	1852	K	1857	R	1861	Y	1853
E	1855	L	1856	S	1849	Z	1860
F	1847	M	1859	T	1867		
G	1863	N	1864	U	1848		

1868-83

① class ② day ③ parcel number ④ year ⑤ month

The index to year letters 1868-83:

A	1871	F	1873	K	1883	U	1874
C	1870	H	1869	L	1882	V	1876
D	1878	I	1872	P	1877	X	1868
E	1881	J	1880	S	1875	Y	1879

The months for both periods:

A	December	D	September	H	April	M	June
B	October	E	May	I	July	R	August
C/O	January	G	February	K	November	W	March

From 1884 consecutive numbers only were used, prefixed in most cases by "Rd" or "Rd No." A guide to the year of manufacture according to the number featured, is given below:

1	1884	205240	1893	402500	1903*
19754	1885	224720	1894	420000	1904*
40480	1886	246975	1895	447000	1905*
64520	1887	268393	1896	471000	1906*
90483	1888	291241	1897	494000	1907*
116648	1889	311658	1898	519000	1908*
141273	1890	331707	1899	550000	1909*
163767	1891	368154	1901		
185713	1892	385500	1902*		

* Approximate only

The figure for 1995 is around two million.

Derby

From 1882 the Derby Porcelain Works has used year cyphers which appear below the marks shown.

This mark was used c.1878-90 at the time the company was known as the Derby Crown Porcelain Co. Ltd.

Used from 1890 when the company name changed to Royal Crown Derby Porcelain Co. Ltd., this mark also includes the word "England" from 1891, and "Made in England" from c.1920.

1882	1883	1884	1885	1886	1887	1888
1889	1890	1891	1892	1893	1894	1895
1896	1897	1898	1899	1900	1901	1902
1903	1904	1905	1906	1907	1908	1909
1910	1911	1912	1913	1914	1915	1916
1917	1918	1919	1920	1921	1922	1923
1924	1925	1926	1927	1928	1929	1930
1931	1932	1933	1934	1935	1936	1937
I	II	III	IV	V	VI	VII
1938	1939	1940	1941	1942	1943	1944
VIII	IX	X	XI	XII	XIII	XIV
1945	1946	1947	1948	1949	1950	1951
XV	XVI	XVII	XVIII	XIX	XX	XXI ETC
1952	1953	1954	1955	1956	1957	1958

Minton

From 1842 Minton included year cyphers in the marks impressed on their pieces.

J January	**A** April	**H** July	**O** October
F February	**E** May	**Y** August	**N** November
M March	**I** June	**S** September	**D** December

At the beginning of 1943 this system was discontinued and replaced by figures corresponding to the year of production preceded by a number allocated to the actual maker of the piece.

Sèvres

Date letters were used at Sèvres from 1753-93 to show the year of manufacture. The letter appeared within or alongside the interlaced "L" mark. Letters that appear below the mark are usually those of the painter, gilder or potter.

Year marks 1753-93

A	1753	L	1764	X	1775	HH	1785
B	1754	M	1765	Y	1776	II	1786
C	1755	N	1766	Z	1777	JJ	1787
D	1756	O	1767			KK	1788
E	1757	P	1768	AA	1778	LL	1789
F	1758	Q	1769	BB	1779	MM	1790
G	1759	R	1770	CC	1780	NN	1791
H	1760	S	1771	DD	1781	OO	1792
I	1761	T	1772	EE	1782	PP	1793
J	1762	U	1773	FF	1783		
K	1763	V	1774	GG	1784		

Marks of painters, gilders and potters at Sèvres

These are ordered alphabetically by initial or monogram, and then by device or other mark. Potters are marked with an asterisk.

A	Auvillain* 1877-after 1900	ℬ	Belet, Adolphe 1881-1882
A, N, A.	Asselin, Charles-Éloi 1765-1804	ℬ	Briffaut, Alphonse-Théodore-Jean 1848-1890
A	Lapierre, Auguste* 1833-1843	A.C.	Cieutat, Alphonse* 1894-1928
A	Richard, Auguste 1811-1848	C	Coursaget 1881-1886
A	Archelais, Jules 1865-1902	AD	David, Francois-Alexandre 1844-1881
AB	Blanchard, Alexandre 1878-1901	AD	Dumain, Alphonse* 1884-1928
A.B.	Brachard jeune, Alexandre* 1784-1792, 1795-1799, 1802-1827	A.D	Ducluzeau, Mme Marie-Adélaïde 1818-1848
ℬ	Barré, Louis-Désiré 1846-1881	A)	Dammouse, Pierre-Adolphe* 1852-1880
ℬ	Bonnuit, Achille-Louis 1858-1862, 1865-1894	AD	David, François-Alexandre 1844-1881
ℬ	Boullemier, Antoine-Gabriel 1802-1842	AD	Dubois, Alexandre* 1896-1915
		AF	Fournier, Anatole 1878-1926

Mark	Artist / Dates
AL / AL / A	Ligué, Denis 1881-1911
Al	Allard, Jean-Baptiste* 1832-1841
A	Lacour, Armand* 1895-1911
A	Longuet, Alexandre* 1840-1876
AM	Meyer, Alfred 1858-1871
AM	Moriot, François-Adolphe 1843-1844
ap	Percheron, Alexandre* 1827-1864
A	Poupart, Antoine-Achille 1815-1848
A	Apoil, Charles-Alexis 1851-1864
:B	Belet, Émile 1876-1900
B	Bouvrain, Antoine-Louis 1826-1848
B	Boulanger père 1754-1784
B.	Barré 1773-1774, 1776-1778
B	Baldisseroni, Shiridani 1860-1879
B	Barrat l'oncle 1769-1791
B.	Brachard aîné, Jean-Charles-Nicolas* 1782-1824, or one of the Bougons 1754-1812
BT	Boitel, Charles-Marie-Pierre 1797-1822
BD	Baudouin père 1750-1800
BD	
Bf	Boullemier fils, Hilaire-François 1817-1855
BG	Béranger, Antoine 1807-1846
Bh	Boullemier fils, Hilaire-François 1817-1855
Bn	Bulidon 1763-1792
Bo	Bono, Étienne-Henri* 1754-1781
Bt	Boquet, Louis-Honoré* 1815-1860
Bx	Buteux, Théodore 1786-1822
By.	Bailly père 1753-1767
Bv	Bourdois* 1773-1774
C	Couturier, Claude 1762-1775
C.	Castel 1772-1797
B	Barriat, Charles 1848-1883
C.C.	Constans, Charles-Louis 1803-1840
CC	Cabau, Eugène-Charles 1847-1885
C.C.	Constantin, Abraham 1813-1848
CD	Develly, Jean-Charles 1813-1848
CD	Desnoyers-Chapponet aîné 1788-1804, 1810-1828
ch.	Chabry fils, Étienne-Jean 1765-1787
G.L ch.L	Lucas, Charles 1878-1910
CL	Delahaye, Charles-François-Jules* 1818-1852
cm cm	Commelin, Michel-Gabriel 1768-1802

Mark	Maker
cn	Chanou jeune, Henri-Florentin* 1746-1779, 1785
C:P	Capronnier, François 1812-1819
cp	Chappus aîné, Antoine-Joseph* 1761-1787
CR	Robert, Charles* 1889-1930
CV	Villion, Charles* 1894-1941
D	Doré, Pierre 1829-1865
D	Delatre cadet* 1754-1758
D.D..	Dusolle 1768-1774
D..	
D	Tardy, Claude-Antoine 1755-1795
da	Danet père* 1759-after 1780
DE	Drouet, Ernest-Émile 1878-1920
DF	Delafosse, Denis 1804-1815
D.F.	Davignon, Jean-François 1807-1815
DG	Derichweiler, Jean-Charles-Gérard 1855-1884
D.G.	Drouet, Gilbert 1785-1825
D.G.	Godin, Mme Catherine 1806-1828
Dh	Deutsch 1803-1819
D.I	Didier père 1787-1825, or fils, Charles-Antoine 1819-1848
DP DP DP	Devicq, Jules* 1881-1928
D.B	Boullemier, Mlle Virginie 1814-1842
D.P.	Depérais, Claude-Antoine 1794-1822
DR	Drand 1764-1775, 1780
DT	Dutanda, Dutenda, Nicolas 1765-1802
DP	Doat, Taxile 1879-1905
D.y	Durosey, Charles-Christian-Marie 1802-1830
E	Latache, Étienne 1867-1879
E.	Ouint, Édouard* 1888-1893
E·R	Apoil, Mme Suzanne-Estelle 1865-1892
B	Bulot, Eugène-Alexandre 1855-1883
E.D.	Drouet, Ernest-Émile 1878-1920
E de M	Mauisson, Mlle de 1862-1870
E	Escallier, Mme Éléonore 1874-1888
EF	Fromant, Eugène 1855-1885
E	Guillemain, Ambroise-Ernest-Louis 1864-1885
H	Hallion, Eugène 1870,1872-1874, 1876-1893
EL	Leroy, Eugène-Éléonor 1855-1891
M	Moriot, Mlle Élise 1881-1886
P	Porchon 1880-1884
ER	Richard, Eugène 1833-1872

ℜ	Réjoux, Émile-Bernard 1858-1893	๛	Vaubertrand, François 1822-1848
ℰ.𝒮	Simard, Eugène 1880-1908	ƒₓ ℛ	Fumez 1777-1804
ℰ.𝟹.	Humbert, Jules-Eugène 1851-1870	G	Genest, Jean-Baptiste-Étienne 1752-1789
ℱ	Falconet, Étienne-Maurice* 1757-1766	𝒢...	Godin, François-Aimé* 1813-1848
𝖥	Fallot 1773-1790	𝒢ℬ	Boterel, Georges* 1888-1933
𝔽	Fernex, Jean-Baptiste de* c.1756	𝒢𝒟	Derichweiller, Jean-Charles-Gérard 1855-1884
ℱ	Fontaine, Jean-Joseph 1825-1857	𝓰𝖽. 𝒢𝒥.	Gérard, Claude-Charles 1771-1824
ƒ	Lévé, Félixm 1777-1800	𝒢.𝒢.	Georget, Jean 1801-1823
ƒ𝓈	Pfeiffer 1771-1800	GL	Lebarque, Georges* 1895-1916
ℱ.ℬ	Boullemier, François-Antoine 1806-1838	𝒢ℒ	Gébleux, Léonard 1883-1928
ℬ	Barbin, François-Hubert 1815-1849	𝒢ₐℛ	Gobert, Alfred-Thompson 1849-1891
F C	Courcy, Alexandre-Frédéric de 1865-1886	𝒢ℛ	Robert, Mme Louise 1835-1840
ℱ.𝒞.	Charrin, Mlle Fanny 1814-1826	𝒢𝓉	Grémont jeune 1769-1775, 1778-1781
𝔉	Ficquenet, Charles 1864-1881	𝒢ᵤ	Ganeau, Pierre-Louis 1813-1831
ℱℱ	Fischbag, Charles* 1834-1850	𝒢 ℋ	Vignol, Gustave 1881-1909
F.G. F.𝒮	Goupil, Frédéric 1859-1878	H	Houry, Pierre 1752-1755
ℋ	Hallion, François 1865-1895	♭	Laroche, de 1759-1802
ℳ	Mérigot, Maximilien-Ferdinand 1845-1872, 1879-1884	𝒽c.	Hericourt c.1755
𝒫	Paillet, Fernand 1879-1888, 1893	ℋ𝒞ℛ	Renard, Henri c.1881
ℛ	Régnier, Joseph-Ferdinand* 1826-1830, 1836-1870	𝒽.𝒥.	Huard, Pierre 1811-1846

Mark	Attribution	Mark	Attribution
he.	**Héricourt jeune** 1770-1773, 1776-1777	*E E*	**Julienne, Alexis-Étienne** 1837-1849
HF	**Faraguet, Mme** 1857-1879	*H, Jh. R Jh.R*	**Richard, Nicolas-Joseph** 1833-1872
H HL.	**Laserre, Henri*** 1886-1931	*j h.*	**Henrion aîné** 1770-1784
HP.	**Prévost aîné** 1754-1793, or le second 1757-1797	*H*	**Lambert, Henri-Lucien** 1859-1899
HR	**Robert, Henri*** 1889-1933	*JR*	**Régnier, Hyacinthe*** 1825-1863
HS	**Sill** 1881-1887	*J.*	**Legay, Jules-Eugène*** 1861-1895
H	**Trager, Henri** 187-1909	*JL*	**Liance fils aîné*** 1769-1810
HU	**Uhlrich, Henri** 1879-1925	*J.G*	**Gély, Léopold-Jules-Joseph*** 1851-1889
hy	**Huny** (doubtful mark) 1785-1800, 1810	*j.n.*	**Chauveaux fils** 1771-1783
IC	**Chanou, Jean-Baptiste*** 1779-1825	*J2*	**Jaquotot** or **Jacquotot Mme Marie-Victoire** 1801-1842
J. j	**Jubin** 1772-1775	*JR*	**Risbourg, Julien*** 1895-1925
JA	**André, Jules** 1840-1869	*JR*	**Roger, Thomas-Jules*** 1852-1886
J a	**Jacob-Ber, Moïse** 1814-1848	*j t*	**Thévenet fils** 1752-1758
A	**Archelais, Jules** 1865-1902	*KK...*	**Dodin, Charles-Nicolas** 1754-1802
JB	**Boileau fils aîné*** 1773-1781	*L*	**Le Cat*** 1872-after 1900
J.C	**Célos, Jules-François** 1865-1895	*L*	**Lévé, Denis** 1754-1805
J.C.	**Trager, Jules** 1847, 1854-1873	*L*	**Leclerc, Auguste*** 1897-1911
jc.	**Chappuis jeune** 1772-1777	*L.*	**Couturier** entered 1783
JD	**Chanou, Mme Mère** 1779-1800	*B*	**Blanchard, Louis-Étienne-Frédéric** 1848-1880
E E	**Jardel, Bernard-Louis-Émile** 1886-1913	*B*	**Belet, Louis** 1878-1913

ℒℬ	Le Bel jeune 1773-1793	*M*	Moiron 1790-1791
ℒℬ	Le Bel, Nicolas-Antoine 1804-1845	*M*	Moyez, Jean-Louis 1818-1848
LC	Charpentier, Louis-Joseph 1852, 1854-1879	*M*	Michel, Ambroise 1772-1780
ℒᵉ·	Le Bel aîné, Jean-Etienne 1766-1775	*ℳ*	Morin, Jean-Louis 1754-1787
LG	Le Guay, Étienne-Charles 1778-1781, 1783-1785,1808-1840	*ℳ*	Massy 1779-1803
LG	Guéneau, Louis* 1885-1924	MA	Mascret, Achille 1838-1846
ℒℊ	Le Guay père, Étienne-Henri 1748-1749, 1751-1796	*Mas*	Mascret, Jean* 1810-1848
ℒℊ·		MB	Bunel, Mme Marie-Barbe 1778-1816
ℒℊ	Le Grand, Louis-Antoine 1776-1817	*Mℂ*	Micaud, Pierre-Louis 1795-1834
ℓℊ	Langle, Pierre-Jean-Victor-Amable 1837-1845	ME *ℳ*	Maugendre* 1879-1887
ℒℊᶜᵉ	Langlacé, Jean-Baptiste-Gabriel 1807-1844	*Mℒ*	Mascret, Louis* 1825-1864
ℒi	Liance, Antoine-Mathieu* 1754-1777	*m.ℰ*	Moyez, Pierre* 1827-1848
LL*ℒℒ*	Lécot 1773-1802	*Mℛ*	Morin, Charles-Raphaël 1805-1812
LM	Mirey 1788-1792	*ℳℛ*	Moreau, Denis-Joseph 1807-1815
LM	Mimard, Louis 1884-1928	*ℳ̃*	Solon, Marc* 1857-1871
P	Peluché, Léon 1881-1928	*N*	Morin 1880-after 1900
ℒℬ	Parpette jeune, Mlle Louise 1794-1798, 1801-1817	*N*	Aloncle, François 1758-1781
ℒℛ	Laroche, de 1759-1802	*ℬ*	Bestault, Nestor* 1889-1929
ℒℛ	Le Riche, Josse-François-Joseph* 1757-1801	*ng.*	Nicquet 1764-1792
		O	Ouint, Émmanuel* 1877-1889
		o.ch	Ouint, Charles 1879-1886, 1889-1890

o g	Oger, Jacques-Jean* 1784-1800, 1802-1821	*St.*	Pithou aîné 1757-1790
M	Milet, Optat 1862-1879	R	Riton, Pierre 1821-1860
P	Pine or Pline, François-Bernard-Louis 1854-1870 or later	·R	Sioux aîné 1752-1791
P	Perrottin or Perottin 1760-1793 or later	R	Richard, Nicolas-Joseph 1833-1870 or later
P	Parpette, Philippe 1755-1757, 1773-1806	*R*	Robert, Jean-François 1806-1834, 1836-1843
P.A.	Avisse, Alexandre-Pau 1848-1884	*R...*	Richard, Pierre 1815-1848
B.B Pb	Boucot, Philippe 1785-1791	*R*	Girard 1772-1817
P	Pihan, Charles 1879-1928	*R.B.*	Maqueret, Mme 1796-1798, 1817-1820
J F	Fachard, Pierre* 1899-1934	*RB*	Robert, Jean-François 1806-1843
P.H.	Philippine aîné 1778-1791, 1802-1825	*R*	Rémy, Charles 1886-1897, 1901-1928
S . h.	Philippine cadet, François 1783-1791, 1801-1839	*RL*	Roussel 1758-1774
S.j.	Pithou jeune 1760-1795	*R L.*	
P 7. P9.	Pierre jeune, Jean-Jacques 1763-1800	*Rx*	Riocreux, Denis-Désiré 1807-1828
PK	Knip, Mme de Cour-celles 1808-1809, 1817-1826	*Rx*	Riocreux, Isidore 1846-1849
p.o	Pierre aîné 1759-1775	S	Samson, Léon* 1897-1918
P P	Parpette aîné, Mlle 1788-1798	*S*	Méreaud aîné, Pierre-Antoine 1754-1791
R	Perrenot aîné 1804-1809, 1813-1815	*S*	Sandoz, Alphonse* 1881-1920
PR	Robert, Pierre 1813-1832	*Sc*	Chanou, Mlle Sophie, Mme Binet 1779-1798
P.T.	Petit aîné, Nicolas 1756-1806	*SD*	Noualhier, Mme Sophie 1777-1795
		S	Sieffert, Louis-Eugène 1881-1887, 1894-1898

S.h.	Schradre 1773-1775, 1780-1786		1804, 1807-1808, 1811, 1816-1824
SS	Sinsson or Sisson, Jacques 1795-1846	ⓦ	Hileken 1769-1774
SSℓ	Sinsson or Sisson, Louis 1830-1847	𝔀𝔀𝔀𝔀	Hilken (?) Before 1800
SSp	Sinsson or Sisson, Pierre 1818-1848	3𝒱	Weydinger troisième fils, Pierre 1781-1792, 1796-1816
S. W. Sw	Swebach, Jacques-Jose (called Fontaine) 1803-c.1814	W	Walter c.1867-c.1870
T	Binet 1750-1775	X	Micaud, Jacques-François 1757-1810
𝒞	Troyon, Jean-Marie-Dominique 1801-1817	X X	Grison 1749-1771
⊡	Tardy, Claude-Antoine 1755-1795	X	Catrice 1757-1774
Ŧ	Latache, Étienne 1870-1879	XX	Rocher, Alexandre 1758-1759
ℐhℬ	Fragonard, Théophile 1839-1869	Y	Fouré 1749, 1754-1762
I	Letourneur* 1756-1762	ℽ	Bouillat père, Edmé-François 1758-1810
.I.	Trager, Louis 1888-1934	𝒴	Bouillat fils, F. 1800-1811
𝒫r: 𝒱r	Tristan, Étienne-Joseph 1837-1871, 1879-1882	Z.	Joyau 1766-1775
V	Villion, Paul* 1886-1934	⚒	Roisset, Pierre-Joseph 1753-1795
VD	Vandé, Pierre-Jean-Baptiste 1779-1824	⚹ ⚹	Choisy, Apprien-Julien de 1770-1812
VD	Vandé père 1753-1779	⚲	Martinet, Émile-Victor 1847-1878
𝒱.t	Gérard, Mme née Vautrin 1781-1802	⚱	Le Guay, Pierre-André 1772-1818
W	Vavasseur aîné 1753-1770	⌂	Anthaume, Jean-Jacques 1752-1758
W	Weydinger père 1757-1807	T⚚	Aubert aîné 1754-1758
W	Weydinger second fils, Joseph 1778-		

Mark	Name
	Tardy, Claude-Antoine 1755-1795
	Cardin 1749-1793 or later
	Probably Gomery or Gommery, Edme 1756-1758
	Léandre 1779-1785
	Armand cadet 1746-1788
	Génin, Charles 1756-1757
	Xhrouet, Xhrowet or Secroix, Philippe and Mlle 1750-1775
	Fontelliau, F. 1753-1755
	Pajou 1751-1759
	Renard, Emile 1852-1882
	Boucher 1754-1762
	Probably Ledoux, Jean-Pierre 1758-1761
	Bienfait, Jean-Baptiste 1756-after 1770
	Fritsch 1763-1764
	Bouchet, Jean 1763-1793
	Dubois, Jean-René 1756-1757
	Sinsson, Simpson or Sisson, Nicolas 1773-c.1800
	Gautier 1787-1791
	Becquet 1749-1750, 1753-1765

Mark	Name
	Pouillot 1773-1778
	Buteux aîné, Charles 1756-1782
	Mutel 1754-1759, 1765-1766, 1771-1773
	Évans, Étienne 1752-1806
	Yvernel 1750-1759
	Taillandier or Taillandiez, Vincent 1753-1790
	Boulanger fils 1778-1781
	Chevalier, Pierre-François 1755-1757
	Thévenet père 1741-1777
	Cornailles, Antoine-Toussaint 1755-1800
	Chulot, Louis-Gabriel 1755-1800
	Sioux jeune 1752-1759
	Capell 1746-1800
	Buteux fils cadet 1773-1790
	Dieu, Jean-Jacques 1777-1790, 1794-1798, 1801-1811
	Tabary 1754-1755
	Caton 1749-1798
	Chauveaux aîné, Michel-Barnabé 1752-1788
	Rocher, Alexandre 1758-1759

═══	Bardet 1751-1758		Fournier, Anatole 1878-1926
⋰⋱	Fontaine, Jacques 1752-1775, 1778-1807	J.G	Gély, Léopold-Jules-Joseph 1851-1888
⌒	Noël, Guillaume 1755-1804		Goupil, Frédéric 1859-1878
⋰⋱	Raux aîné 1766-1779		Meyer, Alfred 1858-1871
◌	Sioux aîné 1752-1791		Richard, François 1832-1875
•••	Tandart jeune, Charles 1756-1760 or Tandart, Jean-Baptiste 1754-1803	ɤҴ ℛ	Richard, Émile 1867-1900
••••	Théodore 1765-1771 or later	PM	Roussel, Paul-Marie 1850-1871
⊻⊻⊻	Viellard aîné 1752-1790		Sandoz, Alphonse 1881-after 1900
5	Mongenot 1754-1764	P.S	Schilt, Louis-Pierre 1818-1855
5.	Carrié or Carrier 1752-1757		
6	Bertrand 1757-1774		
˙G.	Bertrand 1750-1800		
9.	Buteux fils aîné, Charles-Nicolas 1763-1801		
9	Méreaud jeune, Charles-Louis 1756-1779		
2000	Vincent jeune 1753-1806		
ℬ	Barré, Louis Désiré 1846-1881		
⌂B ⌂	Bieuville or Bienville (Bieauville?), Horace 1879-1925		
⌂ly ℬy.	Brécy, Paul* or Henry* 1881-after 1900		
ℋ	Courcy, Alexandre-Frédéric de 1865-1886		

Wedgwood

From 1860, as well as their usual name-mark, the Wedgwood
factory began to use a system of date-marking using three
impressed letters. The first denotes the month, the second is a
potter's mark, and the third indicates the year of manufacture.
The system went through three year mark cycles before, in 1907,
the system was amended so that the first letter indicated the cycle
of year marks in use.

Monthly marks 1860-64

January	J	April	A	July	V	October	O
February	F	May	Y	August	W	November	N
March	M	June	T	September	S	December	D

Monthly marks 1865-1907

January	J	April	A	July	L	October	O
February	F	May	M	August	W	November	N
March	R	June	T	September	S	December	D

First cycle of year marks

O	1860	R	1863	U	1866	X	1869
P	1861	S	1864	V	1867	Y	1870
Q	1862	T	1865	W	1868	Z	1871

Second cycle of year marks

A	1872	H	1879	O	1886	V	1893
B	1873	I	1880	P	1887	W	1894
C	1874	J	1881	Q	1888	X	1895
D	1875	K	1882	R	1889	Y	1896
E	1876	L	1883	S	1890	Z	1897
F	1877	M	1884	T	1891		
G	1878	N	1885	U	1892		

Third cycle of year marks

A	1898	H	1905	O	1912	V	1919
B	1899	I	1906	P	1913	W	1920
C	1900	J	1907	Q	1914	X	1921
D	1901	K	1908	R	1915	Y	1922
E	1902	L	1909	S	1916	Z	1923
F	1903	M	1910	T	1917		
G	1904	N	1911	U	1918		

Fourth cycle of year marks

A	1924	C	1926	E	1928	
B	1925	D	1927	F	1929	

After 1929 the last two years of the date appear in full.

Worcester

In 1862, the factory based at the Worcester Porcelain Works became known as Royal Worcester. From 1867 a system of dating by year letters was used together with the standard printed mark.

1867-90

A	1867	H	1873	P	1879	W	1885
B	1868	I	1874	R	1880	X	1886
C	1869	K	1875	S	1881	Y	1887
D	1870	L	1876	T	1882	Z	1888
E	1871	M	1877	U	1883	O	1889
G	1872	N	1878	V	1884	a	1890

From 1891 the words "Royal Worcester England" were added around the standard Worcester mark (see p.222). From 1892 dots were added, one for each year

1892	one dot added above "Royal"
1893	two dots, one on either side of "Royal Worcester England"
1894	three dots
1895	four dots
1896	five dots

This continued until 1915 when there were 24 dots, some placed below the main mark.

1916	dot replaced by a star below the mark
1917	one dot added to star
1918	two dots added to star

This continued until 1927 when there were eleven dots with the star.

1928	dots and star replaced by a small square
1929	small diamond
1930	division sign
1931	two inter-linked circles
1932	three inter-linked circles
1933	one dot added to three circles
1934	two dots added to three circles

This continued until 1941 when there were nine dots. Between 1941 and 1948 there were no changes made in year marks.

1949	"V" placed under mark
1950	"W" placed under mark
1951	one dot added to "W"
1952	two dots added to "W"
1953	three dots added to "W"
1954	four dots added to "W"
1955	five dots added to "W"
1956	"W" is replaced by "R", dots are added until
1963	13 dots appear with the circled "R" device

From 1963 all new patterns feature the year in full.

Further reading

Great Britain and Ireland

J. P. Cushion, *British Ceramic Marks*, London, 1988

Geoffrey A. Godden, *Encyclopedia of British Pottery and Porcelain Marks*, London, 1994

Geoffrey A. Godden, *Jewitt's Ceramic Art of Great Britain 1800-1900*, London, 1972

The rest of Europe

Ludwig Danckert, *Directory of European Porcelain*, London, 1981

Carl Christian Dauterman, *Sèvres*, London, 1969

Antoinette Fäy-Hallé and Barbara Mundt, *19th Century European Porcelain*, London, 1983

W. B. Honey, *European Ceramic Art*, London, 1952

W. B. Honey, *European Ceramic Art: An Illustrated Historical Survey*, London, 1959

W. B. Honey, *German Porcelain*, London, 1947

Arthur Lane, *Deutsche Fayencen im Hetjens-Museum Dusseldorf*, 1962

Arthur Lane, *French Faience*, London, 1970

Wendy M. Watson, *Italian Renaissance Maiolica*, London, 1986

USA

Edwin AtLee Barber, *Marks of American Potters*, Philadelphia, 1904

Edwin AtLee Barber, *The Pottery and Porcelain of the United States*, New York, 1909

Ellen and Bert Denker, *Warner's Collector's Guide to North American Pottery and Porcelain*, New York, 1985

Alice Frelinghuysen, *American Porcelain: 1770-1920*, New York, 1989

William C. Gates Jr. and Dana E. Ormerod, *"The East Liverpool Pottery District: Identification of Manufacturers and Marks"*, *Historical Archaeology*, 16 (1982), pp.1-358.

William C. Ketchum, *American Stoneware*, New York, 1991

William C. Ketchum, *Pottery and Potteries of New York State 1650-1900*, Syracuse, New York, 1987

Ralph and Terry Kovel, *American Art Pottery: The Collector's Guide to Makers, Marks and Factory Histories*, New York, 1993

Lois Lehner, *Lehner's Encyclopedia of U.S. Marks on Pottery, Porcelain & Clay*, Paducah, Kentucky, 1988

International

J. P. Cushion, *Handbook of Pottery & Porcelain Marks*, London, 1990

General

Eric Knowles, *Miller's Antiques Checklists: Art Deco*, London, 1991

Eric Knowles, *Miller's Antiques Checklists: Art Nouveau*, London, 1992

Eric Knowles, *Miller's Antiques Checklists: Victoriana*, London, 1991

Eric Knowles, *Victoriana to Art Deco*, London, 1993

Gordon Lang, *Miller's Antiques Checklist: Porcelain*, London, 1991

Gordon Lang, *Miller's Antiques Checklists: Pottery*, London, 1995

Miller's Antiques Fact File, London, 1988

Miller's Understanding Antiques, London, 1989

George Savage and Harold Newman, *An Illustrated Dictionary of Ceramics*, London 1985.

Glossary

Acid gilding A decorative process whereby patterns are etched into porcelain with hydrofluoric acid, then gilded and brushed.

American Belleek A late-19thC American version of the thinly-potted wares originally made at the Irish Belleek factory.

Agate ware A type of pottery revived by Staffordshire potters in the middle of the 18thC which is made to resemble agate by the partial blending of different coloured clays.

Alafia An Arabic word for "benediction" or "blessing", used symbolically by Moorish potters in early Hispano-moresque lustreware.

Albarello A drug jar, generally of waisted cylindrical form originating in Persia in the 12thC but adopted by almost every major European country from the 15thC on. A variation is the so-called "dumb-bell" form popular in northern Italy, especially in the Veneto.

Alla porcellana Literally "in the style of Chinese blue and white porcelain". A type of scrolling foliage derived from Ming wares used by Italian maiolica decorators in the late 15th and 16thC.

Applied moulding Relief decoration made separately from the body and applied later.

Arcanist One who possesses a porcelain formula – from *arcanum*, the Latin for mystery.

Arita An area of western Kyushu, where most early Japanese porcelain was made from c.1610, including Imari, blue and white, Kakiemon, and Nabeshima.

Armorial wares Wares decorated with coats-of-arms or crests, either transfer-printed or painted. Usually refers to Chinese porcelain bearing European coats-of-arms, produced from the 16thC.

Artificial porcelain Another term for soft-paste porcelain.

A tulipano A pattern devised at the Doccia factory, depicting formal sprays of Oriental flowers.

Baluster In ceramics a term employed to describe a shape of a vase or other vessel with the profile of an elongated pear or teardrop.

Baluster vase A vase shape resembling the curved support of a balustrade. See also above.

Baroque A vigorous decorative style that grew out of the Renaissance, characterized by lively figures and symmetrical ornament. Meissen's porcelain of the early 18thC is the most notable.

Basaltes Black basaltes, a fine black stoneware developed by Josiah Wedgwood in the 1760s.

Basketweave A relief pattern resembling woven willow twigs (oziers) used on borders by most European factories in the 1730s.

Bat-printing A type of transfer-printing used by early 19thC Staffordshire firms. The design was transferred from an engraved plate to a glazed surface via slabs of glue or gelatin (bats).

Bellarmine A Rhenish stoneware vessel of generally bulbous form with a narrow neck on which is stamped the bearded face associated later with Cardinal Roberto Bellarmino, a stern anti-Protestant. These vessels were made over a long period from the 15th to the beginning of the 19thC. They are termed *bartmannkrug* in Germany.

Berettino A style of decoration initially associated with Faenza from the 1520s on but was later adopted by north Italian potteries, particularly Venice. The object is entirely covered in pale or dark blue tin-glaze which is then painted in white and other colours.

Bianco-di-Faenza A type of maiolica developed in the middle of the 16thC at Faenza. It is covered in a thick milk-white glaze, and is usually cursorily decorated in a restricted palette of ochre and blue termed *compendiario*.

Bianco-sopra-bianco Literally "white-on-white". A type of maiolica and other, later tin-glazed wares (e.g. Bristol), painted in white enamel on an off-white or bluish ground. The effect is similar to lace-work.

Birnkrug A pear-shaped jug or mug. Originally produced in Dutch or German earthenware and stoneware (in the 17thC), it was later adopted by the early porcelain factories.

Biscuit Unglazed porcelain or earthenware fired once only. The term also refers to white porcelain (especially figures) that has been left unglazed and undecorated.

Blackware A type of ancient Chinese ceramics similar to greenware but with more iron in the formula.

Blanc de Chine A translucent white Chinese porcelain, unpainted and with a thick glaze. It was made at kilns in Dehua in the Fukien province, from the Ming dynasty and often copied in Europe.

Bleu celeste A sky-blue ground colour developed by Jean Hellot at Vincennes in 1752.

Bleu persan A French adaptation of *berettino* decoration, popular in the latter 17thC at Nevers and copied at Rouen, and also in England.

Bleu-du-Roi Also *bleu nouveau*. A rich blue enamel used as a ground colour at Sèvres.

Bleu lapis An intense cobalt blue ground of almost purplish tone, introduced at Vincennes in 1749.

Blue and white The term for any white Oriental or Western porcelain decorated in cobalt blue.

Blue scale A decorative pattern of blue overlapping fish scales. Also termed "imbrication".

Bocage Densely-encrusted flowering tree stumps supporting a group or used as a backdrop.

Body The material from which pottery or porcelain is made (although the term paste is more often used for porcelain). Also refers to the main part of a piece.

Bonbonnière A small box or covered bowl for sweetmeats, often in novelty form.

Bone ash Burnt, crushed animal bone that is added to soft-paste mixture to fuse the ingredients.

Bone china A porcelain recipe consisting of petuntse, kaolin and dried bone, supposedly invented by Josiah Spode II c. 1794. It became the mainstay of the English porcelain industry from c.1820.

Botanical wares Wares decorated with painted flowers, generally copied from prints or engravings.

Bracket lobes Bracket-shaped moulding used on dish rims.

Brocade Decorative patterns derived from textiles, employing repeated geometric motifs, abstract designs, or reserves enclosing animal, figural or floral subjects set against a contrasting (usually floral) ground.

Cachepot An ornamental container for ordinary flower pots. A smaller form of *jardinière*.

Caillouté Literally, "pebbled". An irregular pattern of amorphous oblongs picked out in gilding on a solid ground.

Camaieu Painted decoration in different tones of one colour. See also *grisaille*.

Campana vase An inverted, bell-shaped vase (sometimes with a handle on each shoulder).

Caneware A pale straw-coloured stoneware developed in Staffordshire in the late 18thC and used by many factories including Davenport, Spode and Wedgwood.

Canton porcelain The term for wares produced and enamelled in Canton province for export to the West. Usually heavily decorated with reserves of figures, flowers, birds and butterflies on a complex ground of green, pink and gold scrolling foliage.

Cartouche A decorative motif in the form of a scroll of paper with rolled ends, bearing a picture, motif or monogram. Also used to describe a frame, usually oval, decorated with scrollwork. See also vignette.

Cash pattern A Chinese repeat pattern based on the design of Chinese coins with a square central hole. Also known as coin pattern.

Caudle cup In England the term generally refers to a bulbous side cup used for caudle, a spicy, usually milk-based, porridge.

Celadon Green-glaze stoneware so-named after a character in a French play who wore pale green ribbons. Originally made in China during the Song dynasty (960-1279) both in the north and the south of the country, it remained popular well into the Ming dynasty. It was also produced in Korea, in Thailand and later in Japan.

Chiaroscuro The term for decorative use of contrasting shade and light.

China A general term for porcelain derived from the "China wares" imported into Europe from the 16thC. In 19thC England it came to mean almost any porcelain-type ceramic.

China clay Another term for kaolin, a white clay mixed with petuntse to form true porcelain.

Chinese export porcelain Chinese hard-paste porcelain made from the 16thC to suit European tastes. Also known as "China trade porcelain".

Chinese imari Chinese copies or pastiches of Japanese Imari wares, made largely for export from c.1700. The decoration involves Japanese brocade designs and the typical Imari palette of dark underglaze blue, iron-red and gilt, with no spur marks.

Chinoiserie The European fashion for Chinese decoration and motifs, influential in the decorative arts in the 17th and 18thC.

Cisele **gilding** Thickly-applied gilding with patterns tooled in to increase the decorative effect.

Clobbering The Dutch term for the practice of over-printing blue and white Oriental porcelain in colour enamels with designs rarely compatible with the original theme.

Cloud pattern An incised or painted scrolled design, often of square form, on Chinese porcelain.

Cobalt blue A pigment used in blue and white decoration.

Colloidal gold A form of gold-solution, used in gilding.

Comb pattern A pattern, often painted in underglaze blue, that looks as if it has been made with a toothed comb. Found mainly on Nabeshima porcelain.

Commedia dell'Arte A traditional Italian comedy, with characters extemporising on a general theme. Characters were modelled in porcelain by Meissen, Nymphenburg and others.

Compendiario A form of decoration found on Faentine maiolica, painted in a restricted palette of blue and yellow-ochre, generally with a sketchy design. Popular from about the middle of the 16thC and copied elsewhere.

Coperta A clear lead-glaze used on decorated maiolica to add lustre to the finished product.

Crabstock The form taken by a handle or spout on 18thC English pottery. It is based on the knotty contours of a pruned crab-apple tree.

Crackle A network of fine cracks introduced as decoration into the glazing of some Chinese Song dynasty porcelain and copies.

Craze Tiny, undesirable surface cracks caused by shrinking in the glaze, or other technical defects.

Creamware Finely potted lead-glazed earthenware covered in a cream-coloured glaze, developed over a long period in the 18thC, but brought to refinement by Wedgwood in the 1760s.

Cuspidor A spittoon, usually globular-shaped, with a wide flaring rim or a high, funnel-shaped mouth.

Decal decoration Liothographic transfer printing, also known as *decalomania* in the USA.

Delft The name most closely associated with northern tin-glazed earthenware, or delftware. Although the technique was introduced to the Netherlands by

Italian potters probably towards the end of the 15thC. The town of Delft only became prominent from about 1650 onwards.

Delftware Tin-glazed earthenware made in England (called faience in Germany, France and Scandanavia). When capitalized as Delftware, it refers to the same type of wares made in the Netherlands.

Deutsche Blumen Painted flowers, single or in bunches, used as decoration in the mid-18thC. The style is derived from botanical wood-block prints.

Diaper A pattern of repeated diamonds or other geometrical shapes seen on Chinese porcelain.

Ding Yao A type of porcelain made in China during the 10thC Sung dynasty, with a creamy-white body and an orange translucence.

Documentary piece Wares that bear evidence indicating the origin of the piece, such as the signature of the decorator or modeller, or an armorial mark.

Doucai A form of decoration using overglaze enamels (red, yellow, brown, green and black) within an underglaze blue outline. First used in 15thC China.

Dry edge An unglazed area around the base of some early Derby figures.

Earthenware Non-vitreous pottery that is not stoneware. See also tinglaze.

Encaustic decoration Painting with colours mixed with wax and fused to the body of the ware by heat.

Enghalskrug A type of jug with a bulbous, egg-shaped (ovoid) body surmounted by a tall, narrow neck. It was popular for about 100 years from about the middle of the 17thC in Germany and Holland.

Faience see Delftware

Famille jaune A type of famille verte, featuring a yellow ground.

Famille noire A variant of the 17thC and18thC Chinese *famille verte* palette, with reserves set against a black background.

Famille rose A palette dominated by opaque rose pink enamel.

Famille verte A type of 17th and 18thC Chinese decoration largely based on brilliant green enamels. Much copied on European earthenware and some porcelain.

Fan-shaped or scroll-shaped reserves Reserves in the form of Oriental scrolls, often fan-shaped, bearing writing or printing.

Fazackerley A palette associated with Liverpool delftware from about 1750, and which includes a soft sage-green, manganesebrown, pale blue, yellow and red.

Feldspar A rock-forming mineral (also known as Chinese petuntse) used to make hard-paste porcelain. Feldspar china, a variant of bone china, was made from c.1820. Feldspathic glazes applied to hard-paste porcelain become glassy (vitreous) at high temperatures.

Feronnerie A type of delicate baroque scrollwork inspired by wrought-iron work and used on French faience.

Fêtes galantes The term for open-air scenes of aristocratic amusement that were a favourite theme of French rococo painters.

Fire cracks The term for the splitting in the body that can appear after firing. Usually regarded as acceptable damage.

Firing The process of baking ceramics in a kiln. Temperatures range from 800°C (1472°F) for earthenware to 1450°C (2642°F) for some hard-paste porcelain and stoneware.

Flambé glaze A Chinese glaze made from reduced copper, dating from the Song dynasty. It is usually deep crimson, flecked with blue or purple, and often faintly crackled. It was also used on 18thC Chinese porcelain and copied in Europe.

Flatbacks Mainly Staffordshire pottery figures and groups made from about 1840 until early in the 20thC. As the name implies, the backs are almost flat and undecorated as they were principally intended for the mantelpiece.

Flatware Flat or shallow wares such as plates, dishes and saucers.

Fluting A pattern of concave grooves repeated in vertical parallel lines. The inverse of gadroon.

Footrim A projecting circular base on the underside of a plate or vessel. See also undercut foot.

Frit The powdered glass added to fine white clay to make a type of soft-paste porcelain.

Fritware A silicous clay bodied ware developed in Persia in the 12thC and used extensively throughout the Islamic world.

Gadroon Decorative edging consisting of a series of convex, vertical or spiralling curves.

Galanterien Small portable wares such as snuff boxes, nécessaires, patch boxes and scent bottles, sometimes in the form of figures, animals or fruit.

Galletto A decorative pattern of red and gold Chinese cockerels, devised at the Doccia factory.

Garniture de cheminée A set of three or more contrasting vases, intended for mantelpiece display.

Gilding The application of gold leaf or gold mixed with honey or mercury. See also acid gilding, *cisele* gilding and gloss-gilding.

Glaze A glassy coating painted, dusted or sprayed onto the surface of porcelain and stoneware which becomes smooth and shiny after firing, making the body non-porous.

Gloss-gilding The gilding of porcelain using gold in solution.

Graniteware A type of ironstone with a speckled appearance, designed to imitate granite.

"Green" The term for unfired ware. Not to be confused with Chinese greenware.

Greenware High-fired Chinese ceramics with a green-cloured glaze, dating from the late Han dynasty (25-220 AD).

Grisaille Painted decoration using a mainly black and grey palette and resembling a print.

Grotesque A fantastical type of ornament originally based on the wall decoration of the underground ruins (*grotte*) of Nero's Golden House in Rome rediscovered in about 1480. Raphael and his assistants incorporated these themes into the decorations of the Vatican Loggie in 1518/19. They include a wide variety of strange half-human beasts, masks, scrollwork and threads arranged in any number of ways. Other later designers such as Cornelis Bos, Du Cerceau and Jean Berain adapted these motifs in their respective styles.

Ground The base or background colour on a body, to which decoration and gilding are applied.

Guanyao Official stoneware of the Song dynasty.

Guilloche A neo-classical pattern of twisting bands, spirals, double spirals or linked chains.

Hans Sloane wares Porcelain with a botanical theme produced at the Chelsea factory 1752-57.

Hard-paste porcelain The technical term for porcelain made according to the Chinese formula combining kaolin and petuntse.

Hausmaler The German term for an independent painter or workshop specializing in the decoration of blanks, especially from Meissen.

"Heaping and piling" Accidental concentrations of cobalt blue that appear on 14thC and 15thC Chinese blue and white porcelain.

Hirado A type of Japanese blue and white porcelain made on Kyushu from the 18thC.

The wares have a distinctive, milky-white body, a velvet-like glaze and superlative pictorial decoration.

Hispano-moresque ware A highly important and influential group of lustred pottery, made in Spain from the 13thC onwards. The main centres were at Malaga in Andalusia and Manises, near Valencia.

Historismus A trend in late 19thC European decorative arts which involved the reproduction of many classical and traditional forms and styles, often in an over-elaborate way.

"Hob in the well" A pattern used on Japanese Kakiemon ware and much copied in Europe, based on a Song dynasty legend.

Hongs Warehouses erected in China by European traders, and used for storing goods for export.

Hookah or narghili A type of Middle-Eastern smoking pipe. See also *kendi*.

Huashi Literally, "slippery stone". The Chinese term for a type of soft-paste porcelain most often used for small, finely decorated pieces.

Imari A type of Japanese porcelain made in the Arita district in the 17th and 18thC and exported from the port of Imari. Features dense brocade patterns and a palette of underglaze blue, iron-red and gilding.

Imperial wares Wares produced in China at least as early as the Northern Song dynasty (980-1127) intended for the home market.

Impressed Indented marks and hallmarks, as opposed to incised.

Incised Scratched into the surface of a piece. Used of marks and decoration.

Indianische Blumen The German term for floral decoration on Meissen porcelain derived from Kakiemon styles. Generally 1720-40.

"In the white"/ blanks Undecorated porcelain wares.

Istoriato A style of painting on Italian maiolica from the 16thC. The artist uses the dish or vessel as a canvas on which to represent some narrative subject derived from biblical, allegorical, mythological or genre sources, usually via an engraving. The most important centres were Urbino, Castel Durante and Faenza.

Japonaise or Japanesque The term for European designs c.1862-1900 inspired by Japanese decoration.

Jardinière See *cachepot*.

Jasper ware A highly-refined white-bodied stoneware used by Josiah Wedgwood from about 1775. Jasper can be stained blue, green, yellow or claret. Copied by many other makers.

Jewelled decoration A decorative method whereby drops of translucent enamel are applied over gold or silver foil, in imitation of precious gems.

Kakiemon A much-copied decorative style introduced by the Kakiemon family in the Arita district of Japan during the 17thC. Typically, sparse and asymmetrical decoration is executed in a vivid palette on a dead-white *nigoshide* ground.

Kaolin A fine white china clay used to make true porcelain.

Kendi The Persian word for a globular-bodied drinking vessel with a short spout, made during the 15th and 16thC in China for export to the Middle East. See also hookah.

Kickback terminal A handle that terminates in a flourish away from the body of the piece.

Kinrande The term for a Japanese pattern of gilt on a red ground that originated in mid-16thC China and was much copied in Japan.

Knop Literally, the bud of a flower. Refers to the decorative knobs on teapot and vase covers.

Ko-Kutani See Kutani.

Ko-sumetsuke The Japanese term for "old blue and white" porcelain imported from China during the late Ming dynasty. See also blue and white and hirado.

Kraak-porselein The Dutch term for late Ming Chinese blue and white porcelain that was mass-produced for export to Europe. Also, the segmented patterns which typically decorated the borders of this type of flatware.

Kutani A type of Japanese porcelain. Old, or *"ko" Kutani* was allegedly made at Kutani in Kaga province in the early 17thC although most, if not all, was made in Arita in a so-called Kutani style. The style was revived in the 19thC as *ao-Kutani* (green Kutani).

Kwaart A thin clear lead-glaze applied over already decorated Dutch delftware to intensify the colours and create a shinier finish. It is equivalent to *coperta* in Italy.

Kylin A dragon-headed beast with the body and limbs of a deer and a lion's tail. In Chinese mythology it is a symbol of goodness. Also known as a *ch'ilin* or *qilin*.

Kyoto A centre of porcelain making in 19thC Japan.

Lambrequins Late baroque French ornament resembling delicate lace-work or tracery generally pendant from borders. Very popular with Rouen potters (and at St Cloud) at the end of the 17thC and beginning of the 18thC. It is mainly done in cobalt blue but sometimes heightened with red.

Lang yao See *sang-de-boeuf*.

Laub und bandelwerk Literally "leaf and strapwork". The German term for baroque cartouches that surround a pictorial reserve.

Lead glaze A clear glaze composed of silicous sand, salt, soda, potash and a lead component such as litharge (lead monoxide).

Leys jars A type of large rounded wine-jar with shoulder handles.

Lingzhi A fungus symbolizing longevity; a common 16thC Chinese decorative motif.

Li shui A type of Sung dynasty celadon wares.

Lithophane A kind of thin, low relief pictorial plaque that reveals a chiaroscuro effect when held up to the light. Also called "Berlin transparencies".

Lustre A type of decoration using metallic oxides to produce lustrous surface effects. For example, silver gives a soft golden yellow while copper appears a ruby red colour. These oxides were applied to a fired glazed piece and re-fired at a lower temperature in a reduction kiln. A successful firing would leave a deposit of virtually pure metal on the surface creating the desired lustre. The technique was probably borrowed by Mesopotamian potters from Egyptian glass makers in the 9thC. From then on it was used on Persian, Syrian and Egyptian pottery as well as in post-medieval Spain and Renaissance Italy. The technique was revived by European potters in the latter half of the 19thC.

Luting Joining two or more elements in a ceramic object by means of a semi-liquid clay or slip "glue".

Maiolica Tin-glazed earthenware produced in Italy from 15th-18thC. Although tin-glazed ware was made on the peninsula from the 11th or 12thC, it was not truly developed until the Renaissance.

Majolica The change of one letter in a corruption of the previous maiolica may appear slight but the material is completely different. Developed by Thomas Minton in the middle of the 19thC. It is usually a heavily-potted, complex, moulded type of ware covered in rich but generally sombre coloured lead glazes, including spinach green, dark cobalt blue, brown, ochre, often surprisingly in combination with opaque pastel colours such as turquoise and pink. A number of other factories in England, France, Sweden and North

America subsequently produced this type of ware.

Mandarin pattern A mainly red and purple decoration of figures within complicated diaper borders, often found on Chinese export porcelain of the mid-18th to the early 19thC.

Manganese A mineral used to make purple brown pigments.

Mannerist style A complex and articulate manifestation of the late Renaissance. Employing twisted, exaggerated and bizarre forms often entrapped by strap-work and grotesques, it was highly influential in the decorative arts for almost a century beginning in the 1520s.

Mason's Patent Ironstone China A type of fine porcellaneous stoneware introduced in England in 1813 by Charles James Mason of Lane Delph in Staffordshire. A similar type of ware was later made by many other manufacturers in Britain, Europe and the United States.

Masso bastardo Italian term for a poor-quality hard-paste made at the Doccia factory in the 18thC. Its rough, sticky, grey surface often shows firecracks.

Mazarin blue The English version of Sèvres *gros bleu*, introduced in the late 1750s.

Meiping A high-shouldered, short and narrow-necked Chinese baluster vase, designed to hold a single flower spray.

Millefleurs The French term for a type of dense floral decoration.

Mon A Japanese insignia.

Monochrome Decoration executed in one colour.

Moons Air bubbles in the body (or paste) which expand during the firing of incorrectly formulated porcelain (generally soft-paste), leaving translucent spots.

Mount A decorative metal attachment for porcelain.

Muffle The chamber inside a kiln that prevents wares from being damaged by flames during firing.

Nabeshima wares Arita wares made from the mid-17thC at Okawachi. Palettes consist of blue and white, coloured enamels or celadon.

Neo-classical A decorative style, based on a revival of Etruscan, Greek, Egyptian or Roman ornament.

Nigoshide The dead-white body and colourless glaze used for the best quality Kakiemon porcelain.

Oeil de perdrix Literally, "eye of a partridge"; a pattern of dotted circles in enamel or gilding, used at Sèvres and copied by artists at Meissen.

Ollientopfe A type of ceramic broth bowl.

Onion pattern A popular decorative pattern in blue underglaze employed at Meissen and other Continental factories.

Ormolu A gilded, brass-like alloy of copper, zinc and tin, used for mounts on fine furniture and other decoration.

Overglaze The term for any porcelain decoration painted in enamels or transfer-printed on top of a fired glaze.

Ozier See basketweave.

Palette The range of colours used in the decoration of a piece, or favoured by a factory or decorator. Also includes gilding.

Parian A semi-matt biscuit porcelain made from feldspar and china clay. Originally called "statuary porcelain", it became known as "parian" because of its similarity to the white marble from the Greek island of Paros.

Paste The mixture of ingredients from which porcelain is made.

Pâte-sur-pâte A kind of porcelain decoration involving low-relief designs carved in slip and applied in layers to a contrasting body.

Peach bloom A glaze derived from copper, ranging in hue from red to green. First seen in Chinese wares of the Kangxi period.

Pearlware A fine earthenware, similar to creamware but with a decided blue tint to the glaze. Although developed by Wedgwood in about 1779, it was soon adopted by all the major potters in England and Wales.

Petit-feu Low-fired enamel colours developed in Germany towards the end of the 17thC and in France in the late 1740s. The palette is much broader than the earlier grand-feu colours.

Petuntse or "china stone" A fusible, feldspathic bonding mineral used to make hard-paste porcelain.

Pierced decoration A method of decoration whereby a pattern is cut out of the body with a knife prior to firing.

Plasticity A term to describe the pliability of a china clay.

Pointilliste A style of painting involving the application of tiny dots of colour.

Polychrome Decoration executed in more than two colours. See wucai and doucai.

Porcelain A translucent white ceramic body fired at a high temperature. The formula can be either hard-paste or soft-paste.

Potiche The French word for a small porcelain vase or lidded jar.

Powder-blue A mottled blue ground achieved by blowing dry pigment through gauze.

Porcellaneous A piece with some of the ingredients or features of porcelain but which is not necessarily translucent.

Pratt ware Essentially a creamware decorated in high-fired colours including ochre, yellow, green, brown and blue. Made widely throughout England, Scotland and Wales in the early 19thC.

Press-moulding The moulding of figures or applied ornament achieved by pressing clay into an absorbent mould.

Privilege The granting of a privilege by Royal decree guaranteed monopolistic rights to a potter for a limited number of years. An example is the privilege obtained by Nicholas Poirel at Rouen in 1644 and then transferred to Edme Poterat. This gave Poterat and his family the right to produce faience in the city for the next 50 years. The loss of this monopoly in 1694 allowed other potters to establish their own factories in competition with the Poterat family.

Puce A purple red colour formed from manganese oxide.

Punch'ong A type of greyish coarse celadon stoneware, usually coated in slip, made in South Korea in the 15th and 16thC.

Pu-Tai Ho-Shang Also known as Budai Heshang or the "laughing Buddha". The figure of a grinning pot-bellied monk sitting cross-legged on a cushion. Appears on Chinese porcelain or as a statuette.

Putti Decorative motifs of small, naked, male baby-like figures.

Quatrefoil A shape or design incorporating four foils, or lobes (hence also quatrelobes).

Queen's Ware The name given to Josiah Wedgwood's creamware after it had found favour with Queen Charlotte. Subsequently this type of ware was extensively copied.

Raku ware An individually modelled type of earthenware made in Japan for the Tea Ceremony from the late 16thC up to the present day.

Reign marks Marks applied to some Chinese porcelains to denote the emperor during whose reign the piece was made. In many cases, however, marks were "borrowed" by later potters from earlier, important reigns to add iumposrtance to their wares.

Reserve A self-contained blank area within a pattern reserved for other decoration.

Robin's egg glaze A pale blue, speckled glaze developed in China during the 18thC.

Rococo A decorative European style that evolved in the early 18thC from the baroque. Typically featured asymmetric ornament and flamboyant scrollwork.

Rockingham ware Pottery with a brown glaze, often mottled with yellow. Produced in Britain and the USA.

Rose Pompadour A dealer's term for the rich, deep pink glaze used by Sèvres as a ground colour from c.1757-64. Named after Louise XV's famous mistress, Madame du Pompadour.

Ru ware A Chinese imperial stoneware made towards the end of the Northern Song dynasty (960-1127). Thinly potted of pale buff material, there is no surface decoration other than a fine duck-egg blue or greenish crackled glaze.

Saltglaze A thin, glassy nonporous glaze applied to some stoneware by throwing salt into the kiln at the height of firing. The surface is faintly dimpled like the surface of an orange.

Sang-de-boeuf Literally, "oxblood". A bright red glaze, toning to darker areas, first used during the Qing dynasty in China.

Satsuma A major Japanese port famed for its crackle-glazed earthenware.

Schnabelkanne (or Schnabelkrug) A Rhenish stoneware jug with a tall, diagonally-projecting handle resembling a bird's beak. Made at the Siegburg or Raeren potteries in Germany during the 16th and 17thC.

Schnelle A tall tankard with tapered sides made in the Rhineland, especially at Siegburg, from the 1550s up to c.1600.

Schwarzlot A type of linear painting in black developed in Germany.

Scroll-feet A type of base that incorporates a scroll motif, either in shape or in decoration.

Seladon fond Meissen's sea-green ground used to decorate wares in the 1730s. See also celadon.

Semi-porcelain A term coined in the 19thC and used by ceramics manufacturers to cover hybrid wares similar to ironstone china.

Sgraffiato (or sgraffito) The term for patterns incised into the slip surface of a piece exposing the contrasting body underneath.

Shoki-Imari "Early Imari" wares.

Shonzui A type of high quality 17thC Ming export porcelain made for the Japanese market and often decorated with brocade patterns and diapers.

Shu fu Opaque white porcelain with a matt, blue-tinged glaze, made at Jingdezhen in Yuan dynasty China and incised with the characters "shu fu", meaning "Privy Council".

Sleeve vase A long, thin cylindrical vase.

Slip A mixture of clay and water used for decorating ceramic bodies and for slip-casting and sprigging.

Soapstone or soaprock A type of steatite used instead of kaolin in soft-paste porcelain from 1750.

Soft-paste or artificial porcelain A porcelain formula made from a mixture of kaolin and powdered glass (frit), soapstone or bone ash. See also hard-paste porcelain.

Sprigged wares The term for wares decorated with small, low-relief moulding applied with slip.

Stilt marks or spur marks Small defects on the base or foot rim, made by the supporting stilts (or cockspurs) used during firing.

Stampino An Italian term for blue and white stencil decorations.

Stone china A type of fine, porcelaneous stoneware first developed by John Turner of Lane End, Staffordshire c.1800 and originally called Turner's Stoneware. Josiah Spode subsequently named the formula "Stone China". It is hard and compact, and sometimes slightly translucent. Many firms subsequently began to produce this type of ware.

Stoneware Ceramic ware made from clay, and sand or flint, fired at a higher temperature to earthenware (c.1350°C), making it durable and non-porous. Pieces are often salt-glazed or left unglazed and, if thinly potted, are almost as translucent as porcelain.

"Sumptuary Laws" Laws introduced by Louis XV of France c.1750, forbidding the use of gilding in porcelain decoration and discouraging competition with the Royal factory at Sèvres.

Swag A decorative motif of looped flowers or foliage.

Temmoku The Japanese term for a molasses-coloured glaze used in the Chinese province of Henan and Fujian from the Song period; made from iron oxide.

Thrown wares Hollow wares shaped on a pottery wheel.

Thumbpieces The angled attachment to the upper part of a cup, mug or jug handle.

Tin-glaze An opaque glassy white glaze made from tin oxide; commonly used on earthenware bodies such as delftware, faience and maiolica.

Toby Jug A tankard in the form of a seated toper clutching a mug of foaming ale. It first appeared in Staffordshire in about 1760. The hat is detachable and forms the lid.

Transfer-printing A decorative technique whereby a design can be mass-produced by transferring it from an inked engraving onto paper, and then to a ceramic body.

Transitional porcelain The term for porcelain that was produced in Jingdezhen, China, in the declining years of the Ming and the early Qing dynasty.

Trek The Dutch word for the fine outlining, mainly on blue and white wares, mostly done in dark manganese. It is especially noticeable on wares painted in the so-called "Transitional" style in the latter half of the 17thC.

Trompe l'oeil Pictorial decoration intended to deceive the eye.

Undercut foot The term for an inward-sloping base to a piece.

Underglaze A coloured sheath or pattern applied to biscuit porcelain before glazing and firing.

Veilleuse A food warmer comprising a vessel over a source of heat.

Vert pomme A mid-green enamel ground introduced at Sèvres c.1757.

Vignette An area of design or a picture that merges into the surrounding area.

Violette A violet enamel ground introduced at Sèvres in 1757.

Violeteers A vessel intended to hold herbs or petals.

Vitrifiable colours Coloured enamels which become fixed and glassy when fired.

Wall pocket An 18thC pottery flat-backed vase with small holes for suspension against a wall for the purpose of holding flowers.

Waster A deformed or damaged pot rejected by the factory.

Wreathing Spiral throwing marks following the contours of a vessel.

Wucai A "five coloured" Chinese palette developed in the Ming dynasty; contains underglaze cobalt blue, iron-red, turquoise, yellow and green enamels, usually with black outlines.

Yingquing One of the earliest forms of Chinese porcelain, often with carved or moulded designs.

Index